CAMBRIDGE TEXTS IN THE
HISTORY OF POLITICAL THOUGHT

SIR ROBERT FILMER
Patriarcha and Other Writings

CAMBRIDGE TEXTS IN THE HISTORY OF POLITICAL THOUGHT

Series editors

RAYMOND GEUSS *Columbia University*
QUENTIN SKINNER *Christ's College, Cambridge*
RICHARD TUCK *Jesus College, Cambridge*

The series is intended to make available for students the most important texts required for an understanding of the history of political thought. The scholarship of the present generation has greatly expanded our sense of the range of authors indispensable for such an understanding, and the series will reflect those developments. It will also include a number of less well-known works, in particular those needed to establish the intellectual contexts that in turn help to make sense of the major texts. The principal aim, however, will be to produce new versions of the major texts themselves, based on the most up-to-date scholarship. The preference will always be for complete texts, and a special feature of the series will be to complement individual texts, within the compass of a single volume, with subsidiary contextual material. Each volume will contain an introduction on the historical identity and contemporary significance of the work or works concerned, as well as a chronology, notes on further reading and (where appropriate) brief biographical sketches of significant individuals mentioned in each text.

For a list of titles published in the series, please see end of book

SIR ROBERT FILMER

Patriarcha and Other Writings

EDITED BY

JOHANN P. SOMMERVILLE

Associate Professor of History,
University of Wisconsin-Madison

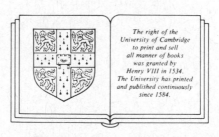

The right of the
University of Cambridge
to print and sell
all manner of books
was granted by
Henry VIII in 1534.
The University has printed
and published continuously
since 1584.

CAMBRIDGE UNIVERSITY PRESS

CAMBRIDGE

NEW YORK   PORT CHESTER

MELBOURNE   SYDNEY

Published by the Press Syndicate of the University of Cambridge
The Pitt Building, Trumpington Street, Cambridge CB2 1RP
40 West 20th Street, New York, NY 10011, USA
10 Stamford Road, Oakleigh, Melbourne 3166, Australia

© Cambridge University Press 1991

First published 1991

Printed in Great Britain by
The Bath Press, Bath, Avon

British Library cataloguing in publication data
Filmer, Sir Robert, *1588–1653*
Patriarcha and other writings. – (Cambridge texts in the
history of political thought).
1. Monarchy
I. Title   II. Sommerville, J. P. (Johann P.), *1953–*
321.6

Library of Congress cataloguing in publication data
Filmer, Robert, Sir, d. 1653
Patriarcha and other writings/Sir Robert Filmer; edited by
Johann P. Sommerville.
p.   cm. – (Cambridge texts in the history of political
thought)
Includes bibliographical references (p.   ).
ISBN 0 521 37491 X – ISBN 0 521 39903 3 (pbk.)
1. Political science – Early works to 1800. 2. Monarchy.
I. Sommerville, J. P., 1953–   . II. Title. III. Series.
JC153.F492 1990
321'.6–dc20 89-70842 CIP

ISBN 0 521 37491 X hard covers
ISBN 0 521 39903 3 paperback

Contents

Contents

Preface

In recent years there has been an explosion of interest in social history and in Women's Studies. Research has shed much light on the history of patriarchal attitudes and practices – not least in seventeenth-century England. The writings of Sir Robert Filmer are classic texts of seventeenth-century patriarchalist political thinking. Until now, the only modern edition of Filmer's political works has been Peter Laslett's. It was published in 1949 and has become quite a scarce book. The purpose of the present edition is to make Filmer's political works readily available.

Laslett's edition drew for the first time on the important Cambridge manuscript of Filmer's longest work, the *Patriarcha*. However, the text which Laslett printed contains a substantial number of mis-readings. For example, it gives the opening words of *Patriarcha* as 'Within the last hundred years' whereas the Cambridge manuscript in fact reads 'Within this last hundred of years', and similar errors occur throughout the book. Moreover, Laslett used *only* the Cambridge manuscript of *Patriarcha*. The present edition is based not just on that manuscript, but also on another important manuscript of *Patriarcha* at Chicago University Library. In the case of works other than *Patriarcha*, Laslett reprinted the text of the 1684 republication of Filmer's writings. The 1684 edition has no textual authority. This edition is based on manuscripts of sections of Filmer's *Observations* on Hobbes, *Directions for Obedience* and *The Necessity of the Absolute Power of all Kings*, and on the authoritative first printed editions of all of Filmer's writings, published in 1648 and 1652. Laslett traced many of Filmer's sources in *Patriarcha*, but only rarely in his other

vii

works. This edition tracks down almost all of Filmer's quotations and citations throughout his writings.

In the course of preparing this edition I have incurred many debts. I would like to thank Mark Goldie, Peter Laslett, Conrad Russell, Gordon Schochet, John M. Wallace and Corinne Comstock Weston for answering my importunate questions on Filmer and all his works. My debt to their writings, and to those of the late James Daly, will be obvious throughout. Colleagues in the History Department here in Madison have been most supportive. In particular, I am indebted to Ken Sacks for his efforts to trace a persistently recalcitrant quotation from Plato. I also owe much to Tim Fehler, who typed the entire text, and to Jack Hexter and the John M. Olin Foundation. A grant of summer support from the Foundation made it possible for me to complete the work on time.

I am grateful to the University of Chicago Library for permission to print Chicago MS 413 (*Patriarcha*), to the Syndics of Cambridge University Library for permission to print the Library's Additional MS 7078 (*Patriarcha*), and to the British Library for permission to print Harleian MS 6867, ff.255a–259a (part of the *Observations* on Hobbes), Harleian MS 4685, f.75a–b (part of the *Directions for Obedience*) and Harleian MS 6867, ff.253a–254b (part of the *Necessity*).

While proofs of this book were being prepared, Professor David Underdown of Yale University kindly drew my attention to a very important document amongst the Trumbull Papers (Misc XLII, 35). It is printed in the Sotheby's catalogue for the sale of the papers on 14 December 1989, pp. 121–2. The document shows that before 8 February 1632 Filmer brought 'a Discourse ... of Government and in praise of Royaltie' (presumably *Patriarcha*) to Charles I's secretary Weckherlin, requesting that it be licensed for publication. Weckherlin asked the king whether a book on such a subject was fit to be published at that time, and received a negative answer.

Introduction

In seventeenth-century England, social theory – and practice – gave
fathers and husbands very wide authority over their wives and children. People said that fatherly (or patriarchal) authority was derived
from God. The father, they claimed, was head of the family according
to the divine law of nature; his wife, children and servants owed him
obedience by the will of God Himself. Fatherly power over the family
was natural, and God was the author of nature. These ideas were
held by people of widely differing political opinions. It was perfectly
possible to argue in favour of an authoritarian and patriarchal family,
and against an authoritarian state. Many theorists did in fact draw
a sharp distinction between family and state, arguing that what was
true of the one institution need not necessarily be true of the other.
But some applied social theory to politics, and claimed that rulers
have fatherly power over their subjects. Just as a father's power over
his children does not stem from their consent, they said, so the king's
power is not derived from the consent of his subjects, but from God
alone. The state, they argued, is a family, and the king its father.
They concluded that kings are accountable to God alone and that
they can never be resisted by their subjects. The most famous of
these theorists was Sir Robert Filmer. His patriarchalist political
theory was set out in several works, of which the longest was *Patriarcha*.
To understand Filmer's ideas it is necessary to know something about
his life, and also about the context (or rather, contexts) of his thought.

1 SIR ROBERT FILMER

Robert Filmer was born into a prosperous gentry family in Kent in 1588, the eldest son of eighteen children. His education was typical of men of his social standing. In 1604 he entered Trinity College, Cambridge, but took no degree. Early in 1605 he gained admission to Lincoln's Inn, and eight years later he was called to the bar, but it is uncertain whether he ever went into legal practice. His writings show that he had some knowledge of English legal history, though much of his material was cribbed from a few recent authors.

In 1618 a marriage settlement was drawn up between Filmer and Anne Heton, whose father had been Bishop of Ely. The couple lived for a number of years in the Porter's Lodge at Westminster Abbey, and it may have been there that Sir Robert (who was knighted in 1619) met and befriended Peter Heylin. Heylin was a clergyman who had a prebend at the Abbey. He later gave high praise to Filmer's political thinking and was responsible for the first printed reference to his friend's *Patriarcha*. Filmer's marriage to a bishop's daughter, and his friendship with Heylin, help to account for the fact that on most points his political ideas closely resembled opinions often expressed by the higher clergy in the decades before the English Civil War. In those years it was high-ranking clergymen and courtiers who most vocally supported the elevated views on royal power of the first two Stuart kings. We have seen that Filmer had connections to the church. He also had a relative at the royal court, for his brother Edward was an esquire of the king's body. In 1629 Ben Jonson addressed a poem to Edward. Another famous poet, George Herbert, was a friend of Sir Robert himself.

On the death of his father in 1629, Filmer inherited the family estate at East Sutton in Kent – though he continued to keep up his household at Westminster. By the 1620s Filmer had begun to turn his hand to writing, composing a short book on the much debated question of whether it was sinful to charge interest on loans. This work was first published in 1653 by Filmer's friend Sir Roger Twysden, another member of the gentry of Kent. In 1642, when Twysden was imprisoned by the House of Commons, Filmer stood bail for him. The two men shared scholarly and antiquarian interests, and they both suffered at the hands of parliament in the 1640s. But their political attitudes were very different, for while Twysden was a moderate, Filmer was an uncompromising absolutist.

During the Civil War, Filmer himself took no part in the fighting, but his writings make it abundantly clear that he was an ideological supporter of the king, and his eldest son Sir Edward did join Charles at York on the eve of the war. Ageing and often unwell, Sir Robert stayed in Kent, which soon fell into parliamentarian hands, though many of the gentry there were royalist sympathisers. Under threat of a worse fate, Filmer was coerced into contributing heavily to the parliament's war effort, and in 1643 an order was issued for his imprisonment. Sir Robert spent the following months in gaol in Leeds castle (not far from East Sutton). The exact date of his release remains uncertain, though he was certainly at liberty in the spring of 1647. A year earlier, the first Civil War had effectively ended when Charles I surrendered to parliament's Scottish allies.

It was in 1647 that Filmer first ventured into print with an essay *Of the blasphemie against the Holy Ghost*. Sir Robert had already penned manuscript treatises for circulation amongst his friends at Westminster and in Kent. But in 1647 he suddenly began to publish – and kept on doing so until his death in 1653. Quite why Filmer changed the habits of a lifetime in his final years is difficult to say. The 1640s did indeed witness an explosion in the number of printed books and pamphlets as a legion of new authors published their views on questions which the Civil War had made topical – such questions as the nature, origins and limitations of royal and parliamentary authority. Perhaps Filmer was merely following fashion in printing his ideas. It is possible, too, that he hoped his writings would advance the Stuart cause, and the secret publisher of his political pamphlets – Richard Royston – did indeed specialise in royalist propaganda.

In February 1648 Royston published *The Free-holders Grand Inquest* – an outspokenly royalist survey of English constitutional history, which may have been written well before it was published – perhaps in 1644. There are good reasons for thinking that this pamphlet is Filmer's, and it is reprinted below. But his authorship has recently been challenged in cogently argued articles by Professor Corinne Comstock Weston. The problem is discussed on p. xxxiv below. In April 1648 Royston brought out Filmer's *The Anarchy of a Mixed or Limited Monarchy*. This anonymous pamphlet replied to one of the best-known works of parliamentarian political theory, Philip Hunton's *Treatise of Monarchie*. Hunton's book was published in 1643, and internal evidence suggests that Filmer's reply was completed no later than 1644. If that is so, the reasons for the delay in publication are unclear, though it is worth noting that Filmer's arguments are far more trenchantly absolutist, and far less moderate in tone, than most royalist writings. Perhaps Filmer's work was considered unsuitable for publication at a time when most of the king's publicists were keen to stress the moderation of the royalist cause.

By issuing the *Anarchy* in April 1648, Filmer (or Royston) may have hoped to contribute to renewed royalist efforts to return Charles to power – efforts which included a major revolt in Kent in May. Filmer himself was invited to take part in this rising, but cautiously refrained. He did, however, bring out another pamphlet, entitled *The Necessity of the Absolute Power of all Kings*, in the summer of 1648. Once more this was published without the name of printer or author. In fact, the printer was Royston and the author the great sixteenth-century French theorist Jean Bodin. The pamphlet, which was compiled by Filmer, consists entirely of quotations from Richard Knolles' English translation of Bodin. The extracts were vigorously monarchical and absolutist in nature.

The *Necessity* appeared too late to aid the royalist war effort – and it is unlikely that it would have contributed much to Charles' cause even if it had been printed earlier. Clement Walker, who favoured compromise with Charles and bitterly denounced those who brought the king to trial and execution, recorded the publication of *The Necessity* on about 19 August. He called it 'a pestilent book' and warned his readers that it was thought to be 'a cockatrice hatched by the antimonarchical faction, to envenom the people against the king and prince' (Clement Walker, *Relations and Observations*, edition of 1660 but dated 1648, p. 135).

In August 1648 the king's supporters were finally vanquished, and in January 1649 Charles was executed. A republic was established, and for several years Filmer lapsed into silence. He did, however, continue to read the latest political writings, including Thomas Hobbes' *Leviathan* and John Milton's defence of England's new government against the criticisms of the learned Huguenot, Claude de Saumaise. Within a few months of the publication of these works Filmer had composed commentaries on them. In February 1652

Royston published these works, together with an essay by Filmer on the *De Jure Belli ac Pacis* of the great Dutch jurist Hugo Grotius. This commentary on Grotius is more difficult to date, and part of it also occurs in the Cambridge manuscript of Filmer's *Patriarcha*. One passage – which is not in the *Patriarcha* manuscript – dates from after 1638, for it mentions Salmasius' *De Usuris*, which was published that year. The book was entitled *Observations concerning the original of government*, and was soon re-issued with the *Anarchy*.

In almost all of his writings Filmer drew heavily upon the work of Bodin and that of Aristotle. His last political publication was a pamphlet entitled *Observations upon Aristotles Politiques touching Forms of Government*. This was an analysis of the political ideas of the Greek philosopher, in which Filmer attempted to show that Aristotle had favoured the doctrine of royal absolutism even if he had sometimes been unclear in expressing the theory. Appended to this pamphlet was a short essay called *Directions for Obedience to Government in dangerous or doubtful times*. In this work Filmer dealt with the topical question of whether a usurping government should be obeyed, concluding that only limited obedience was justified, and that nothing should be done which would prejudice the rights of the true ruler – namely Charles II. The *Observations upon Aristotles Politiques* and the *Directions* were published by Royston in May 1652. A year later Sir Robert was dead.

In addition to the works discussed so far, Filmer produced treatises on a variety of topics. In March 1653 he published *An Advertisement to the Jurymen of England touching Witches*, in which he did not actually deny the existence of witches but certainly came close to doing so. Other writings survived in manuscript. One discusses the Sabbath, while another deals with marriage and adultery, and a third (which has recently been printed) is 'In Praise of a Vertuous Wife'. But by far the most important manuscripts are two different versions of Filmer's longest political treatise, *Patriarcha*. Sir Robert probably added to this book over a period of years, and it is likely that the whole work dates from before the Civil War. The problem is discussed below (p. xxxii). It is the fullest presentation of his political ideas, and its arguments underlie much of what he said in his other writings – while a great deal of what is in those writings is little more than amplification (or repetition) of views expressed in *Patriarcha*.

Peter Heylin lamented the fact that Filmer refused to publish *Patriarcha*, and it is true that a reader of Sir Robert's writings in the 1640s or 1650s could not have gained a fully rounded picture of Filmer's thought. His writings were occasionally noticed. In his *Certaine Considerations upon the Government of England* Sir Roger Twysden politely answered the *Anarchy*'s claim that the power of all monarchs was by definition unlimited, and referred to the book as 'a learned treatise' (*Certaine Considerations*, ed. J. M. Kemble, Camden Society, 1849, p. 17). The cleric Brian Duppa, who became Bishop of Winchester at the Restoration, referred to Filmer far more favourably in 1654. A letter from him to Sir Justinian Isham provides a striking early instance of Filmer's influence. He said:

> in the point of government, I know no man speaks more truth than the knight you mention, who follows it to the right head and spring, from whence the great wits have wandered, and have sought for that in their own fancy which they might have found in the plain Scripture road, where God, having created our first father to be the first monarch of the world, gave him dominion over all His creatures. (*The Correspondence of Bishop Brian Duppa and Sir Justinian Isham*, ed. Sir Gyles Isham, Bart., Northamptonshire Record Society 17 (1951) p. 91)

In 1656 John Hall of Richmond took Filmer's patriarchalism to be typical of English royalism, referring to 'the judicious author of a treatise called *The Anarchy of a Limited Monarchy*', who had 'founded monarchy on patriarchal right' in accordance with 'the most general opinion of the royalist' (*The True Cavalier examined by his Principles*, p. 126). Two years later Edward Gee included a critique of Filmer's views in his *The Divine Right and Originall of the Civill Magistrate*. In 1659 the well-known republican Henry Stubbe referred with respect to 'Sir Robert Filmores discourses upon Aristotles politicks' (*A Letter to an Officer of the Army concerning a Select Senate*, p. 57). These instances indicate that Filmer's views already exercised some sway in the 1650s. But his works did not acquire a really wide vogue until they were republished in 1679–80, at the time of the Exclusion Crisis. In those years a heated ideological struggle between Whigs and Tories arose from moves to exclude the Catholic heir to the throne – James, Duke of York – from succession to the crown of England. In 1679 all of Filmer's political writings except *Patriarcha* and the *Necessity* were reprinted. In 1680 the *Necessity* was re-published, and in the same year *Patriarcha* at last made its appearance in print. These works were issued as Tory propaganda, and they soon attracted responses from Whig publicists. Algernon Sidney and James Tyrell both replied to Filmer's theories. So too did John Locke, who devoted the first of his *Two Treatises of Government* of 1689 to criticising Sir Robert's ideas.

Not long ago, Filmer was read (if he was read at all) only as background to Locke. But if we want to understand Filmer it makes little sense to approach him through Locke (an extremely hostile critic) or through the debates on the Exclusion Crisis (which occurred a quarter of a century after Filmer's death). Rather, we must locate him in the context of his own times.

2 THE CONTEXTS OF FILMER'S THOUGHT

In 1588, the year of Filmer's birth, the Spanish Armada sailed for England. In 1605, when he entered Lincoln's Inn, the Gunpowder Plot was discovered. One of the main threats to England in Filmer's formative years seemed to come from Roman Catholics at home and abroad. Many years later, Filmer continued to equate Catholicism with disobedience to the monarch and with rebellion. 'If we would truly know what popery is', he said, 'we shall find by the laws and statutes of the realm, that the main, and indeed the only point of popery is the alienating and withdrawing of subjects from their obedience to their prince, to raise sedition and rebellion' (*Anarchy*, pp. 132–3). In the opening sections of *Patriarcha* Filmer singled out for special criticism two leading Roman Catholic thinkers – Bellarmine and Suarez. The political ideas of these men lay at the centre of much of the debate between British Protestants (including James I) and Catholics both British and continental, during the first decades of the seventeenth century.

Bellarmine and Suarez argued that the powers of kings were at first derived from the people. The rights of fathers over their families, they held, were granted to them directly by God, and were not a consequence of the consent of their children. But a father's power was very different from a king's, and a family was not a state. In states, power was at first held by the community as a whole and when it transferred authority to a king it could do so on conditions of its own choosing. If the king failed to fulfil the conditions, he might forfeit his power and be removed.

The ideas of original popular sovereignty, of legitimate resistance, and of limited monarchy were expressed not only by Catholics such as Suarez and Bellarmine, but also (as Filmer knew) by Protestants, including the Scottish thinker George Buchanan. Such theories had helped to foment civil war in France where at different times in the later sixteenth century both Catholics and Protestants had taken up arms against the king. In order to help preserve peace, Jean Bodin published *Six Livres de la Republique* (six books of the commonweal) in 1576. Bodin argued that in every state there must be a sovereign who alone makes law, but who is not subject to it, and who is accountable only to God. This sovereign must be absolute and indivisible – for a limited sovereign was a contradiction in terms, and divided sovereignty was a recipe for anarchy. In no circumstances, he held, would subjects be justified in resisting their sovereign. Bodin's book was translated into English in 1606, and it greatly influenced Filmer, who drew on it extensively. Sir Robert fully accepted Bodin's views on sovereignty and resistance. But he did not derive his patriarchal political theory from the Frenchman, for Bodin did not identify royal with fatherly power.

Filmer wrote as though his patriarchal theory was original (*Patriarcha* pp. 4–5). It was not. Many of his most characteristic claims were expressed by critics of Catholic and Protestant resistance theories in late Elizabethan and Jacobean England. An excellent example is Hadrian Saravia, a clergyman of Flemish extraction. Saravia held ecclesiastical livings in Kent and was one of the translators of the Authorised Version of the Bible under James I. In 1593 the Royal Printer published a Latin treatise by Saravia on political authority – *De Imperandi Authoritate*. In this book Saravia accepted the idea of absolute and indivisible sovereignty. Mixed monarchy – in which the king shared power with his subjects – was, he asserted, impossible, and any attempt to institute it would be bound to lead to disaster. Kings, he claimed, were lawmakers, and were not subject to their own laws. Of course, kings ought to rule in the public good, but if they failed to do so their subjects could never use force against them.

On all these points, Saravia's opinions coincided with those of Filmer – and of Bodin. Unlike Bodin, however, Saravia went on to formulate a patriarchalist account of the origins and nature of government, drawing on Scripture (and, in particular, on the book of Genesis) to confirm his views. Resistance theorists grounded their claims upon the idea that free peoples had originally transferred political authority to the king. This transference, they said, took place upon whatever conditions the people desired. Later kings succeeded to the crown of the original monarch – and also to the conditions upon which he had held it. A king who failed to abide by these conditions might be resisted and perhaps even deposed. So the doctrine that the people had at first been free was used to mount an argument in favour of limited monarchy and legitimate resistance.

Saravia challenged the argument by attacking the notion of the original freedom of mankind. 'By nature', he wrote, 'people are not born free' (*De Imperandi Authoritate*, reprint of 1611 in *Diversi Tractatus Theologici*, p. 125). Everyone was born into a family, and subject to its head – the father. The first communities, then, were not free peoples composed of citizens with equal rights. Rather, they were families in which the father ruled. Moreover, these early families were *political* communities. The book of Genesis made it clear that the first fathers had governed as kings over their families – which included not only children but also grandchildren and more remote descendants, and which could grow to be very populous indeed, since the Bible recorded that in those times men might live for many centuries. Even after the death of the first father, the family remained in being as a political entity. Power over the family (or state) now passed to the first father's successor by right of primogeniture. Unlike the original father, this successor might not be the lineal ancestor of all his subjects, but he did inherit fatherly power over them – and one of the hallmarks of this power was that it was not derived from the consent of the subjects. God in His wisdom could even transfer power from the ruling line to someone else, or alter the form of government from monarchy (the original and best variety) to one of the other two valid but less excellent possibilities – aristocracy and democracy. If this happened, the governing authorities would still hold fatherly power, and be accountable to God alone.

Saravia's book was republished in 1611, at a time when controversy over the origins and nature of political authority was at its height between James I and his supporters on the one hand, and such Catholics as Cardinal Bellarmine on the other. In the course of this controversy, a number of authors adopted a patriarchalist view of the origins of kingship. An example is John Buckeridge, Bishop of Rochester in Kent, and later of Ely – the see which Filmer's father-in-law had once held. In a Latin work against Bellarmine, published in 1614, Buckeridge argued that fatherly power was the basis of all just power (*De potestate papae in rebus temporalibus*, 1614, p. 531), and he declared that 'paternal and regal power are the same in substance and essence' (p. 282). Preaching a sermon before James I in 1618, the bishop repeated his patriarchalist message. 'The power of the king', he declared, 'is no other but *patria potestas*, that fatherly power that was placed by God immediately in Adam over all the families that issued from him' (*A sermon preached before his Maiestie at Whitehall*, 1618, p. 7).

Similar ideas occur in writings by Lancelot Andrewes, Thomas Jackson and other leading clergymen, and indeed in the canons adopted by the clergy's representatives in convocation in 1606. Nor was it only clerics who adopted such views. Sir Edward Rodney was a gentleman who in 1626 delivered a speech encouraging payment of a benevolence to the king, though many thought it illegal (Cambridge University Library MS Dd. 3. 84, pp. 149–50). He also wrote an essay 'Of Divine Providence' (pp. 110–25) in which he argued that 'monarchy sprang from paternal government' and that therefore 'the consent of the people was no more necessary than the consent of children to the paternal' (p. 116). Rodney insisted that a father's power over his children continued even after they ceased to be minors (p. 116), and claimed that the government of the Old Testament Jews was paternal and therefore monarchical long before they introduced kings (p. 115). He cited Aristotle to support his contention 'that the best and most natural form of government is that of monarchy, as taken from the paternal' (p. 114).

Patriarchalist political theory was thus common in early seventeenth-century England. It was frequently used to rebut the claims that royal power springs from the consent of the subject, and that kings can therefore sometimes be resisted. Controversy over the origins of royal power lay at the centre of much of the debate between Protestants and Catholics in the years immediately after the Gunpowder Plot – and this debate provides one of the main contexts of Filmer's ideas.

Not all of those who held high views on royal power were patriarchalists. James I, who wrote a good deal on politics, placed little stress on the equation between royal and paternal power. The king's works were frequently cited by Filmer on the interpretation of the prophet Samuel's famous words about monarchy, and especially on the royal power to make laws. James claimed that it was kings, not parliaments, who made laws, and that the monarch could interpret the laws which he had made. Filmer shared these views, and also James' conviction that the privileges of parliament were derived not from any ancient fundamental law but from the grace of the king. Disputes on parliamentary privilege flared up on numerous occasions in the early seventeenth century, and a particularly heated quarrel broke out between the king and the House of Commons in 1621. Tensions between the monarch and the Commons provide the second major context in which it makes sense to locate Filmer's theories. One of the few public events mentioned by Filmer was Charles I's answer to the Petition of Right – an important landmark in the history of relations between crown and Commons.

The financial difficulties of James I and Charles I led them to explore new means of raising revenue. These included impositions – levies on exports and imports – which tapped the wealth of merchants. Impositions did not have parliamentary sanction. They arguably infringed the principle (which was widely accepted, though not by the kings, nor by Filmer) that taxation requires the consent of parliament. They certainly increased suspicions on the part of many members of the House of Commons that James I (and later his son) had little respect for the liberties of the subject. The actions of Charles I went far towards confirming these fears.

Debates on parliament's powers aroused interest in its history. Of course, if kings held sovereign power, derived directly from God, it followed that all the rights and privileges of subjects depended on the royal will, and also that parliament was wholly subordinate to the monarch. Filmer used history to illustrate this conclusion, and drew heavily on the ideologically charged accounts of England's constitutional past given in works by Sir John Hayward and especially Thomas Egerton (Lord Ellesmere) and William Lambarde.

The version of English constitutional history outlined in Filmer's *Patriarcha* and developed in *The Free-holders Grand Inquest* was essentially the same as that put forward by other writers who took the king's side in disputes on parliamentary privilege – for example, Sir Francis Kynaston who, like Filmer's brother, was an esquire of the king's body. In a manuscript dated 1629 and entitled 'The true presentation of forepast parliaments' (British Library, Lansdowne Manuscripts 213, ff. 146a-76b) Kynaston gave a lively survey of parliamentary history, which argued that it was the king who made law, and that the privileges of the House of Commons were derived from the king, who was, indeed, under no obligation to summon the Commons to parliament.

The Free-holders Grand Inquest attacked the constitutional views of the parliamentarian William Prynne, and aimed to show that historically the king alone made laws in parliament, while the Lords advised and the Commons merely signified their consent. Consisting largely of quotations from earlier authors, or from statutes and legal documents, the work proved to be a useful collection of precedents. Prynne himself later drew on it in defending the House of Lords.

Like the *Free-holders Grand Inquest*, Filmer's other political publications adapted material contained in *Patriarcha* to the circumstances of the 1640s and 1650s, and to the particular claims of those whom he attacked. His criticisms of Hobbes, Milton and Grotius were sometimes original and incisive, and his later works added some new weapons to his arsenal of arguments against democracy. On the question of usurpers Filmer shifted ground a little after 1649. In *Patriarcha* (pp. 11, 44) and the *Anarchy* (p. 144) he granted that divine providence could validate the rule of a usurper, while in the *Directions* he argued that the legitimate ruling line never lost its title as a consequence of usurpation. After monarchy was abolished and England was declared a commonwealth he also came to dislike the use of the 'commonwealth' for 'commonweal' (p. 186) – though he himself had earlier used the two terms interchangeably – and he stridently insisted that monarchy was not just the best but the only form of government. But the main lines of Filmer's theory were mapped out in *Patriarcha*, and underwent relatively little change during or after the Civil War. Let us turn to the principal elements of Filmer's theory.

3 FILMER'S THOUGHT: THE TEXTS

Filmer explored the implications of patriarchal political theory in greater detail than any previous writer. But, as we have seen, the theory itself was not original. Indeed, much of Filmer's work was derived from earlier authors, and he often quoted from them at length – especially in *The Free-holders Grand Inquest* and most of all in the

Necessity. Amongst his favourite authorities were Bodin and Aristotle – though Filmer rejected Aristotle's contention that the family and the *polis* were different kinds of institution, and in some senses, at least, he was an anti-Aristotelian (as, indeed, was Bodin). Sir Robert also drew very heavily on the Bible. For Filmer, as for St Thomas Aquinas and many (though by no means all) other scholastics, Scripture and reason were in harmony. But he believed that on questions of political theory, reason by itself was liable to err, so close attention to the Bible was necessary if the truth were to be discovered. The errors of Aristotle and other pagans were to some extent excusable, he held, for they lacked Scriptural knowledge (pp. 252–3). Filmer himself quoted the Bible with great frequency. He approached Scripture directly, and treated it as an easily accessible and wholly consistent source of information. Only rarely did he refer to the Fathers or to more recent commentators on the Bible.

In Filmer's opinion, the most important political facts contained in Scripture occurred in the opening pages of the book of Genesis, where the story of the creation was told. He insisted that 'we must not deny the truth of the history of the creation' (p. 188). The Bible recorded that God gave the world to Adam, and this one simple truth was sufficient to overthrow the whole foundations on which arguments for original sovereignty were built. For if, as Scripture recorded, Adam was lord of the earth, and his descendants by right of primogeniture inherited his power, then the notion that the first human communities were self-governing democracies of free and equal citizens was historically false.

But were these first communities states or merely families? Suarez had argued that Adam ruled over a *family*, but not a commonwealth or state. Filmer rejected the argument. 'I see no reason', he said, 'but that we may call Adam's family a commonwealth, except we will wrangle about words. For Adam, living 930 years and seeing seven or eight descents from himself, he might live to command of his children and his posterity a multitude far bigger than many commonwealths or kingdoms' (p. 16). Adam's family was quite large enough to count as a commonwealth, and there was no reason to deny it that name – 'except we will wrangle about words' (p. 16).

Of course, it was not then known who was the direct descendant of Adam, and Filmer did not think that there was any great need to try to find him – or her. He held that primogeniture had been instituted by God as the natural and ordinary means of succession. However, he argued that fathers were empowered by God to divide the succession amongst their offspring, as Noah had done (p. 7), and even to alienate their fatherly (and thus political) rights (p. 44). Moreover, God could extraordinarily intervene to change the ruling line. Filmer did not pay much attention to how kings acquired their thrones, and indeed declared that 'It skills not which way kings come by their power, whether by election, donation, succession or by any other means, for it is still the manner of the government by supreme power that makes them properly kings, and not the means of obtaining their crowns' (p. 44). His basic claim was that however the government gains power, and whether it consists of just one person, or of a few, or of many, the power 'is the only right and natural authority of a supreme father' (p. 11). Thus, in any state, the rulers are accountable to God alone and not to their subjects.

The sovereign authority (whether one person or more) held fatherly power over the people. What, then, was the status of subjects who were themselves fathers? In Filmer's opinion, the sovereign could use his own fatherly power to limit the powers of these subordinate fathers. But he made it clear that he thought it was unwise to restrict too greatly the powers of these fathers. Like Bodin, he believed that fathers should have the power of life and death over their children, and he was fond of telling the story (which Bodin also told) of Cassius, who in Roman times had thrown his son from a rock, though the son was a tribune of the people (pp. 18, 260). Unless fathers agreed to part with their power, or the state deprived them of it, they could kill their children – even if the latter were adults. In Filmer's opinion it was not nature, but the laws and customs of the state which exempted children over a certain age from their father's authority (p. 228). Filmer favoured strong fatherly and strong royal power, because he believed that without them the love which fallen mankind had for liberty would lead to anarchy. If the Fall had not occurred, he held, there would have been no need for coercion, since everyone would have obeyed their superiors willingly. Before the Fall, directive power – the power to guide – would have been sufficient; but now the ruler also needed coercive or coactive power – the power to enforce his commands by physical penalties. The ruler himself was not subject to coercion, but would do well to be guided or directed by his own laws. This distinction between coercive and directive power was a scholastic commonplace.

Amongst the scholastics, Filmer quoted Bellarmine, Suarez and the Spanish Jesuit, Luis de Molina, but Bodin exercised a far greater influence on him, providing him with arguments in favour of absolute monarchy and against other forms of government. As we have seen, Filmer endorsed Bodin's contention that in every state there must be an absolute and indivisible sovereign. Like Bodin, he held that the key mark of sovereignty was the power to make law. The Bodinian concept of sovereignty was as important in Filmer's theory as the idea of patriarchal origins.

Filmer borrowed many details of modern and ancient history from Bodin, often using them to demonstrate the inadequacies of non-monarchical government. He drew on a wide variety of classical sources to illuminate the same topic. In *Patriarcha*, Filmer tried to demonstrate that democracy led to disastrous consequences, citing many examples from Roman history, and he explored the same theme again in the *Anarchy* and *Observations* on Aristotle. Filmer claimed that aristocratic and democratic governments were riddled with defects and inconsistencies. Though the opponents of absolute monarchy often paid lip-service to the idea that the 'people' held ultimate sovereignty, they generally restricted 'people' to mean only the greater or richer part of the population, thus unjustly excluding a substantial number of free and equal citizens from power. It was self-contradictory to argue that all were free and yet that a majority could bind the rest without their own consent.

If free and equal people held power, said Filmer, no decision could be made unless each and every one of them was consulted – a cumbersome procedure, especially since 'Mankind is like the sea, ever ebbing or flowing, every minute one man is born another dies; those that are the people this minute, are not the people the next minute' (p. 142). The need to keep consulting newly born babies could, of course, be avoided if it were conceded that children were politically subject to their fathers – and that would also explain how people today could be bound by contracts into which their remote ancestors had entered. But to make this admission would at a stroke destroy the foundations of original popular sovereignty, for if people were born into political subjection to their fathers they were manifestly not born free and equal (p. 142).

Filmer is at his most incisive and cogent when attacking the views of his opponents. His patriarchal theory is interesting as a good example of ideas which were commonly – though not universally – held by seventeenth-century royalists and Tories. The theory is historically important not only because it influenced the actions of those who believed it, but also because it helped to shape the outlook of those who rejected it. It is difficult to understand Locke unless we understand Filmer, for Locke's *Two Treatises* were not written as the abstract reflections of a detached philosopher, but were a polemical refutation of Filmer's case. The first treatise, indeed, is a detailed response to Sir Robert's arguments. It is hard to grasp the nuances of Locke's reply unless we know something of what Filmer asserted – and Locke himself is not a trustworthy guide to Sir Robert's ideas. Of course, today the literal truth of Biblical history no longer seems as clear as it did in Filmer's age. But Filmer relied on Scripture *and* reason. He is arguably at his most interesting, and challenging, when he attacks democratic theory, and the notion that government rests upon a contract between ruler and subject. We may no longer find patriarchalism a convincing political philosophy. But much of what Filmer had to say against contractualist theories of government remains compelling.

Principal events in Filmer's life

1588   Birth of Filmer. The Spanish Armada sails for England.

1603   Succession of James I to the throne of England.

1604   Filmer enters Trinity College, Cambridge.

1605   Filmer enters Lincoln's Inn.
Discovery of the Gunpowder Plot, a Catholic conspiracy to blow up James I and parliament.

1606   Parliament enacts that Catholics who refuse to take an oath of allegiance rejecting the pope's claims to be able to depose kings may be punished by loss of goods and imprisonment during the king's pleasure.
The English clergy pass a set of canons condemning the pope's claims to authority over kings, and giving a patriarchalist account of the origins of government. (The canons were published as *Bishop Overall's Convocation-Book*, 1690.)

1608   James I publishes a defence of the oath of allegiance against Catholic criticisms. The king's book is soon answered by Catholics, including Bellarmine and Parsons.

1613   The Jesuit Suarez publishes *Defensio Fidei Catholicae*, attacking the ideas of James I. Suarez's book is burned in London.

1618   A marriage settlement drawn up between Filmer

and Anne Heton. The couple settles in Westminster.

1621   A bitter dispute between the king and the House of Commons over the nature and origins of the Commons' privileges wrecks parliament.

1625   Succession of Charles I.

1628   Grievances against recent royal policies lead the House of Commons to adopt a Petition of Right which attempts to outlaw extra-parliamentary taxation, and imprisonment without cause shown. Because of his financial difficulties, Charles I accepts the Petition, but he soon tries to circumvent its provisions.

1629   Renewed conflict between the king and members of the House of Commons leads Charles to dissolve parliament and rule without it for the next eleven years.

Filmer inherits his father's estate at East Sutton in Kent.

1637–40   Attempts by Charles I to introduce a new Prayer Book in Scotland lead to a Scottish rebellion against him.

Failing to suppress the rebellion, the king is forced to call parliament in England, 1640.

1642   Outbreak of Civil War in England.

Publication of Henry Parker's *Observations upon some of his Majesties late Answers and Expresses*.

Extensive pamphlet controversy on the nature of royal power and similar questions.

1643   Publication of Philip Hunton's *Treatise of Monarchie* and of William Prynne's *The Treachery and Disloyalty of Papists to their Sovereigns*.

1643–7   Filmer imprisoned by the parliamentarians for some of this period.

1644   Publication of *The Fourth Part of the Institutes of the Lawes of England* by Sir Edward Coke.

1646   Surrender of Charles I ends the Civil War.

1647   Publication of Filmer's *Of the Blasphemie against the Holy Ghost* (February).

1648	Publication of *The Free-holders Grand Inquest* (February), replying to Prynne, Coke and others. Carlisle and Berwick seized by the king's supporters (April). Publication of Filmer's *The Anarchy of a Limited or Mixed Monarchy* (April). Royalist rebellion in Kent (21 May–2 June). Publication of Filmer's *The Necessity of the Absolute Power of all Kings* (August). Defeat of Scottish royalist invasion by Oliver Cromwell at Preston (17 August) Surrender of royalist rebels at Colchester (27 August).
1649	Execution of Charles I (30 January). Abolition of monarchy and the House of Lords in England. Establishment of the Commonwealth.
1650	A law passed requiring the adult male population of England to take an Engagement to be faithful to the Commonwealth as established, without king or Lords.
1651	Publication of John Milton's *Pro Populo Anglicano Defensio* and of Thomas Hobbes' *Leviathan*
1652	Publication of Filmer's *Observations concerning the Originall of Government* (February), criticising Hobbes, Milton and Grotius. Publication of Filmer's *Observations upon Aristotles Politics concerning Forms of Government* (May), including *Directions for Obedience to Government in Dangerous and Doubtful Times,* which discusses issues of allegiance raised by the Engagement.
1653	Death of Filmer (30 May).
1660	Restoration of Charles II.
1679–81	Political crisis over attempts by members of the House of Commons to exclude Charles II's Catholic brother James, Duke of York, from succession to the throne.
1679	Publication of a collected edition of Filmer's political works, including all except *Patriarcha* and the *Necessity.*

1680	First publication of *Patriarcha*.
	Publication of a new edition of the *Necessity* under the title *The Power of Kings*.
1685	Publication of an improved edition of *Patriarcha* by Edmund Bohun, aided by Archbishop William Sancroft.

Bibliographical note

The best guide to Filmer's life is Peter Laslett's 'Sir Robert Filmer: the man versus the Whig myth' in *The William and Mary Quarterly* 5 (1948), pp. 523–46. The same author's 'The gentry of Kent in 1640' in *The Cambridge Historical Journal* 9 (1948), pp. 148–64, contains information about Filmer's Kentish neighbours and their scholarly interests, and adds some details on Filmer's life. Laslett's introduction to his edition of *Patriarcha and Other Political Works of Sir Robert Filmer* (Oxford 1949) also includes useful information on Sir Robert and his times, despite some slips and errors.

Filmer's thought is the subject of James Daly's *Sir Robert Filmer and English Political Thought* (Toronto 1979). This is essential reading for anyone with a serious interest in Filmer, and contains a great deal of important material. But Daly rather overstates the case for Filmer's originality. He says much about Filmer's critics and followers, and about royalist opinion during and after the Civil War, but his book is weaker on pre-Civil War thought. English political ideas before 1640 are surveyed in J. P. Sommerville's *Politics and Ideology in England 1603–1640* (1986). The first chapter is especially relevant to Filmer's ideas and their context. Sommerville's 'From Suarez to Filmer: a reappraisal', in *Historical Journal* 25 (1982), pp. 525–40, illuminates the relationship between Filmer's political thinking and that of some of his contemporaries. The same author's 'Richard Hooker, Hadrian Saravia, and the origins of the Divine Right of Kings', in *History of Political Thought* 4 (1983), pp. 229–45, discusses an Elizabethan thinker whose political theory was similar to Filmer's. There is much valuable information on early seventeenth-century political thought in Margaret A. Judson, *The Crisis of the Constitution* (New Brunswick 1949; reprinted with a preface by Jack Hexter, 1988). The best guide to the context and reception of *The Free-holders Grand Inquest* is J. G. A. Pocock's *The Ancient Constitution and the Feudal Law* (Cambridge 1957; new edition, with a retrospect, 1987).

An important work on patriarchalist political ideas in general is Gordon J. Schochet's *Patriarchalism and Political Thought* (Oxford 1975), which also contains much useful material on Filmer and his influence. Some of this material is also available in Schochet's 'Patriarchalism, politics and mass attitudes in Stuart England', in *Historical Journal* 12 (1969), pp. 413–41. Two older articles which make interesting points on Filmer's thinking, but which should be read with caution are J. W. Allen's 'Sir Robert Filmer' in F. J. C. Hearnshaw, ed., *The Social and Political Ideas of some English Thinkers of the Augustan Age*, A.D. *1650–1750* (1928), pp. 27–46, and R. W. K. Hinton's 'Husbands, fathers and conquerors', in *Political Studies* 15 (1967), pp. 291–300.

Filmer wrote a number of works besides those included in this volume, and to grasp the full range of his thought it is well worth reading some of these. *An Advertisement to the Jury-Men of England touching Witches* (1653) is an interesting discussion of the evidence for the existence of witches, but unfortunately is not available in a modern edition. The *Quaestio Quodlibetica; Or a Discourse whether it may be lawfull to take Use for Money* (1653) was reprinted in *The Harleian Miscellany* volume 10, second supplemental volume (1813), and a facsimile of this edition was issued in *The Usury Debate in the Seventeenth Century* (New York 1972), in the series The Evolution of Capitalism. An interesting short manuscript work by Filmer has recently been published in Margaret J. M. Ezell, *The Patriarch's Wife: Literary Evidence and the History of the Family* (Chapel Hill 1987), Appendix I, pp. 169–90. This work, 'In Praise of the Vertuous Wife', illuminates Filmer's attitudes towards women and marriage. These attitudes are discussed by Ezell in *The Patriarch's Wife*, pp. 129–141 (also printed in *Seventeenth-Century News* 42 (1984), pp. 60–6). For descriptions of other manuscript works by Filmer, and for much useful bibliographical information about his published writings, see Gordon J. Schochet's 'Sir Robert Filmer: some new bibliographical discoveries', in *The Library*, fifth series, 26 (1971), pp. 135–60. This is a very important article, though Schochet's attribution of some anonymous political treatises to Filmer is unconvincing. These attributions, and other bibliographical problems associated with Filmer, are discussed in 'The authorship and dating of some works attributed to Filmer' below.

The authorship and dating of some works attributed to Filmer

Recent scholarship has raised and re-opened some important questions of authorship and dating connected with Filmer. Firstly, the date of composition of *Patriarcha* has been variously set at years ranging from 1631 or earlier to 1648 or later. Secondly, the ascription of *The Free-holders Grand Inquest* to Filmer has been challenged, and it has been suggested that it is in fact by Sir Robert Holborne, a lawyer who defended John Hampden in the famous Ship Money trial of 1637–8 but who became a royalist in the Civil War. Thirdly, some anonymous seventeenth-century works of political theory have been attributed to Filmer. Each of these three topics deserves brief discussion here. On the first, see also p. viii above.

1 THE DATE OF FILMER'S *PATRIARCHA*

In the introduction to his *Patriarcha and Other Political Works of Sir Robert Filmer* (Oxford 1949), p. 3, Peter Laslett suggested that *Patriarcha* was written between 1635 and 1642. He argued that it must have been written after 1635, since the Cambridge manuscript 'quotes Selden's *Mare Clausum*, which was published in that year'; and that it dates from before the outbreak of the Civil War in 1642, since the Cambridge manuscript (unlike the printed versions of 1680 and later) refers to only two civil wars in English history – the Barons' Wars and the Wars of the Roses (p. 34 below). The 1680 edition added a reference to a third war, namely 'the late rebellion' – that is to say, the Civil War. Laslett did not know of the Chicago manuscript, but on this point it agrees with the Cambridge manuscript, for it also refers to only two civil wars. Laslett's dating has been widely accepted.

In 1980 John M. Wallace published 'The date of Sir Robert Filmer's *Patriarcha*', *Historical Journal* 23 (1980), pp. 155–65. This provocative reappraisal of the question cast doubt on the idea that 'it would have been possible for anyone to write such a detailed, casuistical tract before the great constitutional debates in 1642, which Henry Parker is usually credited with having initiated' (p. 156). Wallace also pointed to a number of passages in *Patriarcha* which are identical with, or strikingly similar to, sections of *The Free-holders Grand Inquest* and the *Anarchy*, and argued that Patriarcha borrowed from these other works. He concluded that the Chicago manuscript was written in the second half of 1648, and that the Cambridge manuscript was not drawn up until the final year of Filmer's life.

James Daly replied to Wallace's arguments in 'Some problems in the authorship of Sir Robert Filmer's Works', *English Historical Review* 98 (1983), pp. 737–62. He rightly asserted that a plausible context for much of the material in *Patriarcha* may be found in late sixteenth-century and Jacobean debates over the nature and origins of royal authority (p. 749) – a point which is discussed in the introduction above. He also cast doubt on Wallace's contention that internal evidence shows that *Patriarcha* borrows from other works by Filmer, arguing that it is just as likely that those works took material from *Patriarcha* (p. 750), and he re-emphasised the importance of the reference to only two previous civil wars. Daly tentatively concluded that the Chicago manuscript was completed 'by about 1641' and that the Cambridge version was written shortly afterwards (p. 761).

A rather different dating was suggested by Richard Tuck in 'A new date for Filmer's *Patriarcha*', *Historical Journal* 29 (1986), pp. 183–6. Replying to Wallace, Tuck also rejected the contention that the similarities between *Patriarcha* and the other works furnish clear evidence that it borrowed from these works. It is, in fact, perfectly possible that the *Anarchy* and *The Free-holders Grand Inquest* borrowed from *Patriarcha*, or that all three works drew on a single set of notes and extracts which Filmer had made. Tuck went on to argue, on the basis of the sources used by the two manuscripts of *Patriarcha*, that the Chicago manuscript dates from between 1628 and 1631, while the Cambridge manuscript belongs to the years between 1631 and 1642. He also suggested that the Chicago manuscript may not have been the earliest version of the work.

In support of this dating, Tuck pointed out that in the Cambridge manuscript Filmer uses the 1631 edition of Selden's *Titles of Honor*, while in the Chicago manuscript he does not do so – although it would have been highly relevant to his concerns. 'The obvious implication is that he was writing before 1631' (p. 184). At first sight, there is a problem with this argument, for the Chicago manuscript does draw on William Lambarde's *Archeion*, which was written by 1591 but not published until 1635. However, Tuck speculated that Filmer used a manuscript of this work, which is known to have circulated in manuscript (p. 184).

His argument at this point can be substantially strengthened, for a comparison of *Patriarcha*'s quotations from Lambarde with the two printed editions of 1635 reveals that it does not draw on either of them. For example, *Patriarcha* p. 51 has the words 'commanded James Audley', which are missing from both printed editions of *Archeion*; two surviving manuscripts of *Archeion* have 'commandeth James Audley' (Lambarde I, p. 73 n. 80). This and several similar instances (discussed in more detail below, in connection with *The Free-holders Grand Inquest*) prove that Filmer drew on a manuscript of *Archeion*. Perhaps rather less convincing is Tuck's argument that a date close to 1628 is suggested by *Patriarcha*'s reference to Charles I's 'speech after this last answer to the Petition of Right' of that year (p. 184). Though Laslett's edition does indeed mis-print 'this last answer', both manuscripts in fact read 'his last answer'. Had Filmer said '*this* last answer' we might indeed infer that he was writing very soon after the event; but it is difficult to deduce much from 'his last answer'.

We may tentatively conclude that the Chicago manuscript, or the text from which it is copied, was written before 1631, and that the Cambridge manuscript dates from 1635–42. The third chapter of *Patriarcha* is arguably not very well integrated with the first two chapters, and it is possible that it was written a good deal later than them. On p. 5 Filmer refers to 'the new coined distinction of subjects into royalists and patriots'. The word 'royalist' appeared in print in 1627 (Robert Sibthorp, *Apostolike Obedience*, p. 13) and occurs in manuscript earlier in the 1620s. Perhaps the first two chapters of *Patriarcha* were composed in the 1620s and the third chapter about 1630.

2 THE ASCRIPTION OF *THE FREE-HOLDERS GRAND INQUEST* TO FILMER

In 1679 *The Free-holders Grand Inquest* was published as the first item in a collection of works attributed to Filmer. The other works in this collection are unquestionably Filmer's, and the whole collection was several times re-issued under Filmer's name. As far as is known, none of Filmer's family or friends challenged the attribution of *The Free-holders Grand Inquest* to Sir Robert. In 1680 Filmer's *Necessity of the Absolute Power of all Kings* was printed under the title *The Power of Kings*. An anonymous preface to this work gave a list of Filmer's writings which included *The Free-holders Grand Inquest*. All the other titles given in this list are certainly by Filmer – and the list contained titles not in the 1679 collection, so it is not merely derived from that book. However, Anthony Wood (1632–1695) attributed *The Free-holders Grand Inquest* to Sir Robert Holborne: *Athenae Oxonienses*, ed. P. Bliss, 4 vols. (1813–20), volume 4, part 2 (*Fasti*), p. 45. The ascription to Holborne has been vigorously re-asserted by Corinne Comstock Weston in 'The authorship of the *Free-holders Grand Inquest*', *English Historical Review* 95 (1980), pp. 74–98, and again in 'The case for Sir Robert Holbourne reasserted' in *History of Political Thought* 8 (1987), pp. 435–60. The first of these articles attracted a response from James Daly in his 'Some problems in the authorship of Sir Robert Filmer's Works', *English Historical Review* 98 (1983), pp. 737–62.

Weston argued that the *Anarchy* and the *Free-holders* take such different lines on the question of whether the king is one of the three estates of the realm that they cannot be by the same author. The *Anarchy* accepted that the king was one of the estates (p. 137 below), while the *Free-holders* (like much contemporary royalist writing at Oxford, where Holborne was) took pains to stress that the king stood outside and above the estates (p. 89 below). Since the *Anarchy* is by Filmer, Weston concluded that the *Free-holders* is not. In reply, Daly claimed that there is no inconsistency between the two works, asserting that in the *Anarchy* Filmer did *not* accept the idea that the king is one of the estates, and contending that the unquestionably different emphases on this topic of the two works may readily be explained in terms of their overall aims and arguments.

Other characteristics of the *Free-holders* lend some support to Weston's thesis. It is the only work to cite the *Rotuli Parliamentorum* and the Year Books, which may suggest that its author had more legal knowledge than Filmer can be shown to have possessed. It alone cites Coke, and it alone fails to cite Bodin and Aristotle, authors whom Filmer was extremely fond of quoting, even if the quotations were not always of central and immediate relevance to his arguments. Moreover, patriarchal political theory is wholly absent from the *Free-holders*.

These points are, however, inconclusive, and against them must be set some very weighty evidence suggesting that *Patriarcha* and the *Free-holders* are by the same author. As Laslett observed, the *Free-holders* reads like an expansion of the last section of *Patriarcha*, and the two works contain a very substantial amount of common material, including large sections taken from Egerton and Lambarde. A list of parallel passages may be found in James Daly's 'Some problems in the authorship of Sir Robert Filmer's Works', *English Historical Review* 98 (1983), pp. 737–62, at p. 743, and they may easily be traced by consulting the index to the present edition, especially under the entries for Camden, Egerton, Lambarde, Raleigh and Selden. The most decisive piece of evidence is, perhaps, the use which the two works make of Lambarde's *Archeion*, for they both drew not on a printed version but on a manuscript of *Archeion*, and it seems that both used the same manuscript. The evidence follows (with references to *Archeion* being to the edition of Charles H. McIlwain and Paul L. Ward, Harvard 1957 – an edition which includes readings from both printed editions of 1635, and which is the only printed edition other than those two):

> *Free-holders* p. 110 and *Patriarcha* p. 51: and so proceeded
> *Archeion* p. 73, printed versions: and so proceed

> *Free-holders* p. 110 and *Patriarcha* p. 51: Audley, commanded James Audley
> *Archeion* p. 73, printed versions: Audley

> *Free-holders* p. 110 and *Patriarcha* p. 51: appear before him
> *Archeion* p. 73, printed versions: appear before himself

> *Free-holders* p. 119 and *Patriarcha* p. 48: then let him go
> *Archeion* p. 58, printed versions: go

> *Free-holders* p. 118: after that he had
> *Archeion* p. 57, printed versions: after he had

This last quotation is not in *Patriarcha*, which indicates that the *Free-holders* did not simply take its Lambarde material from *Patriarcha* – of which Holborne may conceivably have had a copy – but from a manuscript of *Archeion*. In all the cases listed above, McIlwain and Ward record manuscript readings which are either close to or identical with those of *Patriarcha* and the *Free-holders*, though it can be shown that the manuscript used by Filmer is not the same as either of the two manuscripts on which they drew.

It is extremely unlikely that the copy of *Archeion* which Filmer used in writing *Patriarcha* somehow made its way to Oxford to be used by Holborne in the mid-1640s – at a time when *Archeion* was readily available in print. The obvious conclusion is that Filmer possessed a manuscript of *Archeion* before its publication in 1635, that he used this manuscript (or extracts from it) in writing *Patriarcha*, and that he re-used the same source in composing the *Free-holders*, so that at least some of the *Free-holders* was by Filmer. It is just possible that parts of it were written by another hand, and rather more likely that Filmer obtained material from his acquaintances for inclusion in it. Perhaps the lawyer Holborne was one of those consulted. But the weight of the evidence favours the authorship of Sir Robert Filmer, not Sir Robert Holborne.

3 SOME WORKS ATTRIBUTED TO FILMER

In 'Sir Robert Filmer: some new bibliographical discoveries', *The Library*, fifth series, 26 (1971), pp. 135–60, Gordon J. Schochet suggested that Filmer wrote two works which are usually ascribed to Sir John Monson: *A Discourse concerning Supreme Power and Common Right* and a *Short Answer to Several Questions proposed to a Gentleman of Quality*, published in 1680 and 1678 respectively. He also attributed to Filmer a manuscript treatise on the Engagement of 1650, Bodleian Tanner MS. 233, pp. 135–47. These works have not been included in the present edition since internal evidence renders Schochet's attributions doubtful. Some of this evidence is set out in James Daly, *Sir Robert Filmer and English Political Thought* (Toronto 1979), Appendix B, pp. 194–8.

A note on the text

In conformity with the requirements for this series, the text of this edition of Filmer's political writings has been modernised and standardised throughout, except that the spelling of the titles of Filmer's books has been retained. The original paragraph structure has generally been preserved. Contractions have been silently expanded, and the erratic use of italics in the original editions has been ignored. Filmer's method of referring to the regnal years of kings in legal and other citations was inconsistent. For instance, '7 Henry III' may sometimes appear in the original texts as 'septimo Henry III', or '7° Henry III', or 'in the seventh of Henry III'. In this edition, all these forms have been standardised as '7 Henry III'. Where the original manuscript interpolates words this fact has not been recorded, though it is worth observing here that on a number of occasions interpolated words in the Chicago manuscript of *Patriarcha* have been omitted in the Cambridge manuscript.

The texts used in each work are recorded in the first note to that work. In the case of all Filmer's writings except the *Necessity* and *Patriarcha* (which they do not include) the collected editions of 1679 (Wing 913 and 914) have been consulted, as well as the first editions. All readings given as from the 1679 editions occur in both the printings of that year.

Filmer sometimes quotes *verbatim* from his sources. On other occasions he mis-quotes them slightly, and sometimes he gives summaries which are almost quotations. A number of passages given as quotations in the text below are not wholly accurate renditions of

Filmer's sources, while other passages not in quotation marks may have strong verbal similarities to the sources.

Square brackets indicate editorial material throughout. Citations given in round brackets are usually taken from the margins of Filmer's works, but are sometimes from the body of his text. Filmer's '*lib.*' and '*cap.*' have been slightly expanded and translated as 'book' and 'chapter'.

The Chicago manuscript of *Patriarcha* is referred to as A; the Cambridge manuscript is B; the Chiswell edition dated 1680 is C; and the Bohun edition of 1685 is D. 48F is the first edition of *The Freeholders*. 48A is the first edition of the *Anarchy*. 48B is the first edition of the *Necessity*. BMS is the manuscript of part of the *Necessity*. 80B is the 1680 edition of the *Necessity*, published as *The Power of Kings*. 52H is the first edition of *Observations concerning the Originall of Government*, on Hobbes etc. OMS is the manuscript of part of the *Observations* on Hobbes. 52A is the first edition of *Observations on Aristotles Politiques*. DMS is the manuscript of part of the *Directions for Obedience*. 79 indicates the collected editions of 1679.

Abbreviations and sources

The following list gives bibliographical details of those of Filmer's sources which are referred to by abbreviations in the text below. Where no specific details of publication are given, there are many editions of the book, and in these cases references are usually to chapter and section numbers. In addition, Filmer refers to many classical writers including Aristotle, Cicero, Claudian, Cassius Dio, Livy, Lucan, Orosius, Plato, Plutarch (in Sir Thomas North's translation), Polybius, Sophocles and Tacitus. References to these authors are given in the conventional form. For example, references to works of Aristotle are to the page, column and line numbers of the standard Berlin edition.

Ambrose	Saint Ambrose, *Apologia Prophetae David.* References are to chapters.
Aristotles Politiques	*Aristotles Politiques, or Discourses of Government*, London 1598.
Bellarmine	Bellarmine, Robert, Cardinal and Saint, *De Romano Pontifice.* References are to book and chapter.
	De Laicis. This is book three of Bellarmine's *De Membris Ecclesiae Militantis.* References are to chapters.
	De Verbo Dei. References are to book and chapter.
	All these works were published in *Disputationum*

	de Controversiis, 3 vols., Ingolstadt 1586–9, and many other editions.
Bodin	Bodin, Jean, *The Six Bookes of a Commonweale*, translated by Richard Knolles, London 1606.
Botero	Botero, Giovanni, *Relations of the Most Famous Kingdoms and Common-wealthes thorowout the World*, London 1630.
Bracton	*Henrici de Bracton De Legibus et Consuetudinibus Angliae, libri quinque*, London 1640.
Calvin	Calvin, John, *The Institutes of the Christian Religion*. The final edition was published in 1559, and it was translated into English in 1561. There were many later editions. References are to book and chapter.
Camden	Camden, William, *Britain, or a Chorographicall Description of the most flourishing Kingdomes, England, Scotland, and Ireland*, translated by Philemon Holland, London 1637. This book was first published in Latin in 1586, and the translation – which Filmer used – first appeared in 1610.
Coke 1	Coke, Sir Edward, *The First Part of the Institutes*, London 1628.
Coke 4	Coke, Sir Edward, *The Fourth Part of the Institutes*, London 1644.
Cotton	'That the Kings of England have been pleased, usually, to consult with their peers in the Great Council, and Commons in Parliament, of marriage, of peace, and war' (pp. 11–39). 'That the soveraigns person is required in the Great Councils, or Assemblies of the State' (pp. 41–57). References to both these works, which Filmer used in manuscript, are to *Cottoni Posthuma: divers choice pieces of that renowned antiquary, Sir Robert Cotton, Knight and Baronet*, third edition, London 1679.
Crompton	Crompton, Richard, *L'Authorite et Iurisdiction des cours de la maiestie de la Roygne*, London 1594. This book was reprinted in 1637.
D'Avity	D'Avity, Pierre, *The Estates, Empire, & Princi-*

	palities of the World, translated by Edward Grimstone, London 1615.
Decreti	Decreti prima pars, in Corpus Iuris Canonici, 2 vols., Halle 1747. All the passages cited by Filmer are in columns 1–2 of this edition. Sectional references are given.
D'Ewes	D'Ewes, Sir Simonds, A Compleat Journal of the Votes, Speeches and Debates, both of the House of Lords and House of Commons throughout the whole reign of Queen Elizabeth, London 1693. Filmer drew on manuscripts of these materials, and his manuscripts were not always identical with those later printed by D'Ewes.
Digest	Digestorum et Pandectorum, in Corpus Iuris Civilis, ed. P. Krueger, T. Mommsen, R. Schoell and W. Kroll, 3 vols., Berlin 1954–9, vol. 1, second count. Page references are to this edition, but standard sectional references are also given.
Discourse upon the Questions	A Discourse upon the Questions in debate between the King and Parliament, London 1642.
Duval	Duval, Guillaume, Aristotelis Opera Omnia quae extant, Graece et Latine ... accessit brevis ... Synopsis ... authore Guillelmo Du Val, 2 vols., Paris 1629. The Latin translation of the Politics is by Denis Lambin. References are to volume and page. An earlier edition was printed at Paris in 1619.
Egerton	Egerton, Sir Thomas, Baron Ellesmere and Viscount Brackley, The Speech of the Lord Chancellor of England, in the Eschequer Chamber, touching the Post-nati, second impression, London 1609. The first impression appeared in the same year.
Ferne	Ferne, Henry, A Reply unto Severall Treatises pleading for the Armes now taken up by Subjects, Oxford 1643.
Florence of Worcester	Florence of Worcester, Chronicon ex Chronicis, ab initio mundi usque ad annum Domini. 1118, London 1592.
Fuller	Fuller, Nicholas, The Argument of Master Nicho-

	las Fuller, *in the case of Thomas Lad, and Richard Maunsell his clients*, London 1607. This book was reprinted in 1641.
Gee	Gee, Edward, *An Exercitation concerning Usurped Powers*, London 1650.
Glanville	Glanville, Sir John, *The Copies of two Speeches in Parliament. The one by Iohn Glanville Esquire. The other by Sir Henry Martin Knight. At a Generall Committee of both Houses, the 22. of May. 1628*, no place or date [London 1628].
Grotius	*De Jure Belli ac Pacis*, first published at Paris in 1625. Published again with important revisions in 1631 and frequently reprinted. Filmer used both the first and later editions. References are to book, chapter, section and, where appropriate, subsection.
Hayward 1	Hayward, Sir John, *An Answer to the First Part of a Certaine Conference*, London 1603.
Hayward 2	Hayward, Sir John, *The Lives of the III. Normans, Kings of England*, London 1613.
Hobbes 1	Hobbes, Thomas, *De Cive. The Latin version* ed. Howard Warrender, Oxford 1983. First published in 1642 and again in 1647. References are to pages in Warrender's edition, and also to chapter and section.
Hobbes 2	*Leviathan or the Matter, Forme and Power of a Commonwealth Ecclesiastical and Civil*, London 1651. C. B. Macpherson's readily available Penguin edition includes the page numbers of this edition.
Holinshed	Holinshed, Raphael, *Holinshed's Chronicles of England, Scotland, and Ireland*, 6 vols., London 1807–8. First published in 1577.
Hooker	Hooker, Richard, *Of the Laws of Ecclesiastical Polity*. References are to book, chapter and section. Filmer drew on a manuscript of the eighth book, which was first published in 1648.
Hoveden	Hoveden or Howden, Roger of, *Rogeri de Hovedeni Annalium pars prior & posterior*, in Sir Henry

	Savile, ed. *Rerum Anglicarum Scriptores post Bedam*, London 1596, ff. 229a-471b.
Hunton	Hunton, Philip, *A Treatise of Monarchie*, London 1643.
Institutes	*Iustiniani ... Institutorum*, in P. Krueger, T. Mommsen, R. Schoell and W. Kroll, eds., *Corpus Iuris Civilis*, 3 vols., Berlin 1954–9, vol. 1, first count. Page references are to this edition, but standard sectional references are also given.
James I 1	James I, *A Speech to the Lords and Commons of the Parliament at White-Hall, On Wednesday the XXI. of March. Anno 1609*, in C. H. McIlwain, ed., *The Political Works of James I*, Cambridge, Mass. 1918, pp. 306–25. The speech was first published in 1610.
James I 2	James I, *The Trew Law of Free Monarchies*, in C. H. McIlwain, ed., *The Political Works of James I*, Cambridge, Mass. 1918, pp. 53–70. First published in 1598.
James I 3	James I, *His Maiesties Declaration, touching his Proceedings in the late Assembly and Convention of Parliament*, London 1621.
Lambarde 1	Lambarde, William, *Archeion or, a Discourse upon the High Courts of Justice in England*, ed. C. H. McIlwain and Paul L. Ward, Cambridge, Mass. 1957. *Archeion* was first published in 1635. Filmer used a manuscript version of this book.
Lambarde 2	*A Perambulation of Kent*, second edition, 1596. First published in 1574.
Matthew Paris	Matthew Paris, *Matthaei Paris Historia Maior*, London 1640.
Matthew Westminster	Matthew Westminster, *Matthaeus Westmonasteriensis, Florilegus dictus, praecipue de rebus Britannicis ab exordio mundi usque ad annum Domini. 1307*, London 1570.
Milles	Milles, Thomas, *The Catalogue of Honor or Treasury of True Nobility*, London 1610.
Milton 5	Milton, John, *The Tenure of Kings and Magistrates*, in *The Works of John Milton*, vol. 5, pp. 1–59,

	Columbia edition, New York 1932. First published in 1649.
Milton 7	Milton, John, *Pro Populo Anglicano Defensio*, in *The Works of John Milton*, vol. 7, Columbia edition, New York 1932. Filmer used the first edition of 1651.
Molina	*De Justitia et Jure*, 6 vols., Mainz 1607–9, and many other editions.
Parker	Parker, Henry, *Observations upon some of his Majesties late Answers and Expresses*, London 1642.
Parsons	Parsons, Robert, *A Conference about the next Succession to the Crown of Ingland ... Published by R. Dolman*, 1594.
Prynne	Prynne, William, *The Treachery and Disloyalty of Papists to their Sovereigns, in Doctrine and Practise*, second edition, London 1643. Filmer used the first edition, which was published in the same year.
Raleigh 1	Raleigh, Sir Walter, *The History of the World*, first published at London in 1614 and frequently reprinted. References are to book, chapter and section.
Raleigh 2	*The Prerogative of Parliaments in England*, London 1628. Filmer possessed a manuscript of this work.
R. P.	*Rotuli Parliamentorum; ut et petitiones, et placita in Parliamento*, 6 vols., London 1783. Filmer used manuscripts of these materials.
Salmasius	Salmasius, Claudius (Claude de Saumaise), *De Usuris Liber*, Leiden 1638.
Selden 1	Selden, John, *Titles of Honor*, second edition, London 1631. First published in 1614, but Filmer used the much revised and enlarged second edition.
Selden 2	Selden, John, *Of the Dominion, or Ownership of the Sea*, translated by Marchamont Nedham, London 1652. The Latin original was first published in 1635 as *Mare Clausum seu de Dominio*

	Maris libri duo. Filmer used the Latin version, making his own translations. All Filmer's references are to book 1, chapter 4.
Selden 3	Selden, John, *The Privileges of the Baronage of England*, London 1642.
Selden 4	Selden, John, ed., *Eadmeri Monachi Cantuarensis Historiae Novorum*, London 1623.
Spelman	Spelman, Sir Henry, *Henrici Spelmanni Equit. Anglo-Brit. Archaeologus. In modum Glossarii ad rem antiquam posteriorem*, London 1626.
Starkey	Starkey, Ralph, *The Privileges and Practice of Parliaments in England*, London 1628.
Statutes	*The Statutes at Large*, 2 vols., London 1618. Page references are to vol. 1 of this edition. In addition references are given to monarch, regnal year and chapter.
Statutes of Ireland	*The Statutes of Ireland, beginning the third yere of K. Edward the second*, Dublin 1621.
Stow	Stow, John, *The Survey of London*, Everyman edition, London 1912. This reprints the enlarged text of 1603. The book was first published in 1598.
Suarez	*Tractatus de Legibus ac Deo Legislatore*. References are to book, chapter and section. The work was first published at Coimbra in 1612, and was frequently reprinted.
Vowell	Vowell, John (alias John Hooker), *The Order and Usage of the keeping of a Parliament*, London 1575.
Wing	Wing, Donald G., ed., *Short-Title Catalogue of Books printed in England, Scotland, Ireland, Wales and British America and of English Books printed in other Countries 1641–1700*, 3 vols., New York 1972, 1982, 1951.
Year Book, Edward III 22	*De Termino Hillarii Anno Regni Regis Edwardi tertii post Conquestum xxii*, London 1567.

Patriarcha[a]
The Naturall Power of Kinges Defended against the Unnatural Liberty of the People.

By Arguments { Theological
Rational
Historical
Legall*[1]

*Patriarcha. That the first kings were fathers of families.

Chapter One: (1) The tenet of the natural liberty of mankind new, plausible and dangerous; (2) the question stated out of Bellarmine; some contradictions of his noted; (3) Bellarmine's argument answered out of Bellarmine himself; (4) the royal

[a] *Patriarcha*: texts: A – Regenstein Library, University of Chicago, Codex MS 413.

B – Cambridge University Library MS Add. 7078.

C – Chiswell edition dated 1680 but probably published later (Wing F923 – a corrected reprint of the first (Davis) edition of 1680, Wing F922. In the case of all readings recorded below the Chiswell and Davis editions agree).

D – Bohun's edition of 1685, Wing F928.

B was found by Peter Laslett at the ancestral home of the Filmers at East Sutton Park in 1939, and is now in the Cambridge University Library. It is a fair copy, and Laslett ascribes the hand to Filmer. Manifestly, it is a text of high authority. A was bought by the Chicago University Library from the booksellers Percy Dobell & Son of Tunbridge Wells in 1929. Nothing further is known of its provenance. It is in several hands. Schochet and Wallace argue that at least some of the manuscript was written by Filmer himself, but Tuck claims that the work is a professional scribal copy. In any event, A provides a good text which is clearly not copied from B, and which is seemingly largely free of scribal errors. There is strong evidence for supposing that A is the earlier text. For a fuller discussion of the dating of the two texts, see pp. xxxii–iv of this edition.

Copy-text is A; variant readings in B are given in the notes. An exception is that authority of the patriarchs before the Flood; (5) the dispersion of nations over the world after the confusion of Babel, was by entire families over which the fathers were kings; (6) and from them all kings are descended; (7) all kings are either fathers of their people, (8) or heirs of such fathers or usurpers of the right of such fathers; (9) of the escheating of kingdoms; (10) of regal and paternal power and of their agreement*.[2]

(1)   *Since the time that school divinity began to flourish, there hath been a common opinion maintained as well by divines as by divers other learned men which affirms:*[3] 'Mankind is naturally endowed and born with freedom from all subjection, and at liberty to choose what form of government it please, and that the power which any one man hath over others was at the first by human right bestowed according to the discretion of the multitude.'

This tenet *was*[4] first hatched in the schools,[b] *and hath been fostered by all succeeding papists for good divinity*.[5] The divines *also*[6] of the reformed churches have entertained it, and the common people everywhere tenderly embrace it as being most plausible to flesh and blood, for that it prodigally distributes a portion of liberty to the meanest of the multitude, who magnify liberty as if the height of human felicity were only to be found in it – never remembering that the desire of liberty was the cause of the fall of Adam.

B usually has K. before kings' names, e.g. K. Henry VII; this has not been recorded in the notes. Copy-text for passages omitted in A is B. If a note gives a reading from A, the text is from B and vice versa. Readings from C and D are given only occasionally, and especially where they arguably correct errors in A and B. In general, C is an inferior version of A; D is a version of C with corrections and additions based on B or just possibly on an unknown manuscript closely related to B. The division into sections and the section numbers follow A, and take account of A's list of contents; but where A omits or mis-places numbers this has not been recorded; nor have the revised numbering system and list of contents adopted in B.

Two chapters included in B were printed in Filmer's *Observations* on Grotius in 1652, and are printed with that work in this edition. Elsewhere in the *Observations* Filmer refers to material from those chapters, and the *Observations* are, indeed, incomplete without them. So they have been included here, rather than in *Patriarcha*. The largest difference between A and B is the inclusion in B of the two chapters, and a number of other divergences arose to accommodate the new material. Since the chapters are here printed (as Filmer intended) with the *Observations*, it makes sense to use A as the main text for *Patriarcha*. But it deserves to be reiterated that, with the exception of the altered numbering system and table of contents, all variant readings in B may be recovered in this edition.

[b] [Medieval Roman Catholic universities].

But howsoever this *vulgar*[7] opinion hath of late obtained great reputation, yet it is not to be found in the ancient Fathers and doctors of the primitive church. It contradicts the doctrine and history of the Holy Scriptures, the constant practice of all ancient monarchies, and the very principles of the law of nature. It is hard to say whether it be more erroneous in divinity or dangerous in policy.

Yet[8] upon the grounds of this doctrine both Jesuits and some *over zealous*[9] favourers of the Geneva discipline have built a perilous conclusion, which is 'that the people or multitude have power to punish or deprive the prince if he transgress the laws of the kingdom'. Witness Parsons and Buchanan. The first, under the name of Doleman, in the third chapter of his first book labours to prove that kings have been lawfully chastised by their commonwealths [Parsons pp. 37–63]. The latter in his book *De Jure Regni apud Scotos* maintains a liberty of the people to depose their prince. Cardinal Bellarmine *(book 3 *De Laicis*, chapter 6)*[10] and Mr Calvin *(*Institutes* book 4, chapter 10)*[11] both look asquint this way.

This desperate assertion, whereby kings are made subject to the censures and deprivations of their subjects, follows (as the authors of it conceive) as a necessary consequence of that former position of the supposed natural equality and freedom of mankind, and liberty to choose what form of government it please.

And though Sir John Hayward, Adam Blackwood, John Barclay and some others have learnedly confuted both Buchanan and Parsons, and *bravely*[12] vindicated the right of kings in most points, yet all of them, when they come to the argument drawn from the natural liberty and equality of mankind, *do*[13] with one consent admit it for a *truth*[14] unquestionable, not so much as once denying or opposing it. Whereas if they did but confute this first erroneous principle, the *whole fabric of this vast engine of popular sedition would drop down of itself*.[15]

The rebellious consequence which follows this prime article of the natural freedom of mankind may be my sufficient warrant for a modest examination of the original truth of it. Much hath been said, and by many, for the affirmative. Equity requires that an ear be reserved a little for the negative.

In this discourse I shall give myself these cautions:

First, I have nothing to do to meddle with mysteries of *the present*[16] state. Such *arcana imperii* [state secrets], or cabinet councils, the vulgar may not pry into. An implicit faith is given to the meanest artificer in his own craft. How much more is it, then, due to a prince in the profound secrets of government. The causes and ends of the greatest politic actions and motions of state dazzle the eyes and exceed the capacities of all men, save only those that are hourly versed in managing public affairs. Yet since the rule for each man to know in what to obey his prince cannot be learnt without a relative knowledge of those points wherein a sovereign may command, it is necessary when the commands and pleasures of superiors come abroad and call for an obedience that every man inform himself how to regulate his actions or his sufferings. For according to the quality of the thing commanded an active or passive obedience is to be yielded, and this is not to limit the prince's power, but the extent of the subject's obedience, by giving to Caesar the things that are Caesar's etc. [Matthew xxii, 21].

Secondly, I am not to question or quarrel at the rights or liberties of this or any other nation. My task is chiefly to enquire from whom these *first*[17] came, not to dispute what or how many they are, but whether they are derived from the law of natural liberty or from the grace and bounty of princes. My desire and hope is that the people of England may and do enjoy as ample privileges as any nation under heaven. The greatest liberty in the world (if it be duly considered) is for people to live under a monarch. It is the Magna Carta of this kingdom. All other shows or pretexts of liberty are but several degrees of slavery, and a liberty only to destroy liberty.

If such as maintain the natural liberty of mankind take offence at the liberty I take to examine it, they must take heed that they do not deny by retail that liberty which they affirm by wholesale. For if their thesis be true, the hypothesis will follow, that all men may examine their own charters, deeds, or evidences by which they claim and hold the inheritance or freehold of their liberties.

Thirdly, I *must not detract*[18] from the worth of all those learned men who are of a contrary judgment in the point of natural liberty. The profoundest scholar that *ever was*[19] known hath not been able to search out every truth that is discoverable: neither Aristotle in natural philosophy, nor *Hooker*[20] in divinity. They *were*[21] but men, yet I reverence their judgments in most points, and confess myself beholding even to their errors in this. Something that I found amiss in their opinions guided me in the discovery of that truth which

(I persuade myself) they missed. A dwarf sometimes may see that which a giant looks over, for whilst one truth is curiously searched after, another must necessarily be neglected. Late writers have taken up too much upon trust from the subtle schoolmen,ᶜ who to be sure to thrust down the king below the pope, thought it the safest course to advance the people above the king, that so the papal power may *more easily*[22] take place of the regal. *Thus*[23] many an ignorant subject hath been fooled into this faith, that a man may become a martyr for his country by being a traitor to his prince; whereas the new coined distinction of subjects into royalists and patriots is most unnatural, since the relation between king and people is so great that their well-being is reciprocal.

(2)   To make evident the grounds of this question about the natural liberty of mankind, I will lay down some passages of Cardinal Bellarmine, that may best unfold the state of this controversy. 'Secular or civil power', saith he

> is instituted by men. It is in the people unless they bestow it on a prince. This power is immediately in the whole multitude, as in the subject of it. For this power is by the divine law, but the divine law hath given this power to no particular man. If the positive law be taken away, there is left no reason why amongst a multitude (who are equal) one rather than another should bear rule over the rest. Power is given by the multitude to one man, or to more by the same law of nature, for the commonwealth of itself cannot exercise this power, therefore it is bound to bestow it upon some one man, or some few. It depends upon the consent of the multitude to ordain over themselves a king, or consul, or other magistrate; and if there be a lawful cause, the multitude may change the kingdom into an aristocracy or democracy. (Book 3 *De Laicis*, chapter '4' [=6])

Thus far Bellarmine, in which passages are comprised the strength of all that ever I have read or heard produced for the natural liberty of the subject.

Before I examine or refute these doctrines, I must a little make *some observations upon his*[24] words.

First, he saith that by the law of God power is immediately in the people. Hereby he makes God *to be the immediate*[25] author

ᶜ [medieval Roman Catholic clergy who taught philosophy and theology].

of a democratical estate. For a democracy is nothing else but the power of the multitude. If this be true, not only aristocracies but all monarchies are altogether unlawful, as being ordained (as he thinks) by men, when as God himself hath chosen a democracy.

Secondly, he holds that although a democracy be the ordinance of God, yet the people have no power to use the power which God hath given them, but only power to *give*[26] away their power; whereby it follows *that*[27] there can be no democratical government, because the people, he saith, 'must give their power to one man, or to some few'; which maketh either a regal or aristocratical estate, which the multitude is tied to do, even by the same law of nature which originally gave them the power. And why then doth he say the multitude may change the kingdom into a democracy?

Thirdly, he concludes that 'if there be a lawful cause the multitude may change the kingdom *into an aristocracy or democracy*'.[28] Here I would fain know who shall judge of this *lawful*[29] cause? If the multitude (for I see nobody else can) then this is a pestilent and dangerous conclusion.

(3)   I come now to examine that argument which is used by Bellarmine, and is the one and only argument I can find produced by *any*[30] author for the proof of the natural liberty of the people. It is thus framed: that God hath given or ordained power is evident by Scripture; but God hath given it to no particular man, because by nature all men are equal; therefore he hath given power to the people or multitude.

To answer this reason, drawn from the equality of mankind by nature, I will first use the help of Bellarmine himself, whose *very*[31] words are these: 'if many men had been together created out of the earth, all they ought to have been princes over their posterity' (book I *De Romano Pontifice*, chapter 2). *In these words we have an evident confession that creation made man prince of his posterity.*[32] And indeed not only Adam but the succeeding patriarchs had, by right of fatherhood, royal authority over their children. Nor dares Bellarmine deny this also. 'That the patriarchs', saith he, 'were endowed with kingly power, their deeds do testify' [*De Romano Pontifice* book I, chapter 2]. For as Adam was lord of his children, so his children under him had a command *and power*[33] over their own children, but still with subordination to the first parent, who is lord paramount over his children's children to all generations, *as being the grand-father of his people*.[34]

I see not then how the children of Adam, or of any man else, can be free from subjection to their parents. And this *subjection*[35] of children is the only fountain of all regal authority, by the ordination of God himself. *It*[36] follows that civil power not only in general is by divine institution, but even the *assignment*[37] of it specifically to the eldest parent, which quite takes away that new and common distinction which refers only power universal *as*[38] absolute to God, but power respective in regard of the special form of government to the choice of the people. *Nor leaves it any place for such imaginary pactions between kings and their people as many dream of*.[39]

(4)   This lordship which Adam by creation had over the whole world, and by right descending from him the patriarchs did enjoy, was as large and ample as the absolutest dominion of any monarch which hath been since the creation. For power of life and death we find that Judah, the father, pronounced sentence of death against Thamar, his daughter-in-law, for playing the harlot. 'Bring her forth', saith he, 'that she may be burnt' [Genesis xxxviii, 24]. Touching war, we see that Abraham commanded an army of 318 soldiers of his own family [Genesis xiv, 14]; and Esau met his brother Jacob with 400 men at arms [Genesis xxxiii, 1]. For matter of peace, Abraham made a league with Abimelech, and ratified the articles *by*[40] an oath [Genesis xxi, 23–4]. These acts of judging in capital causes, of making war, and concluding peace, are the chiefest marks of sovereignty that are found in any monarch.

(5)   Not only until the Flood, but after it, this patriarchal power did continue – as the very name of patriarch doth in part prove. The three sons of Noah had the whole world divided amongst them by their father, for of them was the whole world overspread, according to the benediction given to him and his sons: 'Be fruitful and multiply and replenish the earth' *(Genesis ix, [1])*.[41] Most of the civillest nations *in*[42] the world labour to fetch their original from some one of the sons or nephews of Noah, which were scattered abroad after the confusion of Babel. In this dispersion we must certainly find the establishment of regal power throughout the kingdoms of the world.

It is a common opinion that at the confusion of tongues there were seventy-two distinct nations erected. All which were not confused multitudes, without heads or governors, and at liberty to choose what governors or government they pleased, but they were distinct families, which had fathers for rulers over them. Whereby it appears that even in the confusion, God was careful to preserve the fatherly authority by distributing the diversity of languages according to the diversity of families. For so it plainly appears by the text. First, after the enumeration of the sons of Japhet, the conclusion is: 'By these were the isles of the gentiles divided in their lands; every one after his tongue, after their families, in their nations' (Genesis x, 5). So it is said: 'These are the sons of Ham after their families, after their tongues, in their countries, and in their nations' [Genesis x, 20]. The like we read: 'These are the sons of *Shem**43 after their families, after their tongues, in their lands, after their nations. These are the families of the sons of Noah after their generations in their nations, and by these were the nations divided in the earth after the Flood' [Genesis x, 31–2].

In this division of the world, some are of opinion that Noah used lots for the distribution of it. Others affirm *that**44 he sailed about the Mediterranean sea in ten years and as he went about, pointed to each son his part, and so made the division of the then known world into Asia, Africa, and Europe, according to the number of his sons, the limits of which three parts are all found in that midland sea.

(6)   But howsoever the manner of the division be uncertain, yet it is most certain the division itself was by families from Noah and his children, over which the parents were heads and princes.

Amongst these was Nimrod, who no doubt (as Sir Walter Raleigh affirms) was by *good**45 right lord or king over his family [Raleigh I, I, 10, i]. Yet against right did he enlarge his empire by seizing violently on the rights of other lords of families, and in this sense he may be said to be the author and first founder of monarchy. And all those that do attribute unto him the original of regal power do hold he got it by tyranny or usurpation, and not by any due election of the people or multitude, nor by any paction with them.

As this patriarchal power continued in Abraham, Isaac and Jacob, even until the Egyptian bondage, so we find it amongst the sons of Ishmael and Esau. It is said: 'These are the sons of Ishmael, and these are *their names by their**46 castles and towns, twelve princes of their tribes or families' (Genesis xxv, 16). 'And these are the names of the dukes that came of Esau, according to their families and their places by their nations' (Genesis xxxvi, 40).

(7)   Some, perhaps, may think that these princes and dukes of families were but some petty lords under some greater kings, because the number of them are so many that their particular territories could be but small, and not worthy the title of kingdoms. But *they*[47] must consider that at first kings had no such large dominions as they have nowadays. We find in the time of Abraham, which was about 300 years after the Flood, that in a little corner of Asia nine kings at once met in battle, most of which were but kings of cities apiece, with the adjacent territories, as of Sodom, Gomorrha, Shinar, etc. In the same chapter is mention *of*[48] Melchisedek, king of Salem, which was but the city *of*[49] Jerusalem (Genesis xiv). And in the catalogue of the kings of Edom, the name of each king's city is recorded as the only mark to distinguish their dominions (Genesis xxxvi). In the land of Canaan, which was but of *a*[50] small circuit, Joshua destroyed thirty-one kings [Joshua xii, 24], and about the same time Adonibezek had seventy kings whose fingers and toes he had cut off, and made them feed under his table [Judges i, 7]. A few ages after this, thirty-two kings came *to*[51] Benhadad [1 Kings xx, 16], king of Syria, and about seventy kings of Greece went to the wars of Troy. Caesar found more kings in France than there be now provinces there, and at his sailing over into *this*[52] island he found four kings in our county of Kent. These heaps of kings in each nation are an argument *that*[53] their territories were but small, and strongly confirm our assertion that erection of kingdoms came at first only by distinction of families.

By manifest footsteps we may trace this paternal government unto the Israelites coming into Egypt, where the exercise of *supreme*[54] patriarchal jurisdiction was intermitted because they were in subjection to a stronger prince. After the return of these Israelites out of bondage, God, out of a special care of them, chose Moses and Joshua successively to govern as princes in the place and stead of the supreme fathers, and after them likewise for a time He raised up Judges to defend His people in times of peril. But when God gave the Israelites kings, He re-established the ancient and prime right of lineal succession to paternal government. And whensoever He made choice of any special person to be king, He intended that the issue *also*[55] should have benefit thereof, as being comprehended sufficiently in the person of the father – although the father only were named in the grant.

(8)   It may seem absurd to maintain that kings now are the fathers of their people, since experience shows the contrary. It is true, all kings be not the natural parents of their subjects, yet they all *either*[56] are, or are to be reputed as the next heirs *to*[57] those progenitors who were at first the natural parents of the whole people, and in their right succeed to the exercise of supreme jurisdiction. And such heirs are not only lords of their own children, but also of their brethren, and all others that were subject to their fathers.

And therefore we find that God told Cain of his brother Abel: 'His desires shall be subject unto thee, and thou shalt rule over him' (Genesis iv, 7). Accordingly, when Jacob had bought his brother's birthright, Isaac blessed him thus: 'Be lord over thy brethren, and let the sons of thy mother bow before thee' *(Genesis xxvii, 29)*.[58] As long as the first fathers of families lived, the name of patriarchs did aptly belong unto them. But after a few descents, when the true fatherhood itself was extinct and only the right of the father descended to the true heir, then the title of prince or king was more significant to express the power of him who succeeds only to the right of that fatherhood which his ancestors did naturally enjoy. By this means it comes to pass that many a child, by succeeding a king, hath the right of a father over many a grey-headed multitude, *and hath the title of pater patriae [father of the fatherland]*.[59]

(9)   It may be demanded what becomes of the right of fatherhood in case the crown do escheat for want of an heir, whether doth it not then devolve to the people? The answer is:

   1. It is but the negligence or ignorance of the people to lose the knowledge of the true heir, for an heir there always is. If Adam himself were still living, and now ready to die, it is certain that there is one man, and but one in the world, who is next heir, although the knowledge who should be that one man be quite lost.

   2. *This*[60] ignorance of the people being admitted, it doth not by any means follow that for want of heirs the supreme power *devolves*[61] to the multitude, and that they have power to rule, or choose what rulers they please. No: the kingly power escheats in

such cases to the *prime*[62] and independent heads of families, for every kingdom is resolved into those *parts*[63] whereof at first it was made. By the uniting of great families or petty princedoms, we find the greater monarchies were at the first erected, and into such again – as into their first matter – many times they *return*.[64] And because the dependency of ancient families is oft obscure or worn out of knowledge, therefore the wisdom of all or most princes hath thought fit to adopt many times those for heads of families and princes of provinces whose merits, abilities, or fortunes have enabled them, or made them fit and capable of such royal favours. All such prime heads and fathers have power to consent in the uniting or conferring of their fatherly right of sovereign authority on whom they please. And he that is so elected claims not his power as a donative from the people, but as being substituted properly by God, from whom he receives his royal charter of an universal father, though testified by the ministry of the heads of the people.

If it please God, for the correction of the prince or punishment of the people to suffer princes to be removed and others placed in their rooms, either by the factions of the nobility or rebellion of the people, in all such cases the judgment of God – who hath power to give and to take away kingdoms – is most just. Yet the ministry of men who execute God's judgments without commission is sinful and damnable. God doth but use and turn men's unrighteous acts to the performance of His righteous decrees.

(10)   In all kingdoms *or*[65] commonwealths in the world, whether the prince be the supreme father of the people or but the true heir of such a father, or whether he come to the crown by usurpation, or by election of the nobles or of the people, or by any other way whatsoever, or whether some few or a multitude govern the commonwealth, yet still the authority that is in any one, or in many, or in all *of*[66] these, is the only right and natural authority of a supreme father. There is, and always shall be continued to the end of the world, a natural right of a supreme father over every multitude, although, by the secret will of God, many at first do most unjustly obtain the exercise of it.

To confirm this natural right of regal power, we find in the decalogue that the law which enjoins obedience to kings is delivered in the terms of 'honour thy father' [Exodus, xx, 12] as if all power were originally in the father. If obedience to parents be immediately due by a natural law, and subjection to princes but by the mediation of *an*[67] human ordinance, what reason is there that the law of nature should give place to the laws of men, as we see the power of the father over his child gives place and is subordinate to the power of the magistrate?

If we compare the natural duties of a father with those of a king, we find them to be all one, without any difference at all but only in the latitude or extent of them. As the father over one family, so the king, as father over many families, extends his care to preserve, feed, clothe, instruct and defend the whole commonwealth. His wars, his peace, his courts of justice and all his acts of sovereignty tend only to preserve and distribute to every subordinate and inferior father, and to their children, their rights and privileges, so that all the duties of a king are summed up in an universal fatherly care of his people.

Chapter Two: It is unnatural for the people to govern or choose governors. (1) Aristotle examined about the freedom of the people and justified; (2) Suarez disputing against the regality of Adam; (3) families diversely defined by Aristotle, Bodin and others; (4) Suarez contradicting Bellarmine; (5) of election of kings, (6) by the major part of the people, (7) by proxy, and by silent acceptation; (8) no example in the Scripture of the people's choosing their king; Mr Hooker's judgment therein; (9) God governed always by monarchy; Bellarmine's (10) and Aristotle's judgment of monarchy; (11) imperfection of the Roman democracy; (12) Rome began her empire under kings and perfected it under emperors; (13) in danger the people always fled to monarchy; (14) whether democracies were invented to bridle tyrants, or rather that they came in by stealth; (15) democracies vilified by their own historians; (16) popular government more bloody than a tyranny; (17) of a mixed government of the king and people; (18) the people may not judge or correct their king; (19) no tyrants in England since the Conquest.

(1)   By conferring these proofs and reasons drawn from the authority of Scripture, it appears to be little less than a paradox which

Bellarmine and others affirm of the freedom of the multitude to choose what rulers they please.

Had the patriarchs their power given them by their own children? Bellarmine dares not say it, but the contrary. If then, the fatherhood enjoyed this authority for so many ages by the law of nature, when was it lost, or when forfeited, or how is it devolved to the liberty of the multitude?[d]

Because the Scripture is not favourable to the liberty of the people, therefore many fly to natural reason and to the authority of Aristotle. I must crave liberty to examine or explain the opinion of this great philosopher *but briefly*.[68]

I find this sentence in the third of his *Politics*, chapter 16: 'It seems *to some* not to be natural for one man to be lord of all the citizens, since a city consists of equals' [1287[a] 10–12]. *These words seem to favour the equality of mankind*.[69] Lambin, in his Latin interpretation of this text, hath omitted the translation of this word 'τισιν' [to some; Duval ii, p. 359].[e] By that means he makes that to be the opinion of Aristotle which Aristotle allegeth to be the opinion but of some. This negligent or wilful escape of Lambin, in not translating a word so material, hath been an occasion to deceive many, who, looking no further than to the Latin translation, have concluded, and made the world now of late believe, that Aristotle here maintains a *natural equality of men*. And not only our English translator of Aristotle's *Politics* is, in this place, misled by following Lambin [*Aristotles Politiques*, p. 179], but even the learned Monsieur Duval in his analytical *Synopsis* bears them company [Duval ii, p. 53]. And yet this version of Lambin's is esteemed the best, and printed with Casaubon's corrected Greek copy, though in the rendering of this place the other translations have been more faithful. And he that shall compare the Greek text with the Latin will find that Casaubon had just cause in his preface to Aristotle's works to complain that the best *translations*[70] of Aristotle did need correction [Duval i, sig. a5a].

To prove that in these words, which seem to favour the equality

---

[d] [At this point B has three chapters omitted by A and C; D omits the first two of these chapters, but here prints the third. The chapters on Grotius and Selden are printed on pp. 216–27. The chapter on the civil law is in section (1) of the Appendix, p. 64 below. After the three chapters on Grotius, Selden and the civil law, B has sections (2)–(4) – on Suarez and Aristotle – and then the remainder of section (1)].

[e] [Filmer also discusses this passage from Aristotle in an interesting draft letter in British Library, Harleian MS 6867, ff.251a–2a].

of mankind, Aristotle doth not speak according to his own judgment but recites only the opinion of others, we find him clearly deliver his own opinion that the power of government did originally arise from the right of fatherhood, which cannot possibly consist with that natural equality which men dream of. For in the first of his *Politics* he agrees exactly with the Scripture, and lays *this*[71] foundation of government: 'The first society', *saith he*,[72] 'made of many houses is a village, which seems most naturally to be a colony of families or foster brethren of children and children's children. And therefore, at the beginning, cities were under the government of kings, for the eldest in every house is king. And so for kindred sake it is in colonies' [1252[b] 15–21]. And in the fourth of his *Politics*, chapter 2, he gives the title of the 'first and divinest sort of government to the institution of kings' [1289[a] 39–40], by defining tyranny to be a digression from the first and divinest.

Whosoever weighs advisedly these passages will find little hope of natural reason in Aristotle to prove the natural liberty of the multitude. Also, before him the divine Plato concludes 'a commonweal to be nothing else but a large family' [*Statesman* 259b]. I know *that*[73] for this position Aristotle quarrels with his master, but most unjustly. For therein he contradicts his own principles, for they both agree to fetch the original of civil government from the prime government of families. No doubt but Moses' history of the creation guided these two philosophers in finding out of this lineal subjection, deduced from the loins of the first parents according to that rule of St Chrysostom: 'God made all mankind of one man, that he might teach the world to be governed by a king, and not by a multitude' [Suarez III, ii, 3; Bellarmine *De Romano Pontifice* book 1, chapter 2].

The ignorance of the creation occasioned several errors amongst heathen philosophers. Polybius, though otherwise a most profound philosopher and judicious historian, yet here he stumbles. For in searching out the original of civil societies he conceited that 'multitudes of men after a deluge, a famine or a pestilence, met together like herds of cattle without any dependency, until the strongest bodies and boldest minds got the mastery of their fellows, even as it is', saith he, 'among bulls, boars and cocks' (Polybius book 6, [5, 5–8]).

And Aristotle himself, forgetting his first doctrine, tells us the first heroical kings were chosen by the people for their deserving well of the multitude, 'either by teaching them some arts, or by warring for them, or for gathering them together, or for dividing land amongst them' (*Politics* book 3, chapter 14) [1285^b 4–11]. Also Aristotle had another fancy, that those men 'which proved wise of mind were by nature intended to be lords and govern, and those that were strong of body were ordained to obey and be servants' *(Politics* book 1, chapter 2)*[74] [1252^a 34–6]. But this is a dangerous and uncertain rule, and not without some folly. For if a man prove both wise and strong, what will Aristotle have done with him? As he was wise, he could be no servant, as he had strength, he could not be a master. Besides, to speak like a philosopher, nature intends all men to be perfect both in wit and strength. The folly or imbecility proceeds from some error in generation or education, for nature aims at perfection in all her works.

(2)   *Father*[75] Suarez the Jesuit riseth up against the royal authority of Adam in defence of the freedom and liberty of the people, and thus argues: 'by right of creation', saith he,

> Adam had only economical power, but not political. He had power over his wife, and a fatherly power over his sons, whilst they were not made free. He might also, in process of time, have servants and a complete family, and in that family he might have complete economical power. But after that families began to be multiplied, and men to be separated and become heads of several families, they had the same power over their families. But political power did not begin until families began to be gathered together *into*[76] one perfect community. Wherefore, as the community did not begin by the creation of Adam, nor by his will alone, but of all them which did agree in this community, so we cannot say that Adam naturally had political primacy in that community. For that cannot be gathered by *any*[77] natural principles, because by the force of the law of nature alone it is not due *unto*[78] any progenitor to be also king of his posterity. And if this be not gathered out of the principles of nature, we cannot say 'God by a special gift or providence gave him this power'. For there is no revelation of this, nor testimony of Scripture. (*De Legibus* book 3, chapter 2, [3])

Hitherto Suarez.

Whereas he makes Adam to have a fatherly power over his sons, and yet shuts up this power within one family, he seems either to imagine that all Adam's children lived within one house and under a roof with their father, or else that as soon as any of his children lived out of his house, they ceased to be subject, and did thereby become free. For my part I cannot believe that Adam, although he were sole monarch of the world, had any such spacious palace as might contain any considerable part of his children. It is likelier that some mean cottage or tent did serve him to keep his court in; it were a hard case he should lose part of his authority because his children lay not within the walls of his house. But if Suarez will allow all Adam's children to be of his family, howsoever they were separate in dwellings, if their habitations were *either*[79] contiguous or at such distance as might easily receive his fatherly commands, and that all that were under his commands were of his family – although they had many children or servants married, having themselves also children – then I see no reason but that we may call Adam's family a commonwealth, except we will wrangle about words. For Adam, living 930 years and seeing seven or eight descents from himself, he might live to command of his children and *their*[80] posterity a multitude far bigger than many commonwealths or kingdoms.

(3) I know the politicians and civil lawyers do not well agree about the definition of a family, and Bodin doth seem in one place to confine it to a house. Yet in his definition he doth enlarge his meaning to 'all persons under the obedience of one and the same head of the family' (book 1, chapter 2, [p.8]), and he approves better of the propriety of the Hebrew word for a family, which is derived from a word that signifies a head, a prince or lord, than the Greek word for a family, which is derived from '*οἶκος*', which signifies a house. Nor doth Aristotle confine a family to one house, but esteems it to be made of those 'that daily converse together', whereas, before him, Charondas called a family 'homosypioi', those that feed together 'out of one common pannier', and Epimenides, the Cretan, terms a family 'homocapnoi', 'those that sit by *a*[81] common fire or smoke' [1252[b] 11–15]. But let *Father*[82] Suarez understand what he please by Adam's family. If he will but confess, as he needs must, that Adam and the patriarchs had absolute power of life and death, of peace and war and the like, within their houses or families, he must give us leave at least to call them kings of their houses or families. And if they be so by the law of nature, what liberty will be left for their children to dispose of?

Aristotle gives the lie to Plato and those that say that political and economical societies are all one, and do not differ *specie* [in species], but only *multitudine et paucitate* [in greatness and smallness of number], as if there were no difference betwixt a great house and a little city (*Politics* book 1, chapter 2). All the *argument*[83] I find he brings against them is this:

> The community of man and wife differs from the community of master and servant, because they have several ends. The intention of nature, by conjunction of male and female, is generation. But the scope of master and servant is only preservation, so that a wife and a servant are by nature distinguished. Because nature does not work like the cutlers at Delphos, for she makes but one thing for one use. [1252^b 1–4]

If we allow this argument to be sound, nothing doth follow but only this, that conjugal and despotical communities do differ. But it is no consequence that therefore economical and political societies do the like. For though it prove a family to consist of two distinct communities, yet it follows not that a family and commonwealth are distinct, because, as well in the commonwealth as in the family, both these communities are found.

And as this argument comes not home to our point, so it is not able to prove that little which it shows for. For if it should be granted (which yet is false) that generation and preservation differ about the *individuum*, yet they agree in the *general*, and serve both for the *conservation*[84] of mankind. Even as several servants differ in their particular ends or offices, as one to brew and another to bake, yet they agree in the general preservation of the family. Besides Aristotle himself confesseth that among the barbarians (as he calls all them that are not Grecians)

> a wife and a servant are the same, because by nature no barbarian is fit to govern. It is fit the Grecians should rule over the barbarians, for by nature a servant and a barbarian is all one. Their family consists only of an ox for a manservant and a wife for *a*[85] maid, so they are fit only to rule their wives and their beasts. [1252^b 4–21]

Lastly Aristotle, if it had pleased him, might have remembered that nature doth not always make *one thing but for one use*. He knows the tongue serves both to speak and to taste.

(4)   But to leave Aristotle *and*[86] return to Suarez. He saith that 'Adam had fatherly power over his sons whilst they were not made free' [Suarez III, ii, 3]. Here I could wish that the Jesuit had taught us how and when sons become free. I know no means by the law of nature. It is the favour, I think, of the parents only, who, when their children are of age and discretion to ease their parents of part of their fatherly care, are then content to remit some part of their fatherly authority. Therefore the customs of some countries *do*[87] in some cases enfranchise the children of inferior parents, but many nations have no such custom, but on the contrary have strict laws for the obedience of children (Bodin book I, chapter 4, [pp. 20–31]). The *judicial*[88] law of Moses† giveth full power to the father to stone his disobedient son, so it be done in the presence of a magistrate. And yet, *as some say*,[89] it did not belong to the magistrate to enquire or examine the justness of the cause, but it was so decreed lest the father should in his anger suddenly or secretly kill his son. Also, by the laws of the Persians and of the people of the Upper Asia, and of the Gauls, and by the laws of all the West Indies, the parents have power of life and death over their children. The Romans, even in their most popular estate, had this law in force, and this power of parents was ratified and amplified by the laws of the twelve tables, to the enabling of parents to sell their children two or three times over. By the help of this fatherly power Rome long flourished, and oftentimes was freed from great dangers. The fathers have drawn out of the very assemblies their own sons, when, being tribunes, they have published laws tending to sedition.

Memorable is the example of Cassius, who 'threw his son headlong out of the consistory, publishing the law *agraria* for the division of lands in the behoof of the people. And afterwards, by his own private judgment, put him to death' [Bodin p. 23] by throwing him down from the Tarpeian rock, the magistrates and people standing thereat amazed and not daring to resist his fatherly authority, although they would with all their hearts have had that law for the division of land. By which it appears it was lawful for the father to dispose of the

---

† Moses' laws were commonly divided into three groups: (1) the moral law, consisting of eternally binding precepts set out in the Ten Commandments; (2) the ceremonial law, consisting of orders relating to Jewish religious rites, and not binding on Christians; (3) the judicial law, consisting of laws other than those relating to religious rites; these laws were adapted to the circumstances of the ancient Jews, but some early modern theorists claimed they included many principles which continued to bind.

life of his child contrary to the will of the magistrates or people. The Romans also had a law that what the children got was not their own but their father's, although Solon made a law which acquitted the son from the nourishing of his father if his father had taught him no trade whereby to get his living [Bodin p. 23].

Suarez proceeds, and tells us that 'in process of time Adam had complete economical power' [Suarez III, ii, 3]. I know not what *this 'complete economical power' is*,[90] nor how or in what it doth really and essentially differ from political. If Adam did or might exercise in his family the same jurisdiction which a king doth now in a commonweal, then the kinds of power are not distinct, and though they may receive an accidental difference by the amplitude or extent of the bounds of the one beyond the other, yet since the like difference is also found in political estates, it follows that economical and political power differ no otherwise than a little commonweal differs from a great one.

Next saith Suarez, 'community did not begin at the creation of Adam' [Suarez III, ii, 3]. It is true – because he had nobody to communicate with. Yet community did presently follow his creation, and that by his will alone, for it was in his power only, who was lord of all, to appoint what his sons should have in proper and what in common. So *that*[91] *property* and *community* of goods did follow originally from him, and it is the duty of a father to provide as well for the common good of his children as for their particular.

Lastly, Suarez concludes that 'by the law of nature alone it is not due unto any progenitor to be also king of his posterity'. This assertion is confuted point blank by Bellarmine, who expressly affirmeth that 'the first parents ought to have been princes of their posterity' [*De Romano Pontifice* book 1, chapter 2]. And until Suarez bring some reason for what he saith, I shall trust more to Bellarmine's proofs than to his bare denials.[f]

(5)   But let us condescend a while to the opinion of Bellarmine *and*[92] Suarez, and of all those who place supreme power in the whole people, and ask them if their meaning be that there is but one and the same power in all the people of the world, so that no power can be granted except all the *people*[93] upon the earth meet and agree to choose a governor? An answer is here given by Suarez, that:

[f] [in B section (1) resumes here. See p. 13 n.*d*.].

It is scarce possible nor yet expedient that all men in the world should be gathered together into one community. It is likelier that either never, or for a very short time, that this power was in this manner in the whole multitude of men collected; but a little after the creation men began to be divided into several commonwealths, and this distinct power was in each of them. [Suarez III, ii, 5]

This answer of 'scarce possible nor yet expedient ... *It*[94] is likelier', begets a new doubt how this distinct power comes to each particular community when God gave it to the whole multitude only, and not to any particular assembly of men. Can they show or prove that ever the whole multitude met and divided this power, which God gave them in gross, by breaking it into parcels and by apportioning a distinct power to each several commonwealth? Without such a compact, I cannot see, according to their own principles, how there can be any election of a magistrate by *a*[95] commonwealth, but by a mere usurpation upon the privilege of the whole world. If any man think that particular multitudes, at their own discretion, had power to divide themselves into several commonwealths, those that think so have neither reason nor proof for so thinking, and thereby a gap is opened for every petty factious multitude to raise a new commonwealth, and to make more commonweals than there be families in the world.

But let this also be yielded them, that in each particular commonwealth there is a distinct power in the multitude; was a general meeting of a whole kingdom ever known for the election of a prince? *Was*[96] there any example of it ever found in the whole world? To conceit such a thing is to imagine little less *than*[97] an impossibility, and so by consequence no one form of government or king was ever established according to this supposed law of nature.

(6)　It may be answered by some that if either the greatest part of a kingdom; or, if a smaller part only by themselves and all the rest by proxy; or, if the part not concurring in election do after by a tacit assent ratify the act of others, that in all these cases it may be said *to be*[98] the work of the whole multitude.

As to the act of the *major* part of a multitude, it is true that by politic human constitutions it is oft ordained that the voices of the most shall overrule the rest. And such ordinances bind, because where men are assembled by an human power, that power that doth assemble them can also limit and direct the manner of the execution of that power. And by such derivative power, made known by law or custom, either the greater part, or two *thirds*,[99] or three parts of five or the like, have power to oversway the liberty of their opposites. But in assemblies that take their authority from the law of nature it cannot be so. For what freedom or liberty is due to any man by the law of nature, no inferior power can alter, limit or diminish. No one man, nor a multitude, can give away the natural right of another. The law of nature is unchangeable, and howsoever one man may hinder another in the use or exercise of his natural right, yet thereby no man loseth the right itself. For the right and the use of the right may be distinguished, as right and possession are oft distinct. Therefore, unless it can be proved by some law of nature that the major, or some other part, have power to overrule the rest of the multitude, it must follow that the acts of multitudes not entire are not binding to all but only to such as consent unto them.

(7)   As to the point of proxy, it cannot be showed or proved that all those that have been absent from popular elections did ever give their voices to some of their fellows. I ask but one example out of *the history of the whole world*.[100] Let the commonweal be but named where ever the multitude, or so much as the greatest part of it, consented either by voice or by procuration to the election of a prince. The ambition sometimes of one man, sometimes of many, or the faction of a city or citizens, or the mutiny of an army, hath set up or pulled down princes. But they have never tarried for this pretended orderly proceeding of the whole multitude.

Lastly, if the silent acceptation of a governor by part of the people be an argument of their concurring in the election of him, by the same reason the tacit assent of the whole commonwealth may be maintained. From whence it follows that every prince that comes to a crown, either by succession, conquest or usurpation, may be said to be elected by the people. Which inference is too ridiculous, for in such cases the people are so far from the liberty of *specification* that they want even that of *contradiction*.

(8)   But it is vain to argue against the liberty of the people in the election of kings as long as men are persuaded that examples *of it are to be found*[101] in Scripture. It is fit, therefore, to discover the grounds of this error. It is plain by an evident text that it is one thing to choose a king, and another thing to set a king over

the people. This latter power the children of Israel had, but not the former. This distinction is found most evident in Deuteronomy xvii, 15, where the law of God saith: 'Him shalt thou set king over thee whom the Lord shall choose'. So God must *eligere* [choose], and the people only do *constituere* [set up]. Mr Hooker, in his eighth book of *Ecclesiastical Polity* (manuscript), clearly expounds this distinction. His words are worth the citing:

> Heaps of Scripture (saith he) are alleged concerning the solemn coronation or inauguration of Saul, David, Solomon and others, by nobles, ancients and people of the commonwealth of Israel; as if the solemnities were a kind of deed, whereby the right of dominion is given. Which strange, untrue and unnatural conceits set abroad by seedmen of rebellion, only to animate unquiet spirits, and to feed them with possibilities of aspiring unto the thrones, if they can win the hearts of the people, whatsoever hereditary title any other before them may have; I say these unjust and insolent positions I would not mention, were it not thereby to make the countenance of truth more orient. For unless we will openly proclaim defiance unto all law, equity and reason, we must (there is no remedy) acknowledge that in kingdoms hereditary, birthright giveth right unto sovereign dominion, and the death of the predecessor putteth the successor by blood in seisin. Those public solemnities before mentioned do either serve for an open testification of the inheritor's right, or belongeth to the form of inducting of him into possession of that thing he hath right unto. [Hooker VIII, ii, 8]

This is Mr Hooker's judgment of the Israelites' power to set a king over themselves. No doubt but if the people of Israel had had power to choose their king, they would never have made their choice of Joas, a child but of seven years old [2 Kings xi, 21], nor of Manasses, a boy *but*[102] of twelve [2 Kings xxi, 1], since, as Solomon saith, 'Woe to the land whose king is a child' [Ecclesiastes x, 16]. Nor is it probable they would have elected Josias, but a very child, and a son to so wicked and idolatrous a father as that his own servants murdered him. And yet all the people set up this young Josias and slew all the conspirators of the death of Ammon his father [2 Kings xxi, 24], which justice of the people God rewarded by making this Josias the most religious king that ever that nation enjoyed.

(9)   Because it is affirmed that the people have power to choose as well what form of government as what governors they please, of

which mind is Bellarmine in those places we cited at first, therefore it is necessary to examine the strength of what is said in defence of popular commonweals against this natural form of kingdoms which I *maintain*.[103] Here I must first put *the Cardinal in mind of what he affirmeth*[104] in cold blood in other places, where he saith 'God, when *he*[105] made all mankind of one man, did seem openly to signify that He rather approved the government of one man than of many' [Bellarmine, *De Romano Pontifice* book 1, chapter 2]. Again, 'God showed His opinion when he endued not only men, but all creatures, with a natural propensity to monarchy. Neither can it be doubted but a natural propensity is to be referred to God, who is author of nature' [*De Romano Pontifice* book 1, chapter 2]. And again in a third place, 'what form of government God confirmed by His authority may be gathered by *the*[106] commonweal which He instituted among the Hebrews, which was not aristocratical (as Calvin saith) but plainly monarchical' [*De Romano Pontifice* book 1, chapter 2]. Now, if God (as Bellarmine saith) have taught us by natural instinct, signified to us by the creation and confirmed by His own example, the excellency of monarchy, why should Bellarmine or we doubt but that it is natural? Do we not find that in every family the government of one alone is most natural? God did always govern His own people by monarchy only. The patriarchs, dukes, Judges and kings were all monarchs. There is not in all Scripture mention and approbation of any other form of government. At the time when the Scripture saith 'There was no king in Israel, but that every man did that which was right in his own eyes' [Judges xxi, 25], even then, the Israelites were under the kingly government of the fathers of particular families. For in the consultation after the Benjamitical war for providing wives for the Benjamites, we find the elders of the congregation bear only sway, Judges xxi, 16. To them also were complaints to be made, as appears by verse 22. And though mention be made of 'all the children of Israel', 'all the congregation', and 'all the people', yet by that term of '*all*' the Scripture means only all the fathers, and not all the whole multitude, as the text plainly expounds itself in the 2 Chronicles i, 2, where Solomon speaks unto *all* Israel, to the captains, the judges, and to every governor, the chief of the fathers. So the elders of Israel are expounded to be the chief of the fathers of the children of Israel, 1 Kings viii, 1; 2 Chronicles v, 2.

At that time also, when the people of Israel begged a king of Samuel, they were governed by kingly power. God, out *of*[107] special care and love to the house of Israel, did choose to be their king Himself, and did govern them at that time by His viceroy Samuel and his sons. And therefore God tells Samuel: 'They have not rejected thee but Me, that I should not reign over them' *(1 Samuel viii, 7)*.[108] It seems they did not like a king by deputation, but desired one by succession like all the nations. All nations belike had kings then, and those by inheritance, not by election. For we do not find the Israelites prayed that they themselves might choose their own king; they dreamt of no such liberty, and yet they were the elders of Israel gathered together (verse 4). If other nations had elected their own kings, no doubt but they would have been as desirous to have imitated other nations as well in the electing as in the having of a king.

(10)   Aristotle, in his books of *Politics*, when he comes to compare the several kinds of government, he is very reserved in discovering what form he thinks best. He disputes subtly to and fro of many points, and judiciously confutes many errors, but concludes nothing himself. In all those books I find little in commendation of monarchy. It was his hap to live in those times when the Grecians abounded with several commonwealths, who had *then*[109] learning enough to make them seditious. Yet in his *Ethics* he hath so much good manners as to confess in right down words that 'monarchy is the best form of government, and a popular estate the worst' [1160^a 36]. And though he be not so free in his *Politics*, yet the necessity of truth hath here and there extorted from him that which amounts no less to the dignity of monarchy. He confesseth it to *be 'the*[110] first, the natural, and *the*[111] divinest form of government' [1289^a 39–40], and that the gods themselves did live under a monarchy. What can a heathen say more?

Indeed, the world for a long time knew no other sort of government but only monarchy. The best order, the greatest strength, the most stability and easiest government are to be found *all*[112] in monarchy, and in no other form of government. The new platforms of commonweals were first hatched in a corner of the world, amongst a few cities of Greece, which have been imitated by very few other places. Those very cities were first for many years governed by kings, *until*[113] wantonness, ambition or faction made them attempt new kinds of regiment. All which mutations proved most bloody and miserable to the authors of them, happy in nothing but that they continued but a small time.

(11)   A little to manifest the imperfections of popular government, let us but examine the most flourishing democracy that the world hath ever known. I mean that of Rome.

1. First, for the durability, at the most it lasted but 480 years (for so long it was from the expulsion of Tarquin to Julius Caesar), whereas both the Assyrian monarchy lasted, without interruption, at the least twelve hundred years, and the empire of the East continued 1495 years.

2. Secondly, for the order of it, during those 480 years there was not any one settled form of government in Rome. For after they had once lost the natural power of kings, they could not find upon what form of government to rest. Their fickleness is an evidence *that*[114] they found things amiss in every change (see Bodin, *De Republica* book 6, chapter 4, [pp. 700–21]). At the first they choose two annual consuls instead of kings. Secondly, these did not please them long but they must have tribunes of the people to defend their liberty. Thirdly, they leave tribunes and consuls, and choose them ten men to make them laws. Fourthly, they call for consuls and tribunes again; sometimes they choose dictators, which were temporary kings, and sometimes military tribunes, who had consular power. All these shiftings caused such notable alteration in the government, as it poseth both historians and politicians to find out any *perfect*[115] form of regiment in so much confusion. One while the senate made laws, another while the people. The dissensions which were daily between the nobles and the commons bred those memorable seditions about usury, about marriages, and about magistrates. Also the Gracchian, the Apulian and the Drusian seditions filled the market-places, the temples and the capitol itself with blood of the citizens. The Social War was plainly civil; the wars of the slaves and the other of the fencers, the civil wars of Marius and Sulla, of Catiline, of Caesar and Pompey, the triumvirate of Augustus, Lepidus and Antonius, all these shed an ocean of blood within Italy and the streets of Rome.

3. Thirdly, for their government, let it be allowed that for some part of this time it was popular, yet was it popular as to the city of Rome only, and not as *to*[116] the dominions, or whole empire of Rome. For no democracy can extend further than to one city. It is impossible to govern a kingdom, much less many kingdoms, by the whole people, or by the greatest part of them.

(12)   But you will say, yet the Roman empire grew all up under

this kind of popular government, and the city became mistress of the world. It is not so. For Rome began her empire under kings, and did perfect it under emperors; it did only increase under *that*[117] popularity (see Bodin book 6, chapter 4, [pp. 700–21]). Her greatest exaltation was under Trajan, as her longest peace had been under Augustus. Even at those times when the Roman victories abroad did amaze the world, then the tragical slaughter of citizens at home deserved commiseration from their vanquished enemies.

(13) What though in that age of her popularity she bred many admired captains and commanders (each of which was able to lead an army, though many of them were but ill requited by the people) yet all of them were not able to support her in times of danger, but she was forced in her greatest troubles to create a dictator (who was a king for a time), thereby giving this honourable testimony of monarchy, that the last refuge in perils of states is to fly to regal authority. And though Rome's popular estate for a while was miraculously upheld in glory by a greater providence than her own, yet in a short time, after manifold alterations, she was ruined by her own hands. '*Suis et ipsa Roma viribus ruit*' [Rome fell by her own might] for the arms she had prepared to conquer other nations were turned upon herself, and civil contentions at last settled the government again into a monarchy.

(14) The vulgar opinion is that the first cause why the democratical government was brought in was to curb the tyranny of *monarchies*.[118] But the falsehood of this doth best appear by the first flourishing popular estate of Athens, which was founded not because of the vices of their last king, but for that his virtuous deserts were such as the people thought no man worthy enough to succeed him – a pretty wanton quarrel to monarchy! For when their king Codrus understood by the oracle that his country could not be saved unless the king were slain in the battle, he in disguise entered his enemy's camp and provoked a common soldier to make him a sacrifice for his own kingdom. And with his death ended the royal government, for after him was never any more kings of Athens. As Athens thus for the love of their Codrus changed their government, so Rome, on the contrary, out of hatred to their Tarquin, did the like. And though these two famous commonweals did for contrary causes abolish monarchy, yet they both agreed in this, that neither of them

thought it fit to change their state into a democracy. But the one chose archontes and the other consuls to be their governors, both which did most resemble kings, and continued until the people by lessening the authority of their magistrates, did by degrees and stealth bring in their popular government. And I verily believe never any democratical state showed itself *at*[119] first fairly to the world by any elective entrance, but they all secretly crept in by the back door of sedition and faction.

(15)   If we will listen to the judgment of those who should best know the nature of popular government, we shall find no reason for good men to desire or choose it. Xenophon, that brave scholar and soldier, disallowed the Athenian commonweal, for that they followed that form of government wherein 'the wicked are always in greatest credit', and virtuous men kept under (Bodin book 6, chapter 4, [p. 702]). They expelled Aristides the just; Themistocles died in banishment, Miltiades in prison; Phocion, the most virtuous and just man of his age, though he had been chosen forty-five times to be their general, yet was put to death with all his friends, kindred and servants by the fury of the people, without sentence, accusation or any cause at all. Nor were the people of Rome much more favourable to their worthies. They banished Rutilius, Metellus, Coriolanus, the two Scipios and Tully. The worst men sped best – for, as Xenophon saith of Athens, so Rome was a sanctuary for all turbulent, discontented and seditious spirits. The impunity of wicked men was such that upon pain of death it was forbidden all magistrates to condemn to death, or banish any citizen, or to deprive him of his liberty, or so much as to whip him, what offence soever he had committed, either against the gods or men.

The Athenians sold justice as they did other merchandise, which made Plato call a popular *estate*[120] 'a fair, where everything is to be sold' [*Republic* 8.557e]. The officers, when they entered upon their charge, would brag they went to a golden harvest. The corruption at Rome was such that Marius and Pompey durst carry bushels of silver into the *assemblies*[121] to purchase the voices of the people. Many citizens under their grave gowns came armed unto the public meetings, as if they went to war. Often, contrary factions fell to blows, sometimes with stones and sometimes swords. The blood hath been sucked up in the market-place with sponges: the river Tiber hath been filled with the dead bodies of citizens, and the common privies stuffed full with them.

If any man think these disorders in popular states were but casual, or such as may happen under any kind of government, he must know that such mischiefs are unavoidable and of necessity do follow all democratical regiments. The reason is given: because the nature of all people is to desire liberty without restraint, which cannot be but where the wicked bear rule. And if the people should be so indiscreet as to advance virtuous men, they lose their power, for that good men would favour none but the good, which are always the fewer in number; and the wicked and vicious (which is still the greatest part of the people) should be excluded from all preferment, and in the end, by little and little, wise men should seize upon the state and take it from the people.

I know not how to give a better character of the people than can be gathered from such authors as lived among or near to popular states. Thucydides, Xenophon, Livy, Tacitus, Cicero and Sallust have set them out in their colours. I will borrow some of their sentences.

'There is nothing more uncertain than the people. Their opinions are as variable and sudden as tempests. There is neither truth nor judgment in them. They are not led by wisdom to judge of anything, but by violence and by rashness, nor put they any difference between things true and false. After the manner of cattle they follow the herd that goes before. With envious eyes they behold the felicity of others. They have a custom always to favour the worst and weakest. They are most prone to suspicions, and use to condemn men for guilty upon *any*[122] false suggestion. They are apt to believe all news, especially if it be sorrowful, and like Fame, they make it more in the believing. When there is no author, they fear those evils which themselves have feigned. They are most desirous of new stirs and changes, and are enemies to quiet and rest. Whatsoever is giddy or headstrong, they account *manly*[123] and courageous, but whatsoever is modest or prudent seems sluggish. Each man hath a care of his particular, and thinks basely of the common good. They look upon approaching mischiefs as they do upon thunder, only every man wisheth it may not touch his own person. It is the nature of them, they must either serve basely or domineer proudly, for they know no mean.' Thus do *their own friends*[124] paint to the life this beast of many heads. Let me give you the cypher of their form of government. As it is begot by sedition, so it is nourished by arms; it can never stand without wars, either with an enemy abroad, or with friends at home. The only means to preserve it is to have some powerful enemy near, who may serve instead of a king to govern it, that so, though they have not a king among them, yet they may have as good as a king over them, for the common danger of an enemy keeps them in better unity than the laws they make themselves.

(16)   Many have exercised their wits in paralleling the inconveniences of regal and popular government. But if we will trust experience before speculations philosophical, it cannot be denied but that this one mischief of sedition, which necessarily waits upon all popularity, weighs down all the inconveniences that can be found in monarchy, though they were never so many. It is said: 'Skin for skin, yea, all that a man hath will he give for his life' (Job ii, 4); and: 'A man will give his riches for the ransom of his life' (Proverbs xiii, 8). The way then to examine what proportion the mischiefs of sedition and tyranny have one to another, is to enquire in which kind of government most subjects have lost their lives. Let Rome, which is magnified for her popularity and vilified for those tyrannical monsters the emperors, furnish us with examples. Consider whether the cruelty of all the tyrannical emperors that ever ruled in this city, did spill a quarter of that blood that was poured out in the last hundred *years**[125] of her glorious *popular**[126] commonwealth. The murders by Tiberius, Caligula, Nero, Domitian and Commodus, put all together, cannot match that civil tragedy which was acted in that one sedition between Marius and Sulla. Nay, even by Sulla's part alone (not to mention the acts of Marius) were fourscore and ten senators put to death, *fifteen**[127] consuls, two thousand and six hundred gentlemen and a hundred thousand others.

This was the height of the Roman liberty: any man might be killed that would, a favour not fit to be granted under a royal government. The misery of these licentious times are briefly touched by Plutarch in these words. 'Sulla', saith he,

> fell to *the**[128] shedding of blood, and filled all Rome with infinite and unspeakable murders. And this was not only done in Rome, but also in all the cities of Italy throughout. There was no temple of any god whatsoever, no altar in anybody's house, no liberty of hospital, no father's house, which was not imbrued with blood

and horrible murder. The husbands were slain in the wives' arms and the children in the mothers' laps, and yet they that were slain for private malice were nothing in respect of those that were murdered only for their goods ... He openly sold their goods by the crier, sitting so proudly in his chair of state that it grieved the people more to see their goods packed up by them to whom he gave or disposed them than to see them taken away. Sometimes he would give a whole country or the whole revenues of certain cities unto women for their beauty, or to pleasant jesters, minstrels or wicked slaves made free. And to some he would give other men's wives by force, and make them to be married against their wills. [Plutarch, *Sulla* xxxi and xxxiii]

Now let Tacitus and Suetonius be searched, and see if all their cruel emperors can match this popular villain in such an universal slaughter of citizens or civil butchery. God only was able to match him, and overmatched him by fitting him with a most remarkable death, just answerable to his life. For as he had been the death of many *thousands*[129] of his countrymen, so, as many thousands of his own kindred in the flesh were the death of him, for he died of an imposthume[g]

which corrupted his flesh in such sort that it turned all to lice. He had many about him to shift him *continually*[130] night and day, yet the lice they wiped from him were nothing to them that multiplied upon him. There was neither apparel, linen, baths, washings *nor*[131] meat itself, but was presently filled with swarms of this vile vermin. [Plutarch, *Sulla* xxxvi]

I cite not this to extenuate the bloody acts of any tyrannical princes, nor will I plead in defence of their cruelties. Only in the comparative I maintain the mischiefs to a state to be less universal under a tyrant king. For the cruelty of such tyrants extends ordinarily no further than to some particular men that offend them, and not to the whole kingdom. It is truly said by his late majesty of blessed memory: 'A king can never be so notoriously vicious but he will generally favour justice, and maintain some order, except in the particulars wherein his inordinate lust carries him away' [James I 2, p. 66]. Even cruel Domitian, Dionysius the tyrant, and many others are commended

---

[g] [a festering sore].

by historians for great observers of justice. A natural reason is to be *rendered*[132] for it. It is the multitude of people and the abundance of their riches which are the *only*[133] strength and glory of every prince. The bodies of his subjects do him service *in*[134] war, and their goods supply his public wants. Therefore, if not out of affection to his people, yet out of natural love to himself, every tyrant desires to preserve the lives and protect the goods of his subjects, which cannot be done but by justice, and if it be not done, the prince's loss is the greatest.

On the contrary, in a popular state every man knows that the public good doth not depend wholly on his care, but the commonwealth may be well enough governed by others though he tend only his private benefit. He never takes the public to be his own business. Thus, as in a family, where one office is to be done by many servants, one looks upon another, and every one leaves the business for his fellow until it is quite neglected by all. Nor are they much to be blamed for their negligence, since it is an even wager their ignorance is as great. For the magistrates among the people, being for the most part annual, do always lay down their office before they understand it, so that a prince *though*[135] of a duller understanding, by use and experience must needs excel them.

Again, there is no tyrant so barbarously wicked but his own reason and sense will tell him that though he be a god, yet he must die like a man, and that there is not the meanest of his subjects but may find a means to revenge himself of the injustice that is offered him. Hence it is that great tyrants live continually in base fears, as did Dionysius the elder. And Tiberius, Caligula and Nero are all noted by Suetonius to have been frightened with panic fears. But it is not so where wrong is done to any particular person by a multitude. He knows not who hurt him, or who to complain of, or to whom to address himself for reparation. Any man may boldly exercise his malice and cruelty in all popular assemblies. There is no tyranny to be compared to the tyranny of a multitude.

(17) What though the government of the people be a thing not to be endured, much less defended, yet many men please themselves with an opinion that though the people may not govern, yet they may partake and join with a king in *the*[136] government, and so make a state mixed of popular and regal power, which they take to

be the best tempered and equallest form of government. But the vanity of this fancy is too evident. It is a mere impossibility or contradiction. For if a king but once admit the people to be his companions, he leaves to be a king, and the state becomes a democracy. At least, he is but a titular and no real king, that hath not the sovereignty to himself. For the having of this alone, and nothing but this, makes a king to be a king. As for that show of popularity which is found in such kingdoms as have general assemblies for consultation about making public laws, it must *needs*¹³⁷ be remembered that such meetings do not share or divide the sovereignty with the prince, but do only deliberate and advise their supreme head, who still reserves the absolute power in himself. For if in such assemblies the king, the nobility, and people have equal shares in the sovereignty, then the king *hath*¹³⁸ but one voice, the nobility likewise one, and the people one, and then any two of these voices *should*¹³⁹ have power to overrule the third. Thus the nobility and commons together should have power to make a law to bind the king, which was never yet seen in any kingdom, but if it could, the state must needs be popular and not regal.

(18) If it be unnatural for the multitude to choose their governors, or to govern or to partake in the government, what can be thought of that damnable conclusion which is made by too many, that the multitude may correct or depose their prince if need be? Surely the unnaturalness and injustice of this position cannot sufficiently be expressed. For admit that a king make a contract or paction with his people, either originally in his ancestors, or personally at his coronation (for both these pactions some dream of but cannot offer any proof *for*¹⁴⁰ either) yet by no law of any nation *can

> a contract*¹⁴¹ be thought broken, except that first a lawful trial be had by the ordinary judge of the breakers thereof, or else every man may be both party and judge in his own case, which is absurd once to be thought. For then it will lie in the hands of the headless multitude when they please to cast off the yoke of government (that God hath laid upon them) to judge and punish him by whom they should be judged and punished. (*True Law of Free Monarchy*) [James I 2, pp. 68–9]

Aristotle can tell us what judges the multitude are in their own case:† (*Politics* book 3, chapter 9) [1280ᵃ 15] – *the multitude are ill judges in their own cause*.[142]

The judgment of the multitude in disposing of the sovereignty may be seen in the Roman history, where we *may*[143] find many good emperors murdered by the people, and many bad elected by them. Nero, Heliogabalus, Otho, *Vitellius*[144] and such other monsters of nature were the minions of the multitude, and set up by them. Pertinax, Alexander Severus, Gordianus, Gallus, Aemilianus, Quintilius, Aurelianus, Tacitus, Probus and Numerianus, all of them good emperors in the judgment of all historians, yet murdered by the multitude.

(19)   Whereas many out of *an*[145] imaginary fear pretend the power of the people to be necessary for the repressing of the insolencies of tyrants, herein they propound a remedy far worse than the disease. Neither is the disease so frequent as they would have us think. Let us be judged by the history of our own nation. We have enjoyed a succession of kings from the Conquest now near about 600 years (a time far longer than ever yet any popular state could continue). We reckon to the number of twenty-five of these princes of the Norman race, and yet not one of these is taxed by our histories for tyrannical government. It is true, two of these kings have been deposed by the people and barbarously murdered, but neither of them for tyranny. *For*,[146] as a learned historian *of our age*[147] saith, Edward II and Richard II were not insupportable either in their nature or rule, and yet the people more upon wantonness than for any want, did take an unbridled course against them:

> Edward II, by many of our historians is reported to be of a good *and virtuous nature*,[148] and not unlearned. They impute his defects rather to fortune than either to counsel or carriage of his affairs. The deposition of him was a violent fury, led by a wife both cruel and unchaste, and can with no better countenance of right be justified than may his lamentable both indignities and death. Likewise the deposition of King Richard II was a tempestuous rage, neither led nor restrained by any rules of reason or of state. Examine his actions without distempered judgment, and you will not condemn him to be exceeding either insufficient or evil; weigh the imputations that were objected against him, and you shall find nothing either of any truth or of great moment.

† οἱ πλεῖστοι φαῦλοι κριταὶ περὶ τῶν οἰκείων.᾽

Holinshed writeth that he was most unthankfully used by his subjects; for, although through the frailty of his youth he demeaned himself more dissolutely than was agreeable to the royalty of his estate, yet in no king's days the commons were in greater wealth, the nobility more honoured, and the clergy less wronged, who, notwithstanding, in the evil-guided strength of their will, took head against him, to their own headlong destruction afterwards, partly during the reign of Henry his next successor, whose greatest achievements were against his own people in executing those who conspired with him against King Richard, *but most*[149] especially in succeeding times, when, upon occasion of this disorder, more English blood was *spent*[150] than was in all the foreign wars which had been since the Conquest. (Sir John Hayward in answer to Doleman [Hayward I, sig. K1a-b])

Twice hath this kingdom been miserably wasted with civil war, but neither of them occasioned by the tyranny of any prince. The cause of the barons' wars is by good historians attributed to the stubbornness of the nobility, as the bloody variance of the houses of York and Lancaster sprang from the wantonness of the people. These two unnatural wars have dishonoured our nation amongst strangers, so that in the censure of kingdoms the king of Spain is said to be the king of men, because of his subjects' willing obedience; the king of France, king of asses, because of their infinite taxes and impositions; but the king of England is said to be the king of devils, because of his subjects' often insurrections against, and depositions of their princes.

Chapter Three: Positive laws do not infringe the natural and fatherly power of kings. (1) Regal authority not subject to positive laws; kings were before laws; the kings of Judah and Israel not tied to laws: (2) of Samuel's description of a king, 1 Samuel viii; (3) the power ascribed to kings in the New Testament; (4) whether laws were invented to bridle tyrants; (5) the benefit of laws; (6) kings keep the laws though not bound by the laws; (7) of the oaths of kings; (8) of the benefit of the king's prerogative over laws; (9) the king the author and interpreter and corrector of the common laws; (10) the king judge in all causes both before the Conquest and since; (11) the king and his council anciently determined causes in the Star Chamber; (12) of parliaments; (13)

the people when first called to parliament; (14) the liberty of parliament not from nature but from the grace of princes; (15) the king alone makes laws in parliament, [and] (16) governs both Houses by himself, (17), or by his council, (18) or by his judges.

(1)   Hitherto I have endeavoured to show the natural institution of regal authority, and to free it from subjection to an arbitrary election of the people. It is necessary also to enquire whether human laws have a superiority over princes, because those that maintain the acquisition of royal jurisdiction from the people do subject the exercise of it to *human*[151] positive laws. But in this also they err. For as kingly power is by the law of God, so it hath no inferior law to limit it. The father of a family governs by no other law *than*[152] by his own will, not by the laws or wills of his sons or servants. There is no nation that allows children any action or remedy for being unjustly governed; and yet for all this every father is bound by the law of nature to do his best for the preservation of his family. But *much*[153] more is a king always tied by the same law of nature to keep this general ground, that the safety of his kingdom be his chief law. He must remember that the profit of every man in particular, and of all together in general, is not always one and the same, *and*[154] that the public is to be preferred before the private, and that the force of laws must not be so great as natural equity itself – which cannot fully be comprised in any laws, but is to be left to the religious arbitrament of those who know how to manage the affairs of state, and wisely to balance the particular profit with the counterpoise of the public, according to the infinite variety of times, places, persons.

A proof unanswerable for the superiority of princes above laws is this, that there were kings long before there were any laws. For a long time the word of the king was the only law. 'And if practice', as saith Sir Walter Raleigh, 'declare the greatness of authority, even the best kings of Judah and Israel were not tied to any law, but they did whatsoever they pleased in the greatest matters' ([Raleigh 1] book 2, part 1, chapter 16, section 1).

(2)   The unlimited jurisdiction of kings is so amply described by Samuel [1 Samuel viii, 11–18] that it hath given occasion to some to imagine that it was but either a plot or trick of Samuel to keep the government in himself and family by frighting the Israelites with the

mischiefs in monarchy, or else a prophetical description *only*[155] of the future ill government of Saul. But the vanity of these conjectures are judiciously discovered in *the*[156] majestical discourse of *The True Law of Free Monarchy* [James I 2, pp. 56–9], wherein it is evidently showed that the scope of Samuel was to teach the people a dutiful obedience to their king, even in those things which themselves did esteem mischievous and inconvenient. For, by telling them what a king would do, he instructs them what a subject must suffer, yet not so that it is right for kings to do injury, but it is right for them to go unpunished by the people if they do it. So that in this point it is all one whether Samuel describe a king or a tyrant, for patient obedience is due to both. No remedy in the text against tyrants, but *in*[157] crying and praying unto God in that day. But howsoever in a rigorous construction Samuel's description be applied to a tyrant, yet the words by a benign interpretation may agree with the manners of a just king, and the scope and coherence of the text doth best imply the more moderate or qualified sense of the words. For, as Sir Walter Raleigh confesseth, 'all those inconveniences and miseries' (which are reckoned up by Samuel as belonging to kingly government) 'were not intolerable, but such as have been borne, and are still borne, by free consent of subjects towards their princes' [Raleigh 1, II, 16, i]. Nay, at this day and in this land, many tenants by their tenures and services are tied to the like subjection to subordinate and inferior lords. To serve the king in his wars and to till his ground is not only agreeable to the nature of subjects but much desired by them, according to their several births and conditions. The like may be said for the offices of women servants, confectioners, cooks and bakers. For we cannot think that the king would use their labours without giving them wages, since the text itself mentions a liberal reward of his servants. As for the taking the tenth of their seed, of their vines and of their sheep [1 Samuel viii, 15, 17], it might be a necessary provision for their king's household, and so belong to the right of tribute. For whereas it mentions the taking of the tenth, it cannot well agree to a tyrant, who observes no proportion in fleecing his people.

Lastly, the taking of their fields, vineyards and olive trees [1 Samuel viii, 14], if it be by force or fraud, or without just recompense to the damage of private persons only, it is not to be defended. But if it be upon the public charge and by general consent, it might be justified as necessary at the first erection of a kingdom. For those who will have a king are bound to allow him royal maintenance by providing revenues for the crown, since it is both for the honour, profit and safety of the people to have their king glorious, powerful and abounding in riches. Besides, we all know the lands and goods of many subjects may be ofttimes legally taken by the king, either by forfeitures, escheat, attainder, outlawry, confiscation or the like. Thus we see Samuel's character of a king may *literally*[158] well bear a mild sense. For greater probability that Samuel so meant, and the Israelites so understood it, this may be added: Samuel tells the Israelites 'this will be the manner of the king that shall reign over you' [1 Samuel viii, 11], 'and ye shall cry because of your king which ye shall have chosen you' [1 Samuel viii, 18]. That is to say, this shall be the common custom or fashion or proceeding of Saul your king. Or, as the vulgar Latin renders it, this shall be the right or law of your king, not meaning, as some expound it, the casual event *or act*[159] of some *individuum vagum*, or indefinite king, that might happen one day to tyrannise over them. So that Saul, and the constant practice of Saul, doth best agree with the literal sense of the text.

Now that Saul was no tyrant, we may note that the people asked a king as all nations had [1 Samuel viii, 5]. God answers, and bids Samuel to hear the voice of the people in all things which they spake, and appoint them a king [1 Samuel viii, 7]. They did not ask a tyrant, and to give them a tyrant when they asked a king had not been to hear their voice in all things, but when they asked an egg to have given them a scorpion, unless we will say that all nations had tyrants. Besides, we do not find in all Scripture that Saul was punished, or so much as blamed, for committing *any of*[160] those acts which Samuel describes. And if Samuel's drift had been only to terrify the people, he would not have forgotten to foretell Saul's bloody cruelty in murdering eighty-five innocent priests, and smiting with the edge of the sword the city of Nob, both man, woman and child (1 Samuel xxii, [18–19]). Again, the Israelites, it seems, never shrank at these conditions proposed by Samuel, but accepted of them as such as all other nations were bound unto. For their conclusion is: 'Nay, but we will have a king over us, that we also may be like all the nations, and that our king may judge us, and go out before us to fight our battles' [1 Samuel viii, 19–20] – meaning he should earn his privileges by doing their work for them, by judging them, and fighting for them. Lastly, whereas the mention of the people's *crying*[161] unto the Lord argues they should be under some tyrannical oppression, we may remember that the people's complaints and cries are not always an argument of their living under a tyrant. No man can say King Solomon was a tyrant, yet all the congregation of Israel complained that Solomon made their yoke grievous, and therefore their prayer to Rehoboam is, 'Make thou the grievous service of thy father Solomon, and his heavy yoke which he put upon us, lighter, and we will serve thee' [2 Chronicles x, 4]. To conclude, it is true Saul lost his kingdom, but not for being too cruel or tyrannical to his subjects, but for being too merciful to his enemies. His sparing Agag when he should have slain him [1 Samuel xv, 9] was the cause why the kingdom was torn from him.[h]

(3)   If any desire the direction of the New Testament, he may find our Saviour limiting and distinguishing royal power, 'By giving to Caesar those things that were Caesar's, and to God those things that were God's' [Matthew xxii, 21]. Let St Basil expound this text: '*Obediendum est in quibus mandatum Dei non impeditur*: we must obey princes in those things wherein the commandment of God *is*[162] not hindered.' There is no other law but God's law to hinder our obedience. It was the answer of a Christian to the emperor: 'We only worship God, in other things we gladly serve you.' And it seems Tertullian thought whatsoever was not God's was the emperor's, when he saith: '*Bene *apposuit*[163] Caesari pecuniam, te ipsum Deo, alioqui quid erit Dei, si omnia Caesaris*: our Saviour hath well apportioned our money for Caesar, and ourselves for God, for otherwise what shall God's share be if all be Caesar's?' The Fathers mention no reservation of any power to the laws of the land, or to the people. St Ambrose, in his *Apology for David*, expressly saith: 'He was a king, and therefore bound to no laws, because kings are free from the bonds of any fault' [Ambrose, chapter 10]. St Augustine also resolves: '*Imperator non est subjectus legibus, qui habet in potestate alias leges ferre*: the emperor is not subject to laws, who hath power to make other laws.' For, indeed, it is the rule of Solomon that, 'We must keep the king's commandment, and not say to him, what dost thou?, because where the word of a king is, there is power, and all that he pleaseth he will do' (Ecclesiastes viii, [2–4]).

[h] [A passage inserted here in B is printed in the Appendix, section (2), pp. 65–6].

38

If any dislike this divinity in England, let him but hearken to Bracton, chief justice in King Henry III's days, *which was*[164] since the institution of parliaments. His words are, speaking of the king: '*Omnes sub eo, et ipse sub nullo, nisi tantum sub Deo*', *etc*:[165]

> all are under him, and he under none but God only. If he offend, since no writ can go against him, their remedy is by petitioning to him to amend his fault. Which, if he shall not do, it will be punishment sufficient for him to expect God as a revenger. Let none presume to search into his deeds, much less to oppose them. [Bracton ff. 5b-6a]

When the Jews asked our blessed Saviour whether they should pay tribute, He did not first demand what the law of the land was, or whether there was any statute against it, nor enquired whether the tribute were given by act of parliament, nor advised them to stay their payment until a parliament should grant it. He did no more but look upon the superscription, and concluded, 'This image you say is Caesar's, therefore give it *to*[166] Caesar' [Matthew xxii, 21]. Nor must it here be said that Christ taught this lesson only to the conquered Jews, for in this He gave direction for all nations, who are bound as much in obedience to their lawful kings as to any conqueror or usurper whatsoever.

Whereas St Paul bids us 'be subject *to*[167] the higher powers' [Romans xiii, 1], some have strained these words *to*[168] signify the laws of the land, or else to mean the highest power, as well aristocratical *and*[169] democratical as regal. It seems St Paul looked for such interpreters, and therefore thought fit to be his own expositor, and to let it be known that by power he understood a monarch that carried a sword: 'Wilt thou not be afraid of the power?' that is the ruler that carrieth the sword, for 'he is the minister of God to thee, for he beareth not the sword in vain' [Romans xiii, 3–4]. It is not the law that is the 'minister of God', or that 'carries the sword', but the ruler or magistrate. So that they that say the law governs the kingdom, may as *well*[170] say that the carpenter's rule builds *the*[171] house and not the carpenter, for the law is but the rule or instrument of the ruler. And St Paul concludes: 'For this cause pay you tribute also, for they are God's ministers, attending continually upon this very thing. Render therefore tribute to whom tribute is due, custom to whom custom' [Romans xiii, 6–7]. He doth not say, give tribute as a gift to God's minister, but ἀπόσυτε, render or restore tribute as a due. Also, St Peter doth most clearly expound this place of St Paul, where he saith: 'Submit yourselves to every ordinance of man for the Lord's sake, whether it be to the king as supreme or unto governors, as unto them that are sent by him' [1 Peter ii, 13–14]. Here the very self same word 'supreme' or 'ὑπερέχοντι' which St Paul coupleth with power, St Peter conjoineth with the king, 'βασιλεῖ ὡς ὑπερέχον', thereby to manifest that king and power are both one. Also St Peter expounds his own words of human ordinance to be the king, who is *lex loquens* – a speaking law. He cannot mean that kings themselves are an human ordinance, since St Paul calls the supreme power the ordinance of God, and the wisdom of God saith 'By me kings reign' [Proverbs viii, 15]. But his meaning must be that the commands or laws of kings are human ordinances. Next, the governors that are sent by him: that is, by the king, not by God as some corruptly would wrest the text to justify popular governors as authorised by God, whereas in grammatical construction 'him', the relative, must be referred to the next antecedent, which is 'the king'. Besides, the antithesis between 'supreme' and 'sent' proves plainly that the governors were sent by kings. For, if the governors were sent by God and the king be an human ordinance, then it follows that the governors were supreme and not the king. Or, if it be said that *both king*[172] and governors are sent by God, then they are both equal, and so neither of them 'supreme'. Therefore St Peter's meaning is in short: 'Obey the laws of the king or of his ministers.' By which it is evident that neither St Peter nor St Paul intended any other form of government than only monarchical, much less any subjection of princes to human laws.

That familiar distinction of the schoolmen,[i] whereby they subject kings to the *directive* but not to the *coactive* power of laws, is a confession *that*[173] kings are not bound by the positive laws of any nation – since the compulsory power of laws is that which properly makes laws to be laws, by binding men by rewards or punishment to an obedience; whereas the direction of the law is but like the advice and direction which the king's council gives the king, which no man can say is a law to the king.

(4)   There want not those who believe that the first invention of

---

[i] [medieval Roman Catholic clergy who taught philosophy and theology].

laws was to bridle and moderate the over-great power of kings. But the truth is, the original of laws was for the keeping of the multitude in order. Popular *states*[174] could not subsist at all without laws, whereas kingdoms were governed many ages without them. The people of Athens, as soon as they gave over kings, were forced to give power to Draco first, then to Solon, to make them laws not to bridle kings but themselves. And though many of their laws were very severe and bloody, yet for the reverence they bore to their lawmakers they willingly submitted to them. Nor did the people give any limited power to Solon, but an absolute jurisdiction at his pleasure to abrogate and confirm what he thought fit, the people never challenging any such power to themselves. So the people of Rome gave to the ten men, who were to choose and correct their laws for the twelve tables, an absolute power without any appeal to the people.

(5)   The reason why laws have been also made by kings was this: when kings were either busied with wars or distracted with public cares, so that every private man could not have access to their persons to learn their wills and pleasure, then of necessity were laws invented, that so every particular subject might find his prince's pleasure deciphered unto him in the tables of his laws, that so there might be no need to resort to the king but either for the interpretation or mitigation of obscure or rigorous laws, or else, in new cases, for a supplement where the law was defective. By this means both king and people were in many things eased:

1. The king, by giving laws, doth free himself of great and intolerable troubles, as Moses did himself *by*[175] choosing elders (Exodus xviii, [13–26]).

2. The people have the law as a familiar admonisher and interpreter of the king's pleasure, which being published throughout the kingdom doth represent the presence and majesty of the king.

Also, the judges and magistrates (whose help in giving judgment in many causes kings have need to use) are restrained by the common rules of the law from using their own liberty to the injury of others, since they are to judge according to *the*[176] laws, and not follow their own opinions.

(6)   Now albeit kings who make the laws be, as his late majesty teacheth us, above the laws, yet will they rule their subjects by the law [James I 2, p. 63]; 'And a king, governing in a settled kingdom,

leaves to be a king and degenerates into a tyrant so soon as he leaves to rule according to his laws' [James I 1, p. 309].

Yet where he sees the laws rigorous or doubtful he may mitigate *or*[177] interpret. General laws made by parliament may, upon known respects to the king, by his authority be mitigated or suspended upon causes only known to him. And although a king do frame all his actions to be according to the laws, yet *is he*[178] not bound thereto but at his good will and for good example [James I 2, p. 63],

or so far forth as the general law of the safety of the commonweal doth naturally bind him. For in such sort only positive laws may be said to bind the king, not by being positive but as they are naturally the best *or*[179] only means for the preservation of the commonwealth. By this means are all kings, even tyrants and conquerors, bound to preserve the lands, goods, liberties and lives of all their subjects, not by any municipal law of the land, but by the natural law of a father, which binds them to ratify the acts of their forefathers and predecessors in things necessary for the public good of their subjects.

(7)   Others there be that affirm that although laws of themselves do not bind kings, yet the oaths of kings at their coronation tie them to keep all the laws of their kingdoms. How far this is true, let us but examine the oath of the kings of England at their coronation, the words whereof are these: 'Art thou pleased to cause to be administered in all thy judgments, indifferent and upright justice, and to use discretion with mercy and verity? Art thou pleased that our upright laws and customs be observed, and dost thou promise that those shall be protected and maintained by thee?' [Milles p. 53]. These two are the articles of the king's oath which concern the laity or subjects in general, to which the king answers affirmatively, being first demanded by the Archbishop of Canterbury, 'Pleaseth it you to confirm and observe the laws and customs of ancient times, granted *from*[180] God by just and devout kings unto the English nation, by oath unto the said people, specially the laws, customs and liberties granted unto the clergy and laity by the famous King Edward?' (Milles, *Of Nobility* [p. 53]). We may observe, in these words of the articles of the oath, that the king is required to observe not *all* the laws, but only the *upright laws*, and that with discretion and mercy. The word *upright* cannot mean *all* laws, because in the oath of Richard

II I find 'evil and unjust laws' mentioned, which the king swears to abolish. And in the old abridgement of statutes set out in Henry VIII's days, the king is to swear wholly to 'put out evil laws', which he cannot do if he be bound to keep *all* laws. Now what laws are upright and what evil, who shall judge but the king, since he swears to administer upright justice with discretion and mercy, or, as Bracton hath it, *'aequitatem praecipiat, et misericordiam'* [let him command justice and mercy; Bracton f. 107a]. So that in effect the king doth swear to keep no laws but such as in his judgment are upright, and those not literally always, but according to the equity of his conscience joined with mercy, which is properly the office of a chancellor rather than of a judge. And if a king did strictly swear to observe all the laws, he could not without perjury give his consent to the repealing *or*[181] abrogating of any statute by act of parliament, which would be very *mischevable*[182] to the state.

Let it be supposed for truth that kings do swear to observe all the laws of their kingdoms, yet no man can think it reason that kings should be more bound by their voluntary oaths than common persons are by theirs. If a private person make a contract either with oath or without oath, he is no further bound than the equity and justice of the contract ties him. For a man may have relief against an unreasonable and unjust promise, if either deceit, or error, or force or fear induced him thereunto, or if it be hurtful or grievous in the performance. Since the laws in many cases give the king a prerogative above common persons, I see no reason why he should be denied the privilege which the meanest of his subjects doth enjoy.

Here is a fit place to examine a question which some have moved, whether it be a sin for a subject to disobey the king if he command anything contrary to his laws? For satisfaction in this point we must resolve that not only in human laws, but even in divine, a thing may be commanded contrary to law, and yet obedience to such a command is necessary. The sanctifying of the sabbath is a divine law, yet if a master command his servant not to go to church upon *a sabbath*[183] day, the best divines teach us that the servant must obey this command, though it may be sinful and unlawful in the master; because the servant hath no authority or liberty to examine and judge whether his master sin or no in so commanding, for there may be a just cause for a master to keep his servant from church, *as*[184] appears Luke xiv, 5. Yet it is not fit to tie the master to acquaint his servant with his secrets, counsels or present necessity, and in such cases the servant's not going to church becomes the sin of the master, and not of the servant. The like may be said of the king's commanding a man to serve him in the wars. He may not examine whether the war be just or unjust, but must obey, since he hath no commission to judge of the titles of kingdoms or causes of war, nor hath any subject power to condemn his king for breach of his own laws.

(8) Many will be ready to say it is a slavish and a dangerous condition to be subject to the will of any one man who is not subject to the laws. But such men consider not:

1. That the prerogative of a king is to be above all laws, for the good only of them that are under the laws, and to defend the people's liberties – as his majesty graciously affirmed in his speech after his last answer to the Petition of Right. Howsoever some are afraid *of**185 the name of prerogative, yet they may assure themselves the case of subjects would be desperately miserable without it. The court of chancery itself is but a branch of the king's prerogative to relieve men against the inexorable rigour of the law, which without it is no better than a tyrant, since *summum jus* [law pushed to extremes] is *summa injuria* [extreme injustice]. General pardons at the coronation and at parliaments are but the bounty of the prerogative.

2. There can be no laws without a supreme power to command or make them. In all aristocracies the nobles are above the laws, and in all democracies the people. By *the**186 like reason, in a monarchy the king must of necessity be above the laws. There can be no sovereign majesty in him that is under them. That which giveth the very being to a king is the power to give laws; without this power he is but an equivocal king. It skills not which way kings come by their power, whether by election, donation, succession or by any other means, for it is still the manner of the government by supreme power that makes them properly kings, and not the means of obtaining their crowns. Neither doth the diversity of laws, nor contrary customs – whereby each kingdom differs from another – make the forms of commonweal different, unless the power of making laws be in several subjects.

For confirmation of this point, Aristotle saith that 'a perfect kingdom is that wherein the king rules all things according to his own will, for he that is called a king according to the law makes no kind of kingdom at all' (*Politics* book 3, chapter 16) [1287ª 8–10]. This, it seems, also the Romans well understood to be most necessary in monarchy. For though they were a people most greedy of liberty, yet the senate did free 'Augustus from all necessity of laws, that he might be free of his own authority and of absolute power over himself and over the laws to do what he pleased and leave undone what he list. And this decree was made while Augustus was yet absent' (Dio book 53, [chapter 28, 2–3]). Accordingly we find that Ulpian, that great lawyer, delivers it for a rule of the civil law: '*princeps legibus solutus est*: the prince is not bound by the laws' [*Digest* I, iii, 31; p. 34].

(9)   If the nature of laws be advisedly weighed, the necessity of the prince's being above them may more manifest itself. We all know that a law in general is the command of a superior power. Laws are divided (as Bellarmine divides the word of God) into written and unwritten [Bellarmine, *De Verbo Dei* book 4, chapter 1]. *'τῶν νόμον, οἱ μεν ἐγγραφοι, οἱ δε ἀγραφοι*', saith Ulpian in the Civil Law*,[187] 'The common law unwritten and the statute law written' [*Digest* I, i, 6; p. 29]. The common law is called unwritten not for that it is not written at all, but because it was not written by the *first*[188] devisers or makers of it. The common law (as the lord chancellor Egerton teacheth us) is the 'common custom of the realm' ([Egerton] *Postnati* page 35*).[189] Now concerning customs, this must be considered, that for every custom there was a time when it was no custom, and the first precedent we now have, had no precedent when it began. When every custom began, there was something else than custom that made it lawful, or else the beginning of all customs were unlawful. Customs at first became lawful only by some superior power which did either command or consent unto their beginning. And the first power which we find (as is confessed by all men) is kingly power, which was both in this nation and in all other nations of the world long before any laws or any other kind of government was thought of. From whence we must necessarily infer that the common law itself, or common customs of this land, were originally the laws and commands of kings at first unwritten.

Nor must we think *that*[190] the common customs (which are the principles of the common law, and are but few) to be such or so many as are able to give special rules to determine every particular cause. Diversity of cases are infinite, and impossible to be *regulated*[191] by any law. And therefore we find even in the divine laws which were delivered by Moses, there be only certain principal laws which did not determine but only direct the high priest or magistrate, whose judgment in special cases did determine what the general law intended.

It is so with the common law, for when there is no perfect rule judges do resort to those principles or common law axioms whereupon former judgments in cases somewhat like have been delivered by former judges, who all receive authority from the king, in his right and name, to give sentence according to the rules and precedents of ancient times. And where precedents have failed, the judges have resorted to the general law of reason, and accordingly given judgment without any common law to direct them. Nay, many times where there have been precedents to direct, they upon better reason only have changed the law both in causes criminal and civil, and have not insisted so much on the examples of former judges as examined and corrected their reasons. Hence it is that some laws are now *obsolete*[192] and out of use, and the practice quite contrary to what it was in former times, as the lord chancellor Egerton proves by several instances.

Nor is this spoken to derogate from the common law, for the case standeth so with the laws of all nations, although some of them have their laws and principles written and established. For witness in this we have Aristotle his testimony in his *Ethics*, and in several places in his *Politics*. I will cite some of them:

> Every law (saith he) is in the general, but of some things there can be no general law† ... When therefore the law speaks in general, and *something falls*[193] out after *beside*[194] the general rule, then it is fit that what the lawmaker hath omitted, or where he hath erred by speaking generally, it should be corrected or supplied, as if the lawmaker himself were present to ordain it. [1137[b] 13–14, 19–24].

> The governor, whether *it*[195] be one man or more, ought to be lord over all those things whereof it was impossible the law should exactly speak, because it is not easy to comprehend all things under general rules ... Whatsoever the law cannot determine, it leaves to the governors to give judgment therein, and permits

† [B adds in the margin:] '*ὁ μὲν νόμος καθόλου πᾶς.*' *Ethics* book 5, chapter 14.

them to rectify whatsoever upon trial they find to be better than the written laws. (*Politics* book 3, chapter 11) [1282ᵇ 3–6]ʲ

Besides, all laws are of themselves dumb, and some or other must be trusted with the application of them to particulars, *who*,¹⁹⁶ by examining all circumstances, *are*¹⁹⁷ to pronounce when they are broken or by whom. This work of right application of laws is not a thing easy or obvious for ordinary capacities, but requires profound abilities of nature for the beating out of the truth. Witness the diversity and sometimes the contrariety of opinions of the learned judges in some difficult points.

(10) Since this is the common condition of laws, it is most reasonable that the lawmaker should be trusted with the application or interpretation of the laws. *And for*¹⁹⁸ this cause anciently the kings of this land have sitten personally in courts of judicature, and are still representatively present in all courts. The judges are but substituted and called the king's justices, and their power ceaseth when the king is in place. To this purpose Bracton, that learned chief justice in the reign of Henry III, saith in express terms, 'In doubtful and obscure points the interpretation and will of the lord our king is to be expected, since it is his part to interpret who made the law' [Bracton f. 34a; Egerton p. 108]. For, as he hath it in another place, '*Rex et non alius debet judicare si solus ad *id*¹⁹⁹ sufficere possit*', etc:

the king and nobody else ought to give judgment if he were

ʲ [B here adds: And the civil law agrees with Aristotle, for it saith: '*Jura constitui oportet (ut dixit Theophrastus) in his quae ἔπι τὸ πλεῖστον accidunt, non quae ἐκ παραλόγου*' [laws should be made concerning what usually happens, not concerning exceptions; *Digest* I, iii, 3; p. 34]. They are the words of Pomponius. Again: '*Ex his quae forte uno aliquo casu accidere possunt jura non constituuntur ... nam ad ea potius debet aptari jus quae et frequenter et facile, quam quae perraro eveniunt*' [laws are not made on things which might happen in just one case, for laws should be fitted to what occurs commonly and readily rather than to what occurs very rarely; *Digest* I, iii, 5; p. 34], saith Celsus. '*Quae semel aut bis accidunt praetereunt legislatores*' [lawmakers pass over things that happen just once or twice; *Digest* I, iii, 6n4; p. 34]. '*Neque leges ita scribi possunt, ut omnes casus qui quandoque inciderint comprehendantur, sed sufficit et ea quae plerumque accidunt contineri*' [nor can laws be drawn up to cover all cases which might possibly occur, but it is enough that they deal with what happens for the most part; *Digest* I, iii, 10; p. 34], saith Julianus. '*Cum in aliqua causa sententia eorum est manifesta, is qui jurisdictioni praeest, ad similia procedere atque ita jus dicere debet*' [if the reason for a judgment is clear in one case, the judge should extend it to other cases, and pronounce judgment accordingly; *Digest* I, iii, 12; p. 34].

able, since by virtue of his oath he is bound to it. Therefore the king ought to exercise power as the vicar or minister of God. But if our lord the king be not able to determine every cause, to ease part of his pains by distributing the burden to more persons, he ought to choose wise men, fearing God, etc., and make justices of them. [Bracton f. 107a]

Much to the same purpose are the words of King Edward I in the beginning of *the*[200] book of laws written by his appointment by John Britton, Bishop of Hereford. '"We will", saith the king, "that our own jurisdiction be above all the jurisdictions of our realm, so as in all manner of felonies, trespasses, contracts and in all other actions, personal or real, we have power to yield such judgments as do appertain, without other process, wheresoever we know the right truth as judges."' [Lambarde 1, p. 57]. Neither may this be taken to be meant of an imaginary presence of the king's person in his courts, because he doth immediately after in the same place severally set forth by themselves the jurisdictions of his ordinary courts; but must necessarily be understood of a jurisdiction remaining in the king's royal person. 'And that this then was no new made law, or first brought in by the Norman Conquest' [Lambarde 1, p. 58], appears by a Saxon law made by King Edgar in these words, as I find them in Mr Lambarde: '*Nemo in lite regem appellato, nisi quidem domi justitiam consequi, aut *impetrare*[201] non poterit, sin summo jure domi urgeatur, ad regem, ut is onus aliqua ex parte allevet, provocato*: Let no man in suit appeal to the king unless he may not get right at home. But if that right be too heavy for him, then let him go to the king to have it eased' [Lambarde 1, p. 58].

As the judicial power of kings was exercised before the Conquest, so in those settled times after the Conquest wherein parliaments were much in use, there was a high court following the king, which was the place of sovereign justice both for the matter of law and conscience – as may appear by *a parliament*[202] in King Edward I's time taking order 'that the chancellor and the justices of the bench should follow the king, to the end that he might have always at hand able men' for his direction in suits that came before him [Lambarde 1, pp. 28, 63]. And this was after the time that the court of common pleas was made stationary, which is an evidence the king reserved a sovereign power by which he did supply the want, or correct the rigour of the common law, because the positive law, being grounded upon that which happens for the most part, cannot foresee every particular which time and experience bring forth.

(11)   Therefore, though the common law be generally good and just, yet in some special case it may *need*[203] correction by reason of some considerable circumstance falling out which at the time of the law-making was not thought of. Also sundry things do fall out both in war and peace that require extraordinary help, and cannot wait for the usual care of common law, the which is not performed but alto-gether after one sort, and that not without delay of help and expense of time. So that, although most causes are and ought to be referred to the ordinary process of common law, yet rare matters from time to time do grow up meet, for just reasons, to be referred to the aid of the *absolute and indefinite*[204] authority of the prince. And the statute of Magna Carta *hath and must be*[205] understood of the institution then made of the ordinary jurisdiction in common causes, and not for restraint of the absolute authority *which serves in*[206] 'rare and singular cases' [Lambarde 1, p. 62]. For though the subjects were put to great damage by false *accusations*[207] and malicious suggestions made to the king and his council, especially during the time of King Edward III whilst he was absent in the wars in France, insomuch as in his reign divers statutes were made that provided none should be put to answer before the king and his council without due process, yet it is apparent the necessity of such proceedings was so great that both before Edward III's days and in his time and after his death, several statutes were made to help and order the proceedings of the king and his council [Lambarde 1, pp. 63–4].

As the parliament in 28 Edward I, c. 5, did provide 'that the chancel-lor and justices of the king's bench should follow the king so that he may have near unto him some that be learned in the laws, which be able to order all such matters as shall come unto the court at all times when need shall *require*'[208] [Statutes p. 51]. By the statute of 37 Edward III, c. 18, taliation was ordained in case the suggestion to the king proved untrue [Lambarde 1, p. 64]. Then 38 Edward III, c. 9, takes away *the*[209] taliation and appoints imprisonment till the king and party grieved be satisfied [Lambarde 1, p. 64]. In the statutes of *17*[210] Richard II, c. 6, and 15 Henry VI, c. 4, damages and expenses are awarded in such cases [Lambarde 1, pp. 64–5]. In all these statutes it is necessarily implied that complaints upon just causes might be moved before the king and his council. At a parliament at Gloucester, 2 Richard II, when the Commons made petition that none might be forced by writ out of chancery or by privy seal to appear before the king and his council to answer touching freehold, the king's answer was

he thought it not reasonable that he should be restrained to send for his lieges upon causes reasonable. And albeit he did not purpose that such as were sent for should answer *finalment*, peremptorily, touching their freehold, but should be remanded for trial thereof as law required, 'Provided always' (saith he) 'that at the suit of the party where the king and his council shall be credibly informed that because of maintenance, oppression or other outrages, the common law cannot have duly her course, in such case the council may send for the party'. [Lambarde I, p. 70]

Also, in the thirteenth year of his reign, when the Commons did pray that, upon pain of forfeiture, the chancellor or council of the king should not after the end of the parliament make any ordinance against the common law, the king answered: 'Let it be used as it hath been used before this time, so as the regality of the king be saved; for the king will save his regalities as his progenitors have done'. [Lambarde I, p. 71]

Again, in the fourth year of Henry IV, when the Commons complained against subpoenas and other writs grounded upon false suggestions, the king answered:

'That he would give in charge to his officers that they should abstain more than before time they had to send for his subjects in that manner. But yet', saith he, 'it is not our intention that our officers shall so abstain that they may not send for our subjects in matters and causes necessary, as it hath been used in the time of our good progenitors'. [Lambarde I, p. 72]

Likewise, when for the same cause complaint was made by the Commons *anno* [in the year] 3, Henry V, *the king's answer was*:[211] '*Le roi s'advisera*: the king will be advised', which amounts to a denial for the present, by a phrase peculiar for the king's denying to pass any act that hath passed the Lords and Commons [Lambarde I, p. 72].

These[212] complaints of the Commons, and the answers of the kings, discover that such moderation should be used that the course of the common law be ordinarily maintained *lest subjects be convented before the king and his council without just cause, that the proceedings of the council table be not upon every slight suggestion, nor to determine finally concerning freehold of inheritance*.[213] And yet that, *for causes*[214] reasonable, 'upon credible information in matters of weight, the king's regality or prerogative in sending for his subjects be maintained, as of right it ought' and in former times hath been constantly used [Lambarde 1, pp. 72–3].

King Edward I, finding 'that Bogo de Clare was discharged of an accusation brought against him in parliament, for that some formal imperfections *were*[215] found in *the*[216] complaint, commanded him nevertheless to appear before him and his council, '*ad faciendum et recipiendum quod per regem et ejus consilium fuerit faciendum*' [to do and undergo what the king and his council decreed], and so proceeded to an examination of the whole cause (*anno* [in the year] 18 Edward I)' [Lambarde 1, p. 73].

Edward III in the Star Chamber (which was the ancient council chamber at Westminster) upon the complaint of Elizabeth Audley, 'commanded James Audley to appear before him and his council, and determined a controversy between them touching lands contained in the covenants of her jointure. (*Rotulo clauso de Anno* [in the close roll of the year] 41 Edward III)' [Lambarde 1, pp. 73–4].

Henry V,

> in a suit before him and his council for the titles of the manors of Serre and St Lawrence in the Isle of Thanet in Kent, took order for the sequestering *of*[217] the profits till the right were tried, as well for the avoiding the breach of the peace as for prevention of waste and spoil. (*Rotulo patenti anno* [in the patent roll of the year] 6 Henry V) [Lambarde 1, p. 74].

Henry VI 'commanded the justices of the bench to stay the arraignment of one Verney *of*[218] London till they had other commandment from him and his council. Because Verney, being indebted to the king and others, practised to be indicted of felony, wherein he might have his clergy, and make his purgation of intent to defraud his creditors (34 Henry VI *rotulo* [in roll] 37 *in banco regis* [in the king's bench])' [Lambarde 1, p. 75].

Edward IV and his council in the Star Chamber

> heard the cause of the master and poor brethren of St Leonards in York, complaining that Sir Hugh Hastings and others withdrew

from them a great part of their living, which consisted chiefly upon the having of a thrave of corn of every plough-land within the counties of York, Westmorland, Cumberland and Lancashire (*rotulo patenti de anno* [in the patent roll of the year] 8 Edward IV, part 3, membrane 14). [Lambarde 1, p. 75]

Henry VII and his council, in the Star Chamber,

> decreed that Margery and Florence Backet should sue no further in their cause against Alice Radley, widow, for lands in Woolwich and Plumsted, forasmuch as the matter had been heard, first before the council of King Edward IV, after that before the president of the requests of that King Henry VII, and then lastly before the council of the said king (1 Henry VII). [Lambarde p. 76]

What is hitherto affirmed of the dependency and subjection of the common law to the sovereign prince, the same may be said as well of all statute laws. For the king is the sole immediate author, corrector and moderator of them also. So that neither of these two kinds of laws are, or can be, any diminution of that natural power which kings have over their people by right of fatherhood, but are *an*[219] argument to strengthen the truth of it. For evidence whereof we may in some points consider the nature of parliaments, because by them only all statutes are enacted.

(12)   Though the name of 'parliament', as Mr Camden saith, be 'of no great antiquity', but brought in out of France, yet our ancestors the English Saxons had a meeting which they called the 'assembly of the wise', termed in Latin ' *conventum magnatum*, or *praesentia regis*, *procerumque, praelatorum collectorum*; the meeting of the nobility, or the presence of the king, prelates and peers assembled' [Camden p. 177], or in general, *magnum concilium* [the great council], or *commune concilium* [the common council]. And many of our kings in elder times made use of such great assemblies for to consult of important affairs of state, all which meetings in a general sense may be termed parliaments.

Great are the advantages which both the king and people may receive by a well ordered parliament. There is nothing more expresseth the majesty and supreme power of a king than such an assembly, wherein all his people acknowledge him for sovereign lord, and make *their*[220] addresses to him by humble petition and supplication, and by their consent and approbation do strengthen all the laws which the king at their request, and by their advice and ministry, shall ordain. Thus they facilitate the government of the king by making the laws unquestionable, either to the subordinate magistrates or refractory multitude. Then the benefit which accrues to the subject by parliaments is, that by their prayers and petitions kings are drawn many times to redress their just grievances, and are overcome by their importunity to grant many things which otherwise they would not yield unto – for the voice of a multitude is easilier heard. Many vexations of the people are without the knowledge of the king, who in parliament seeth and heareth his people himself, whereas at other times he commonly useth the eyes and ears of other men.

(13)   Against the antiquity of parliaments we need not dispute, since the more ancient they be, the more they make for the honour of monarchy. Yet there be certain circumstances touching *the forms of*[221] parliaments which are fit to be considered.

   1. We are to remember that until about the time of the Conquest there could be no parliaments assembled of the general states of the whole kingdom of England, because till those days we cannot *learn*[222] it was entirely united into one kingdom, but it was either divided into several kingdoms, or governed by several laws. When Julius Caesar landed he found four kings in Kent [Caesar, *De Bello Gallico* book 5, 22], and the British names of Danmonii, Durotriges, Belgae, Attrebatii, Trinobantes, Iceni, Silures and the rest are plentiful testimonies of the several kingdoms of the Britons when the Romans became our lords. As soon as ever the Romans left us, the Saxons divided us into seven kingdoms. When these Saxons were united into a monarchy, they had always the Danes their companions or masters in the empire till Edward the Confessor's days, since whose time the kingdom of England hath continued united as now it doth. But for a thousand years before, we cannot find it was entirely settled during the time of any one king's reign. As for laws, we find the middle parts of the kingdom under the Mercian law; the West Saxons were confined to the Saxon laws; Essex, Norfolk, Suffolk and some other places were vexed with the Danish laws. The Northumbrians also had their laws apart, and until Edward the Confessor's reign, who was the next but one before the Conqueror, the laws of the kingdom were so several and uncertain that he was forced to cull

a few of the most indifferent and best of them, which were from him called St Edward's laws. Yet some say that Edgar made those laws, and that the Confessor did but restore and amend them. Alfred also gathered out of Malmutius' laws such as he translated into the Saxon tongue. Thus, during the time of the Saxons the laws were so variable that there is little or no likelihood to find any constant form of parliaments of the whole kingdom.

A second point considerable is whether in such parliaments as were in the Saxons' times the *nobility and clergy*²²³ only were of those assemblies, or whether the Commons were also called *(Mr Lambarde, *Archion*)*.²²⁴ Some are of the opinion that though none of the Saxon laws do *expressly*²²⁵ mention the Commons, yet it may be gathered by the word *'*witena*', 'wisemen', that the*²²⁶ Commons are intended to be of those assemblies. And they bring (as they conceive) probable arguments to prove it from the antiquity of some boroughs that *were decayed before the Conquest and*²²⁷ yet send burgesses, and from the proscription of those in *ancient demesne* not to send any burgesses to parliament *or pay knights' wages*.²²⁸

*If it be true that the West Saxons had a custom to assemble burgesses out of some of their towns, yet it may be doubted whether other kingdoms had the same usage. But sure it is that during the Heptarchy the people could not elect any knights of the shire, because England was not then divided into shires.*²²⁹

On the contrary there be *of our*²³⁰ historians who do affirm that King Henry I 'caused the commons first to be assembled by knights and burgesses of their *own*²³¹ appointment, for before his time only certain of the nobility and prelates of the realm were called to consultation about the most important affairs of state' *(Sir John Hayward in Henry I)*²³² [Hayward 2, pp. 283–4]. *If this assertion be true it seems a mere matter of grace of this king, and proves not any natural right of the people to be admitted to choose their knights and burgesses of parliament*.²³³ And it had been more for the honour of parliaments if a king whose title to the crown had been *better*²³⁴ had been author of the *form of it*,²³⁵ because he made use of it for his unjust ends. For thereby he secured himself against his competitor and elder brother, by taking the oaths of the nobility in parliament and *getting*²³⁶ the crown to be settled upon his children. And as the king made use of the people, so they, by colour of a parliament, served their own turns. For after the establishment of parliaments by strong hand

and by the sword, they drew from him the great charter, which he granted the rather to flatter the nobility and people, as Sir Walter Raleigh in his dialogue of parliaments doth affirm in these words:

> The great charter was not originally granted regally and freely, for Henry I did but usurp the kingdom, and therefore the better to assure himself against Robert his elder brother, *he*[237] flattered the nobility and people with these charters. Yea, King John that confirmed them had the like respect, for Arthur Duke of Britain was the undoubted heir of the crown, upon whom King John usurped. And so, to conclude, these charters had their original from kings *de facto* but not *de jure* ... The great charter had first an obscure birth by usurpation, and was secondly fostered and showed to the world by rebellion. [Raleigh 2, pp. 4, 6]

(14) A third consideration must be that in the form of parliaments instituted and continued since King Henry I's *and King Henry III's*[238] times is not to be found the usage of any natural liberty of the people. For all those liberties that are claimed in parliaments are the liberties of grace from the king, and not the liberties of nature to the people. For if the liberty were natural it would give power to the multitude to assemble themselves *when* and *where* they please, to bestow sovereignty and by pactions to limit and direct the exercise of it, whereas the liberties of favour and grace which are claimed in parliaments are restrained both for time, place, persons and other circumstances, to the sole pleasure of the king. The people cannot assemble themselves, but the king, by his writs, calls them to what place he pleases, and then again scatters them with his breath at an instant, without any other cause showed them than his will. Neither is the whole summoned, but only so many as the king's writs appoint. *The prudent King Edward I summoned always those barons of ancient families that were most wise in his parliaments but omitted their sons after their death if they were not answerable to their parents in understanding*[239] [Camden p. 169]. Nor have the whole people voices in the election of knights of the shire or burgesses, but only freeholders in the counties and freemen in the cities and boroughs. Yet in the city of Westminster, all the householders, though they be neither freemen nor freeholders, have voices in their election of burgesses.

Also, during the time of parliament those privileges of the House of Commons – of freedom of speech, power to punish their own members, to examine the proceedings and demeanour of courts of justice and officers, to have access to the king's person and the like – are not due by any natural right, but are derived from the bounty or indulgence of the king, as appears by a solemn recognition of the House. For at the opening of the parliament, when the Speaker is presented to the king, he, in the behalf and name of the whole House of Commons, humbly craves of his majesty that he would be pleased to grant them their accustomed liberties of freedom of speech, of access to his person and the rest. These privileges are granted with a condition implied that they keep themselves within the bounds and limits of loyalty and obedience, for else why do the House of Commons inflict punishment themselves upon their own members for transgressing in some of these points? And the king as head hath many times punished the members for the like offences. The power which the king giveth in all his courts to his judges or others to punish doth not exclude him from doing the like by way of prevention, concurrence or evocation, even in the same point which he hath given in charge by a delegated power. For they who *give*[240] authority by commission do always retain more than they grant. Neither of the two houses claim infallibility of not erring, no more than a general council can. It is not impossible but that the greatest part may be in fault, or at least interested or engaged in the delinquency of one particular member. In such cases it is most proper for the head to correct, and not to expect the consent of the members, or for the parties peccant to be their own judges. Nor is it needful to confine the king in such cases within the circle of any one court of justice, who is supreme judge in all courts. And in rare and new cases rare and new remedies must be sought out, for it is a rule of the common law in '*novo casu, novum remedium est apponendum*' [in a new case a new remedy is to be applied], and the Statute of Westminster II, c. 24, giveth power even to the clerks of the chancery to make new forms of writ in new cases, lest any man that came to the king's court of chancery for help should be sent away without remedy [Statutes pp. 34–5]. A precedent cannot be found for every case, and of things that happen seldom and are not common there cannot be a common custom. Though crimes exorbitant do pose the king and council in finding a precedent for a condign punishment, yet they must not therefore pass unpunished.

I have not heard that the people by whose voices the knights and burgesses are chosen did ever call to an account those whom they had elected. They neither give them instructions or directions what to say or do in parliament, therefore they cannot punish them, when they come home, for doing amiss. If the people had any such power over their burgesses, then we might *have some colour to call it the natural liberty of the people*.[241] But they are so far from punishing that they may be punished themselves for intermeddling *with*[242] parliamentary business. They must only choose, and trust those whom they choose to do what they list, and that is as much liberty as many of us deserve for our irregular elections of burgesses.

(15)   A fourth point to be considered is that in parliament all statutes or laws are made properly by the king alone at the rogation of the people, as his late majesty of happy memory affirms in his *True Law of Free Monarchy* [James I 2, p. 62], and as Mr Hooker teacheth us that 'Laws do not take their constraining force from the quality of such as devise them but from the power that doth give them the strength of laws' [Hooker I, x, 8]. '*Le roi le veult*: the king will have it so' is the imperative phrase pronounced at the king's passing of every act of parliament. And it was the ancient custom for a long time, till the days of King Henry IV, that the kings, when any bill was brought unto them that had passed both houses, to take and pick out as much or as little thereof *as they pleased*[243] and to leave out what they liked *not*[244] and so much as they *chose*[245] was enacted for a law. *But the custom of later kings hath been so gracious as to allow always of the entire bill as it had passed both houses*.[246]

(16)   The parliament is the king's court, for so all the oldest statutes call it, 'The king in his parliament'. But neither of the two houses are that supreme court, not yet both of them together. They are only members and a part of the body, whereof the king is the head and ruler. The king's governing of this body of the parliament we may find most significantly proved, both by the statutes themselves, as also by such precedents as expressly show us how the king sometimes by himself, sometimes by his council, and other times by his judges, *hath*[247] overruled and directed the judgments of the Houses of parliament. For the king, we find that Magna Carta and the charter of forests and many other statutes about those times had only the form of the king's letters-patents, or grant under the great seal, testifying those great liberties to be the sole act and bounty of the king. The words of Magna Carta begin thus: 'Edward, by the grace of God,

etc. To all our archbishops, etc., and *to*[248] our faithful subjects, greeting. Know ye that we, *of*[249] our *mere freewill* have granted to all freemen these liberties' [Statutes p. 1].

In the same *style*[250] goeth the charter of forests and other statutes. *Statutum Hiberniae* [the statute of Ireland], made at Westminster, February 9th, 14 Henry III, is but a letter of the king to Gerard son of Maurice, justiciar of Ireland [Statutes pp. 4–5]. The statute *de anno bisextili* begins thus: 'The king to his justices of the bench, greeting, etc' (6 Edward I) [Statutes p. 25]. *Explanationes statuti Glocestriae* [explanations of the statute of Gloucester], made by the king and his justices only, were received always as statutes, and are still printed amongst them [Egerton p. 15].

The statute made for correction of the twelfth chapter of the statute of Gloucester was signed under the great seal, and sent to the justices of the bench after the manner of a writ patent, with a certain writ closed, dated by the king's hand at Westminster, that 'they should do and execute all and everything contained in it, although the same do not accord with the statute of Gloucester in all things' [Statutes p. 26].

The statute of Rutland is the king's letters to his treasurer and barons of his exchequer and to his chamberlain [Statutes pp. 26–7]. The statute of *circumspecte agatis* saith: 'The king to his judges sendeth greeting' [Statutes p. 43].

There are many other statutes of the same form, and some of them which run only in the majestic terms of 'The king commands', or 'The king wills', or 'Our Lord the king hath established', or 'Our Lord the king hath ordained', or 'Of his special grace hath granted', without mention of consent of the Commons or people; insomuch that some statutes rather resemble proclamations than acts of parliament. And indeed some of them were no other than mere proclamations, as the provisions of Merton, made by the king at an assembly of the prelates and nobility for the coronation of the king and his Queen Eleanor, which begins: '*Provisum est in curia domini regis apud Merton*' [it is provided in the court of the lord king at Merton] [Egerton p. 14]. Also a provision was made, 19 Henry III, '*De assisa ultimae praesentationis*' (20 Henry III), which 'was continued and allowed for law until Westminster II, *anno* [in the year] 13 Edward I, c. 5, which provides the contrary by express words' [Egerton p. 15]. This provision begins: ' *Provisum fuit coram domino rege, archiepiscopis, episcopis et baronibus, Quod,*' etc. [it is provided before the king, archbishops, bishops and barons, That, etc.] [Egerton p. 15]. It seems originally the difference was not great between a proclamation and a statute. This latter the king made by the common council of the kingdom. In the former he had but the advice only of his great council of the peers, or of his privy council only. That the king had a great council besides his parliament appears by a record of 5 Henry IV about an exchange between the king and the Earl of Northumberland, whereby the king promiseth to deliver to the earl lands to the value, *etc.*,[251] by the advice of parliament, or otherwise by the advice of his grand council and other estates of the realm, which the king will assemble in case the parliament do not meet [Lambarde 1, pp. 59–60].

We may find what judgment of later times parliaments have had of proclamations by the statute of 31 Henry *VIII*,[252] c. 8, in these words:

> Forasmuch as the king, by the advice of his council, hath set forth proclamations which obstinate persons have contemned, not considering what a king by his royal power may do; considering that sudden causes and occasions fortune many times which do require speedy remedies, and that by abiding for a parliament in the meantime might happen great prejudice to ensue to the realm; and weighing also that his majesty, which by the kingly power and regal power given him by God may do many things in such cases, *should*[253] not be driven to intend[k] the liberties and supremacy of his *royal*[254] power and dignity by wilfulness of froward subjects; it is therefore thought fit that the king with the advice of his honourable council should set forth proclamations for the good of the people and defence of his regal dignity, as necessity shall require. [Statutes p. 640]

This opinion of a House of parliament *was confirmed afterwards by a second parliament*,[255] and the statute made proclamations of as great validity as if they had been made by parliament (34 Henry VIII, c. 23) [Statutes pp. 807–8]. This law continued until the government of the state came to be under a protector during the minority of Edward VI, and in his first year it was repealed (1 Edward VI [c. 12; Statutes p. 918]).

I find also that a parliament in the eleventh year of Henry VII

---

[k] [increase].

did so great reverence to the actions or ordinances of the king, that by statute they provided a remedy or means to levy a benevolence granted to the king [Statutes p. 363; 11 Henry VII, c. 10], although by *a*[256] statute made not long before, all benevolences were damned and annulled for ever (1 Richard III, c. 2) [Statutes p. 328].

Mr Fuller in his *Argument* against the proceedings of the High Commission court affirms that the statute of 2 Henry IV, c. 15, which giveth power to ordinaries to imprison and set fines on subjects, was made without the assent of the Commons because they are not mentioned in the act [Fuller pp. 7–8]. *If this argument be good we shall*[257] find very many *ancient*[258] statutes of the same kind, for the assent of the Commons was seldom mentioned in the elder parliaments. *The most usual title of parliaments in Edward III, Richard II, the three Henries, IV, V, VI, in Edward IV and Richard III's days was: 'The king in his parliament with the assents of the prelates, earls and barons, and at the petition, or at the special request or instance, of the Commons, doth ordain'*.[259] The same Mr Fuller saith that the statute made against Lollards was without the assent of the Commons, as appears by their petition in these words: 'The Commons beseech that whereas a statute was made in the last parliament etc., which was never assented to nor granted by the Commons, but that which was done therein was done without their assent' (5 Richard II, c. 5) [Fuller p. 8].[/]

(17) How far the king's council hath directed and swayed in parliament hath in part appeared by what hath been already produced. For further evidence we may add the statute of Westminster the first, which saith: 'These be the acts of King Edward I, made at his first parliament general by his council, and by the assent of bishops, abbots, priors, earls, barons and all the commonalty of the realm, etc.' (3 Edward I) [Statutes p. 15]. The statute of bigamy saith: 'In the presence of certain reverend fathers, bishops of England and others of the king's council, the *constitutions*[260] underwritten were recited and after published before the king and his council. Forasmuch as all the king's council, as well justices as others, did agree that they should be put in writing and observed' (4 Edward I) [Statutes p. 23].

The statute of Acton Burnell saith: "The king, for himself and

---

[/] [B places this paragraph at the end of section 15 above].

by[261] his council, hath ordained and established' (13 Edward I) [Statutes p. 27].

In *articuli super chartas*, when the great charter was confirmed 'at the request of his prelates, earls and barons', we find these passages (28 Edward I): 1. 'Nevertheless the king and his council do not intend by reason of this estatute to diminish the king's right', etc. (chapter 2) [Statutes p. 50]. 2. 'And notwithstanding all these before mentioned or any part of them, both the king and his council and all *they*[262] that were present at the making of this ordinance, will and intend that the right and prerogatives of *his*[263] crown shall be saved to him in all things' (chapter 20) [Statutes p. 52]. Here we may see in the same parliament the charter of the liberties of the subjects confirmed, and a saving of the king's prerogative. Those times neither stumbled at the name, nor conceived any such antipathy between the terms as should make them incompatible.

The statute of escheators hath this title: 'At the parliament of our sovereign lord the king, by his council it was agreed, and also by the king himself commanded' (29 Edward I) [Statutes p. 52].

And the ordinance of inquest goeth thus: 'It is agreed and ordained by the king and all his council' (33 Edward I) [Statutes p. 54].

The statute made at York 9 Edward III saith:

> Whereas the knights, citizens and burgesses desired our sovereign lord the king in his parliament by their petition, that for his profit and the commodity of his prelates, earls, barons and commons, it may please him to provide remedy; our sovereign lord the king desiring the profit of his people by the assent of his prelates, earls, barons and other nobles of *his*[264] realm, summoned at *his*[265] parliament, and by the advice of his council being there, hath ordained (9 Edward III). [Statutes p. 74]

In the parliament 2 Edward III, where Magna Carta was confirmed, I *find*[266] this preamble: 'At the request of the commonalty by their petition made before the king and his council in parliament, by the assent of the prelates, earls, barons and other great men assembled, it was granted' [Statutes p. '55'=67; 1 Edward III].

The Commons presenting a petition unto the king which the king's council did mislike, were content thereupon to *amend*[267] and explain their petition; the form of which petition is in these words:

> To their most redoubted sovereign lord the king, praying the

said Commons, that whereas they have prayed him to be discharged of all manner of articles of the eyre, etc; which petition seemeth to his council to be prejudicial unto him and in disinherison of his crown if it were so generally granted; his said Commons, not willing nor desiring to demand things of him which should fall in *disinherison*[268] of him or of his crown perpetually, as of escheats, etc., but of trespasses, misprisions, negligences and ignorances, etc ... (27 Edward III). [Statutes pp. 119–20; 36 Edward III]

In the time of Henry III an order or provision was made by the king's council, and it was pleaded at the common law *in bar*[269] to a writ of dower (4 Henry III). 'The plaintiff's attorney could not deny it and thereupon the judgment was *ideo sine die* (Fitzherbert *Dower* 179)' [Egerton pp. 13–14]. It seems in those days an order of the council board was either parcel of the common law or above it.

'The reverend judges have had regard in their proceedings that before they would resolve or give judgment in new cases they consulted with the king's privy council' [Egerton p. 50]. In the case of Adam Brabson, who was assaulted by R.W. in the presence of the justices of assize at Winchester, the judges would have 'the advice of the king's council, for in a like case, because R.C. did strike a juror at Westminster, which passed in an inquest against one of his friends, it was adjudged by all the council that his right hand should be cut off and his lands and goods forfeited to the king' [Egerton p. 51].

'Green and Thorpe were sent by the judges *of the bench*[270] to the king's council to demand of them whether by the statute of 14 Edward III, c. 6, a word may be amended in a writ. And it was answered that a word may well be amended, although the statute speak but of a letter or syllable' [Egerton pp. 52–3].

In the case of Sir Thomas Ughtred, knight, who

> brought a formedon against a poor man and his wife, they came and yielded to the demandant, which seemed suspicious to the court, whereupon judgment was stayed (39 Edward III). And Thorpe said that in the like case of Giles *Blacket*[271] it was spoken of in parliament, and we were commanded that when any like case should come we should not go to judgment without good advice. [Egerton p. 52]

Therefore the judges' conclusion was[m]: 'Sue to the Council, and as they will have us to do, we will; and otherwise not in this case'.

(18)   In the last place we may consider how much hath been attributed to the opinions of the king's judges by parliaments, and so *find*[272] that the king's council hath guided and ruled the judges, and the judges guided the parliament.

> In the parliament of 28 Henry VI, the Commons made suit that William de la Pole, Duke of Suffolk, should be committed to prison for many treasons and other crimes. The lords of the higher house were doubtful what answer to give. The opinion of the judges was demanded. Their opinion was that he ought not to be committed, for that the Commons did not charge him with any particular offence, but with general reports and slanders. This opinion was allowed. [Egerton p. 19]

In another parliament (which was prorogued) (31 Henry VI) in the vacation the Speaker of the House of Commons

> was condemned in a thousand pounds damages in an action of trespass, and was committed to prison in execution for the same. When the parliament was reassembled the Commons made suit to the king and Lords to have their Speaker delivered. The Lords demanded the opinions of the judges whether he might be delivered out of prison by privilege of parliament. [Egerton p. 20]

Upon the judges' answer it was concluded that the Speaker

> should still remain in prison according to the law, notwithstanding the privilege of parliaments and that he was the Speaker. Which resolution was declared to the Commons by Moyle, the king's serjeant at law, and the Commons were commanded in the king's name by the Bishop of Lincoln (in the absence of the Archbishop of Canterbury, then chancellor) to choose another Speaker. [Egerton p. 21]

In 7 of Henry VIII

> a question was moved in parliament, whether spiritual persons might be convented before temporal judges for criminal causes? There Sir John Fineux and the other judges delivered their

---

[m] '*Sues au conseil et comment ils voilent que nous devomus faire, nous volomus faire, et auterment nient en cest case.*' [This law French passage is not in Egerton, but the English translation given by Filmer is identical with that printed in Egerton p. 52].

opinion that they might and ought to be. And their *opinion*[273] was allowed and maintained by the king and Lords. And Dr Standish, who before had holden the same opinion, was delivered from the bishops. [Egerton, (*Post-nati* p. 22)]

If a writ of error be sued in parliament upon a judgment given in the king's bench, the lords of the higher house alone (without the Commons) are to examine the errors. The Lords are to proceed *according to the law, and*[274] for their judgment therein they are to be informed by the advice and counsel of the judges, who are to inform them what the law is, and so to direct them in their judgment. For the Lords are not to follow their own opinions or discretions otherwise. (*Ibidem*) [Egerton pp. 22–3].

*'So it was in a writ of error brought in parliament by the Dean and chapter of Lichfield against the Prior and convent of *Newtonpanell*,[275] as appeareth by the record (17 Richard II)' [Egerton p. 23]. See Flower Dew's case, P. 1 Henry VII, fol. 19 [Egerton p. 23]*.[276]

Appendix: Three passages omitted in the Chicago manuscript but included in the Cambridge manuscript.

(1)   Two Passages in the Civil Law Cleared. (C.U.L. Add. MS 7078; title at p. ix; text at pp. 43–5; also printed, with omissions and errors, in the Bohun edition, 1685. This chapter is inserted after the two chapters on Grotius: see p. 13 above and note *d*. Text is B):

There are two places cited out of the civil law which do seem much to strengthen the opinion of Grotius about natural community. Though they be not alleged by him, yet they are fit to be considered because they are authorities of the greatest antiquity in this point, and the foundation upon which the late schoolmen have built. In the digests there is first this principle: '*Jure naturali omnes homines liberi nascuntur*' [by natural law all men are born free; *Digest*, 1, i, 4; p. 29]. Secondly, the law there, speaking of the prince, saith: '*Populus ei et in eum omne suum imperium et potestatem confert*' [the people confer to and upon him all their power and authority]. For a general answer to these two texts of the civil law, it must be remembered that the grounds of this law are but the opinions and sayings of heathens that knew not, or at least believed not, the history of the Scriptures or of the creation, and that this law was fitted properly for the commonwealth and empire of the Romans. For these causes it is no great wonder if the principles of the Roman laws vary from the rules of Scripture, and customs of other nations.

To answer in particular to the first text, it may be said the sense of these words, 'by the law of nature all are born free', must needs mean a freedom only that is opposite to such subjection as was between *master* and *servant*, and not a freedom from such subjection as is between *father* and *son*. This is made manifest by the text of the law, for Ulpian in that place speaketh only of manumission, which is setting at liberty of servants from servitude, and not of emancipation, which is the freeing of children from their fathers' tuition. 'Servitude', as the law teacheth, 'is a constitution of the law of nations, by which a man is subjected to the dominion of any other man against nature' [*Digest* I, v, 4; p. 35]. So not every subjection is servitude, but subjection contrary to the law of nature. No man is born a servant, or subject to the power of a master by the law of nature, yet every man is born subject to the power of a father. This the law itself saith: '*In potestate nostra liberi nostri sunt*' [our children are in our power; *Institutes* I, ix]. And Ulpian teacheth that the education of children is by the law of nature, so that '*qui ex me et uxore mea nascitur in potestate mea est*' [he who is born of me and my wife is in my power; *Digest* I, vi, 4; p. 36].

For answer to the second text, 'that the people bestow all the power upon the prince', certainly the law there intends no more than to note *the particular fact* of the people of Rome, and not *a general right* of all other people. When Julius and Augustus had successively taken the power into their hands, the people of Rome very bountifully, by a royal law, bestowed that power upon Augustus which he before had taken upon him. This act of the people the law mentioned, not to prove the right of all people to give power to princes, but produceth it against the people, to show them that by their own act the prince was free from all laws. And therefore in the very same place the civil law doth conclude that 'what pleaseth the prince had the vigour of the law, or whatsoever the emperor ordained by his epistles, or rescripts, or commanded upon mature deliberation, or by edict, was a law'. The title of the law *De constitutione principum* [on the ordaining of princes] is not concerning the ordaining of princes by the people, but the ordaining of laws by the princes.

(2)   A passage omitted in A (cf. above chapter 3, section 2, p. 38; text is B, pp. 95–6, corrected in the light of D):

It was objected that when Saul was made king, Samuel gave him a written law by which he was to govern, so that Saul was subject to that law. The answer is, the law which Samuel writ was to instruct the *people in*[277] their duty, not to teach the king his office. For the text saith 'That Samuel told the people the manner of the kingdom' (1 Samuel x, 25). There is no speech of reading to the king what Samuel had formerly told the people when they desired a king. Of the manner of the king and the *things*[278] they must suffer he now *writes*,[279] and leaves it to remain upon record to all posterity, and laid it up before the Lord. Thus saith Josephus (book 6, chapter 5) [*Jewish Antiquities* VI, 66], who should best know the Jewish records. Those err that think that the law in Deuteronomy xvii concerning the duty of a king was the same law that Samuel writ and laid up. If it had been the same, what need Samuel have writ and laid it up? – since that was writ and laid up long before in the ark, Deuteronomy xxxi. Secondly, the law in Deuteronomy concerns properly the king, and should have been read to him rather than to the people. Thirdly, the law itself in Deuteronomy xvii was but some few general precepts which did properly concern the particular kings of the Jews, as the not multiplying of horses or wives, not returning into Egypt. And though there be no question but that God may give laws to all kings, though the people may not, yet the laws in Deuteronomy xvii were only laws for the kings of the particular commonwealth of the Hebrews.

(3)   A passage omitted in A (cf above, Chapter 3, section 13, p. 54 and n. 233; the text is B, pp. 128–31, corrected in the light of D):

What the ancientiest usage of the Normans *was*[280] may best appear by such testimonies as Mr Selden produceth in his *Titles of Honor*. King William the Conqueror in the fourth year of his reign by the consent of his barons had twelve men out of every county who showed what the customs of the kingdom were and by the assent of the barons those customs were confirmed for laws. Which appears also by the laws of King Henry I, where it is said 'I restore you the laws of King Edward with those amendments by which my father amended them by the counsel of his barons' [Selden 1, p. 701]. It is probable, if there had been any custom in the Saxon times to have summoned knights and burgesses, that the Conqueror (who was so desirous to know and confirm the ancient customs) would rather have called such knights and burgesses than twelve men out of every county. Mr Selden citeth proofs for other parliaments in King William I's reign, but in none of them any mention of any other but *comites et primates et principum conventus* [earls and nobles and a meeting of the leading men], which was only earls and barons.

In the second year of King William II there was a parliament by *cunctis regni principibus*, and another which had *quosque regni proceres*. 'At the coronation of King Henry I', all the people of the kingdom were called, and laws then made '*per commune consilium baronum*' [Selden 1, p. 702].

3 Henry I *proceres regni* [the nobles of the kingdom] were called, and another parliament a while after *consensu comitum et baronum* [by the consent of the earls and barons] and in his tenth year of *comites* and *proceres* [earls and nobles] [Selden 1, p. 703]. In the eleventh year, at a parliament at Northampton, were summoned *omnes qui tenebant de rege in capite* [all who held land from the king as tenants-in-chief] [Selden 1, p. 705]. In the twenty-third year, *earls and barons*. The year following the same king held a parliament or great council with his *barons spiritual and temporal* [Selden 1, p. 706].

In the fifth year of King John, '*Rex et magnates convenerunt* [the king and the magnates met] and the roll of that year hath *commune consilium baronum meorum* [the common council of my barons] at Winchester' [Selden 1, p. 707]. The grand charter made in the last year of King John mentions *maiores barones regni, et qui in capite tenent de nobis* [the greater barons of the kingdom, and those who hold land from us as tenants-in-chief] [Selden 1, p. 709]. King Henry III, *anno* [in the year] 1225, called *omnes clericos et laicos totius regni* [all the clergy and laymen of the whole kingdom]. King Edward I in his third year summoned the *communaltie* [commonalty] of the land. King Edward II in his fourteenth year had *tout le cominaltie de son royaume* [all the commonalty of his kingdom].

By these testimonies it appears that the ancientest and most usual summons was of earls and barons, and that kings did vary their summons at their pleasure. Which may be further confirmed out of Mr Camden, who, speaking of barons, saith that

> King Henry III out of a great multitude which was seditious and turbulent called out the best of them by his writ to parliament. And the prudent King Edward I summoned always those barons of ancientest families that were most wise to his parliaments, but omitted their sons after their death if they were not answerable to their parents in understanding. [Camden p. 169]

King Henry III commanded '*duos milites gladio cinctos magis discretos et idoneos*' [two most discreet and suitable knights, girt with swords] to be chosen to serve for knights of the shire. And it is the acknowledgment of Mr Selden that the 'first writs we find accompanied with the other circumstances of a summons to parliament, as well for the Commons as Lords, is in the forty-ninth year of King Henry III' [Selden 1, p.

717]. Amongst all those proofs which I can find produced for the antiquity of parliaments, I see nothing for the choosing of knights and burgesses by popular elections before the times of this King Henry III, although King Henry I were the first that summoned all the people.

THE[n]
FREE-HOLDERS
GRAND INQUEST
TOUCHING
Our Soveraigne LORD the KING
AND
HIS PARLIAMENT.

Claudian. *de laudibus Stiliconis.*

Fallitur egregio quisquis sub Principe credit
Servitium: Nunquam LIBERTAS gratior extat,
Quam sub rege pio – –
[Claudian, *De Consulatu Stilichonis* III, 113–15]

[Anyone who believes that it is servitude to live under a prince is badly mistaken: there is no more welcome liberty than to be under a righteous king[o]]

THE PREFACE

There is a general belief that the parliament of England was at first an imitation of the assembly of the three estates in France. Therefore, in order to prepare the understanding in the [research][p] we have in hand, it is proper to give a brief account of the mode of France in those assemblies. Scotland and Ireland being also under the dominion of the king of England, a touch of the manner of their parliaments shall be by way of preface.

1. In France the king's writ goeth to the bailiffs, seneschals or stewards of liberties, who issue out warrants to all such as have fees

---

[n] [Copy-text is the first edition (Wing F910), which is referred to in the notes as 48F. Where the notes record readings or omissions in this edition, the text is taken from the editions of 1679 (Wing F913 and 914), referred to in the notes as 79].
[o] [a version of part of the same quotation occurs on the title-page of the *The Anarchy of a Limited or Mixed Monarchy*].
[p] [48F, 79: recerche].

and lands within their liberties, and to all towns, requiring all such as have any complaints to meet in the principal city, there to choose two or three delegates in the name of that province to be present at the general assembly.

At the day appointed they meet at the principal city of the bailiwick. The king's writ is read, and every man called by name and sworn to choose honest men for the good of the king and commonwealth, to be present at the general assembly as delegates, faithfully to deliver their grievances and demands of the province. Then they choose their delegates and swear them. Next they consult what is necessary to be complained of, or what is fit to be desired of the king, and of these things they make a catalogue or index. And because every man should freely propound his complaint or demands, there is a chest placed in the town hall into which every man may cast his writing. After the catalogue is made and signed, it is delivered to the delegates to carry to the general assembly.

All the bailiwicks are divided into twelve classes. To avoid confusion, and to the end there may not be too great delay in the assembly by the gathering of all the votes, every classis compiles a catalogue or book of the grievances and demands of all the bailiwicks within that classis. Then these classes at the assembly compose one book of the grievances and demands of the whole kingdom. This being the order of the proceedings of the third estate, the like order is observed by the clergy and nobility. When the three books for the three estates are perfected, then they present them to the king by their presidents. First, the president for the clergy begins his oration on his knees, and the king commanding he stands up bare-headed and proceeds. And so the next president for the nobility doth the like. But the president for the commons begins and ends his oration on his knees. Whilst the president for the clergy speaks, the rest of that order rise up and stand bare, till they are bid by the king to sit down and be covered, and so the like for the nobility. But whilst the president of the commons speaks, the rest are neither bidden to sit *[nor]*[281] be covered. Thus the grievances and demands being delivered, and left to the king and his council, the general assembly of the three estates endeth, *atque ita totus actus concluditur* [and so the whole business is concluded].

Thus it appears the general assembly was but an orderly way of presenting the public grievances and demands of the whole kingdom to the consideration of the king – not much unlike the ancient usage of this kingdom for a long time, when all laws were nothing else but the king's answers to the petitions presented to him in parliament, as is apparent by very many statutes, parliament rolls and the confession of Sir Edward Coke.

2. In Scotland, about twenty days before the parliament begins, proclamation is made throughout the kingdom to deliver into the king's clerk or master of the rolls all bills to be exhibited that sessions, before a certain day. Then are they brought to the king and perused by him, and only such as he allows are put into the chancellor's hand to be propounded in parliament, and none others. And if any man in parliament speak of another matter than is allowed by the king, the chancellor tells him there is no such bill allowed by the king. When they have passed them for laws, they are presented to the king, who with his sceptre put into his hand by the chancellor, ratifies them. And if there be anything the king dislikes they raze it out before.

3. In Ireland the parliament, as appears by a statute made in the tenth year of Henry VII, c. 4, is to be after this manner:

> No parliament is to be holden but at such season as the king's lieutenant and council there do first certify the king, under the great seal of that land, the causes and considerations, and all such acts as *them seemeth*²⁸² should pass in the said parliament. And such causes and considerations, and acts affirmed by the king and his council to be good and expedient for that land: and his licence thereupon as well in affirmation of the said causes and acts, as to summon the parliament under his great seal of England had and obtained. That done, a parliament to be had and holden after the form and effect afore rehearsed, and if any parliament be holden in that land contrary to the form and provision aforesaid, it is deemed void, and of none effect in law. [Statutes of Ireland pp. 55–6]

It is provided that all such bills as shall be offered to the parliament there shall first be transmitted hither under the great seal of that kingdom, and having received allowance and approbation here, shall be put under the great seal of this kingdom, and so returned thither to be preferred to the parliament. By a statute of 3 and 4 of Philip and Mary for the expounding of Poynings' Act, it is ordered for the king's 'passing of the said acts in such form and tenor as they should be sent into England, or else for the change of them, or of any part of them' [Statutes of Ireland p. 253].

After this shorter narrative of the usage of parliaments in our neighbour and fellow kingdoms, it is time the *inquisitio magna* of our own be offered to the verdict or judgment of a moderate and intelligent reader.

THE ARGUMENT

A presentment of divers statutes, records and other precedents, explaining the writs of summons to parliament; showing:

    I. That the Commons by their writ are only to perform and consent to the ordinances of parliament.

    II. That the Lords or common council by their writ are only to treat and give counsel in parliament.

    III. That the king himself only ordains and makes laws, and is supreme judge in parliament.

With the suffrages of

Henry de Bracton	Henry Spelman
John Britton	John Glanville
Thomas Egerton	William Lambarde
Edward Coke	Richard Crompton
Walter Raleigh	William Camden, and
Robert Cotton	John Selden

THE FREEHOLDER'S GRAND INQUEST TOUCHING OUR SOVEREIGN LORD THE KING, AND HIS PARLIAMENT

Every freeholder that hath a voice in the election of knights, citizens or burgesses for the parliament ought to know with what power he trusts those whom he chooseth, because such trust is the foundation of the power of the House of Commons.

A writ from the king to the sheriff of the county is that which gives authority and commission for the freeholders to make their election at the next county court day after the receipt of the writ; and in the writ there is also expressed the duty and power of the knights, citizens and burgesses that are there elected.

The means to know what trust or authority the country or freeholders confer or bestow by their election is in this as in other like

72

cases, to have an eye to the words of the commission or writ itself. Thereby it may be seen whether that which the House of Commons doth act be within the limit of their commission. Greater or other trust than is comprised in the body of the writ, the freeholders do not or cannot give if they obey the writ. The writ being Latin and not extant in English, few freeholders understand it and fewer observe it. I have rendered it in Latin and English:*

The king to the sheriff of greeting.

Whereas by the advice and consent of our council, for certain difficult and urgent businesses concerning us, the state and defence of our kingdom of England and the English church, we have ordained a certain parliament of ours to be held at our city of the day of next ensuing, and there to have conference, and to treat with the prelates, great men and peers of our said kingdom; we command and straitly enjoin you, that making proclamation at the next county court after the receipt of this our writ, to be holden the day, and place aforesaid, you cause two knights, girt with swords, the most fit and discreet of the county aforesaid; and of every city of that county two citizens; of every borough, two burgesses of the discreeter and most sufficient; to be freely, and

* 'Rex vicecomiti salutem, etc.

Quia de advisamento et assensu concilii nostri pro quibusdam arduis et urgentibus negotiis, nos, statum et defensionem regni nostri Angliae, et ecclesiae Anglicanae concernentibus, quoddam parliamentum nostrum apud civitatem nostram Westmonasterii duodecimo die Novembris proxime futuro teneri ordinavimus, et ibidem cum praelatis, magnatibus et proceribus dicti regni nostri colloquium habere et tractatum; tibi praecipimus, firmiter injungentes, quod facta proclamatione in proximo comitatu tuo post receptionem hujus brevis nostri tenendo die et loco praedictis duos milites gladiis cinctos magis idoneos et discretos comitatus praedicti, et de qualibet civitate comitatus illius duos cives, et de quolibet burgo duos burgenses de discretioribus et magis sufficientibus, libere et indifferenter per illos, qui proclamationi hujusmodi interfuerint juxta formam statutorum inde editorum et provisorum, eligi, et nomina eorundem militum, civium et burgensium, sic electorum in quibusdam indenturis, inter te et illos, qui hujusmodi electioni interfuerint, inde conficiendis, sive hujusmodi electi praesentes fuerint vel absentes, inferi: eosque ad dictos diem et locum venire facias. Ita quod iidem milites plenam et sufficientem potestatem pro se et communitate comitatus praedicti, ac dicti cives et burgenses pro se et communitate civitatum et burgorum praedictorum, divisim ab ipsis habeant, ad faciendum, et consentiendum his, quae tunc ibidem de communi consilio dicti regni nostri (favente Deo) contigerint ordinari super negotiis antedictis: Ita quod, pro defectu potestatis hujusmodi, seu propter improvidam electionem militum civium, aut burgensium praedictorum, dicta negotia infecta non remaneant quovismodo. Nolumus autem, quod tu, nec aliquis alius vicecomes dicti regni nostri, aliqualiter sit electus. Et electionem illam, in pleno comitatu factam, distincte et aperte, sub sigillo tuo et sigillis eorum qui electioni illi interfuerint, nobis in cancellariam nostram ad dictos diem et locum certifices indilate, remittens nobis alteram partem indenturarum praedictarum, praesentibus consutam, una cum hoc breve. Teste meipso apud Westmonasterium.'

indifferently chosen by them who shall be present at such proclamation, according to the tenor of the statutes in that case made
and provided; and the names of the said knights, citizens and
burgesses so chosen, to be inserted in certain indentures to be
then made between you and those that shall be present at such
election, whether the parties so elected be present or absent; and
shall make them to come at the said day and place. So that the
said knights for themselves and for the county aforesaid; and
the said citizens and burgesses for themselves and the commonalty
of the aforesaid cities and boroughs, may have severally from
them full and sufficient power to *perform* and to *consent* to those
things which then by the favour of God shall there happen to
be ordained by the common council of our said kingdom, concerning the businesses aforesaid. So that the business may not
by any means remain undone for want of such power or by reason
of the improvident election of the aforesaid knights, citizens and
burgesses. But we will not in any case you or any other sheriff
of our said kingdom shall be elected. And at the day and place
aforesaid, the said election made in the full county court, you
shall certify without delay to us in our chancery, under your
seal and the seals of them which shall be present at that election,
sending back unto us the other part of the indenture aforesaid
affiled to these presents, together with this writ. Witness our self
at Westminster.

By this writ we do not find that the Commons are called to be
any part of the common council of the kingdom, or of the supreme
court of judicature, or to have any part of the legislative power, or
to consult *de arduis regni negotiis*, of the difficult businesses of the
kingdom. The writ only says the king would have conference and
treat with the prelates, great men and peers – but not a word of
treating or conference with the Commons. The House of Commons,
which doth not minister an oath, nor fine, nor imprison any but
their own members (and that but of late in some cases) cannot properly
be said to be a court at all, much less to be a part of the supreme
court or highest judicature of the kingdom. The constant custom,
even to this day, for the members of the House of Commons to stand
bare, with their hats in their hands in the presence of the Lords,
while the Lords sit covered at all conferences, is a visible argument
that the Lords and Commons are not fellow commissioners or fellow
counsellors of the kingdom.

The duty of knights, citizens and burgesses, mentioned in the writ, is only *ad faciendum et consentiendum*, to perform and to consent to such things as should be ordained by the common council of the kingdom. There is not so much mentioned in the writ as a power in the Commons to dissent. When a man is bound to appear in *a*²⁸³ court of justice, the words are '*ad faciendum et recipiendum quod ei per curiam injungetur*' [to do and undergo what is imposed upon him by the court]: which shows that this word '*faciendum*' is used as a term in law, to signify 'to give obedience'. For this we meet with a precedent even as ancient as the parliament-writ itself, and it is concerning proceedings in parliament 33 Edward I:* 'Our lord the king commands the sheriff to summon Nicholas Segrave to appear before the lord our king in the next parliament, to hear the will of the lord our king himself, and to perform and receive what the king's court shall further consider of the premises' [R.P. 1, p. 172].

Sir Edward Coke, to prove the clergy hath no voice in parliament, saith that by the words of their writ their consent was only to such things as were ordained by the common council of the realm (Coke 4, p. 4). If this argument of his be good, it will deny also voices to the Commons in parliament. For in their writ are the selfsame words, viz. to consent to such things as were ordained by the common council of the kingdom. Sir Edward Coke concludes that the '*procuratores cleri* have many times appeared in parliament as spiritual assistants to consider, consult and to consent' [Coke 4, p. 4], but never had voice there. How they could consult and consent without voices he doth not show. Though 'the clergy', as he saith, 'oft appeared in parliament' yet was it only *ad consentiendum* [to consent] as I take it, and not *ad faciendum* [to act], for the word *faciendum* is omitted in their writ. The cause as I conceive is the clergy, though they were to assent, yet by reason of clerical exemptions they were not required to perform all the ordinances or acts of parliament.

But some may think, though the writ doth not express a calling of the knights, citizens and burgesses to be part of the common council of the kingdom, yet it supposeth it a thing granted, and not to be questioned but that they are a part of the common council.

---

* 'Dominus rex mandavit vicecom. quod, etc., summon' Nicolaum de Segrave, et ex parte domini regis firmiter ei injungeret, quod esset coram domino rege in proximo parliamento etc., ad audiendum voluntatem ipsius domini regis etc. Et ad faciendum et recipiendum ulterius quod curia domini regis consideraret in praemissis.'

Indeed, if their writ had not mentioned the calling of prelates, great men and peers to council, there might have been a little better colour for such a supposition. But the truth is, such a supposition doth make the writ itself vain and idle. For it is a senseless thing to bid men assent to that which they have already ordained, since ordaining is an assenting, and more than an assenting.

For clearing the meaning and sense of the writ, and satisfaction of such as think it impossible but that the Commons of England have always been a part of the common council of the kingdom, I shall insist upon these points: 1. That anciently the barons of England were the common council of the kingdom. 2. That until the time of Henry I the Commons were not called to parliament. 3. Though the Commons were called by Henry I, yet they were not constantly called, nor yet regularly elected by writ until Henry III's time.

For the first point, Mr Camden in his *Britannia* doth teach us that 'in the time of the English Saxons and in the ensuing age a parliament was called *commune concilium* [a common council]', which was, saith he, '*praesentia regis, praelatorum, procerumque collectorum*: the presence of the king, prelates and peers assembled' [Camden p. 177]. No mention of the Commons: the prelates and peers were all barons.

The author of the chronicle of the church of Lichfield, cited by Mr Selden, saith, '*postquam rex Edwardus*, etc., *concilium baronum Angliae*, etc.: After King Edward was king, by the council of the barons of England he revived a law which had lain asleep threescore and seven years, and this law was called the law of St Edward the king' [Selden 4, p. 171].

In the same chronicle it is said that William the Conqueror '*anno regni sui quarto apud Londinias*' [in the fourth year of his reign, at London] had '*concilium baronum suorum*', a council of his barons. And of this parliament it is that his son Henry I speaks, saying, 'I restore you the laws of King Edward the Confessor, with those amendments wherewith my father amended them by the council of his barons' [Selden 1, p. 701].

In the fifth year (as Mr Selden thinks) of the Conqueror, was a parliament, or *principum conventus*, an assembly of earls and barons at Pinenden Heath in Kent, in the cause between Lanfranc the Archbishop of Canterbury and Odo, Earl of Kent [Selden 1, p. 702]. The king 'gave commission to Godfrid, then Bishop of Constance in Normandy, to represent his own person for hearing the controversy', as saith Mr Lambarde,

> and caused Egelric, the Bishop of Chichester (an aged man, singularly commended for skill in the laws and customs of the realm) to be brought thither in a wagon for his assistance in council, commanded Haymo the sheriff of Kent, to summon the whole county to give in evidence; three whole days spent in debate. In the end Lanfranc and the Bishop of Rochester were restored to the possession of Detling and other lands which Odo had withholden. [Lambarde 2, pp. 222–3]

21 Edward III, folio 60. There is mention of a parliament held under the same King William the Conqueror, wherein all the bishops of the land, earls and barons, made an ordinance touching the exemption of the Abbey of Bury from the Bishops of Norwich (*Apud* Selden [1, p. 702]).

In the tenth year of the Conqueror, '*episcopi, comites et barones regni regia potestate ad universalem synodum pro causis audiendis et tractandis convocati*' [the bishops, earls and barons of the kingdom were called together by royal authority to hear and deal with cases in a general assembly], saith the Book of Westminster.

In the second year of William II, there was a parliament *de cunctis regni principibus* [of all the leading men of the kingdom]; another which had *quosque regni proceres*: all the peers of the kingdom (Selden [1, p. 702]).

In the seventh year was a parliament at Rockingham Castle in Northamptonshire, '*episcopis, abbatibus *cunctisque**[284] *regni principibus una coeuntibus*' [the bishops, abbots and all the leading men of the kingdom coming together] [Selden 1, p. 702].

A year or two after, the same king, '*de statu regni acturus*' [to deal with the state of the kingdom], etc. 'called thither by the command of his writ, the bishops, abbots and all the peers of the kingdom' (Selden [1, p. 702]).

'At the coronation of Henry I' all the people of the kingdom of England were called and laws were then made; but it was *per 'commune concilium baronum meorum*, by the common council of my barons' (Selden [1, p. 702]).

In his third year, the peers of the kingdom were called without any mention of the Commons; and another a while after, '*consensu comitum et baronum*, by the consent of earls and barons' (Selden [I, p. 703]).

Florentius Wigor[n]iensis saith, these are statutes which Anselm and all the other bishops in the presence of King Henry, by the assent of his barons ordained [Florence of Worcester p. 478]; and in his tenth year, of earls and peers; and in his twenty-third of earls and barons. In the year following the same king held a parliament or great council with 'his barons spiritual and temporal'.

King Henry II in his tenth year had a great council or parliament at Clarendon, which was an assembly of prelates and peers [Holinshed ii, pp. 119–20].

22 Henry II, saith Hoveden, was a great council at Nottingham, and by the common council of the archbishops, bishops, earls and barons, the kingdom was divided into six parts. And again, Hoveden saith that the same king at 'Windsor (*apud Windeshores*) *communi concilio* [in a common council] of bishops, earls and barons, divided England into four parts'. And in his twenty-first year a parliament at Windsor of bishops, earls and barons. And another of like persons at Northampton [Hoveden ff. 312b–314b].

King Richard I had a parliament at Nottingham in his fifth year, of bishops, earls and barons. This parliament lasted but four days, yet much was done in it. The first day the king disseiseth Gerard de Canvil of the sheriffwick of Lincoln, and Hugh Bardolph of the castle and sheriffwick of York. The second day he required judgment against his brother John, who was afterwards king, and Hugh de Novant, Bishop of Coventry. The third day was granted to the king of every ploughland in England two shillings. He required also the third part of the service of every knight's fee for his attendance into Normandy, and all the wool that year of the monks [of] Cisteaux, which, for that it was grievous and unsupportable, they fine for money. The last day was for hearing of grievances, and so the parliament broke up. And the same year held another at Northampton of the nobles of the realm [Holinshed ii, pp. 247–8].

King John, in his fifth year, he and his great men met – '*rex et magnates convenerunt*': and the roll of that year hath '*commune concilium baronum meorum*, the common council of my barons at Winchester' (Selden [I, p. 707]).

In the sixth year of King Henry III the nobles granted to the king 'of every knight's fee, two marks in silver' [Holinshed ii, p. 351].

In his seventh year he had a parliament at London, an assembly of barons [Holinshed ii, p. 353]. In his thirteenth year an assembly of the Lords at Westminster [Holinshed ii, p. 364]. In his fifteenth year, of nobles both spiritual and temporal.

Matthew Paris saith that 20 Henry III '*Congregati sunt magnates ad colloquium de negotiis regni tractaturi*: The great men were called to confer and treat of the business of the kingdom' [Matthew Paris p. 429]. And at Merton 'our lord the king granted, by the consent of his great men, that hereafter usury should not run against a ward from the death of his ancestor' [Matthew Paris p. 422].

21 Henry III. The king sent his 'royal writs, commanding all belonging to his kingdom, that is to say, archbishops, bishops, abbots and priors installed, earls and barons, that they should all meet at London to treat of the king's business touching the whole kingdom', and 'at the day prefixed the whole multitude of the nobles of the kingdom met at London', saith Matthew Westminster [p. 143].

In his twenty-first year, 'at the request and by the council of the Lords' the charters were confirmed [Holinshed ii, p. 380].

22 Henry III at 'Winchester, the king sent his royal writs to archbishops, bishops, priors, earls and barons, to treat of business concerning the whole kingdom'.

32 Henry III 'the king commanded all the nobility of the whole kingdom to be called to treat of the state of his kingdom'. Matthew Westminster [pp. 228–9].

49 Henry III the king had a treaty at Oxford with the peers of the kingdom. Matthew Westminster [p. 330].

At a parliament at Marlborough, 55 Henry III, statutes were made 'by the assent of earls and barons'.

Here the place of Bracton, chief justice in this king's time, is worth the observing, and the rather for that it is much insisted on of late to make for parliament's being above the king. The words in Bracton are, 'The king hath a superior, God; also the law by which he is made king; also his court, viz. the earls and barons' [Bracton f. 34a]. The court that was said in those days to be above the king was a court of earls and barons, not a word of the Commons or the representative body of the kingdom being any part of the superior court. Now for the true sense of Bracton's words, how the law and the court of earls and barons are the king's superiors, they must of necessity be understood to be superiors so far only as to advise and direct the king out of his own grace and good will only, which appears plainly by the words of Bracton himself where, speaking of the king, he resolves thus, *'Nec potest ei necessitatem aliquis imponere quod injuriam suam corrigat et *emendet**[285], *cum superiorem non habeat nisi Deum, et satis ei erit ad poenam, quod Dominum expectat ultorem*: Nor can any man put a necessity upon him to correct and amend his injury unless he will himself, since he hath no superior but God; it will be sufficient punishment for him to expect the Lord an avenger' [Bracton ff. 368b–369a]. Here the same man who, speaking according to some men's opinion, saith the law and court of earls and barons are superior to the king, in this place tells us himself, the 'king hath no superior but God'. The difference is easily reconciled according to the distinction of the schoolmen, 'the king is free from the coactive power of laws or counsellors, but may be subject to their directive power' [Egerton p. 106] according to his own will – that is, God can only compel, but the law and his courts may advise him.

(*Rotuli parliamentorum* 1 Henry IV, number 79) The Commons expressly affirm, judgment in parliament belongs to the king and Lords [R.P. 3, p. 451].

These precedents show that from the Conquest until a great part of Henry III's reign (in whose days it is thought the writ for election of knights was framed) which is about two hundred years, and above a third part of the time since the Conquest to our days, the barons made the parliament or common council of the kingdom. Under the name of barons, not only the earls but the bishops also were comprehended, for the Conqueror made the bishops barons. Therefore it is no such great wonder that in the writ we find the Lords only to be the counsellors, and the Commons called only to perform and consent to the ordinances.

Those there be who seem to believe that under the word barons, anciently the lords of court-barons were comprehended, and that they were called to parliament as barons. But if this could be proved to have been at any time true, yet those lords of court-barons were not the representative body of the commons of England, except it can be also proved that the commons or freeholders of the kingdom chose such lords of court-barons to be present in parliament. The lords of manors came not at first by election of the people – as Sir Edward Coke, treating of the institution of court-barons, resolves us in these words:

By the laws and ordinances of ancient kings, and especially of King Alfred, it appeareth that the first kings of this realm had all the lands of England in demesne; and *les grand* [the great] manors and royalties they reserved to themselves, and of the remnant they, for the defence of the realm, enfeoffed the barons of the realm with such jurisdiction as the court-baron now hath. (Coke's *Institutes*, Part I, folio 58) [Coke 1, f. 58a–b]

Here, by the way, I cannot but note that if the 'first kings had all the lands of England in demesne', as Sir Edward Coke saith they had; and if the first kings were chosen by the people (as many think they were), then surely our forefathers were a very bountiful (if not a prodigal) people to give all the lands of the whole kingdom to their kings, with liberty for them to keep what they pleased and to give the remainder to their subjects, clogged and cumbered with a condition to defend the realm. This is but an ill sign of a limited monarchy by original constitution or contract. But to conclude the former point, Sir Edward Coke's opinion is that 'in the ancient laws, under the name of barons, were comprised all the nobility' [Coke 1, f. 58b].

This doctrine of the barons being the common council doth displease many, and is denied as tending to the disparagement of the Commons, and to the discredit and confutation of their opinion who teach that the 'Commons are assigned counsellors to the king by the people'. Therefore I will call in Mr Prynne to help us with his testimony. He in his book of *Treachery and Disloyalty*, etc., proves that before the Conquest, by the laws of Edward the Confessor, chapter 17, the king by his oath was 'to do justice by the council of the nobles of his realm' [Prynne p. 51]. He also resolves that the 'earls and barons in parliament are above the king, and ought to bridle him' [Prynne p. 37] when he exorbitates from the laws. He further tells us, the 'peers and prelates have often translated the crown from the right heir' [Prynne p. 9]:

1   'Electing and crowning Edward, who was illegitimate, and putting by Ethelred, the right heir after Edgar's decease' [Prynne p. 9].

2   'Electing and crowning Canutus, a mere foreigner, in opposition to Edmund, the right heir to King Ethelred' [Prynne p. 9].

3   'Harold and Hardicanute, both elected kings successively without title, Edmund and Alfred (the right heirs) being dispossessed' [Prynne p. 9].

4   'The English nobility, upon the death of Harold enacted that
     none of the Danish blood should any more reign over them'
     [Prynne p. 9].

5   'Edgar Atheling, who had best title, was rejected, and Harold
     elected and crowned king' [Prynne p. 9].

6   In the second and third year of Edward II the 'peers and nobles
     of the land, seeing themselves contemned, entreated the king
     to manage the affairs of the kingdom by the council of his
     barons. He gave his assent, and swore to ratify what the nobles
     ordained'; and one of their articles was that 'he would thence-
     forward order all the affairs of the kingdom by the council
     of his clergy and lords' [Prynne p. 20–1].

7   William Rufus, 'finding the greatest part of the nobles against
     him, swore to Lanfranc that if they would choose him for king
     he would abrogate their over-hard laws' [Prynne p. 52].

8   The beginning, saith Mr Prynne, of the charter of Henry I
     is observable: 'Henry by the grace of God, of England, etc.,
     know ye, that by the mercy of God and common council of
     the barons of the kingdom, I am crowned king' [Prynne p. 53].

9   'Maud the Empress, the right heir, was put by the crown by
     the prelates and barons, and Stephen Earl of Mortain, who
     had no good title, assembling the bishops and peers, promising
     the amendment of the laws according to all their pleasures and
     liking, was by them all proclaimed king' [Prynne p. 53].

10   'Lewis of France crowned king by the barons', instead of King
     John [Prynne p. 55].

All these testimonies from Mr Prynne may satisfy that anciently the
barons were the common council or parliament of England. And if
Mr Prynne could have found so much antiquity and proof for the
knights, citizens and burgesses, being of the common council, I make
no doubt but we should have heard from him in capital characters.
But alas! he meets not with so much as these names in those elder
ages. He dares not say the barons were assigned by the people counsellors to the king, for he tells us 'every baron in parliament doth represent his own person, and speaketh in behalf of himself alone. But in
the knights, citizens and burgesses are represented the commons of
the whole realm' (Prynne p. 43). Therefore every one of the Commons
hath a greater voice in parliament than the greatest earl in England.

Nevertheless, Mr Prynne will be very well content if we will admit and swallow these parliaments of barons for the representative body of the kingdom, and to that purpose he cites them, or to no purpose at all, but to prove the treachery and disloyalty of popish parliaments, prelates and peers, to their kings, which is the main point that Mr Prynne, by the title of his book, is to make good and to prove.

As to the second point, which is that until the time of Henry I the Commons were not called to parliament, besides the general silence of antiquity which never makes mention of the Commons coming to parliament until that time, our histories say before his time only certain of the nobility were called to consultation about the most important affairs of the state; he caused the Commons also to be assembled by knights, citizens and burgesses of their own appointment. Much to the same purpose writes Sir Walter Raleigh, saying it is held that the kings of England 'had no formal parliaments till about the eighteenth year of King Henry I. For in his third year, for the marriage of his daughter, the king raised a tax upon every hide of land, by the advice of his privy council alone' [Raleigh 2, pp. 2–3]. And 'the subjects', saith he, 'soon after this parliament was established, began to stand upon terms with their king, and drew from him by strong hand, and their swords, their great charter. It was after the establishment of the parliament, by colour of it, that they had so great daring' [Raleigh 2, p. 3]. If any desire to know the cause why Henry I called the people to parliament, it was upon no very good occasion, if we believe Sir Walter Raleigh. 'The grand charter', saith he,

> was not originally granted regally and freely, for King Henry I did but usurp the kingdom, and therefore the better to assure himself against Robert his elder brother, he flattered the people with those charters. Yea, King John that confirmed them, had the like respect: for Arthur Duke of Britain*q* was the undoubted heir of the crown, upon whom John usurped. So these charters had their original from kings *de facto*, but not *de jure*. [Raleigh 2, p. 4]

And then afterwards his conclusion is that the 'great charter had first an obscure birth by usurpation, and was fostered, and showed to the world by rebellion' [Raleigh 2, p. 6]. In brief, the king called

q [Britanny].

the people to parliament and granted them Magna Carta that they might confirm to him the crown.

The third point consists of two parts. First, that the Commons were not constantly called unto parliament until Henry III['s] days. This appears by divers of the precedents formerly cited to prove that the barons were the common council. For though Henry I called all the people of the land to his coronation, and again in the fifteenth or eighteenth year of his reign, yet always he did not so; neither many of those kings that did succeed him, as appeareth before.

Secondly, for calling the Commons by writ, I find it acknowledged in a book entitled *The Privilege and Practice of Parliaments* in these words:

> In ancient times, after the king had summoned his parliament innumerable multitudes of people did make their access thereunto, pretending that privilege of right to belong to them. But King Henry III having experience of the mischief and inconveniences by occasion of such popular confusion, did take order that none might come to his parliament but those who were specially summoned. [Starkey pp. 6–7]

To this purpose it is observed by Mr Selden that 'the first writs we find accompanied with other circumstances of a summons to parliament, as well for the Commons as Lords, is in the forty-ninth of Henry III' (Selden I, p. 717). In the like manner Mr Camden speaking of the dignity of barons, hath these words:

> King Henry III out of a great multitude which were seditious and turbulent, called the very best by writ or summons to parliament. For he, after many troubles and vexations between the king himself and Simon de Montfort, with other barons, and after appeased, did decree and ordain that all those earls and barons unto whom the king himself vouchsafed to direct his writs of summons should come to his parliament, and no others. But that which he began a little before his death, Edward I and his successors constantly observed and continued. The said prudent King Edward summoned always those of ancient families, that were most wise, to his parliament; and omitted their sons after their death if they were not answerable to their parents in understanding. [Camden p. 169]

Also Mr Camden in another place saith that in the time of 'Edward I select men for wisdom and worth among the gentry were called to parliament, and their posterity omitted, if they were defective there-in'.

As the power of sending writs of summons for elections was first exercised by Henry III, so succeeding kings did regulate the elections upon such writs, as doth appear by several statutes which all speak in the name and power of the kings themselves – for such was the language of our forefathers.

In 5 Richard II, c. 4, these be the words: 'The king willeth and commandeth all persons which shall have summons to come to parliament, and every person that doth absent himself (except he may reasonably and honestly excuse him to our lord the king) shall be amerced, and otherwise punished' [Statutes p. 140].

7 Henry IV, c. 15:

> Our lord the king at the grievous complaint of his Commons of the undue election of the knights of counties, sometimes made of affection of sheriffs, and otherwise against the form of the writs, to the great slander of the counties, etc. Our lord the king, willing therein to provide remedy, by the assent of the Lords and Commons hath ordained that election shall be made in the full county court, and that all that be there present, as well suitors as others, shall proceed to the election freely, notwithstanding any request or command to the contrary. [Statutes p. 194]

11 Henry IV, c. 1: Our lord the king ordained, that a sheriff that maketh an *untrue*[286] return, etc. 'shall incur the penalty of one hundred pounds to be paid to our lord the king' [Statutes p. 197].

1 Henry V, c. 1:

> Our lord the king, by the advice and assent of the Lords, and the special instance and request of the Commons, ordained that the knights of the shire be not chosen unless they be resiant[r] within the shire the day of the date of the writ, and that citizens and burgesses be resiant, dwelling, and free in the same cities and boroughs, and no others in any wise. [Statutes p. 200]

6 Henry VI, c. 4: 'Our lord the king, willing to provide remedy' for knights chosen for parliament, and sheriffs, 'hath ordained that they shall have their answer and traverse to inquest of office found against them' [Statutes p. 226].

8 Henry VI, c. 7:

[r] [resident].

Whereas elections of knights have been made by great outrages, and excessive number of people, of which most part was of people of no value, whereof every of them pretend a voice equivalent to worthy knights and esquires, whereby manslaughters, riots and divisions among gentlemen shall likely be: Our lord the king hath ordained that knights of shires be chosen by people dwelling in the counties, every of them having lands or tenements to the value of forty shillings the year at the least, and that he that shall be chosen shall be dwelling and resiant within the counties. [Statutes p. 230]

10 Henry VI, [c. 2]: 'Our lord the king ordained that knights be chosen by people dwelling, and having forty shillings by the year within the same county' [Statutes p. 243].

11 Henry VI, c. 11:

The king, willing to provide for the ease of them that come to the parliaments and councils of the king by his commandment, hath ordained that if any assault or fray be made on them that come to parliament or other council of the king, the party which made any such affray or assault shall pay double damages, and make fine and ransom at the king's will. [Statutes p. 248]

23 Henry VI, c. 15. The king, considering the statutes of 1 Henry V, c. 1 and 8 Henry VI, c. 7 and the defaults of sheriffs in returning knights, citizens and burgesses, ordained:

1   That the said statutes should be duly kept.

2   That the sheriffs shall deliver precepts to mayors and bailiffs to choose citizens and burgesses.

3   The penalty of one hundred pounds for a sheriff making an untrue return concerning the election of knights, citizens and burgesses.

4   The penalty of forty pounds for mayors or bailiffs, making untrue returns.

5   Due election of knights must be in the full county court, between the hours of eight and eleven before noon.

6   The party must begin his suit within three months after the parliament began.

7   Knights of the shire shall be notable knights of the county, or such notable esquires or gentlemen, born of the said counties, as shall be able to be knights, and no man to be such knight

which standeth in the degree of a yeoman and under. [Statutes pp. 271–2]

The last thing I observe in the writ for election of members of parliament is that by the express words of the writ, citizens and burgesses for the parliament were eligible at the county court, as well as knights of the shire. And that not only freeholders, but all others, whosoever were present at the county court, had voices in such elections: see the Statute 7 Henry IV, c. 15 [Statutes p. 194].

I have the longer insisted on the examination of the writ, because the power and actions of the House of Commons are principally justified by the trust which the freeholders commit unto them by virtue of this writ.

I would not be understood to determine what power the House of Commons doth or may exercise if the king please. I confine myself only to the power in the writ. I am not ignorant that King Henry VII in the cause of the Duke of Britain,⁵ and King James in the business of the Palatinate, asked the counsel of the House of Commons. And not only the House of Commons, but every subject in particular, by duty and allegiance is bound to give his best advice to his sovereign when he is thought worthy to have his counsel asked.

13 Edward III, number 10: All the merchants of England were summoned by writ to appear at Westminster, in proper person, to confer upon great business concerning the king's honour, the salvation of the realm, and of themselves [R.P. 2, p. 108].

In passages of public counsel it is observable, saith Sir Robert Cotton, that in ancient times the kings of England did 'entertain the Commons with weighty causes, thereby to apt and bind them to a readiness of charge; and the Commons to shun expense have warily avoided to give advice' (Cotton [p. 34]).

13 Edward III. The Lords and Commons were called to consult how the domestic quiet may be preserved, the marches of Scotland defended, and the sea secured from enemies. The peers and Commons having apart consulted, the Commons desired 'not to be charged to counsel of things of which they had no cognizance; *de queux ils n'ont pas cognisance*' [R.P. 2, p. 105].

---

⁵ [Britanny].

21 Edward III. Justice Thorpe, declaring to the peers and Commons that the French war began by their advice, the truce after by their assent accepted and now ended; the king's pleasure was to have their counsel in the prosecution. The Commons, being commanded to assemble themselves, and when they were agreed, to give notice to the king and the lords of the council, after four days' consultation 'humbly desire of the king that he would be advised therein by the lords and others of more experience than themselves in such affairs' [R.P. 2, p. 165].

6 Richard II. The parliament was called to consult whether the king should go in person to rescue Gaunt, or send an army. The Commons after two days' debate crave a conference with the Lords, and Sir Thomas Puckering (their Speaker) protests that counsels for war did aptly belong 'to the king and his lords', yet since the Commons were commanded to give their advice 'they humbly wished a voyage by the king' [R.P. 3, p. 145].

7 Richard II. At the second session, the Commons are willed to advise upon view of articles of peace with the French, whether war or such amity should be accepted. They modestly excuse themselves, as too weak to counsel in so weighty causes. But charged again, as they did tender their honour and the right of the king, they make their answer, giving their opinions rather for peace than war [R.P. 3, p. 170].

For fuller manifestation of what hath been said touching the calling, election and power of the Commons in parliament, it is behoveful to observe some points delivered by Sir Edward Coke in his treatise of the jurisdiction of parliaments (Coke); where,

First, he fairly begins, and lays his foundation that 'the high court of parliament consisteth of the king's majesty sitting there, and of the three estates' [Coke 4, p. 1]:

1   The lords spiritual
2   The lords temporal
3   And the Commons

Hence it is to be gathered, that truly and properly it cannot be called the high court of parliament but whilst the king is sitting there in person. So that the question nowadays, whether the parliament be above the king, is either false or idle: false, if you exclude, and idle if you include the king's person in the word parliament. The case truly put, and as it is meant, is whether the three estates (or, which is all one, the Lords and Commons) assembled in parliament be above the king, and not whether the king with the three estates be above the king. It appears also that they are much mistaken who reckon the king one of the three estates, as Mr Prynne, page 20 (Prynne [p. 41]), and many others do. For the three estates make the body, and the king is '*caput, principium et finis parliamentorum*' [the head, originator and end of parliaments], as confesseth Sir Edward Coke (Coke [4, p. 3]).

Secondly, Sir Edward Coke delivers that 'certain it is, both Houses at first sat together', and that it appears in Edward III's time 'the Lords and Commons sat together, and the Commons had no continual Speaker' [Coke 4, p. 2]. If he mean, the Lords and Commons did sit and vote together in one body, few there be that will believe it, because the Commons never were wont to *loose**287 or forgo any of their liberties or privileges. And for them to stand now with their hats in their hands (which is no magistratical posture) there, where they were wont to sit and vote, is an alteration not imaginable to be endured by the Commons. It may be, in former times, when the Commons had no constant Speaker, they were oft, and perhaps for the most part, in the same chamber, and in the presence of the Lords, to hear the debates and consultations of *that**288 great council, but not to sit and vote with them. For when the Commons were to advise among themselves, the chapter house of the abbey of Westminster was ofttimes their place to meet in before they had a settled House. And their meetings not being very frequent may be the reason, I conceive, why the name of the House of Commons is not of such great antiquity, or taken notice of. But the House of the Lords was only called the parliament house. And the treatise called *Modus Tenendi Parliamentum* [the manner of holding parliament]ʹ speaks of the parliament as but of one House only. The House where now the Commons sit in Westminster is but of late use or institution. For in Edward VI's days it was a chapel of the College of St Stephen, and had a dean and secular canons and chorists, who were the king's choir at his palace at Westminster, and at the dissolution were translated to the king's chapel at Whitehall (Stow [pp. 418–19]).

ʹ The *Modus tenendi parliamentum* is a treatise on parliament dating from the 1320s. It was very influential in the early modern period. A recent edition is in Nicholas Pronay and John Taylor, *Parliamentary Texts of the Later Middle Ages*, Oxford 1980.

Also I read that Westminster Hall being out of repair, Richard II caused

> a large house to be builded betwixt the clock tower and the gate of the great old hall in the midst of the palace court. The house was long and large, made of timber covered with tiles, open on both sides, that all might see and hear what was both said and done. Four thousand archers of Cheshire, which were the king's own guard, attended on that house and had *bouche a court* [food and drink at court] and sixpence by the day. [Stow pp. 415–16]

Thirdly, he saith the 'Commons are to choose their Speaker, but seeing after their choice the king may refuse him, the use is (as in the *conge *d'eslier*²⁸⁹*† of a bishop) that the king doth name a discreet, learned man, whom the Commons elect'. 'When the Commons have chosen', 'the king may allow of his excuse, and disallow him, as Sir John Popham was' [Coke 4, p. 8], saith his margin.

Fourthly, he informs us that the first day of the parliament four justices' assistants and two civilians (masters of the chancery) are appointed receivers of petitions, which are to be delivered within six days following; and 'six of the nobility, and two bishops, calling to them the king's learned council, when need should be, to be triers of the said petitions, whether they were reasonable, good, and necessary to be offered and propounded to the Lords' [Coke 4, pp. 10–11]. He doth not say that any of the Commons were either receivers or triers of petitions, nor that the petitions were to be propounded to them, but to the Lords.

Fifthly, he teacheth us that 'a knight, citizen or burgess, cannot make a proxy, because he is elected and trusted by multitudes of people' [Coke 4, p. 12]. Here a question may be, whether a committee, if it be trusted to act anything, be not a proxy? since he saith, 'the high power of parliament to be committed to a few, is holden to be against the dignity of parliaments; and that no such commission ought to be granted' [Coke 4, p. 42].

Sixthly, he saith 'the king cannot take notice of anything said or done in the House of Commons, but by the report of the House' [Coke 4, p. 15]. Surely, if the Commons sat with the Lords, and

---

† [The king granted cathedral chapters a licence to elect bishops, but also appointed who should be elected].

the king were present, he might take notice what was done in his presence. And I read in Vowell that 'the old usage was that all the degrees of parliament sat together, and every man that had there to speak did it openly, before the king and his whole parliament' [Vowell p. 22].

In the 35 Elizabeth there was a report that the Commons were against the subsidies, which was told the Queen. Whereupon, Sir Henry Knyvet said it should be a thing 'answerable at the bar for any man to report anything of speeches, or matters done in the House' [D'Ewes p. 487]. Sir John Wolley 'liked the motion of secrecy, except only the Queen – from whom, he said, there is no reason to keep anything', and Sir Robert Cecil did 'allow that the counsel of the House should be secretly kept, and nothing reported in *malam partem* [to evil ends]. But if the meaning be that they might not report anything done here to the Queen, he was altogether against it' [D'Ewes p. 488].

Seventhly, he voucheth 'an indictment or information in the king's bench against thirty-nine of the Commons for departing without licence from parliament, contrary to the king's inhibition; whereof six submitted to their fines, and Edmund Plowden pleaded he remained continually from the beginning to the end of the parliament' [Coke 4, p. 17]. Note, he did not plead to the jurisdiction of the court of king's bench, but pleaded his constant attendance in parliament, which was an acknowledgment and submitting to the jurisdiction of that court, and had been an unpardonable betraying of the privileges of parliament by so learned a lawyer, if his case ought only to be tried in parliament.

Eighthly, he resolves that 'the House of Lords in their House have power of judicature, and the Commons in their House, and both Houses together' [Coke 4, p. 23]. He brings records to prove the power of judicature of both Houses together, but not of either of them by itself. He cites the 33 Edward I for the judicature of both Houses together, where Nicholas de Segrave was adjudged *per praelatos, comites et barones, et alios de concilio*, by the prelates, earls and barons, and others of the council [R.P. 1, p. 172]. Here is no mention of the judgment of the Commons. 'Others of the council' may mean the king's privy council or his council learned in the laws, which are called by their writs to give counsel, but so are not the Commons. The judgment itself saith,

Nicholas de Segrave confessed his fault in parliament, and submitted himself to the king's will. Thereupon the king, willing to have the advice of the earls, barons, great men and others of his council, enjoined them by the homage, fealty and allegiance which they owed, that they should faithfully counsel him what punishment should be inflicted for such a fact; who all, advising diligently, say that such a fact deserves loss of life and members. [R.P. 1, p. 173]

Thus the Lords (we see) did but advise the king what judgment to give against him that deserted the king's camp to *go*[290] fight a duel in France.

Ninthly, he saith 'of later times, see divers notable judgments at the prosecution of the Commons, by the Lords' [Coke 4, p. 23]. Where the Commons were prosecutors they were no judges, but (as he terms them) 'general inquisitors' [Coke 4, p. 24], or the grand inquest of the kingdom. The judgments he cites are but in king James' days, and no elder.

Tenthly, also he tells us of the judicature in the House of Commons alone. His most ancient precedent is but in Queen Elizabeth's reign, of one 'Thomas Long, who gave the mayor of Westbury ten pounds to be elected burgess' [Coke 4, p. 23].

Eleventhly, he hath a section entitled 'The House of Commons (to many purposes) a distinct court', and saith, '*Nota* [note], the House of Commons to many purposes a distinct court'. Of those many purposes he tells but one, that is, 'it uses to adjourn itself' [Coke 4, p. 28]. Commissioners that be but to examine witnesses may adjourn themselves, yet are no court.

Twelfthly, he handles the privileges of parliament, where the great wonder is that this great master of the law, who hath been oft a parliament-man, could find no other, nor more privileges of parliament but one, and that is freedom from arrests; which, he saith, holds unless in three cases, treason, felony and the peace. And for this freedom from arrests he cites ancient precedents for those in the House of Lords, but he brings not one precedent at all for the Commons' freedom from arrests [Coke 4, pp. 24–5].

It is behoveful for a freeholder to consider what power is in the house of peers. For although the freeholder have no voice in the election of the Lords, yet if the power of that house extend to make ordinances that bind the freeholders, it is necessary for him to enquire what and whence that power is, and how far it reacheth. The chief writ of summons to the peers was in these words:*

Charles by the grace of God, etc. To the most reverend father in Christ William, by the same grace Archbishop of Canterbury, primate and metropolitan of all England, health. Whereas by the advice and assent of our council, for certain difficult and urgent businesses concerning us, the state, and defence of our kingdom of England, and of the English church, we have ordained a certain parliament of ours to be holden at Westminster etc., and there to have conference, and to treat with you the prelates, great men and peers of our said kingdom. We straitly charge and command, by the faith and love by which you are bound to us, that considering the difficulties of the businesses aforesaid, and the imminent dangers, and setting aside all excuses, you be personally present at the day and place aforesaid, with us and the other prelates, great men, and peers aforesaid, to treat and give your counsel concerning the said businesses. And this, as you love us and our honour, and the safeguard of the foresaid kingdom and church, and the expedition of the said businesses, you must no way omit. Forewarning the dean and chapter of your church of Canterbury, and the archdeacons and all the clergy of your diocese, that the same dean, and the archdeacons in their proper persons, and the said chapter by one, and the said clergy by two fit proctors, having full and sufficient power from them the chapter and clergy, be personally present at the foresaid day and place, to consent to those things, which then and there shall

---

* Carolus Dei gratia, etc., Reverendissimo in Christo patri G. eadem gratia Archiepiscopo Cantuariensi totius Angliae primati et metropolitano, salutem. Quia de advisamento et assensu concilii nostri, pro quibusdam arduis et urgentibus negotiis, nos et statum et defensionem regni nostri Angliae, et ecclesiae Anglicanae concernentibus, quoddam parliamentum nostrum apud W. etc. teneri ordinavimus, et ibidem vobiscum, et cum caeteris praelatis, magnatibus et proceribus dicti regni nostri Angliae colloquium habere, et tractatum: vobis in fide, et dilectione quibus nobis te nemini firmiter injungendo mandamus, quod consideratis dictorum negotiorum arduitate, et periculis imminentibus, cessante quacunque excusatione dictis die et loco personaliter intersitis, nobiscum et cum caeteris praelatis, magnatibus, et proceribus praedictis, super dictis negotiis tractaturi, vestrumque concilium impensuri, et hoc sicut nos et honorem nostrum ac salvationem regni praedicti, ac ecclesiae sanctae, expeditionemque dictorum negotiorum diligitis, nullatenus omittatis; praemonentes decanum et capitulum ecclesiae vestrae Cantuariensis, ac archidiaconos, totumque clerum vestrae diocesis, quod idem decanus et archidiaconi in propriis personis suis, ac dictum capitulum per unum, idemque clerus per duos procuratores idoneos, plenam et sufficientem potestatem ab ipsis capitulo et clero habentes, praedictis die et loco personaliter intersint, ad consentiendum hiis quae tunc ibidem de commune concilio ipsius regni nostri, divina favente clementia, contigerit ordinari. Teste meipso apud Westmonasterium, etc.

happen by the favour of God to be ordained by the common council of our kingdom. Witness ourself at Westminster.

The same form of writ, *mutatis mutandis*, concluding with 'you must no way omit. Witness, etc.', is to the temporal barons. But whereas the spiritual barons are required by the faith and love, the temporal are required by their allegiance or homage.

The difference between the two writs is that the Lords are to treat and to give counsel; the Commons are to perform and consent to what is ordained.

By this writ the Lords have a deliberative or a consultative power to treat and give counsel in difficult businesses, and so likewise have the judges, barons of the exchequer, the king's council and the masters of the chancery, by their writs. But over and besides this power, the Lords do exercise a decisive or judicial power, which is not mentioned or found in their writ.

For the better understanding of these two different powers, we must carefully note the distinction between a judge and a counsellor in a monarchy. The ordinary duty or office of a judge is to give judgment, and to command in the place of the king. But the ordinary duty of a counsellor is to advise the king what he himself shall do, or cause to be done. The judge represents the king's person in his absence; the counsellor in the king's presence gives his advice. Judges by their commission or institution are limited [in] their charge and power, and in such things they may judge and cause their judgments to be put in execution. But counsellors have no power to command their consultations to be executed, for that were to take away the sovereignty from their prince, who by his wisdom is to weigh the advice of his council, and at liberty to resolve according to the judgment of the wiser part of his council, and not always of the greater. In a word, regularly a councillor hath no power but in the king's presence, and a judge no power but out of his presence. These two powers thus distinguished, have yet such correspondency, and there is so near affinity between the acts of judging and counselling, that although the ordinary power of the judge is to give judgment yet by their oath they are bound in causes extraordinary, when the king pleaseth to call them, to be his counsellors. And on the other side, although the proper work of a counsellor be only to make report of his advice to his sovereign, yet many times for the ease only, and by the permission of the king, councillors are allowed to judge and command in points wherein ordinarily they know the mind of the prince, and what they do is the act of the royal power itself. For the council is always presupposed to be united to the person of the king, and therefore the decrees of the council are styled 'by the king in his privy council'.

To apply this distinction to the house of peers, we find originally they are called as councillors to the king, and so have only a deliberative power specified in their writ. And therefore the Lords do only then properly perform the duty for which they are called, when they are in the king's presence, that he may have conference and treat with them. The very words of the writ are,* 'with us and with the prelates, great men and peers, to treat and give your counsel'. The word '*nobiscum*' [with us] implieth plainly the king's presence. It is a thing in reason most absurd, to make the king assent to the judgments in parliament and allow him no part in the consultation. This were to make the king a subject. Counsel loseth the name of counsel, and becomes a command, if it put a necessity upon the king to follow it. Such imperious counsels make those that are but counsellors in name to be kings in fact, and kings themselves to be but subjects. We read in Sir Robert Cotton that 'towards the end of the Saxons and the first times of the Norman kings, parliaments stood in custom-grace fixed to Easter, Whitsuntide and Christmas', and that at the king's court or palace, parliaments sat in the presence or privy chamber (Cotton [pp. 44–5]). From whence he infers 'an improbability to believe the king excluded his own presence; and unmannerly for guests to bar him their company who gave them their entertainment' [Cotton p. 44]. And although nowadays the parliament sit not in the court where the king's household remains, yet still even to this day, to show that parliaments are the king's guests, the lord steward of the king's household keeps a standing table to entertain the peers during the sitting of parliament. And he alone, or some from or under him – as the treasurer or comptroller of the king's household – takes the oaths of the members of the House of Commons the first day of the parliament.

Sir Richard Scroop, steward of the household of our sovereign

---

* 'Nobiscum ac cum praelatis, magnatibus et proceribus praedictis super dictis negotiis tractaturi vestrumque concilium impensuri.'

lord the king, by the commandment of the Lords sitting in full parliament in the great chamber, put John Lord Gomeniz and William Weston to answer severally to accusations brought against them (Selden [3, pp. 14–28]).

The necessity of the king's presence in parliament appears by the desire of parliaments themselves in former times, and the practice of it Sir Robert Cotton proves by several precedents. Whence he concludes that 'in the consultations of state, and decisions of private plaints, it is clear from all times the king was not only present to advise but to determine also' [Cotton p. 56]. Whensoever the king is present, all power of judging – which is derived from his – ceaseth. The votes of the Lords may serve for matter of advice; the final judgment is only the king's. Indeed, of late years Queen Mary and Queen Elizabeth, by reason of their sex being not so fit for public assemblies, have brought it out of use. By which means it is come to pass that many things which were in former times acted by kings themselves, have of late been left to the judgment of the peers – who, in quality of judges extraordinary, are permitted for the ease of the king, and in his absence, to determine such matters as are properly brought before the king himself sitting in person, attended with his great council of prelates and peers. And the ordinances that are made there, receive their establishment either from the king's presence in parliament – where his chair of state is constantly placed – or at least from the confirmation of him, who in all courts and in all causes is supreme judge. All judgment is by or under him; it cannot be without, much less against his approbation. 'The king only and none but he, if he were able, should judge all causes' (Bracton [f. 107a]) saith Bracton, that ancient chief justice in Henry III's time.

An ancient precedent I meet with, cited by Mr Selden, of a judicial proceeding in a criminal cause of the barons before the Conquest. Wherein I observe the king's will was that the lords should be judges in the cause wherein himself was a party, and he ratified their proceedings. The case was thus, Earl Godwin having had a trial before the lords under King Hardicanute

> touching the death of Alfred (son to King *[Ethelred]*[291] and brother to him who was afterward Edward the Confessor) had fled out of England. And upon his return, with hope of Edward the Confessor's favour he solicited the lords to intercede for him with the king, who (consulting together) brought Godwin with

them before the king to obtain his grace and favour. But the king presently, as soon as he beheld him, said, 'Thou traitor Godwin, I do appeal thee of the death of my brother Alfred whom thou hast most traitorously slain'. Then Godwin, excusing it, answered, 'My lord the king, may it please your grace, I neither betrayed nor killed your brother, whereof I put myself upon the judgment of your court'. Then the king said, 'You noble lords, earls and barons of the land, who are my liege men now gathered here together, and have heard my appeal and Godwin's answer, I will that in this appeal between us, ye decree right judgment and do true justice'. The earls and barons treating of this among themselves were of differing judgments. Some said that Godwin was never bound to the king, either by homage, service or fealty, and therefore could not be his traitor, and that he had not slain Alfred with his own hands. Others said that neither earl nor baron nor any other subject of the king could wage his war by law against the king in his appeal, but must wholly put himself into the king's mercy, and offer competent amends. 'Then Leofric consul of Chester, a good man before God and the world, said, Earl Godwin next to the king is a man of the best parentage of all England, and he cannot deny but that by his counsel Alfred the king's brother was slain, therefore for my part I consider that he and his son, and all we twelve earls who are his friends and kinsmen, do go humbly before the king, laden with so much gold and silver as each of us can carry in our arms, offering him that for his offence, and humbly praying for pardon; and he will pardon the earl, and taking his homage and fealty, will restore him all his lands.' All they in this form lading themselves with treasure, and coming to the king, did show the manner and order of their consideration, to which the king not willing to contradict, did ratify all that they had judged. (Selden [I, pp. 634–5])

23 Henry II,

in Lent there was an assembly of all the spiritual and temporal barons at Westminster for the determination of that great contention between Alfonso, king of Castile, and Sancho, king of Navarre, touching divers castles and territories in Spain, which was by compromise submitted to the judgment of the king of England. And the king, consulting with his bishops, earls and barons, determined it, as he saith himself, in the first person, in the exemplification of the judgment. (Selden [I, p. 706])

'2 of King John also, that great controversy touching the barony that William of Mowbray claimed against William of Stuteville, which had depended from the time of King Henry II, was ended by the council of the kingdom and will of the king': '*concilio regni, et voluntate regis*' (Selden [1, p. 707]).

The Lords in parliament adjudge William de Weston to death for surrendering Berwick Castle, but for that our lord the king was not informed of the manner of the judgment, the constable of the tower, Alan Buxhull, 'was commanded safely to keep the said William until he hath other commandment from our lord the king', 4 Richard II (Selden [3, pp. 14–26]).

Also, the Lords adjudged John Lord of Gomeniz for surrendering the towns and castles of Arde, and for that he was a gentleman and banneret and had served the late king 'he should be beheaded, and for that our lord the king was not informed of the manner of the judgment, the execution thereof shall be respited until our lord the king shall be informed'. It is commanded to the 'constable of the tower, safely to keep the said John, until he hath other commandment from our lord the king' (Selden [3, p. 28]).

In the case of Henry Spencer, Bishop of Norwich, 7 Richard II, who was accused for complying with the French, and other failings; the bishop complained what was done against him did not pass by the assent and knowledge of the peers. Whereupon it was said in parliament that 'the cognisance and punishment of his offence did of common right and ancient custom of the realm of England, solely and wholly belong to our lord the king, and no other't [R.P. 3, p. 56].

In the case of the Lord de la Warr, the judgment of the Lords was 'that he should have place next after the Lord Willoughby of Eresby', by consent of all except the Lord Windsor; and the 'lord keeper was required to acquaint her majesty with the determination of the peers and to know her pleasure concerning the same' [D'Ewes p. 528].

The inference from these precedents is that the decisive or judicial power exercised in the chamber of peers is merely derivative, and subservient to the supreme power which resides in the king, and

---

† 'Le cognisance et punissement de commune droit et auntienne custome de royalme de Engleterre, seul et per tout apperteine au Roy nostre Seignieur, et a nul autre.'

is grounded solely upon his grace and favour. For howsoever the House of Commons do allege their power to be founded on the principles of nature – in that they are the representative body of the kingdom, as they say, and so, being the whole, may take care and have power by nature to preserve themselves; yet the house of peers do not nor cannot make any such the least pretence, since there is no reason in nature why amongst a company of men who are all equal, some few should be picked out to be exalted above their fellows and have power to govern those who by nature are their companions. The difference between a peer and a commoner is not by nature but by the grace of the prince, who creates honours, and makes those honours to be hereditary (whereas he might have given them for life only, or during pleasure, or good behaviour), and also annexeth to those honours the power of having votes in parliament as hereditary councillors, furnished with ampler privileges than the Commons. All these graces conferred upon the peers are so far from being derived from the law of nature, that they are contradictory and destructive of that natural equality and freedom of mankind which many conceive to be the foundation of the privileges and liberties of the House of Commons. There is so strong an opposition between the liberties of grace and nature, that it had never been possible for the two houses of parliament to have stood together without mortal enmity and eternal jarring, had they been raised upon such opposite foundations. But the truth is, the liberties and privileges of both houses have but one and the self-same foundation, which is nothing else but the mere and sole grace of kings.

Thus much may serve to show the nature and original of the deliberative and decisive power of the peers of the kingdom.

The matter about which the deliberative power is conversant is generally the consulting and advising upon any urgent business which concerns the king or defence of the kingdom, and more especially sometimes in preparing new laws; and this power is grounded upon the writ.

The decisive power is exercised in giving judgment in some difficult cases, but for this power of the peers I find no warrant in their writ.

Whereas the parliament is styled the supreme court, it must be understood properly of the king sitting in the house of peers in person, and but improperly of the Lords without him. Every supreme court must have the supreme power, and the supreme power is always arbitrary – for that is arbitrary which hath no superior on earth to control it. The last appeal in all government must still be to an arbitrary power, or else appeals will be *in infinitum*, never at an end. The legislative power is an arbitrary power, for they are *termini convertibiles* [convertible terms].

The main question in these our days is where this power legislative remains or is placed? Upon conference of the writs of summons for both houses, with the bodies and titles of our ancient acts of parliament, we shall find the power of making laws rests solely in the king. Some affirm that a part of the legislative power is in either of the houses. But besides invincible reason from the nature of monarchy itself, which must have the supreme power alone, the constant ancient declaration of this kingdom is against it. For howsoever of later years in the titles and bodies of our acts of parliament it be not so particularly expressed who is the author and maker of our laws, yet in almost all our elder statutes it is precisely expressed that they are made by the king himself. The general words used of later times, that laws are made by authority of parliament, are particularly explained in former statutes to mean that the king ordains, the Lords advise, the Commons consent – as by comparing the writs with the statutes that expound the writs, will evidently appear.

Magna Carta begins thus, 'Henry by the grace of God, know ye that we of our mere and free will have given these liberties' [Statutes p. 1].

In the self-same style runs *Carta de Foresta*, and tells us the author of it.

The statute *de scaccario*, 41 Henry III, begins in these words: 'the king commandeth that all bailiffs, sheriffs and other officers', etc. And 'concerning the justices of Chester, the king willeth', etc., and again, he 'commandeth the treasurer and barons of the exchequer upon their allegiance' [Statutes pp. 7–8; 51 Henry III].

The statute of Marlborough, 52 Henry III, goeth thus: 'The king hath made these acts, ordinances and statutes, which he willeth to be observed of all his subjects, high and low' [Statutes p. 9].

3 Edward I [Westminster I]: the title of this statute is, 'These are the acts of King Edward', and after it follows, 'The king hath ordained these acts', and in the first chapter, 'the king forbiddeth and commandeth, that none do hurt, damage or grievance to any

religious man or person of the church' [Statutes p. 15]. And in the thirteenth chapter, 'the king prohibiteth that none do ravish or take away by force any maid within age' [Statutes p. 17].

6 Edward I [Gloucester]: it is said, 'our sovereign lord the king hath established these acts, commanding they be observed within this realm' [Statutes p. 23], and in the fourteenth chapter the words are, 'the king of his special grace granteth that the citizens of London shall recover in an assize, damage with the land' [Statutes p. 25].

The statute of Westminster II [chapter one] saith, 'our lord the king hath ordained that the will of the giver be observed' [Statutes p. 28]. And in the third chapter, 'our lord the king hath ordained that a woman after the death of her husband shall recover by a writ of entry' [Statutes p. 29].

The statute of *Quo Warranto* saith 'our lord the king at his parliament, of his special grace and for affection which he beareth to his prelates, earls and barons and others, hath granted' that they that have liberties by prescription shall enjoy them [Statutes p. 44].

In the statute *de finibus levatis* the king's words are, 'We intending to provide remedy in our parliament, have ordained', etc. [Statutes p. 48].

28 Edward I, c. 5: 'The king wills that the chancellor and the justices of the bench shall follow him, so that he may have at all times some near unto him that be learned in the laws' [Statutes p. 51], and in chapter twenty-four the words are 'our lord the king after full conference and debate had with his earls, barons, nobles and other great men, by their whole consent, hath ordained', etc.

The statute *de tallagio* (if any such statute there be) speaks in the king's person, 'no officer of ours; no tallage shall be taken by us; we will and grant' [Statutes p. 56].

1 Edward II begins thus, 'our lord the king willeth and commandeth' [Statutes p. 57].

The statute of 9 the same king, saith, 'our lord the king by the assent of the prelates, earls and other great states, hath ordained' [Statutes p. 59].

10 Edward II: 'It is provided by our lord the king and his justices' [Statutes p. 59].

The statute of Carlisle saith, 'We have sent our command in writing firmly to be observed' [Statutes p. 61; 15 Edward II].

1 Edward III begins thus, 'King Edward III at his parliament, at

the request of the commonalty by their petition before him and his council in parliament, hath granted', etc. [Statutes p. '54'=66].

And in the fifth chapter, 'The king willeth that no man be charged to arm himself otherwise than he was wont' [Statutes p. '55'=67].

5 Edward III: 'Our lord the king, at the request of his people, hath established these things, which he wills to be kept' [Statutes p. 72].

9 of the same king there is this title, 'Our lord the king by the assent, etc., and by the advice of his council being there, hath ordained', etc. [Statutes p. 74].

In his tenth year it is said, 'Because our lord King Edward III hath received by the complaint of the prelates, earls, barons, also at the showing of the knights of the shires and his commons by their petition put in his parliament, etc. Hath ordained, by the assent, etc., at the request of the said knights and commons, etc.' [Statutes p. 76].

The same year in another parliament you may find, 'these be the articles accorded by our lord the king, with the assent, etc., at the request of the knights of the shires and the commons by their petition put in the said parliament' [Statutes p. 76].

In the Year Book 22 Edward III, 3. pl. 25, it is said, 'The king makes the laws by the assent of the peers and Commons; and not the peers and Commons' [Year Book, Edward III 22, f. 3b].

The statute of 1 Richard II hath this beginning: 'Richard II, by the assent of the prelates, dukes, earls and barons, and at the instance and special request of the Commons, ordained' [Statutes p. 129].

There being a statute made 5 Richard II, c. 5, against Lollards, in the next year the Commons petition him, '*Supplient les Commons que come un estatute fuit fait*, etc.: The Commons beseech, that whereas a statute was made in the last parliament, etc. which was never assented to nor granted by the Commons, but that which was done therein was done without their assent' [Statutes p. 140]. In this petition the Commons acknowledge it a statute, and so call it, though they assented not to it.

17 Richard II, number 44: The Commons desire, some pursuing to make a law which they conceive hurtful to the commonwealth, that his majesty will not pass it [R.P. 3, p. 321].

As for the parliaments in Henry IV's, Henry V's, Henry VI's, Edward IV's and Richard III's reigns, the most of them *do*[292] agree in this one title, 'our lord the king, by the advice and assent of his Lords, and at the special instance and request of the Commons, hath ordained'. The precedents in this point are so numerous that it were endless to cite them.

The statutes in Henry VII's days do for the most part agree, both in the titles and bodies of the acts, in these words: 'Our Lord the king by the assent of the lords spiritual and temporal, and the Commons in parliament assembled, and by the authority of the same hath ordained'.

Unto this king's time we find the Commons very often petitioning, but not petitioned unto. The first petition made to the Commons that I meet with among the statutes, is but in the middle of this King Henry VII's reign, which was so well approved that the petition itself is turned into a statute. It begins thus, 'To the right worshipful Commons in this present parliament assembled: showeth to your discreet wisdoms the wardens of the fellowship of the craft of Upholsters within London', etc. This petition, though it be directed to the Commons in the title, yet the prayer of the petition is turned to the king, and not to the Commons; for it concludes, 'therefore it may please the king's highness, by the advice of the Lords spiritual and temporal, and his Commons in parliament', etc. [Statutes p. 367; II Henry VII, c. 19].

Next for the statutes of Henry VIII, they do most part agree both in their titles and the bodies of the acts with those of his father King Henry VII.

Lastly, in the statutes of Edward VI, Queen Mary, Queen Elizabeth, King James, and of our sovereign lord the king that now is, there is no mention made in their titles of any assent of Lords and Commons, or of any ordaining by the king, but only in general terms it is said, 'acts made in parliament'; or thus, 'at the parliament were enacted'. Yet in the bodies of many of the acts of these last princes there is sometimes mention made of consent of Lords and Commons, in these or the like words: 'It is enacted by the king, with the assent of the Lords and Commons'; except only in the statutes of our lord King Charles, wherein there is no mention, that I can find, of any consent of the Lords and Commons, or ordaining by the king. But the words are, 'Be it enacted by authority of parliament'; or else, 'Be it enacted by the king, the lords spiritual and temporal, and Commons', as if they were all fellow-commissioners.

Thus it appears that even till the time of King Edward VI, who lived but in our fathers' days, it was punctually expressed in every king's laws that the statutes and ordinances were made by the king. And withal we may see by what degrees the styles and titles of acts of parliament have been varied, and to whose disadvantage. The higher we look, the more absolute we find the power of kings in ordaining laws; nor do we meet with at first so much as the assent or advice of the Lords mentioned. Nay, if we cast our eye upon many statutes of those that be of most antiquity, they will appear as if they were no laws at all. But as if they had been made only to teach us that the punishments of many offences were left to the mere pleasure of kings. The punitive part of the law, which gives all the vigour and binding power to the law, we find committed by the statutes to the king's mere will and pleasure, as if there were no law at all. I will offer a few precedents to the point:

3 Edward I [Westminster I], c. 9 saith 'that sheriffs, coroners and bailiffs, for concealing of felonies shall make grievous fines at the king's pleasure' [Statutes p. 16].

Chapter thirteen ordains that 'such as be found culpable of ravishing of women, shall fine at the king's pleasure' [Statutes p. 17].

Chapter fifteen saith the penalty for detaining a prisoner that is mainpernable is a fine at the king's pleasure, or a grievous amercement to the king; and he that shall take reward for deliverance of such shall be at the great mercy of the king [Statutes p. 17].

Offenders in parks or ponds 'shall make fines at the king's pleasure' (chapter twenty) [Statutes p. 18].

Committers of champerty, and extortioners are to be punished 'at the king's pleasure' (chapter twenty-five) [Statutes p. 19].

Purveyors, not paying for what they take, shall be grievously punished at the king's pleasure (chapter thirty-one) [Statutes p. 19].

'The king shall punish grievously the sheriff, and him that doth maintain quarrels' (chapter thirty-two) [Statutes p. 19].

'The king shall grant attaint in plea of land where it shall seem to him necessary' (chapter thirty-seven) [Statutes p. 20].

7 Edward I saith,

> Whereas of late, before certain persons deputed to treat upon debates between us and certain great men, it was accorded that in our next parliament provision shall be made by us, and the

common assent of the prelates, earls and barons, that in all parliaments for ever, every man shall come without force and armour. And now in our next parliament the prelates, earls, barons and commonalty have said that to 'us it belongeth, through our royal signory, straitly to defend force of armour at all times when it shall please us, and to punish them which shall do otherwise, and hereunto they are bound to aid us their sovereign lord at all seasons when need shall be'. [Statutes p. 25]

13 Edward I: 'Takers away of nuns from religious houses, fined at the king's will' [Statutes p. 37; Westminster II, c. 32].

'If *by*[293] default of the lord that will not avoid the dyke, underwoods and bushes in highways, murder be done, the lord shall make fine at the king's pleasure' [Statutes p. 41; Winchester, c. 5].

28 Edward I, [c. 20]: 'If a goldsmith be attainted for not assaying, touching and working vessels of gold, he shall be punished by ransom at the king's pleasure' [Statutes p. 52].

2 Henry IV:

> The Commons desire they may have answer of their petitions before the gift of any subsidy; to which the king answers, he would confer with the Lords, and do what should be best according to their advice; and the last day of parliament he gave this answer, that that manner of doing had not been seen, nor used in no time of his progenitors or predecessors, that they should have any answer of their petitions, or knowledge of it before they have showed and finished all their other business of parliament, be it of any grant, business, or otherwise, and therefore the king would not in any ways change the good customs and usages made and used of ancient times. [R.P. 3, p. 458]

5 Henry IV, c. 6: Whereas one Savage did beat and maim one Richard Cheddar, esquire, menial servant to Thomas Brook, knight of the shire for Somersetshire, the statute saith Savage 'shall make fine and ransom at the king's pleasure' [Statutes p. 189].

8 Henry IV: It is said, '*potestas principis non est inclusa legibus*, the power of the prince is not included in the laws'.

13 Henry IV, number 20: we read of a 'restitution in blood and lands of William Lasenby, by the king, by the assent of the lords spiritual, and Commons' [R.P. 3, pp. 655–6]; omitting the lords temporal.

2 Henry V: in a law made, there is a clause that 'it is the king's regality to grant or deny such of their petitions as pleaseth himself'.

6 Henry VI, c. 6: An ordinance was made for to endure 'as long as it shall please the king' [Statutes p. 254; 15 Henry VI, c. 6].

11 Henry VII, c. 1, hath this law:

> The king our sovereign lord, calling to his remembrance the duty of allegiance of his subjects of this his realm, and that by reason of the same they are bound to serve their prince and sovereign lord for the time being in his wars, for the defence of him and the land against every rebellion, power and might reared against him, and with him to enter and abide in service in battle, if case so require; and that for the same service, what fortune ever fall by chance in the same battle, against the mind and will of the prince (as in this land *some time past*[294] hath been seen) that it is not reasonable, but against all laws, reason and good conscience, that the said subjects, going with their sovereign lord in wars, attending upon him in his person, or being in other places by his commandment within the land, or without, any thing should lose or forfeit, for doing their true duty and service of allegiance. It be therefore enacted that no person that shall attend upon the king and do him true service, shall be attainted therefore of treason, or any other offence by act of parliament or otherwise. [Statutes pp. 356–7]

Also the eighteenth chapter of the same year saith:

> Where every subject by the duty of his allegiance is bounden to serve and assist his prince and sovereign lord at all seasons when need shall require, and bound to give attendance upon his royal person, to defend the same when he shall fortune to go in person in war for defence of the realm, or against his rebels and enemies, for the subduing and repressing of them and their malicious purpose. [Statutes p. 367]

Christopher Wray, serjeant at law, chosen Speaker 13 Elizabeth, in his speech to her majesty said that for the orderly government of the commonwealth three things were necessary:

1   Religion
2   Authority
3   Law

'By the first, we are taught not only our duty to God, but to obey the Queen, and that not only in temporals but in spirituals, in which her power is absolute' [D'Ewes p. 141].

Mr Greville in the 35 Elizabeth said in parliament, he wished not the making of many laws, since 'the more we make, the less liberty we have ourselves', her majesty not being bound by them [D'Ewes p. 490].

For further proof that the legislative power is proper to the king, we may take notice that in ancient time, as Sir Edward Coke saith, 'All acts of parliament were in form of petitions' (Coke [4, p. 25]). If the petitions were from the Commons, and the answer of them the king's, it is easy thereby to judge who made the act of parliament. Also Sir John Glanville affirms that

> in former times the course of petitioning the king was this, the Lords and Speaker, either by words or writing, preferred their petition to the king; this then was called the bill of the Commons, which being received by the king, part he received, *and part*[295] he put out, *part*[296] he ratified; for as it came from him, it was drawn into a law. [Glanville p. 3]

Also it appears that provisions, ordinances, and proclamations, made heretofore out of parliament, have been always acknowledged for laws and statutes (Chancellor Egerton [pp. 12–16]). We have amongst the printed statutes one called the statute of Ireland, dated at Westminster, 9th February, 14 Henry III, which is nothing but a letter of the king to Gerard son of Maurice, justiciar of Ireland [Statutes pp. 4–5].

The explanations of the statute of Gloucester, made by the king and his justices only, were received always for statutes, and are still printed with them [Egerton p. 15].

Also the statute made for the correction of the twelfth chapter of the Statute of Gloucester was signed under the great seal and sent to the justices of the bench after the manner of a writ patent, with a certain writ closed, dated by the king's hand at Westminster, 2 May, 9 Edward I, requiring that 'they should do and execute all and everything contained in it, though the same do not accord with the statute of Gloucester in all things' [Statutes p. 26].

The provisions of Merton, made by the king at an assembly of prelates, and the greater part of the earls and barons, for the coronation of the king and his Queen Eleanor, are in the form of a proclamation, and begin, '*provisum est in curia domini regis apud Merton*' [it is provided in the court of the lord king at Merton] [Egerton p. 14].

19 Henry III, a provision was made *de assisa ultimae praesentationis*, which 'was continued and allowed for a law until the statute of Westminster II, which provides the contrary in express words' [Egerton p. 15].

In the old statutes it is hard to distinguish what laws were made by kings in parliament, and what out of parliament. When kings called peers only to parliament, and of those how many or whom they pleased (as it appears anciently they did) it was no easy matter to put a difference between a council table and a parliament, or between a proclamation and a statute. Yet it is most evident that in old times there was a distinction between the king's special or privy council, and his common council of the kingdom; and his special council did sit with the peers in parliament, and were of great and extraordinary authority there.

In the statute of Westminster I it is said, 'these are the acts of king Edward I made at his first parliament by his council, and by the assent of bishops, abbots, priors, earls, barons and all the commonalty of the realm' [Statutes p. 15].

The statute of Acton Burnell hath these words: 'The king for himself, and by his council, hath ordained and established' [Statutes p. 27].

In *articulis super chartas*, when the great charter was confirmed at the request of the prelates, earls and barons, are found these two provisions:

1. 'Nevertheless the king and his council do not intend by reason of this statute to diminish the king's right' [Statutes p. 50].
2. Notwithstanding all these things before-mentioned, or any part of them, both the king and his council, and all they that were present, will and intend that the right and prerogative of his crown shall be saved to him in all things' [Statutes p. 52].

The statute of escheators hath this title: 'At the parliament of our sovereign lord the king, by his council it was agreed, and also by the king himself commanded' [Statutes p. 52].

1 Edward III where Magna Carta was confirmed, this preamble is found, 'At the request of the commonalty, by their petition made

before the king and his council in parliament, by the assent of the prelates, earls and barons, etc.' [Statutes p. 54].

The statute made at York, 9 Edward III, goeth thus: 'Whereas the knights, citizens and burgesses desired our sovereign lord the king in his parliament by their petition, etc. Our sovereign lord the king, desiring the profit of his people, by the assent of his prelates, earls, barons and other nobles of his realm, and by the advice of his council being there, hath ordained' [Statutes p. 74].

25 Edward III, in the statute of purveyors, where 'the king, at the request of the Lords and Commons, made a declaration what offences should be adjudged treason', it is there further said, 'if per-case any man ride armed with men of arms against any other to slay him, or rob him, it is not the mind of the king or of his council that in such cases it shall be adjudged treason'. By this statute it appears that even in the case of treason, which is the king's own cause, as, 'whereas a man doth compass or imagine the death of our lord the king, or a man do wage war against our lord the king in his realm, or be adherent to the king's enemies in his realm, giving to them aid or comfort in the realm, or elsewhere'; in all these cases it is the 'king's declaration only' that makes it to be treason. And though it be said that difficult points of treason shall be brought and showed to the king and his parliament, yet it is said it is the mind of the king and his council that determines what shall be adjudged treason, and what felony or trespass [Statutes p. 96].

27 Edward III. The Commons presenting a petition to the king, which the king's council did mislike, were content thereupon to amend and explain their petition. The petition hath these words:

> To their most redoubted sovereign lord the king, praying, your said Commons, that whereas they have prayed him to be discharged of all manner of articles of the eyre, etc., which petition seemeth to his council to be prejudicial unto him, and in disinherison of his crown if it were so generally granted. His said Commons not willing nor desiring to demand things of him, or of his crown perpetually, as of escheats, etc.; but of trespasses, misprisions, negligences, ignorances, etc. [Statutes pp. 119–20; 36 Edward III]

And as in parliaments the king's council were of super-eminent power, so out of parliament kings made great use of them.

'King Edward I finding that Bogo de Clare was discharged of an accusation brought against him in parliament, commanded him nevertheless to appear before him and his council, '*ad faciendum et recipiendum quod per regem et ejus concilium fuerit faciendum*' [to do and undergo what the king and his council decreed], and so proceeded to the examination of the whole cause, [1]8 Edward I' [Lambarde 1, p. 73].

Edward III. In the Star Chamber (which was the ancient council-table at Westminster) upon the complaint of Elizabeth Audley, commanded James Audley to appear before him and his council; and determined a controversy between them touching land contained in her jointure (*Rotulo clauso de anno* [in the close roll of the year] 41 Edward III) [Lambarde 1, pp. 73–4].

Henry V. 'In a suit before him and his council for the titles of the manors of Serre and St Lawrence in the Isle of Thanet in Kent, took order for the sequestering the profits till the right were tried' [Lambarde 1, p. 74].

Henry VI 'commanded the justices of the bench to stay the arraignment of one Verney in London till they had other commandment from him and his council (34 Henry VI, *rotulo* [in roll] 37 *in banco* [in the king's bench])' [Lambarde 1, p. 75].

Edward IV and his council, in the Star Chamber

> heard the cause of the master and poor brethren of Saint Leonard's in York, complaining that Sir Hugh Hastings and others withdrew from them a great part of their living, which consisted chiefly upon the having of a thrave of corn of every plough-land within the counties of York, Westmorland, Cumberland and Lancashire (*rotulo patente* [in the patent roll] 8 Edward IV, part three, membrane 14) [Lambarde 1, p. 75].

Henry VII and his council, in the Star Chamber,

> decreed that Margery and Florence Becket should sue no further in their cause against Alice Radley, widow, for lands in Woolwich and Plumsted in Kent, forasmuch as the matter had been heard first before the Council of Edward IV, after that before the *president*[297] of the Requests of that King Henry VII, and then lastly before the council of the said king, 1 Henry VII. [Lambarde 1, p. 76]

In the time of Henry III an order or provision was made by the king's council, and it was pleaded at the common law in bar to a writ of dower. 'The plaintiff's attorney could not deny it, and thereupon the judgment was *ideo sine die*' [Egerton pp. 13–14]. It seems in those days an order of the king's council was either parcel of the common law, or above it.

Also we may find the 'judges have had regard that before they would resolve or give judgment in new cases, they consulted with the king's privy council'.

In the case of Adam Brabson who was assaulted by R.W. in the presence of the justices of assize at Westminster, the judges would have 'the advice of the king's council, for in a like case, because R.C. did strike a juror at Westminster which passed against one of his friends, it was adjudged by all the council that his right hand should be cut off, and his lands and goods forfeited to the king' [Egerton pp. 50–1].

'Green and Thorpe were sent by the judges to the king's council to demand of them whether by the statute of 14 Edward III, [c.] 16, a word may be amended in a writ. And it was answered that a word may be well amended, although the statute speaks but of a letter or syllable' [Egerton pp. 52–3].

In the case of Sir Thomas Ughtred, who

> brought a formedon against a poor man and his wife, they came and yielded to the demandant, which seemed suspicious to the court. Whereupon judgment was stayed. And Thorpe said that in the like case of Giles Blacket it was spoken of in parliament, and we were commanded that when any like should come we should not go to judgment without good advice. [Egerton p. 52]

Therefore the judges' conclusion was,† 'sue to the council, and as they will have us to do, we will do; and otherwise not in this case' (39 Edward III).

Thus we see the judges themselves were guided by the king's council, and yet the opinions of judges have guided the Lords in parliament in point of law.

'All the judges of the realm, barons of exchequer, of the quoif, the king's learned council, and the civilians, masters of chancery,'

---

† '*Sues au counseil et comment ils voilent que nous devomus faire, nous volums faire, et autrement nient en cest case.*'
[the same passage is in *Patriarcha* at p. 63 above].

are called 'temporal assistants' by Sir Edward Coke, and though he deny them voices in parliament, yet he confesseth that by their writ they have power both to 'treat, and to give counsel' (Coke [4, p. 4]). I cannot find that the Lords have any other power by their writ. The words of the Lords' writ are, 'That you be present with us, the prelates, great men and peers, to treat and give your counsel'. The words of the judges' writ are, 'that you be present with us, and others of the council (and sometimes with us only) to treat and give your counsel'.

The judges usually joined in committees with the Lords in all parliaments, even in Queen Elizabeth's reign, until her thirty-ninth year; and then upon the 7th of November the judges were appointed to 'attend the Lords' [D'Ewes p. 527]. And whereas the judges have liberty in the upper house itself, upon leave given them by the Lord Keeper, to cover themselves, now at committees they sit always uncovered.

The power of judges in parliament is best understood if we consider how the judicial power of peers hath been exercised in matter of judicature. We may find it hath been the practice that though the Lords in the king's absence give judgment in point of law, yet they are to be directed and regulated by the king's judges, who are best able to give direction in the difficult points of the law; which ordinarily are unknown to the Lords. And therefore, if any error be committed in the king's bench, which is the highest ordinary court of common law in the kingdom, that error must be redressed in parliament. And the manner is, saith the lord chancellor Egerton,

> if a writ of error be sued in parliament upon a judgment given by the judges in the king's bench, the lords of the higher house alone (without the Commons) are to examine the errors. The Lords are to proceed according to the law, and for their judgments therein they are to be informed by the advice and counsel of the judges, who are to inform them what the law is, and to direct them in their judgment; for the Lords are not to follow their own discretion or opinion otherwise. (Egerton [pp. 22–3])

28 Henry VI:

> The Commons made suit that William de la Pole, Duke of Suffolk, should be committed to prison for many treasons and other crimes. The lords of the higher house were doubtful what answer

to give. The opinion of the judges was demanded. Their opinion was that he ought not to be committed, for that the Commons did not charge him with any particular offence, but with general reports and slanders. This opinion was allowed. [Egerton p. 19]

31 Henry VI. A parliament being prorogued in the vacation the Speaker of the House of Commons:

> was condemned in a thousand pounds damages in an action of trespass, and committed to prison in execution for the same. When the parliament was re-assembled, the Commons made suit to the king and Lords to have their Speaker delivered. The Lords demanded the opinion of the judges, whether he might be delivered out of prison by privilege of parliament

Upon the judges' answer it was concluded that the Speaker

> should remain in prison according to the law, notwithstanding the privilege of parliament, and that he was Speaker. Which resolution was declared to the Commons by Moyle the king's serjeant at law, and the Commons were commanded in the king's name by the Bishop of Lincoln (in the absence of the Archbishop of Canterbury, then chancellor) to choose another Speaker. [Egerton p. 21]

7 Henry VIII:

> A question was moved in parliament 'whether spiritual persons might be convented before temporal judges for criminal causes? There Sir John Fineux and the other judges delivered their opinion that they might and ought to be; and their opinion allowed and maintained by the king and Lords. And Dr Standish, who before had holden the same opinion, was delivered from the bishops.' [Egerton p. 22]

I find it affirmed that in causes which receive determination in the House of Lords, the king hath no vote at all, no more than in other courts of ministerial jurisdiction. True it is, the king hath no vote at all, if we understand by vote a voice among others – for he hath no partners with him in giving judgment. But if by no vote is meant he hath no power to judge, we despoil him of his sovereignty. It is the chief mark of supremacy to judge in the highest causes, and last appeals. This the children of Israel full well understood when they petitioned for a king to judge them [1 Samuel viii, 5].

If the *dernier resort* [last resort] be to the Lords alone, then they have the supremacy. But as Moses, by choosing elders to judge in small causes, did not thereby lose his authority to be judge himself when he pleased, even in the smallest matters – much less in the greatest, which he reserved to himself; so kings by delegating others to judge under them, do not thereby denude themselves of a power to judge when they think good.

There is a distinction of these times, that kings themselves may not judge, but they may see and look to the judges, that they give judgment according to law; and for this purpose only (as some say) kings may sometimes sit in the courts of justice. But it is not possible for kings to see the laws executed, except there be a power in kings both to judge when the laws are duly executed, and when not; as also to compel the judges if they do not their duty. Without such power a king sitting in courts is but a mockery, and a scorn to the judges. And if this power be allowed to kings, then their judgments are supreme in all courts. And indeed our 'common law to this purpose doth presume that the king hath all laws within the cabinet of his breast, *in scrinio pectoris*', saith Crompton's *Jurisdiction*, (Crompton) 108.

When several of our statutes leave many things 'to the pleasure of the king', for us to interpret all those statutes 'of the will and pleasure of the king's justices only', is to give an absolute arbitrary power to the justices in those cases wherein we deny it to the king.

The statute of 5 Henry IV, c. 2, makes a difference between the king and the king's justices in these words, 'Divers notorious felons be indicted of divers felonies, murders, rapes: and as well before the king's justices, as before the king himself, arraigned of the same felonies' [Statutes p. 189].

I read that in the year 1256 Henry III sat in the 'exchequer, and there set down order for the appearance of sheriffs, and bringing in their accounts. There was five marks set on every sheriff's head for a fine, because they had not distrained every person that might dispend fifteen pounds lands by the year, to receive the order of knighthood, according as the same sheriffs were commanded' [Holinshed ii, p. 439].

In Michaelmas Term, 1462, Edward IV 'sat three days together in open court in the king's bench'.

For this point there needs no further proofs, because Mr Prynne doth confess that kings themselves have sat in person in the king's bench and other courts, and there given judgment, p. 32. *Treachery and disloyalty*, etc. [Prynne p. 92].

Notwithstanding all that hath been said for the legislative and judicial power of kings, Mr Prynne is so far from yielding the king a power to make laws that he will not grant the king a power to hinder a law from being made. That is, he allows him not a *negative voice* in most cases, which is due to every other – even to the meanest member of the House of Commons in his judgment.

To prove the king hath not a *negative voice*, his main, and in truth his only argument insisted on, is a coronation oath, which is said anciently some of our kings of England have taken, wherein 'they grant to defend and protect the just laws and customs, which the vulgar hath, or shall choose: *justas leges et consuetudines quas vulgus elegerit*'. Hence Mr Prynne concludes that the king cannot deny any law which the Lords and Commons shall make choice of; for so he will have *vulgus* to signify [Prynne p. 56].

Though neither our king nor many of his predecessors ever took this oath, nor were bound to take it, for ought appears; yet we may admit that our king hath taken it, and answer, we may be confident that neither the bishops, nor privy council, nor parliament, nor any other, whosoever they were, that framed or penned this oath, ever intended in this word *vulgus* the Commons in parliament, much less the Lords. They would never so much disparage the members of parliament as to disgrace them with a title both base and false. It had been enough, if not too much, to have called them *populus*, the people; but *vulgus*, the vulgar, the rude multitude (which hath the epithet of *ignobile vulgus* [the low-born masses]) is a word as dishonourable to the composers of the oath to give, or for the king to use, as for the members of the parliament to receive – it being most false, for the peers cannot be *vulgus* because they are the prime persons of the kingdom. Next, the knights of the shires are or ought to be 'notable' knights, 'or notable esquires, or gentlemen born in the counties, as shall be able to be knights'; then 'the citizens and burgesses are to be most sufficient'. None of these can be *vulgus*."
Even those freeholders that choose knights are the best and ablest men of their counties, there being for every freeholder above ten of the common people to be found to be termed the vulgar. Therefore

" [cf. pp. 73–4 above].

115

it rests that *vulgus* must signify the vulgar or common people, and not the Lords and Commons.

But now the doubt will be what the common people or *vulgus*, out of parliament, have to do to choose laws? The answer is easy and ready. There goeth before *quas vulgus* the antecedent *consuetudines*, that is, 'the customs which the vulgar hath, or shall choose'. Do but observe the nature of custom, and it is the *vulgus* or common people only who choose customs. Common usage time out of mind creates a custom; and the commoner an usage is, the stronger and the better is the custom. Nowhere can so common an usage be found, as among the vulgar, who are still the far greatest part of every multitude. If a custom be common through the whole kingdom, it is all one with the common law of England, which is said to be common custom. Thus in plain terms, to protect the customs which the vulgar choose is to swear to protect the common laws of England.

But grant that *vulgus* in the oath signifies Lords and Commons, and that *consuetudines* doth not signify customs but statutes (as Mr Prynne, for a desperate shift affirms), and let *elegerit* be the future, or preterperfect tense, even which Mr Prynne please (Prynne [p. 56]), yet it cannot exclude the king's negative voice. For as *consuetudines* goeth before *quas vulgus*, so doth *justas* stand before *leges et consuetudines*: so that not all laws, but only all just laws are meant. If the sole choice of the Lords and Commons did oblige the king to protect their choice, without power of denial, what need, or why is the word *justas* put in, to raise a scruple that some laws may be unjust? Mr Prynne will not say that a decree of a general council or of a pope is infallible, nor, I think, a bill of the Lords and Commons is infallibly just, and impossible to err. If he do, Sir Edward Coke will tell him that parliaments have been utterly deceived, and that in cases of greatest moment, even in case of high treason [Coke 4, pp. 37–8]; and he calls the statute of 11 Henry VII 'an unjust and strange act' (Coke [4, p. 41]). But it may be Mr Prynne will confess that laws chosen by the Lords and Commons may be unjust, so that the Lords and Commons themselves may be the judges of what is just or unjust. But where a king by oath binds his conscience to protect just laws, it concerns him to be satisfied in his own conscience that they be just, and not by an implicit faith or blind obedience. No man can be so proper a judge of the justness of laws as he whose soul must lie at the stake for the defence and safeguard of them.

Besides, in this very oath the king doth swear 'to do equal and right justice and discretion in mercy and truth in all his judgment'.† If we allow the king discretion and mercy in his judgments, of necessity he must judge of the justness of the laws.

Again, the clause of the oath *quas vulgus elegerit* doth not mention the assenting unto or granting any new laws, but of 'holding, protecting, and strengthening with all his might, the just laws that were already in being'. There were no need of might or strength, if assenting to new laws were there meant.

Some may wonder why there should be such labouring to deny the king a negative voice, since a negative voice is in itself so poor a thing that if a man had all the negative voices in the kingdom it would not make him a king, nor give him power to make one law. A negative voice is but a *privative* power, that is, no power at all to do or act anything, but a power only to hinder the power of another. Negatives are of such a malignant or destructive nature that if they have nothing else to destroy, they will, when they meet, destroy one another – which is the reason why two negatives make an affirmative, by destroying the negation which did hinder the affirmation. A king with a negative voice only is but like a syllogism of pure negative propositions, which can conclude nothing. It must be an affirmative voice that makes both a king and a law, and without it there can be no imaginable government.

The reason is plain why the king's negative voice is so eagerly opposed, for though it give the king no power to do anything, yet it gives him a power to hinder others; though it cannot make him a king, yet it can help him to keep others from being kings.

For conclusion of this discourse of the negative voice of the king, I shall oppose the judgment of a chief justice of England to the opinion of him that calls himself an utter barrister of Lincoln's Inn,ʳ and let others judge who is the better lawyer of the two. The words are Bracton's, but concern Mr Prynne to lay them to heart:

> Concerning the charters and deeds of kings, the justices nor private men neither ought nor can dispute. Nor yet, if there rise a doubt in the king's charter, can they interpret it. And in doubtful and obscure points, or if a word contain two senses, the interpre-

---

† 'facies fieri in omnibus judiciis tuis aequam et rectam justitiam et discretionem in misericordia et veritate'.
ʳ [Prynne].

tation and will of our lord the king is to be expected, seeing it is his part to interpret who makes the charter. [Bracton f. 34a; Egerton p. 108]

Full well Mr Prynne knows that when Bracton writ, the laws that were then made and strived for were called the king's charters, as Magna Carta, *Carta de Foresta*, and others. So that in Bracton's judgment the king hath not only a negative voice to hinder, but an affirmative to make a law, which is a great deal more than Mr Prynne will allow him.

Not only the law-maker, but also the 'sole judge of the people is the king', in the judgment of Bracton. These are his words: '*Rex et non alius debet judicare, si solus ad id sufficere possit*: the king and no other ought to judge, if he alone were able' [Bracton f. 107a; Lambarde 1, p. 56].

Much like the words of Bracton speaketh Britton, where, after that he had showed that the king is the viceroy of God and that he hath distributed his charge into *sundry*[298] portions, because he alone is not sufficient to hear all complaints of his people, then he addeth these words in the person of the king: '*Nous volons que nostre jurisdiction soit sur touts jurisdictions*, etc. We will that our jurisdiction be above all the jurisdictions of our realm, so as in all manner of felonies, trespasses, contracts, and in all other actions personal or real, we have power to yield, or cause to be yielded, such judgments as do appertain without other process, wheresoever we know the right truth as judges'. [Lambarde 1, p. 57]

'Neither was this to be taken', saith Mr Lambarde,

to be meant of the king's bench, where there is only an imaginary presence of his person, but it must necessarily be understood of a jurisdiction remaining and left in the king's royal body and breast, distinct from that of his bench and other ordinary courts. Because he doth immediately after, severally set forth by themselves as well the authority of the king's bench as of the other courts. [Lambarde 1, pp. 57–8]

'And that this was no new made law', Mr Lambarde puts us in mind of a Saxon law of King Edgar's:

'*Nemo in lite regem appellato*', etc: 'Let no man in suit appeal unto the king unless he cannot get right at home. But if that right be too heavy for him, then let him go to the king to have it eased'. By which it may evidently appear that even so many years ago there might be appellation made to the king's person whensoever the cause should enforce it. [Lambarde I, p. 58]

'The very like law in effect is to be seen in the laws of Canutus the Dane, sometimes king of this realm' [Lambarde I, p. 16]. Out of which law Mr Lambarde gathers 'that the king himself had a high court of justice, wherein it seemeth he sat in person. For the words be, "Let him not seek to the king", and the same court of the king did judge not only according to mere right and law, but also after equity and good conscience' [Lambarde I, p. 17].

For the close, I shall end with the suffrage of our late antiquary Sir Henry Spelman. In his *Glossary* he saith, '*Omnis regni justitia solius regis est*', etc.

All justice of the kingdom is only the king's, and he alone, if he were able, should administer it. But that being impossible, he is forced to delegate it to ministers whom he bounds by the limits of the laws. The positive laws are only about generals; in particular cases they are sometimes too strict, sometimes too remiss; and so, oft wrong instead of right will be done if we stand to strict law. Also, causes hard and difficult daily arise which are comprehended in no law books. In those there is a necessity of running back to the king, the fountain of justice, and the vicegerent of God himself, who in the commonwealth of the Jews took such causes to his own cognisance, and left to kings not only the example of such jurisdiction, but the prerogative also. [Spelman p. 129]

OF PRIVILEGE OF PARLIAMENT

What need all this ado, will some say, to sift out what is comprised in the writ for the election of the Commons to parliament, since it is certain, though the writ *do**[299] not, yet privilege of parliament gives sufficient power for all proceedings of the two Houses? It is answered, that what slight esteem soever be made of the writ, yet in all other cases the original writ is the foundation of the whole business or action, and to vary in substance from the writ makes a nullity in the cause and the proceedings thereupon. And where a commissioner exerciseth more power than is warranted by his commission, every such act is void, and in many cases punishable. Yet we will lay aside the writ, and apply ourselves to consider the nature of privilege of parliament. The task is the more difficult for that we are not told what the number of privileges are, or which they be. Some do think that as there be dormant articles of faith in the Roman church, which are not yet declared; so there be likewise privileges dormant in the House of Commons, not yet revealed. We must therefore be content in a generality to discourse of the quality or condition of privilege of parliament, and to confine ourselves to these three points:

1. That privilege of parliament gives no power, but only helps to the execution of the power given by the writ.
2. That the freeholders by their elections give no privilege.
3. That privilege of parliament is the gift of the king.

First, the end or scope of privilege of parliament is not to give any power to do any public act not warranted by the writ, but they are intended as helps only, to enable to the performance of the duty enjoined, and so are subservient to the power comprised in the writ. For instance, the grand privilege of freedom from arrests doth not give any power at all to the House of Commons to do any act, but by taking away from the freeholders and other subjects the power of arrests, the Commons are the better enabled to attend the service to which they are called by the king.

In many other cases the servants or ministers of the king are privileged, and protected much in the same nature. The servants in household to the king may not be arrested without special licence. Also, the officers of the king's courts of justice have a privilege not to be sued in any other court but where they serve and attend, and to this purpose they are allowed a writ of privilege. Likewise all such as serve the king in his wars, or are employed on foreign affairs for him, are protected from actions and suits. Nay, the king's protection descends to the privileging even of laundresses, nurses and midwives, if they attend upon the camp, as Sir Edward Coke saith, '*quia lotrix, seu nutrix, seu obstetrix*' (Coke [1, f. 396]). Besides, the king protects his debtors from arrests of the subject till his own debts be paid.

These sorts of protections are privileges the common law takes notice of, and allows, and hath several distinctions of them; and some are protections, *quia profecturus* [because he is about to set out], and others are *quia moraturus* [because he will be delayed]. Some are with a clause of *volumus* for stay of suits, others with a clause of *nolumus* for the safety of men's persons, servants and goods. And the king's writs do vary herein according to the nature of the business [Coke 1, f. 394–5].

But none of these privileges or protections do give any power. They are not *positive*, but **privative**:[300] they take away and deprive the subject of the power or liberty to arrest or sue, in some cases only. No protection or privilege doth defend in point of treason, felony or breach of the peace. Privileges are directly contrary to the law, for otherwise they should not be privileges, and they are to be interpreted in the strictest manner, as being odious and contrary to law. We see the use of privileges: they do but serve as a dispensation against law, intended originally and principally for the expediting of the king's business, though secondarily and by accident there do sometimes redound a benefit by them to the parties themselves that are protected. Strictly and properly every privilege must be against a public or common law, for there is no use or need of a private law to protect where there is no public law to the contrary. Favours and graces which are only besides but not against the law do not properly go under the name of privileges, though common use do not distinguish them. I know no other privilege that can be truly so called, and to belong to the House of Commons, which is so vast and great as this privilege of their persons, servants and goods. This being indeed against the common law, and doth concern the whole kingdom to take notice of it, if they must be bound by it.

Touching this grand privilege of freedom from arrests, I read that in the 33 Henry VIII, the Commons did not proceed to the punishment of offenders for the breach of it until the Lords referred the punishment thereof to the lower house. The case is thus reported: George Ferrers, gentleman, servant to the king, and burgess for Plymouth, going to the parliament house was arrested in London by process out of the king's bench for debt, wherein he had before been condemned as surety for one Weldon, at the suit of one White. Which arrest, signified to Sir Thomas Moyle, Speaker, and to the rest, the serjeant (called St John) was sent to the Counter in Bread Street to demand Ferrers. The officers of the Counter refuse to deliver him and gave the serjeant such ill language that they fall to an affray.

The sheriff coming, taketh the officers' part. The serjeant returned without the prisoner. This being related to the Speaker and burgesses, they would sit no more without their burgess, and rising, repaired to the upper house where the case was declared by the Speaker before Sir Thomas Audley, chancellor, and the lords and judges there assembled, who judging the contempt to be very great, referred the punishment thereof to the House of Commons itself [Holinshed 3, pp. 824–5].

This privilege of freedom from arrests is the only privilege which Sir Edward Coke finds to belong to the House of Commons (Coke [4, p. 24]). He cannot, or at least he doth not, so much as name any other in his section of the privileges of parliament, neither doth he bring so much as one precedent for the proof of this one privilege for the House of Commons – which may cause a doubt that this sole privilege is not so clear as many do imagine. For in a parliament in the 27 Elizabeth, Richard Coke, a member, being served with a subpoena of chancery, 'the lord chancellor thought the House had no such privilege for subpoenas as they pretended' [D'Ewes p. 347]. Neither would he allow of any precedents of the House committed unto them, formerly used in that behalf, unless the House of Commons could also prove the same to have been likewise thereupon allowed and ratified also by precedents in the court of chancery.

In the 39 Elizabeth, Sir Edward Hoby and Mr Brograve, attorney of the duchy, were sent by the House to the lord keeper,

in the name of the whole House, to require his lordship to revoke two writs of subpoenas, which were served upon Mr Thomas Knyvet, a member of the House, since the beginning of parliament. The lord keeper demanded of them whether they were appointed by any advised consideration of the House to deliver this message unto him with the word "required", in such manner as they had done, or no. They answered his lordship, yea. His lordship then said, as he thought reverently and honourably of the House, and of their liberties and privileges of the same, so to revoke the said subpoenas in that sort was to restrain her majesty in her greatest power, which is, justice in the place wherein he serveth under her

and therefore he concluded, as they required him to revoke his writ so he did require to deliberate [D'Ewes p. 554].

Upon the 22nd of February, being Wednesday, 18 Elizabeth,

report was made by Mr Attorney of the duchy, upon the committee for the delivering of one Mr Hall's man, that the committee found no precedent for setting at large by the mace any person in arrest, but only by writ. And that by divers precedents of records perused by the said committee, it appeareth that every knight, citizen or burgess which doth require privilege hath used in that case to take a corporal oath before the lord chancellor, or lord keeper, that the party for whom such writ is prayed came up with him and was his servant at the time of the arrest made.

Thereupon Mr Hall was moved by the House to repair to the lord keeper, and make oath, and then take a warrant for a writ of privilege for his servant [D'Ewes p. 249].

It is accounted by some to be a privilege of parliament to have power to examine misdemeanours of courts of justice and officers of state. Yet there is not the meanest subject but hath liberty upon just cause to question the misdemeanour of any court or officer, if he suffer by them. There is no law against him for so doing. So that this cannot properly be called a privilege, because it is not against any public law. It hath been esteemed a great favour of princes to permit such examinations. For, when the Lords were displeased with the greatness of Piers Gaveston, it is said that in the next parliament 'the whole assembly obtain of the king to draw articles of their grievances', which they did. Two of which articles were, first, that 'all strangers should be banished the court and kingdom', of which Gaveston was one. Secondly, that 'the business of the state should be treated of by the council of the clergy and nobles'.

In the reign of King Henry VI, one Mortimer, an instrument of the Duke of York, by promising the Kentish men a reformation and freedom from taxations, wrought with the people that they drew to a head, and made this Mortimer (otherwise Jack Cade) their leader, who styled himself Captain Mend-all. He presents to the parliament the complaints of the commons, and he petitions that the Duke of York and some other lords might be received by the king into favour, by the undue practices of Suffolk and his complices commanded from his presence, and that all their opposites might be banished the court and put from their offices, and that there might be a general amotion of corrupt officers. These petitions are sent from the lower house to the upper, and from thence committed to the lords of the king's privy council, who, having examined the particulars, explode them as frivolous, and the authors of them to be presumptuous rebels.

Concerning liberty or freedom of speech, I find that at a parliament at Blackfriars in the 14 of Henry VIII, Sir Thomas More being chosen Speaker of the House of Commons, he first disabled himself, and then petitioned the king that 'if in communication and reasoning any man in the Commons House should speak more largely than of duty they ought to do, that all such offences should be pardoned and to be entered of record; which was granted' [Holinshed 3, pp. 682–3].

It is observable in this petition that liberty or freedom of speech is not a power for men to speak what they will or please in parliament, but a privilege not to be punished but pardoned for the offence of speaking 'more largely than in duty ought to be', which in an equitable construction must be understood of rash, unadvised, ignorant, or negligent escapes and slips in speech, and not for wilful, malicious offences in that kind. And then the pardon of the king was desired to be upon record, that it might be pleaded in bar to all actions. And it seemeth that Richard Strode and his complices were not thought sufficiently protected for their free speech in parliament unless their pardon were confirmed by the king in parliament. For there is a printed statute to that purpose in Henry VIII's time.

Touching freedom of speech, the Commons were warned in Queen Elizabeth's days not to meddle with the 'queen's person, the state, or church government'. In her time the discipline of the church was so strict that the litany was read every morning in the House of Commons during the parliament, and when the Commons first ordered to have a fast in the Temple upon a Sunday, the queen hindered it.

21 January, Saturday, 23 Elizabeth, the case is thus reported: Mr Paul Wentworth moveth for a public set fast and for a preaching every morning at seven of the clock, before the House sat. The House was divided about the fast, one hundred and fifteen were for it, and a hundred against it. It was ordered that as

> many of the House as conveniently could, should on Sunday
> fortnight after, assemble and meet together in the Temple church,
> there to hear preaching and to join together in prayer, with humi-
> liation and fasting, for the assistance of God's spirit in all their
> consultations during this parliament, and for the preservation
> of the queen's majesty and her realms. And the preachers to
> be appointed by the privy council that were of the House, that

they may be discreet, not meddling with innovation or unquietness. [D'Ewes pp. 282–3]

This order was followed by a message from her majesty to the House, declared by Mr Vice-chamberlain, that 'her highness had *great*[301] admiration of the rashness of this House in committing such an apparent contempt of her express command as to put in execution such an innovation, without her privity or pleasure first known'. Thereupon Mr Vice-chamberlain moved 'the House to make humble submission to her majesty, acknowledging the said offence and contempt, craving *the*[302] remission of the same, with a full purpose to forbear the committing of the like hereafter'. And by the consent of the whole House, Mr Vice-chamberlain carried their submission to her majesty [D'Ewes p. 284].

35 Elizabeth,

> Mr Peter Wentworth and Sir Henry Bromley delivered a petition to the lord keeper, desiring the lords of the upper house to be suppliants with them of the lower house unto her majesty, for entailing the succession of the crown, whereof a bill was ready drawn by them. Her majesty was highly displeased herewith, as contrary to her former strait command, and charged the council to call the parties before them. Sir Thomas Heneage sent for them, and after speech with them commanded them to forbear the parliament and not to go out of their several lodgings. After, they were called before the lord treasurer the Lord Buckhurst and Sir Thomas Heneage. Mr Wentworth was committed by them to the Tower. Sir Henry Bromley, with Mr Richard Stephens – to whom Sir Henry Bromley had imparted the matter – were sent to the Fleet, as also Mr Welch, the other knight for Worcestershire. [D'Ewes p. 470]

In the same parliament 'Mr Morrice, attorney of the court of wards, moved against the hard courses of the bishops, ordinaries and other ecclesiastical judges in their courts, used towards sundry learned and godly ministers and preachers' and spake against subscription and oaths, and offered a bill to be read against imprisonment for refusal of oaths. Mr Dalton opposed the reading of it, as a thing expressly against her majesty's command to meddle in [D'Ewes p. 474]. Doctor Lewin showed that subscription was used even at Geneva [D'Ewes p. 475]. At two of the clock the same day, the Speaker, Mr Coke (afterwards Sir Edward Coke), was sent for to the court where the queen herself gave him in command a message to the House. She told him:

it being wholly in her power to call, to determine, to assent or dissent to anything done in parliament, that the calling of this was only that the majesty of God might be more religiously observed, by compelling by some sharp laws such as neglect that service; and that the safety of her majesty's person and the realm might be provided for. It was not meant they should meddle with matters of state, or causes ecclesiastical (for so her majesty termed them). She wondered that any could be of so high commandment to attempt (they were her own words) a thing so expressly contrary to that which she had commanded. Wherefore with this she was highly offended. And because the words spoken by my lord keeper are not now perhaps well remembered, or some be now here that were not then present, her majesty's present charge and express command is that no bill touching the said matter of state, or reformation in causes ecclesiastical, be exhibited. And upon my allegiance (saith Mr Coke) I am charged, if any such bill be exhibited, not to read it. [D'Ewes pp. 478-9]

I have been credibly informed that the queen sent a messenger or serjeant-at-arms into the House of Commons, and took out Mr Morrice, and committed him to prison. Within few days after, I find Mr Wroth moved in the House that they might be humble suitors to her majesty that she would be pleased to set at liberty those members of the House that were restrained. To this it was answered *by all*[303] the privy councillors that her majesty had committed them for causes best known to herself, and to press her highness with this suit would but hinder them whose good is sought [D'Ewes p. 497]; that the House must not call the queen to account for what she doth of her royal authority, that the causes for which they are restrained may be high and dangerous, that her majesty liketh no such questions; neither doth it become the House to search into such matters.

In the 39 Elizabeth, the Commons were told their privilege was 'yea' and 'no', and that her majesty's pleasure was that if the Speaker perceived any idle heads which would not stick to hazard their own estates, which will meddle with reforming the church and transforming the commonweal, and do exhibit bills to that purpose, the Speaker should not receive them till they were viewed and considered by those whom it is fitter should consider of such things, and can better judge of them. And at the end of this parliament the queen refused to pass forty-eight bills which had passed both Houses.

In the 28 of Elizabeth, the queen said 'She was sorry the Commons meddled with choosing and returning knights of the shire for Norfolk, a thing impertinent for the House to deal withal, and only belonging to the office and charge of the lord chancellor, from whom the writs issue and are returned' [D'Ewes p. 393].

4 Henry IV:

> The 10th of October, the chancellor before the king declared the Commons had sent to the king, praying him that they might have advice and communication with certain lords about matters of business in parliament, for the common good of the realm. Which prayer our lord the king graciously granted, making protestation he would not do it of duty, nor of custom, but of his special grace at this time. And therefore our lord the king charged the clerk of the parliament that this protestation should be entered on record upon the parliament roll,

which the king made known to them by the Lord Say, and his secretary:

> how that neither of due nor of custom our lord the king ought to grant any lords to enter into communication with them of matters touching the parliament. But by his special grace at this time he hath granted their request in this particular. Upon which matter, the said steward and secretary made report to the king in parliament, that the said Commons knew well that they could not have any such lords to commune with them of any business of parliament, without special grace and command of the king himself. [R.P. 3, p. 486]

It hath heretofore been a question whether it be not an infringing and prejudice to the liberties and privileges of the House of Commons for them to join in conference with the Lords in cases of benevolence or contribution, without a bill.

In 35 Elizabeth, on Tuesday, the 1st of March, Mr Egerton, attorney general, and Doctor Cary came with a message from the Lords. Their lordships desired to put the House in remembrance of the speech delivered by the lord keeper, the first day, for consultation and provision of treasure to be had against the great and imminent dangers of the realm. Thereupon their lordships did look to have something from the Houses touching those causes before this time (and yet the parliament had sat but three days, for it began February 26th), and therefore their lordships had hitherto omitted to do anything therein themselves. And thereupon their lordships desired that according to former laudable usages between both Houses in such like cases, a committee of Commons may have conference with a committee of Lords touching provision of treasure against the great dangers of the realm, which was presently resolved by the whole House, and they signified to their lordships the willing and ready assent of the whole House. At the meeting, the Lords negatively affirm not to assent to less than three subsidies, and do insist for a second conference. Mr Francis Bacon yielded to the subsidy, but opposed the joining with the Lords as contrary to the privileges of the House of Commons [D'Ewes p. 483]. Thereupon the House resolved to have no conference with the Lords, but

> to give their lordships most humble and dutiful thanks with all reverence for their favourable and courteous offer of conference, and to signify that the Commons cannot in those cases of benevolence or contribution join in conference with their lordships without prejudice to the liberties and privileges of the House; and to request their lordships to hold the members of this House excused in their not-assenting to their lordships' said motion for conference, for that so to have assented without a bill had been contrary to the liberties and privileges of this House, and also contrary to the former precedents of the same House in like cases had. [D'Ewes p. 486]

This answer delivered to the Lords by the chancellor of the exchequer, their lordships said they 'well hoped to have had a conference according to their former request, and desired to see those precedents by which the Commons seem to refuse the said conference' [D'Ewes p. 486]. But in conclusion it was agreed unto, upon the motion of Sir Walter Raleigh, who moved that without naming a subsidy it might be propounded in general words to have a 'conference touching the dangers of the realm, and the necessary supply of treasure to be provided speedily for the same, according to the proportion of the necessity' [D'Ewes p. 488].

In 43 Elizabeth Serjeant Heal said in parliament,

> he marvelled the House stood either at the granting of a subsidy or time of payment, when all we have is her majesty's, and she may lawfully at her pleasure take it from us; and that she had as much right to all our lands and goods as to any revenue of

the crown; and he said he could prove it by precedents in the
time of Henry III, King John and King Stephen. [D'Ewes p. 633]

The ground upon which this serjeant-at-law went may be thought
the same Sir Edward Coke delivers in his *Institutes*, where he saith
'the first kings of this realm had all the lands of England in demesne,
and the great manors and royalties they reserved to themselves, and
of the remnant for the defence of the kingdom enfeoffed the barons'
[Coke 1, f. 58a-b]. From whence it appears that no man holds any
lands but under a condition to defend the realm. And upon the self-
same ground also the king's prerogative is raised, as being a pre-
eminence in cases of necessity above and before the law of property,
or inheritance. Certain it is, before the Commons were ever chosen
to come to parliament, taxes or subsidies were raised and paid without
their gift. The great and long continued subsidy of Danegeld was
without any gift of the Commons, or of any parliament at all that
can be proved. In the 8 Henry III a subsidy of two marks in silver
upon every knight's fee was granted to the king by the nobles, without
any Commons. At the passing of a bill of subsidies, the words of
the king are, 'the king thanks his loyal subjects, accepts their good
will, and also will have it so: *le roy remercie ses loyaux subjects, accept
leur benevolence, et ausi ainsi le veult*': which last words of *ainsi le
veult*, 'the king wills it to be so', are the only words that makes the
act of subsidy a law to bind every man to the payment of it.

In the 39 Elizabeth, the Commons by their Speaker complaining
of monopolies, the queen spake in private to the lord keeper, who
then made answer touching monopolies, that 'her majesty hoped her
dutiful and loving subjects would not take away her prerogative, which
is the chiefest flower in her garland, and the principal and head
pearl in her crown and diadem'; but 'that they will rather leave that
to her disposition' [D'Ewes p. 547].

The second point is, that the freeholders or counties do not nor
cannot give privilege to the Commons in parliament. They that are
under the law cannot protect against it, they have no such privilege
themselves as to be free from arrests and actions. For if they had,
then it had been no privilege, but it would be the common law. And
what they have not, they cannot give: *Nemo dat quod non habet* [no
one gives what he does not have]. Neither do the freeholders pretend
to give any such privilege either at their election or by any subsequent

act. There is no mention of any such thing in the return of the writ, nor in the indentures between the sheriff and the freeholders.

The third point remains: that privilege of parliament is granted by the king. It is a known rule: 'that which gives the form, gives the consequences of the form'. The king by his writ gives the very essence and form to the parliament. Therefore privileges, which are but consequences of the form, must necessarily flow from the king. All other privileges and protections are the acts of the king, and by the king's writ. Sir Edward Coke saith that the protection of men's persons, servants and goods, is done by a writ of grace from the king [Coke 1, ff. 394–5]. At the presentment of the Speaker of the House of Commons to the king upon the first day of parliament, the Speaker in the name and behoof of the Commons humbly craveth that his majesty would be graciously pleased to grant them their accustomed liberties and privileges; which petition of theirs is a fair recognition of the primitive grace and favour of kings in bestowing of privilege, and it is a shrewd argument against any other title. For our ancestors were not so ceremonious nor so full of compliment as to beg that by grace, which they might claim by right. And the renewing of this petition every parliament argues the grant to be but temporary, during only the present parliament; and that they have been accustomed when they have been accustomably sued or petitioned for. I will close this point with the judgment of King James, who in his *Declaration Touching his Proceedings in Parliament*, 1621, resolves 'that most privileges of parliament grew from precedents, which rather show a toleration than an inheritance'. Therefore he 'could not allow of the style, calling it their ancient and undoubted right and inheritance, but could rather have wished that they had said their privileges were derived from the grace and permission of his ancestors and him'. And thereupon he concludes he cannot 'with patience endure his subjects to use such antimonarchical words concerning their liberties, except they had subjoined that they were granted unto them by the grace and favours of his predecessors' [James I 3, p. 47]. Yet he promiseth 'to be careful of whatsoever privileges they enjoy by long custom and uncontrolled and lawful precedents' [James I 3, p. 48].

THE[w]
ANARCHY
OF
A LIMITED
OR
MIXED MONARCHY
OR,

A succinct Examination of the Fundamentals of
Monarchy, both in this and other Kingdoms,
as well about the Right of Power in Kings, as of the
Originall or Naturall Liberty of the
People.

A Question never yet disputed, though most necessary in these Times

Lucan Lib. 3.
Libertas (–) populi quem regna cohercent
Libertate perit: –
[Lucan *Pharsalia* III, 145–6: the liberty of a people which is subject
to royal government is lost if they gain too great liberty]
– neque enim libertas gratior ulla est
Quam domino servire bono –

Claudian

[Claudian, *De Consulatu Stilichonis* III, 114–15: nor is there any more
welcome liberty than to be subject to a good master).[x]

---

[w] [Copy-text is the first edition of 1648 (Wing F910), referred to in the notes as 48A.
Where the notes record readings or omissions in this edition, the text is taken from
the editions of 1679 (Wing F913 and 914), referred to in the notes as 79].
[x] [this quotation also occurs in a more accurate version on the title-page of *The Free-holders
Grand Inquest*].

THE PREFACE

We do but flatter ourselves, if we hope ever to be governed without an arbitrary power. No, we mistake. The question is not, whether there shall be an arbitrary power, but the only point is who shall have that arbitrary power, whether one man or many? There never was, nor *ever**304 can be any people governed without a power of making laws, and every power of making laws must be arbitrary. For to make a law according to law, is *contradictio in adjecto* [self-contradictory].

It is generally confessed that in a democracy the supreme or arbitrary power of making laws is in a multitude, and so in an aristocracy the like legislative or arbitrary power is in a few, or in the nobility. And therefore by a necessary consequence, in a monarchy the same legislative power must be in one, according to the rule of Aristotle, who saith 'government is in one, or in a few, or in many' [1279ª27–8].

This ancient doctrine of government, in these latter days, hath been strangely refined by the Romanists, and wonderfully improved since the reformation, especially in point of monarchy, by an opinion, that the people have originally a power to create several sorts of monarchy, to limit and compound them with other forms of government, at their pleasure.

As for this natural power of the people, they find neither Scripture, reason, *[nor]**305 practice to justify it. For though several kingdoms have several and distinct laws one from another, yet that doth not make several sorts of monarchy, nor doth the difference of obtaining the supreme power – whether by conquest, election, succession or by any other way – make different sorts of government. It is the difference only of the authors of the laws, and not of the laws themselves, that alters the form of government – that is, whether one man, or more than one, make the laws.

Since the growth of this new doctrine of the limitation and mixture of monarchy, it is most apparent that monarchy hath been crucified (as it were) between two thieves, the pope and the people. For what principles the papists make use of for the power of the pope above kings, the very same (by blotting out the word pope, and putting in the word people), the plebists take up to use against their sovereigns.

If we would truly know what popery is, we shall find by the laws and statutes of the realm, that the main, and indeed the only point of popery is the alienating and withdrawing of subjects from their obedience to their prince, to raise sedition and rebellion. If popery and popularity agree in this point, the kings of Christendom that have shaken off the power of the pope have made no great bargain of it, if in place of one lord abroad, they get many lords at home within their own kingdoms.

I cannot but reverence that form of government which was allowed and made use of for God's own people, and for all other nations. It were impiety to think that God, who was careful to appoint judicial laws for his chosen people, would not furnish them with the best form of government, or to imagine that the rules given in divers places in the gospel by our blessed Saviour and his apostles for obedience to kings should now, like almanacs out of date, be of no use to us, because it is pretended we have a form of government now not once thought of in those days. It is a shame and scandal for us Christians to seek the original of government from the inventions or fictions of poets, orators, philosophers and heathen historians, who all lived thousands of years after the creation, and were (in a manner) ignorant of it; and to neglect the Scriptures, which have with more authority most particularly given us the true grounds and principles of government.

These considerations caused me to scruple this modern piece of politics touching limited and mixed monarchy, and finding no other that presented us with the nature and means of limitation and mixture, but an anonymous author, I have drawn a few brief observations upon the most considerable part of his *Treatise*, in which I desire to receive satisfaction from the author himself, if it may be, according to his promise in his preface; or if not from him, from any other for him.

THE ANARCHY OF A LIMITED OR MIXED MONARCHY

There is scarce the meanest man of the multitude but can now in these days tell us that the government of the kingdom of England is a limited and mixed monarchy, and it is no marvel, since all the disputes and arguments of these distracted times both from the pulpit and the press do tend and end in this conclusion.

The author of the *Treatise of Monarchy*[y] hath copiously handled the nature and manner of limited and mixed monarchy and is the

[y] [Philip Hunton].

first and only man (that I know) hath undertaken the task of describing it. Others only mention it, as taking it for granted.

Doctor Ferne gives the author of this *Treatise of Monarchy* this testimony, that 'the mixture of government is more accurately delivered and urged by this treatise' than by the author of the *Fuller Answer* ([Ferne] p. 3). And in another place Doctor Ferne saith he allows his 'distinction of monarchy into limited and mixed' ([Ferne] p. [12–]13).

I have with some diligence looked over this *Treatise*, but cannot approve of these distinctions which he propounds. I submit the reasons of my dislike to others' judgments. I am somewhat confident that his doctrine of limited and mixed monarchy is an opinion but of yesterday, and of no antiquity, a mere innovation in policy, not so old as New England, though calculated properly for that meridian. For in his first part of the treatise which concerns monarchy in general, there is not one proof, text or example in Scripture that he hath produced to justify his conceit of limited and mixed monarchy. Neither doth he afford us so much as one passage or reason out of Aristotle, whose books of *Politics*, and whose natural reasons are of greatest authority and credit with all rational men, next to the sacred Scripture. Nay, I hope I may affirm and be able to prove that Aristotle doth confute both limited and mixed monarchy, howsoever Doctor Ferne think these new opinions to be raised upon Aristotle's principles ([Ferne] p. 6). As for other politicians or historians, either divine or human, ancient or modern, our author brings not one to confirm his opinions. Nor doth he, nor can he, show that ever any nation or people were governed by a limited or mixed monarchy.

Machiavelli is the first in Christendom that I can find that wrote of a mixed government, but not one syllable of a mixed monarchy. He, in his discourses or disputations upon the decades of Livy, falls so enamoured with the Roman commonwealth that he thought he could never sufficiently grace that popular government unless he said there was something of monarchy in it. Yet he was never so impudent as to say it was a mixed monarchy. And what Machiavelli hath said for Rome, the like hath Contarini for Venice. But Bodin hath laid open the errors of both these, as also of Polybius and some few others that held the like opinions. As for the kingdom of England, if it have found out a form of government (as the *Treatise* layeth it down) of such perfection as never any other people could, it is both a glory to the nation and also to this author who hath first deciphered it.

I now make my approach to the book itself. The title is, *A Treatise of Monarchy*. The first part of it is of 'Monarchy in general', where first I charge the author that he hath not given us any definition or description of monarchy in general. For by the rules of method he should have first defined, and then divided. For if there be several sorts of monarchy, then in something they must agree, which makes them to be monarchies; and in something they must disagree and differ, which makes them to be several sorts of monarchies. In the first place he should have showed us in what they all agreed, which must have been a definition of monarchy in general, which is the foundation of the treatise – and except that be agreed upon, we shall argue upon we know not what. I press not this main omission of our author out of any humour of wrangling, but because I am confident that had he pitched upon any definition of monarchy in general, his own definition would have confuted his whole treatise. Besides, I find him pleased to give us a handsome definition of absolute monarchy, from whence I may infer that he knew no other definition that would have fitted all his other sorts of monarchy; it concerned him to have produced it, lest it might be thought there could be no monarchy but absolute.

What our author hath omitted I shall attempt to supply, and leave to the scanning. And it shall be a real as well as nominal definition of monarchy. A monarchy is the government of one alone. For the better credit of this definition, though it be able to maintain itself, yet I shall deduce it from the principles of our author of the *Treatise of Monarchy*.

We all know that this word monarch is compounded of two Greek words, μόνος and ἀρχεῖν; ἀρχεῖν is *imperare*, to govern and rule; μόνος signifies one alone. The understanding of these two words may be picked out of our author. First, for government he teacheth us it is '*potestatis exercitium*, the exercise of a moral power' ([Hunton] p. 1); next he grants us, that every monarch (even his limited monarch) must 'have the supreme power of the state in him, so that his power must no way be limited by any power above his; for then he were not a monarch, but a subordinate magistrate' ([Hunton] p. 12). Here we have a fair confession of a supreme unlimited power in his limited monarch. If you will know what he means by these words 'supreme power', turn to his 26(th) page, there you will find 'Supreme power' is 'either legislative, or gubernative' and that the 'legislative power is the chief of the two' [Hunton p. 26]. He makes both supreme, and yet one chief. The like distinction he hath before, where he saith the power of magistracy 'in respect of its degrees, is *nomothetical* or *architectonical*; and *gubernative* or *executive*' ([Hunton] p. 5). By these words of legislative, nomothetical and architectonical power, in plain English, he understands a power of making laws. And by gubernative and executive, a power of putting those laws in execution by judging and punishing offenders.

The result we have from hence is that by the author's acknowledgment every monarch must have the supreme power, and that supreme power is a power to make laws. And howsoever the author makes the gubernative and executive power a part of the supreme power, yet he confesseth the legislative to be chief, or the highest degree of power, for he doth acknowledge degrees of supreme power. Nay, he afterwards teacheth us that 'the legislative power is the height of power, to which the other parts are subsequent and subservient' ([Hunton] p. 40). If gubernative be subservient to legislative, how can gubernative power be supreme?

Now let us examine the author's limited monarch by these his own rules. He tells us that in a moderated, limited, stinted, conditionate, legal or allayed monarchy (for all these terms he hath for it) the 'supreme power must be restrained by some law according to which this power was given and by direction of which this power must act' ([Hunton] p. 12); when in a line before he said that 'the monarch's power must not be limited by any power above his'. Yet here he will have his supreme power restrained – not limited, and yet restrained. Is not a restraint a limitation? And if restrained, how is it supreme? And if restrained by some law, is not the power of that law, and of them that made that law, above his supreme power? And if by the direction of such law only he must govern, where is the legislative power, which is the chief of supreme power? When the law must rule and govern the monarch, and not the monarch the law, he hath at the most but a gubernative or executive power. If his authority 'transcends its bounds if it command beyond the law, and the subject is not bound legally to subjection in such cases' ([Hunton] p. 14), and if 'the utmost extent of the law of the land' be the measure of the limited monarch's power, and subject's duty (p. 16) [Hunton p. 14], where shall we find the supreme power, that *culmen* or *apex potestatis*, that prime ἀρχὴ, which our author saith must be in every monarch? The word ἀρχὴ, which signifies principality and power, doth also signify *principium*, beginning – which doth teach us that by the word prince or principality the *principium* or beginning of government is meant. This, if it be given to the law, it robs the monarch, and makes the law the *primum mobile* – and so that which is but the instrument, or servant to the monarch, becomes the master. Thus much of the word ἀρχεῖν.

The other word is μόνος, *solus*, one alone. The monarch must not only have the supreme power unlimited, but he must have it alone – without any companions. Our author teacheth us he is 'no monarch if the supreme power be not in one' ([Hunton] p. 15). And again he saith, if 'you put the *apex postestatis*' or supreme power 'in the whole body, or a part of it', you 'destroy the being of monarchy' ([Hunton] p. 17).

Now let us see if his mixed monarchy be framed according to these his own principles. First, he saith, in a mixed monarchy 'the sovereign power must be originally in all three' estates ([Hunton] p. 25). And again his words are, 'the three estates are all sharers in the supreme power; the primity[z] of share in the supreme power is in one' [Hunton p. 25]. Here we find that he that told us the supreme power must be in one will now allow his mixed monarch but one share only of the supreme power, and gives other shares to the estates. Thus he destroys the being of monarchy by putting the supreme power, or *culmen potestatis*, or a part of it, in the whole body or a part thereof. And yet formerly he confesseth that 'the power of magistracy cannot well be divided, for it is one simple thing or indivisible beam of divine perfection' ([Hunton] p. 5). But he can make this indivisible beam to be divisible into three shares. I have done with the word μόνος, *solus*, alone.

I have dwelt the longer upon this definition of monarchy because the apprehending of it out of the author's own grounds quite overthrows both his monarch limited by law and his monarch mixed with the states. For to govern is to give a law to others, and not to have a law given to govern and limit him that governs. And to govern alone is not to have sharers or companions mixed with the governor. Thus the two words of which monarchy is compounded, contradict the two sorts of monarchy which he pleads for, and by consequence

---

[z] [priority].

his whole treatise. For these two sorts of limited and mixed monarchy take up (in a manner) his whole book.

I will now touch some few particular passages in the *Treatise*. Our author first confesseth, 'It is God's express ordinance there should be government' ([Hunton] p. 2), and he proves it by Genesis iii, 16, where God ordained Adam to rule over his wife, and her desires were to be subject to his; and as hers, so all theirs that should come of her. Here we have the original grant of government, and the fountain of all power, placed in the father of all mankind. Accordingly we find the law for obedience to government given in the terms of 'honour thy father'. Not only the constitution of power in general, but the limitation of it to one kind (that is, to monarchy, or the government of one alone) and the determination of it to the individual person and line of Adam, are all three ordinances of God. Neither Eve nor her children could either limit Adam's power or join others with him in the government. And what was given unto Adam, was given in his person to his posterity. This paternal power continued monarchical to the Flood, and after the Flood to the confusion of Babel. When kingdoms were first erected, planted or scattered over the face of the world, we find [Genesis x, 11] it was done by colonies of whole families, over which the prime fathers had supreme power, and were kings, who were all the sons or grandchildren of Noah, from whom they derived a fatherly and regal power over their families. Now if this supreme power was settled and founded by God himself in the fatherhood, how is it possible for the people to have any right or title to alter and dispose of it otherwise? What commission can they show that gives them power either of limitation or mixture? It was God's ordinance, that supremacy should be unlimited in Adam, and as large as all the acts of his will; and as in him, so in all others that have supreme power, as appears by the judgment and speech of the people to Joshua when he was supreme governor. These are their words to him: 'All that thou commandest us we will do; whosoever he be that doth rebel against thy commandment and will not hearken unto thy words in all that thou commandest him, he shall be put to death' [Joshua i, 16–18]. We may not say that these were evil councillors or flattering courtiers of Joshua, or that he himself was a tyrant for having such arbitrary power. Our author, and all those who affirm that power is conveyed to persons by public consent, are forced to confess that it is the fatherly power that first enables a people to make such conveyance. So that admitting (as they hold) that our ancestors did at first convey power, yet the reason why we now living do submit to such power is, for that our forefathers, every one for himself, his family and posterity, had a power of resigning up themselves and us to a supreme power. As the Scripture teacheth us that supreme power was originally in the fatherhood without any limitation, so likewise reason doth evince it, that if God ordained that supremacy should be, that then supremacy must of necessity be unlimited. For the power that limits must be above that power which is limited. If it be limited it cannot be supreme. So that if our author will grant supreme power to be the ordinance of God, the supreme power will prove itself to be unlimited by the same ordinance – because a supreme limited power is a contradiction.

The monarchical power of Adam, the father of all flesh, being by a general binding ordinance settled by God in him and his posterity by right of fatherhood, the form of monarchy must be preferred above other forms, except the like ordinance for other forms can be showed. Neither may men according to their relations to the form they live under, to their affections and judgments in divers respects, prefer or compare any other form with monarchy. The point that most perplexeth our author and many others is that if monarchy be allowed to be the ordinance of God, an absurdity would follow, that we should uncharitably condemn all the communities which have not that form for violation of God's ordinance, and pronounce those other powers unlawful. If those who live under a monarchy can justify the form they live under to be God's ordinance, they are not bound to forbear their own justification because others cannot do the like for the form they live under. Let others look to the defence of their own government. If it cannot be proved or showed that any other form of government had ever any lawful beginning, but was brought in or erected by rebellion, must therefore the lawful and just obedience to monarchy be denied to be the ordinance of God?

To proceed with our author, in the third page he saith 'The higher power is God's ordinance: that it resideth in one, or more; in such or such a way is from human designment': God by 'no word' binds any people to this or that form till they by their own act bind themselves [Hunton p. 3]. Because the power and consent of the people in government is the burden of the whole book, and our author expects it should be admitted as a magisterial postulation without any other proof than a naked supposition; and since others also maintain that originally power was or now is in the people, and that the first kings were chosen by the people, they may not be offended if they be asked in what sense they understand the word 'people', because this – as many other words – hath different accept[at]ions, being sometimes taken in a larger, other whiles in a stricter sense. Literally, and in the largest sense, the word people signifies the whole multitude of mankind. But figuratively and synecdochically[a] it notes many times the major part of a multitude, or sometimes the better, or the richer, or the wiser, or some other part. And oftentimes a very small part of the people, if there be no other apparent opposite party, hath the name of the people by presumption.

If they understand that the entire multitude or whole people have originally by nature power to choose a king, they must remember that by their own principles and rules, by nature all mankind in the world makes but one people, who they suppose to be born alike to an equal freedom from subjection – and where such freedom is, there all things must of necessity be common. And therefore without a joint consent of the whole people of the world, no one thing can be made proper to any one man, but it will be an injury and an usurpation upon the common right of all others. From whence it follows that natural freedom being once granted, there cannot be any one man chosen a king without the universal consent of all the people of the world at one instant, *nemine contradicente*. Nay, if it be true that nature hath made all men free, though all mankind should concur in one vote, yet it cannot seem reasonable that they should have power to alter the law of nature. For if no man have power to take away his own life without the guilt of being a murderer of himself, how can any people confer such a power as they have not themselves upon any one man, without being accessories to their own deaths, and every particular man become guilty of being *felo de se* [his own killer]?

If this general signification of the word people be disavowed and men will suppose that the people of particular regions or countries have power and freedom to choose unto themselves kings, then let them but observe the consequence. Since nature hath not distinguished the habitable world into kingdoms, nor determined what

---

[a] [by taking a part for the whole].

part of a people shall belong to one kingdom and what to another, it follows that the original freedom of mankind being supposed, every man is at liberty to be of what kingdom he please. And so every petty company hath a right to make a kingdom by itself; and not only every city but every village and every family, nay, and every particular man, a liberty to choose himself to be his own king if he please. And he were a madman that being by nature free would choose any man but himself to be his own governor. Thus to avoid the having but of one king of the whole world, we shall run into a liberty of having as many kings as there be men in the world, which upon the matter is to have no king at all, but to leave all men to their natural liberty – which is the mischief the pleaders for natural liberty do pretend they would most avoid.

But if neither the whole people of the world nor the whole people of any part of the world be meant, but only the major part, or some other part, of a part of the world, yet still the objection will be the stronger. For besides that nature hath made no partition of the world or of the people into distinct kingdoms, and that without an universal consent at one and the same instant no partition can be made, yet if it were lawful for particular parts of the world by consent to choose their kings, nevertheless their elections would bind none to subjection but only such as consented. For the major part never binds but where men at first either agree to be so bound or where a higher power so commands. Now, there being no higher power than nature but God himself, where neither nature nor God appoints the major part to bind, their consent is not binding to any but only to themselves who consent.

Yet for the present to gratify them so far as to admit that either by nature or by a general consent of all mankind the world at first was divided into particular kingdoms, and the major part of the people of each kingdom assembled, allowed to choose their king: yet it cannot truly be said that ever the whole people, or the major part, or indeed any considerable part of the whole people of any nation ever assembled to any such purpose. For except by some secret miraculous instinct they should all meet at one time and place, what one man or company of men less than the whole people hath power to appoint either time or place of elections, where all be alike free by nature? And without a lawful summons, it is most unjust to bind those that be absent. The whole people cannot summon itself. One man is sick, another is lame, a third is aged, and a fourth is under age of discretion. All these at some time or other, or at some place or other, might be able to meet if they might choose their own time and place, as men naturally free should.

In assemblies that are by human politic constitution, the superior power that ordains such assemblies can regulate and confine them, both for time, place, persons and other circumstances. But where there is an equality by nature, there can be no superior power. There every infant at the hour it is born in, hath a like interest with the greatest and wisest man in the world. Mankind is like the sea, ever ebbing or flowing, every minute one is born another dies. Those that are the people this minute, are not the people the next minute. In every instant and point of time there is a variation. No one time can be indifferent for all mankind to assemble. It cannot but be mischievous always at the least to all infants and others under age of discretion – not to speak of women, especially virgins, who by birth have as much natural freedom as any other and therefore ought not to lose their liberty without their own consent.

But in part to salve this, it will be said that infants and children may be concluded by the votes of their parents. This remedy may cure some part of the mischief, but it destroys the whole cause and at last stumbles upon the true original of government. For if it be allowed that the acts of parents bind the children, then farewell the doctrine of the natural freedom of mankind. Where subjection of children to parents is natural, there can be no natural freedom. If any reply that not all children shall be bound by their parents' consent but only those that are under age, it must be considered that in nature there is no nonage. If a man be not born free she doth not assign him any other time when he shall attain his freedom, or if she did then children attaining that age should be discharged of their parents' contract. So that in conclusion, if it be imagined that the people were ever but once free from subjection by nature, it will prove a mere impossibility ever lawfully to introduce any kind of government whatsoever without apparent wrong to a multitude of people.

It is further observable that ordinarily children and servants are far a greater number than parents and masters, and for the major part of these to be able to vote and appoint what government or governors their fathers and masters shall be subject unto is most unnatural, and in effect to give the children the government over their parents.

To all this it may be opposed: what need dispute how a people can choose a king since there be multitude of examples that kings have been, and are nowadays chosen by their people? The answer is: 1. The question is not of the fact, but of the right – whether it have been done by a natural or by an usurped right. 2. Many kings are and have been chosen by some small part of a people. But by the whole or major part of a kingdom not any at all. Most have been elected by the nobility, great men, and princes of the blood, as in Poland, Denmark and in Sweden – not by any collective or representative body of any nation. Sometimes a factious or seditious city, or a mutinous army hath set up a king, but none of all those could ever prove they had right or just title either by nature or any otherwise for such elections. We may resolve upon these two propositions: 1. That the people have no power or right of themselves to choose kings. 2. If they had any such right, it is not possible for them any way lawfully to exercise it.

You will say 'there must necessarily be a right in somebody to elect, in case a king die without an heir'. I answer, no king can die without an heir as long as there is any one man living in the world. It may be the heir may be unknown to the people, but that is no fault in nature, but the negligence or ignorance of those whom it concerns. But if a king could die without an heir, yet the kingly power in that case shall not escheat to the whole people, but to the supreme heads and fathers of families. Not as they are the people, but *quatenus* they are fathers of people, over whom they have a supreme power devolved unto them after the death of their sovereign ancestor. And if any can have a right to choose a king, it must be these fathers, by conferring their distinct fatherly powers upon one man alone. Chief fathers in Scripture are accounted as all the people, as 'all the children of Israel', as 'all the congregation', as the text plainly expounds itself (2 Chronicles i, 2) where Solomon speaks to 'all Israel', that is, 'to the captains, the judges, and to every governor, the chief of the fathers', and so the elders of Israel are expounded to be the chief of the fathers of the children of Israel, 1 Kings viii, 1 and the 2 Chronicles v, 2.

If it be objected, that kings are not now (as they were at the first planting or peopling of the world) the fathers of their people or kingdoms and that the fatherhood hath lost the right of governing, an answer is that all kings that now are or ever were are or were either fathers of their people, or the heirs of such fathers, or usurpers of the right of such fathers. It is a truth undeniable that there cannot be any multitude of men whatsoever, either great or small, though gathered together from the several corners and remotest regions of the world, but that in the same multitude considered by itself there is one man amongst them that in nature hath a right to be the king of all the rest, as being the next heir to Adam, and all the others subject unto him. Every man by nature is a king, or a subject. The obedience which all subjects yield to kings is but the paying of that duty which is due to the supreme fatherhood. Many times by the act either of an usurper himself, or of those that set him up, the true heir of a crown is dispossessed, God using the ministry of the wickedest men for the removing and setting up of kings. In such cases the subjects' obedience to the fatherly power must go along and wait upon God's providence, who only hath right to give and take away kingdoms, and thereby to adopt subjects into the obedience of another fatherly power, according to that of Aristotle, 'πατρικη γὰρ ἀρχὴ βούλεται ἡ βασιλεία εἶναι: A monarchy or kingdom will be a fatherly government' (*Ethics* book 8, chapter 12) [1160^b26–7].

However the natural freedom of the people be cried up as the sole means to determine the kind of government and the governors, yet in the close, all the favourers of this opinion are constrained to grant that the obedience which is due to the fatherly power is the true and only cause of the subjection which we that are now living give to kings – since none of us gave consent to government, but only our forefathers' act and consent hath concluded us.

Whereas many confess that government only in the *abstract* is the ordinance of God, they are not able to prove any such ordinance in the Scripture, but only in the fatherly power; and therefore we find the commandment that enjoins obedience to superiors, given in the terms of 'honour thy father'. So that not only the power or right of government, but the form of the power of governing, and the person having that power, are all the ordinance of God. The first father had not only simply power, but power monarchical, as he was a father, immediately from God. For by the appointment of God, as soon as Adam was created he was monarch of the world, though he had no subjects. For though there could not be actual government until there were subjects, yet by the right of nature it was due to Adam to be governor of his posterity. Though not in *act* yet at least in *habit* Adam was a king from his creation, and in the state of innocency he had been governor of his children. For the integrity or excellency of the subjects doth not take away the order or eminency of the governor. Eve was subject to Adam before he sinned; the angels, who are of a pure nature, are subject to God – which confutes their saying who, in disgrace of civil government or power say it was brought in by sin. Government as to *coactive* power was after sin, because coaction supposeth some disorder, which was not in the state of innocency: but as for *directive* power, the condition of human nature requires it, since civil society cannot be imagined without power of government. For although as long as men continued in the state of innocency they might not need the direction of Adam in those things which were necessarily and morally to be done, yet things indifferent[b] – that depended merely on their free will – might be directed by the power of Adam's command.

If we consider the first plantations of the world (which were after the building of Babel, when the confusion of tongues was), we may find the division of the earth into distinct kingdoms and countries by several families, whereof the sons or grandchildren of Noah were the kings or governors by a fatherly right. And for the preservation of this power and right in the fathers, God was pleased upon several families to bestow a language on each by itself, the better to unite it into a nation or kingdom. As appears by the words of the text, Genesis x, [31–2], 'These are the families of the sons of Noah, after their generations in their nations, and by these were the nations divided in the earth after the Flood, every one after his tongue, after their families in their nations'.

The kings of England have been graciously pleased to admit and accept the Commons in parliament as the representees of the kingdom, yet really and truly they are not the representative body of the whole kingdom.

The Commons in parliament are not the representative body of the whole kingdom. They do not represent the king, who is the head and principal member of the kingdom. Nor do they represent the lords, who are the nobler and higher part of the body of the realm,

---

[b] [things indifferent: things neither commanded nor forbidden by God. In these matters the perfect moral sense which people had in the 'state of innocency' (which existed before the Fall) would be no guide, and they would therefore need to follow the direction of Adam].

and are personally present in parliament, and therefore need no representation. The Commons only represent a part of the lower or inferior part of the body of the people, which are the freeholders worth forty shillings by the year, and the commons or freemen of cities and boroughs, or the major part of them. All which are not one quarter, nay, not a tenth part of the commons of the kingdom. For in every parish, for one freeholder there may be found ten that are no freeholders, and anciently – before rents were improved – there were nothing near so many freeholders of forty shillings by the year as now are to be found.

The scope and conclusion of this discourse and argument is that the people taken in what notion or sense soever – either diffusively, collectively or representatively – have not, nor cannot exercise any right or power of their own by nature, either in choosing or in regulating kings. But whatsoever power any people doth lawfully exercise, it must receive it from a supreme power on earth, and practise it with such limitations as that superior power shall appoint. To return to our author.

He divides monarchy into $\begin{cases} \text{absolute,} \\ \text{limited.} \end{cases}$

'Absolute monarchy', saith he, 'is when the sovereignty is so fully in one, that it hath no limits or bounds under God but his own will' ([Hunton] p. 6). This definition of his I embrace. And as before I charged our author for not giving us a definition of monarchy in general, so I now note him for not affording us any definition of any other particular kind of monarchy but only of absolute. It may peradventure make some doubt that there is no other sort but only that which he calls absolute.

Concerning absolute monarchy, he grants that 'such were the ancient eastern monarchies, and that of the Turk and Persian at this day' [Hunton p. 6]. Herein he saith very true. And we must remember him, though he do not mention them, that the monarchs of Judah and Israel must be comprehended under the number of those he calls the eastern monarchies. And truly, if he had said that all the ancient monarchies of the world had been absolute, I should not have quarrelled at him, not do I know who could have disproved him.

Next it follows that absolute monarchy is 'when a people are absolutely resigned up or resign up themselves to be governed by the will of one man ... Where men put themselves into this utmost degree of subjection by oath and contract, or are borne and brought unto it by God's providence' [Hunton p. 6]. In both these places he acknowledgeth there may be other means of obtaining a monarchy besides the contract of a nation or people's resigning up themselves to be governed – which is contrary to what he after says, that 'the sole mean or root of all sovereignty is the consent and fundamental contract of a nation of men' ([Hunton] p. 12).

Moreover, the author determines that 'absolute monarchy is a lawful government' and that men may be 'borne and brought unto it by God's providence, it binds them and they must abide it, because an oath to a lawful thing is obligatory' [Hunton p. 6]. This position of his I approve, but his reason doth not satisfy. For men are bound to obey a lawful governor though neither they nor their ancestors ever took oath.

Then he proceeds, and confesseth that in Romans xiii 'the power which then was, was absolute. Yet the apostle not excluding it, calls it *God's ordinance*, and commands subjection to it. So Christ commands tribute to be paid, and pays it himself. Yet it was an arbitrary tax, the production of an absolute power' ([Hunton] p. 7). These are the loyal expressions of our author touching absolute or arbitrary monarchy. I do the rather mention these passages of our author because very many in these days do not stick to maintain that an arbitrary or absolute monarch not limited by law is all one with a tyrant; and to be governed by one man's will is to be made a slave. It is a question whether our author be not of that mind when he saith 'absolute subjection' is 'servitude' [Hunton p. 7]. And thereupon a late friend to limited monarchy affirms in a discourse upon the question in debate between the king and parliament, 'That to make a king by the standard of God's word, is to make the subjects slaves for conscience sake' (p. 54) [*Discourse upon the Questions*, p. 3] – a hard saying, and I doubt whether he that gives this censure can be excused from blasphemy. It is a bold speech to condemn all the kings of Judah for tyrants, or to say all their subjects were slaves. But certainly the man doth not know *[either]*[306] what a tyrant is, or what a slave is. Indeed the words are frequent enough in every man's mouth, and our old English translation of the Bible useth sometimes the word tyrant. But the authors of our new translation have been so careful, as not once to use the word, but only for the proper name of a man – Acts xix, 9 – because they find no Hebrew word in the

Scripture to signify a tyrant or a slave. Neither Aristotle, Bodin nor Sir Walter Raleigh (who were all men of deep judgment) can agree in a definition or description of tyranny, though they have all three laboured in the point. And I make some question whether any man can possibly describe what a tyrant is, and then tell me any one man that ever was in the world that was a tyrant according to that description.

I return again to our *Treatise of Monarchy*, where I find 'three degrees' of absolute monarchy:

1. Where 'the monarch, whose will is the law, doth set himself no law to rule by, but by commands of his own judgment as he thinks fit' [Hunton p. 7].

2. 'When he sets a law by which he will ordinarily govern, reserving to himself a liberty to vary from it as oft as in his discretion he thinks fit; and in this the sovereign is as free as the former' [Hunton p. 7].

3. Where 'he not only sets a rule but promiseth in many cases not to alter it. But this promise or engagement is an after condescent or act of grace, not dissolving the absolute oath of subjection which went before it' [Hunton p. 7].

For the first of these three there is no question but it is a pure absolute monarchy. But as for the other two, though he say they be absolute, yet in regard they set themselves limits or laws to govern by, if it please our author to term them limited monarchs, I will not oppose him. Yet I must tell him, that his third degree of absolute monarchy is such a kind as I believe never hath been nor ever can be in the world. For a monarch to promise and engage in many cases not to alter a law, it is most necessary that those many cases should be particularly expressed at the bargain-making. Now he that understands the nature and condition of all human laws knows that particular cases are infinite and not comprehensible within any rules or laws. And if many cases should be comprehended, and many omitted, yet even those that were comprehended would admit of variety of interpretations and disputations. Therefore our author doth not, nor can tell us of any such reserved cases promised by any monarch.

Again, where he saith 'an after condescent or act of grace' doth not dissolve 'the absolute oath of subjection which went before it' [Hunton p. 7], though in this he speak true, yet still he seems to insinuate that an oath only binds to subjection – which oath, as he would have us believe, was at first arbitrary. Whereas subjects are bound to obey monarchs though they never take oath of subjection, as well as children are bound to obey their parents though they never swear to do it.

Next, his distinction between the 'rule of power' and the 'exercise of it' ([Hunton] p. 7), is vain. For to rule is to exercise power – for himself saith that 'government is *potestatis exercitium*, the exercise of a moral power' ([Hunton] p. 1).

Lastly, whereas our author saith a monarch 'cannot break' his promise 'without sin' [Hunton p. 7], let me add that if the safety of the people – *salus populi* – require a breach of the monarch's promise, then the sin, if there be any, is rather in the making, than breaking of the promise. The safety of the people is an exception implied in every monarchical promise.

But it seems these three degrees of monarchy do not satisfy our author. He is not content to have a monarch have a law or rule to govern by, but he must have this limitation or law to be '*ab externo*', from somebody else, and not from 'the determination' of the monarch's 'own will' ([Hunton] p. 12). And therefore he saith 'by original constitution the society public confers on one man a power by limited contract, resigning themselves to be governed by such a law' ([Hunton] p. 13). Also, before, he told us 'the sole means' of sovereignty is 'the consent and fundamental contract, which consent puts them in their power – which can be no more nor other than is conveyed to them by such contract of subjection' [Hunton p. 12]. If the sole means of a limited monarchy be the consent and fundamental contract of a nation, how is it that he saith a monarch may be limited 'by after condescent' [Hunton p. 13]? Is an after condescent all one with a fundamental contract, with original and radical constitution? Why yea: he tells us 'it is a secondary original constitution' [Hunton p. 13]. A secondary original, that is, a second first. And if that condescent be an act of grace, doth not this condescent to a limitation come from the free determination of the monarch's will if he either 'formally or virtually' (as our author supposeth) desert his absolute or arbitrary power which he hath 'by conquest or other right' [Hunton p. 13]?

And if it be from the free will of the monarch, why doth he say the limitation must be *ab externo*? He told us before, that subjection cannot be 'dissolved or lessened by an act of grace coming afterwards' ([Hunton] p. 8). But he hath better bethought himself, and now he will have acts of grace to be of two kinds, and the latter kind may 'amount', as he saith, 'to a resignation' of absolute monarchy [Hunton p. 13]. But can any man believe that a monarch who by conquest or other right hath an absolute arbitrary power, will voluntarily resign that absoluteness and accept so much power only as the people shall please to give him, and such laws to govern by as they shall make choice of? Can he show that ever any monarch was so gracious or kind-hearted as to lay down his lawful power freely at his subjects' feet? Is it not sufficient grace if such an absolute monarch be content to set down a law to himself by which he will ordinarily govern, but he must needs relinquish his old independent commission and take a new one from his subjects, clogged with limitations?

Finally, I observe that howsoever our author speak big of the radical, fundamental and original power of the people as the root of all sovereignty, yet in a better mood he will take up and be contented with a monarchy limited by an after condescent and act of grace from the monarch himself.

Thus I have briefly touched his grounds of limited monarchy. If now we shall ask what proof or examples he hath to justify his doctrine, he is as mute as a fish: only Pythagoras hath said it, and we must believe him. For though our author would have monarchy to be limited, yet he could be content his opinion should be absolute, and not limited to any rule or example.

The main charge I have against our author now remains to be discussed, and it is this – that instead of a treatise of *monarchy* he hath brought forth a treatise of *anarchy*. And that by his own confessions shall be made good.

First, he holds a limited monarch 'transcends his bounds if he commands beyond the law, and the subject legally is not bound to subjection in such cases' [Hunton p. 14].

Now if you ask the author who shall be judge whether the monarch *transcend*[307] his bounds, and of the excesses of the sovereign power, his answer is: 'there is an impossibility of constituting a judge to determine this last controversy (p. 16) [Hunton p. 17] ... I conceive in a limited legal monarchy there can be no stated internal judge of the monarch's actions, if there grow a fundamental variance betwixt him and the community ... There can be no judge legal and constituted within that form of government' ([Hunton] p. 17). In these answers it appears there is no judge to determine the sovereign's or the monarch's transgressing his fundamental limits. Yet our author is very cautelous^c and supposeth only a fundamental variance betwixt the monarch and the community. He is ashamed to put the question home. I demand of him if there be a variance betwixt the monarch and any of the meanest *persons**308 of the community, who shall be the judge? For instance, the king commands me, or gives judgment against me; I reply, his commands are illegal and his judgment not according to law. Who must judge? If the monarch himself judge, then you destroy the frame of the state and make it absolute, saith our author; and he gives his reason: for, to define a monarch to a law, and then to make him judge of his own deviations from that law, is to absolve him from all law. On the other side, if any, or all the people may judge, then you put the sovereignty in the whole body, or part of it, and destroy the being of monarchy. Thus our author hath caught himself in a plain dilemma: if the king be judge, then he is no limited monarch; if the people be judge, then he is no monarch at all. So farewell limited monarchy. Nay, farewell all government if there be no judge.

Would you know what help our author hath found out for this mischief? First, he saith that 'a subject is bound to yield to a magistrate when he cannot *de jure* challenge obedience if it be in a thing in which he can possibly without subversion, and in which his act may not be made a leading case, and so bring on a prescription against public liberty' ([Hunton] p. 14).^d Again he saith, 'if the act in which the exorbitance or transgression of the monarch is supposed to be, be of lesser moment, and not striking at the very being of that government, it ought to be borne by public patience, rather than to endanger the being of the state' ([Hunton] p. 17). The like words he uses in another place, saying, 'if the will of the monarch exceed the limits of the law, it ought to be submitted to, so it be not contrary to God's law, nor bring with it such an evil to ourselves or the public that we cannot be accessory to it^e by obeying' ([Hunton] p.49). These are but fig leaves to cover the nakedness of our author's limited monarch,

---

^c [wily, circumspect].

^d [Hunton argues that even in cases where the king's command is contrary to the law of the land – and in which he therefore has no right to his subjects' obedience – subjects should still obey him provided that by doing so they do not allow him to subvert public liberties, for example by establishing crucial legal precedents].

^e [accessory to it: only subordinately and incidentally responsible for it].

formed upon weak supposals in cases of lesser moment. For if the monarch be to govern only according to law, no transgression of his can be of so small moment, if he break the bounds of law, but it is a subversion of the government itself, and may be made a leading case, and so bring on a prescription against public liberty. It strikes at the very being of the government, and brings with it such an evil as the party that suffers, or the public cannot be accessory to. Let the case be never so small, yet if there be illegality in the act, it strikes at the very being of limited monarchy, which is to be legal. Unless our author will say, as in effect he doth, that his limited monarch must govern according to law in great and public matters only, and that in smaller matters which concern private men, or poor persons, he may rule according to his own will.

Secondly, our author tells us, if the monarch's act of exorbitancy or transgression

> be mortal, and such as suffered dissolves the frame of government and public liberty, then the illegality is to be set open, and redress-ment sought by petition; which if failing, prevention by resistance ought to be; and if it be apparent, and appeal be made to the consciences of mankind, then the fundamental laws of that monarchy must judge and pronounce the sentence in every man's conscience, and every man (so far as concerns him) must follow the evidence of truth in his own soul to oppose or not to oppose, according as he can in conscience acquit or condemn the act of the governor or monarch. ([Hunton] p. 17[–18])

Whereas my author requires that the destructive nature of illegal commands should be set open, surely his mind is that each private man in his particular case should make a public remonstrance to the world of the illegal act of the monarch; and then if upon his petition he cannot be relieved according to his desire, he ought, or it is his duty to make resistance. Here I would know, who can be the judge whether the illegality be made apparent? It is a main point, since every man is prone to flatter himself in his own cause and to think it good, and that the wrong or injustice he suffers is apparent, when other moderate and indifferent men can discover no such thing. And in this case the judgment of the common people cannot be gathered or known by any possible means, or if it could, it were like to be various and erroneous.

Yet our author will have an appeal made to the conscience of all mankind, and that being made, he concludes 'the fundamental laws must judge and pronounce sentence in every man's conscience' ([Hunton] p. 18). Whereas he saith 'the fundamental laws must judge'. I would very gladly learn of him, or of any other for him, what a fundamental law is, or else have but any one law named me that any man can say is a fundamental law of the monarchy. I confess he tells us that the common laws are the foundation, and the statute laws are 'superstructive' ([Hunton] p. 38). Yet I think he dares not say that there is any one branch or part of the common law but that it may be taken away by an act of parliament. For many points of the common law *de facto* have; and *de jure* any point may be taken away. How can that be called fundamental which hath and may be removed, and yet the statute laws stand firm and stable? It is contrary to the nature of fundamental for the building to stand when the foundation is taken away.

Besides, the common law is generally acknowledged to be nothing else but common usage or custom, which by length of time only obtains authority. So that it follows in time after government, but cannot go before it and be the rule to government by any original or radical constitution.

Also the common law being unwritten, doubtful and difficult, cannot but be an uncertain rule to govern by, which is against the nature of a rule – which is and ought to be certain.

Lastly, by making the common law only to be the foundation, Magna Carta is excluded from being a fundamental law, and also all other statutes from being limitations to monarchy, since the fundamental laws only are to be judge.

Truly the conscience of all mankind is a pretty large tribunal for the fundamental laws to pronounce sentence in. It is very much that laws – which in their own nature are dumb and always need a judge to pronounce sentence – should now be able to speak and pronounce sentence themselves. Such a sentence surely must be upon the hearing of one party only, for it is impossible for a monarch to make his defence and answer, and produce his witnesses in every man's conscience, in each man's cause who will but question the legality of the monarch's government. Certainly the sentence cannot but be unjust, where but one man's tale is heard. For all this, the conclusion is, every man must oppose or not oppose the monarch according to his own conscience. Thus at the last, every man is brought by this doctrine of our author's to be his own judge. And I also appeal to the consciences of all mankind, whether the end of this be not utter confusion and anarchy.

Yet after all this, the author saith this power of every man's judging the illegal acts of the monarch 'argues not a superiority of those who judge over him who is judged' ([Hunton] p. 18). And he gives *us a*[309] profound reason for it: his words are 'it is not *authoritative*[310] and civil, but moral, residing in reasonable creatures, and lawful for them to execute' [Hunton p. 18]. What our author means by these words 'not authoritative and civil, but moral' perhaps I understand not, though I think I do. Yet it serves my turn that he saith that 'resistance ought to be made, and every man must oppose or not oppose, according as in conscience he can acquit or condemn the acts of his governor' [Hunton p. 18]. For if it enable a man to resist and oppose his governor, without question it *is* authoritative and civil. Whereas he adds that 'moral judgment is residing in reasonable creatures, and lawful for them to execute', he seems to imply that authoritative and civil judgment doth not reside in reasonable creatures, nor can be lawfully executed. Such a conclusion fits well with anarchy, for he that takes away all government and leaves every man to his own conscience, and so makes him an independent in state, may well teach that authority resides not in reasonable creatures, nor can be lawfully executed.

I pass from his absolute and limited monarchy to his division or partition (for he allows no division) of monarchy into simple and mixed, viz. of a monarch, the nobility and community.

Where first, observe a doubt of our author's whether a 'firm union can be in a mixture of equality'. He rather thinks there must be a 'priority of order in one of the three or else there can be no unity' ([Hunton] p. 25). He must know that priority of order doth not hinder but that there may be an equality of mixture if the shares be equal, for he that hath the first share may have no more than the others. So that if he will have an inequality of mixture, a primity*[f]* of share will not serve the turn. The first share must be greater or better than the others, or else they will be equal, and then he cannot call it a mixed monarchy, where only a primity*[g]* of share in the supreme

---

[f] [priority].   *[g]* [priority].

power is in one. But by his own confession he may better call it a mixed aristocracy or mixed democracy than a mixed monarchy, since he tells us the Houses of parliament 'sure have two parts of the greatest legislative authority' ([Hunton] p. 56); and if the king have but a third part, sure their shares are equal.

The first step our author makes is this: 'the sovereign power must be originally in all three'. Next he finds that if there be an equality of shares in three estates, there can be no ground to denominate a monarch, and then his mixed monarch might be thought but an empty title [Hunton p. 25]. Therefore in the third place he resolves us that to salve all 'a power must be sought out wherewith the monarch must be invested, which is not so great as to destroy the mixture, nor so titular as to destroy the monarchy' ([Hunton] p. 25[–6]). And therefore he conceives it may be in these particulars:

First, a monarch in a mixed monarchy may be said to be a monarch, as he conceives, 'if he be the head and fountain of the power which governs and executes the established laws' ([Hunton] p. 26). That is, a man may be a monarch though he do but give power to others to govern and execute the established laws. Thus he brings his monarch one step or peg lower still than he was before. At first he made us believe his monarch should have the supreme power, which is the legislative. Then he falls from that, and tells us a limited monarch must govern according to law only. Thus he is brought from the legislative to the gubernative or executive power only. Nor doth he stay here, but is taken a hole lower, for now he must not govern but he must constitute officers to govern by laws [Hunton p. 26]. If choosing officers to govern be governing, then our author will allow his monarch to be a governor, not else. And therefore he that divided supreme power into legislative and gubernative, doth now divide it into legislative, and power of constituting officers for governing by laws – and this, he saith, is left to the monarch. Indeed you have left him a fair portion of power. But are we sure he may enjoy this? It seems our author is not confident in this neither, and some others do deny it him. Our author speaking of the government of this kingdom, saith the choice of the officers is entrusted to the judgment of the monarch 'for ought I know' ([Hunton] p. 38). He is not resolute in the point, but for ought he knows, and for ought I know, his monarch is but titular – an empty title, certain of no power at all.

The power of choosing officers only is the basest of all powers. Aristotle, as I remember, saith the common people are fit for nothing but 'to choose officers and to take accounts' [1281^{b}32–3]. And indeed, in all popular governments the multitude perform this work, and this work in a king puts him below all his subjects and makes him the only subject in a kingdom, or the only man that cannot govern. There is not the poorest man of the multitude but is capable of some office or other, and by that means may some time or other perhaps govern according to the laws. Only the king can be no officer, but to choose officers; his subjects may all govern, but he may not.

Next I cannot see how in true sense our author can say his monarch is 'the head and fountain of power' [Hunton p. 26], since his doctrine is that in a limited monarchy 'the public society by original constitution confer on one man power' [Hunton p. 13]. Is not then the public society the head and fountain of power, and not the king?

Again, when he tells us of his monarch that 'both the other states, as well *conjunctim* [jointly] as *divisim* [individually] be his sworn subjects and own obedience to his commands' [Hunton p. 26], he doth but flout his poor monarch. For why are they called his subjects and his commons? He (without any compliment) is their subject. For they, as officers, may govern and command according to law, but he may not, for he must judge by his judges in courts of justice only – that is, he may not judge or govern at all.

2. As for the second particular, the 'sole or chief power in capacitating persons' for the supreme power [Hunton p. 26], and

3. As to this the third particular, the power of 'convocating' such persons [Hunton p. 26], they are both so far from making a monarch that they are the only way to make him none, by choosing and calling others to share in the supreme power.

4. Lastly, concerning his authority being 'the last and greatest' in the establishing every act, it makes him no monarch except he be sole that hath that authority. Neither his primity^h of share in the supreme power, nor his authority being last, no, nor his having the greatest authority, doth make him a monarch unless he have that authority *alone*.

Besides, how can he show that in his mixed monarchy the monarch's power is the greatest? The greatest share that our author allows him

^{h} [priority].

156

in the legislative power is a negative voice, and the like is allowed
to the nobility and commons. And truly, a negative voice is but a base
term to express a legislative power. A negative voice is but a privative
power, or indeed no power at all to do anything, only a power to
hinder an act from being done.

Wherefore I conclude, not any of his four nor all of them put
into one person makes the state monarchical ([Hunton] p. 26).

This mixed monarchy, just like the limited, ends in confusion and
destruction of all government. You shall hear the author's confession

> That one inconvenience must necessarily be in all mixed govern-
> ments, which I showed to be in limited governments: there can
> be no constituted legal authoritative judge of the fundamental
> controversies arising between the three estates. If such do rise,
> it is the fatal disease of those governments, for which no salve
> can be applied. It is a case beyond the possible provision of such
> a government; of this question there is no legal judge. The
> accusing side must make it evident to every man's conscience
> ... The appeal must be to the community, as if there were no
> government; and as by evidence consciences are convinced, they
> are bound to give their assistance. ([Hunton] p. 28[-9])

The wit of man cannot say more for anarchy.

Thus have I picked out the flowers out of his doctrine about limited
monarchy, and presented them with some brief annotations. It were
a tedious work to collect all the learned contradictions, and ambiguous
expressions that *occur*[311] in every page of his platonic monarchy.
The book hath so much of fancy that it is a better piece of poetry
than policy.

Because many may think that the main doctrine of limited and
mixed monarchy may in itself be most authentical, and grounded
upon strong and evident reason, although our author perhaps have
failed in some of his expressions and be liable to exceptions, therefore
I will be bold to enquire whether Aristotle could find either reason
or example of a limited or mixed monarchy – and the rather, because
I find our author altogether insists upon a rational way of justifying
his opinion. No man I think will deny, but that Aristotle was sufficiently curious in searching out the several forms of commonwealths
and kingdoms. Yet I do not find that he ever so much as dreamed
of either a limited or mixed monarchy. Several other sorts of

monarchies he reckons up. In the third book of his *Politics* he spends three whole chapters together, upon the several kinds of monarchy. First, in his fourteenth chapter he mentions four kinds of monarchy:

The Laconic or Lacedaemonian[i]
The barbaric
The Aesymnetical
The heroic

The Laconic or Lacedaemonian king, saith he, had only supreme power when he was out of the bounds of the Lacedaemonian territories. Then he had absolute power, his kingdom was like to a perpetual lord general of an army [1285ª2–7].

The barbaric king (saith Aristotle) had a power very near to tyranny. Yet they were lawful and paternal, because the barbarians are of a more servile nature than the Grecians, and the Asiatics than the Europeans. They do willingly, without repining, live under a masterly government. Yet their government is stable and safe because they are paternal and lawful kingdoms, and their guards are royal and not tyrannical. For kings are guarded by their own subjects, and tyrants are guarded by strangers. [1285ª18–27]

'The Aesymnetical king', saith Aristotle, 'in old time in Greece was an elective tyrant, and differed only from the barbarian kings in that he was elective and not paternal' [1285ª31–3]. 'These sorts of kings, because they were tyrannical, were masterly. But because they were over such as voluntarily elected them, they were regal' [1285ᵇ2–3].

The heroic were those (saith Aristotle) which flourished in the heroical times, to whom the people did willingly obey; and they were paternal and lawful because these kings did deserve well of the multitude, either by teaching them arts, or by warring for them, or by gathering them together when they were dispersed, or by dividing lands amongst them. These kings had supreme power in war, in sacrifices, in judicature. [1285ᵇ4–11]

These four sorts of monarchy hath Aristotle thus distinguished, and after sums them up together, and concludes his chapter as if he had forgot himself, and reckons up a fifth kind of monarchy – which is, saith he, 'when one alone hath supreme power of all the

---

[i] [Spartan].

158

rest; for as there is a domestical kingdom of one house, so the kingdom of a city, or of one or many nations, is a family' [1285^b29–33].

These are all the sorts of monarchy that Aristotle hath found out, and he hath strained hard to make them so many. First, for his Lacedaemonian king, himself confesseth that he was but a kind of military commander in war, and so in effect no more a king than all generals of armies; and yet this no-king of his was not limited by any law nor mixed with any companions of his government. When he was in the wars out of the confines of Lacedaemon, he was, as Aristotle styles him 'Αυτοκράτωρ – 'of full and absolute command' [1285^a7], no law, no companion to govern his army but his own will.

Next, for Aristotle's Aesymnetical king, it appears he was out of date in Aristotle's time. For he saith he was 'amongst the ancient Greeks',* [1285^a30]. Aristotle might well have spared the naming him (if he had not wanted other sorts) for the honour of his own nation. For he that but now told us the barbarians were of a more servile nature than the Grecians, comes here and tells us that these old Greek kings were elective tyrants. The barbarians did but suffer tyrants in show but the old Grecians chose tyrants indeed; which then must we think were the greater slaves, the Greeks or the barbarians? Now if these sorts of kings were tyrants, we cannot suppose they were limited either by law, or joined with companions. Indeed, Aristotle saith some of these tyrants were limited to certain times and actions, for they had not all their power for term of life, nor could meddle but in certain businesses. Yet during the time they were tyrants, and in the actions whereto they were limited, they had absolute power to do what they list according to their own will, or else they could not have been said to be tyrants.

As for Aristotle's heroic king, he gives the like note upon him that he did upon the Aesymnet, that he was in old time: 'in the heroic times'† [1285^b4–5]. The thing that made these heroical kingdoms differ from other sorts of kingdoms was only the means by which the first kings obtained their kingdoms, and not the manner of government. For in that they were as absolute as other kings were, without either limitation by law, or mixture of companions.

Lastly, as for Aristotle's barbaric sort of kings, since he reckoned

---

* 'ἐν τοις ἀρχαίοις Ἕλλησιν'.   † 'κατὰ τοὺς ἡρωικοὺς χρόνους'.

all the world barbarians except the Grecians, his barbaric king must extend to all other sorts of kings in the world, besides those of Greece, and so may go under Aristotle's fifth sort of kings, which in general comprehends all other sorts, and is no special form of monarchy. Thus upon a true account it is evident that the five several sorts of kings mentioned by Aristotle are at the most but different and accidental means of the first obtaining or holding of monarchies, and not real or essential differences of the manner of government, which was always absolute, without either limitation or mixture.

I may be thought perhaps to mistake or wrong Aristotle in questioning his diversities of kings. But it seems Aristotle himself was partly of the same mind. For in the very next chapter, when he had better considered of the point, he confessed, that to speak the truth, 'there were almost but two sorts of monarchies worth the considering' [1285ᵇ34–5], that is, his first or Laconic sort, and his fifth or last sort, where one alone hath supreme power over all the rest. Thus he hath brought his five sorts to two. Now for the first of these two, his Lacedaemonian king, he hath confessed before that 'he was no more than a generalissimo' [1285ᵃ7] of an army, and so upon the matter no king at all; and then there remains only his last sort of kings, 'where one alone hath the supreme power' [1285ᵇ29–30]. And this in substance is the final resolution of Aristotle himself. For in his sixteenth chapter, where he delivers his last thoughts touching the kinds of monarchy, he first dischargeth his Laconic king from being any sort of *[monarch]*³¹² and then gives us two exact rules about monarchy, and both these are point blank against limited and mixed monarchy. Therefore I shall propose them to be considered of, as concluding all monarchy to be absolute and arbitrary:

1. The one rule is that 'he that is said to be a king according to law is no sort of government or kingdom at all'* (Aristotle, *Politics*, book 3, chapter 16 [1287ᵃ3–4]).

2. The second rule is that a true king 'is he that ruleth all according to his own will'† [1287ᵃ1].

This latter frees a monarch from the mixture of partners or sharers in government, as the former rule doth from limitation by laws.

Thus in brief I have traced Aristotle in his crabbed and broken

---

* "Ὁ κατὰ νόμον βασιλεὺς οὐκ ἔστιν εἶδος πολιτείας".
† 'κατὰ τὴν αὐτοῦ βούλησιν'.

passages touching diversities of kings. Where first he finds but four sorts, and then he stumbles upon a fifth, and in the next chapter contents himself only with two sorts of kings, but in the chapter following concludes with one – which is the true perfect monarch who rules all by his own will. In all this we find nothing for a regulated or mixed monarchy, but against it.

Moreover, whereas the author of the *Treatise of Monarchy* affirms it as a prime principle that all monarchies (except that of the Jews) depend upon human designment, when the consent of a society of men, and a fundamental contract of a nation, by original or radical constitution confers power, he must know that Aristotle – searching into the original of government – shows himself in this point a better divine than our author, and as if he had studied the book of Genesis, teacheth that monarchies fetch their pedigree from the right of fathers and not from the gift or contract of people. His words may thus be Englished: 'At the first, cities were governed by kings, and so even to this day are nations also. For such as were under kingly government did come together, for every house is governed by a king, who is the eldest; and so also colonies are governed for kindred sake'. And immediately before, he tells us that the 'first society made of many houses is a village, which naturally seems to be a colony of a house, which some call foster-brethren, or children and children's children' [1252^{b}15–21].

So in conclusion we have gained Aristotle's judgment in three main and essential points:

1   A king according to law makes no kind of government.

2   A king must rule according to his own will.

3   The original of kings is from the right of fatherhood.

What Aristotle's judgment was two thousand years since, is agreeable to the doctrine of the great modern politician Bodin. Hear him touching limited monarchy:

> Unto majesty or sovereignty (saith he) belongeth an absolute power, not subject to any law ... chief power given unto a prince with condition, is not properly sovereignty, or power absolute, except such conditions annexed to the sovereignty be directly comprehended within the laws of God and nature ... Albeit by the sufferance of the king of England, controversies between the king and his people are sometimes determined by the high

court of parliament, and sometimes by the lord chief justice of England; yet all the estates remain in full subjection to the king, who is no ways bound to follow their advice, neither to consent to their requests ... It is certain that the laws, privileges, and grants of princes, have no force but during their life, if they be not ratified by the express consent, or by sufferance of the prince following, especially privileges ... Much less should a prince be bound unto the laws he maketh himself; for a [p. '73'=91] man may well receive a law from another man, but impossible it is in nature for to give a law unto himself, no more than it is to command a man's self in a matter depending of his own will. The law saith, '*Nulla obligatio consistere potest, quae a voluntate promittentis statum capit*' [there can be no obligation which arises from the will of the promisor] [p. 92]. The sovereign prince may derogate unto the laws that he hath promised and sworn to keep, if the equity thereof be ceased; and that of himself, without the consent of his subjects [p. 93] ... The majesty of a true sovereign prince is to be known when the estates of all the people assembled, in all humility present their requests and supplications to their prince, without having power in anything to command, determine, or give voice, but that that which it pleaseth the king to like or dislike, to command or [for]bid, is holden for law; wherein they which have written of the duty of magistrates have deceived themselves, in maintaining that the power of the people is greater than the prince; a thing which causeth oft true subjects to revolt from their obedience to their prince, and ministereth matter of great troubles in commonwealths; of which their opinion, there is neither reason nor ground. For if the king be subject unto the assemblies and decrees of the people, he should neither be king nor sovereign, and the commonwealth neither realm nor monarchy, but a mere aristocracy [p. 95] ... So we see the principal point of sovereign majesty and absolute power, to consist principally in giving laws unto the subjects in general without their consent [p. 98]. (Bodin *De Republica*, book I, chapter 8)

To confound the state of monarchy with the popular or aristocratical estate is a thing impossible, and in effect incompatible, and such as cannot be imagined. For sovereignty being of itself indivisible, how can it at one and the same time be divided betwixt one prince, the nobility and the people in common? The first mark of sovereign majesty is to be of power to give laws, and to command over them unto the subjects; and who should those subjects be that should yield their obedience to the law, if they should have also power to make the laws? Who should he be that could give the law, being himself constrained to receive it of them unto whom himself gave it? So that of necessity we must conclude that as no one in particular hath the power to make the law in such a state, that then the state must needs be a state popular [p. 185] ... Never any commonwealth hath been made of an aristocracy and popular estate, much less of the three estates of a commonweal [p. 193] ... Such states wherein the rights of sovereignty are divided are not rightly to be called commonweals, but rather the corruption of commonweals, as Herodotus has most briefly but truly written [p. 194] ... Commonweals which change their state, the sovereign right and power of them being divided, find no rest from civil wars and broils till they again recover some one of the three forms, and the sovereignty be wholly in one of the states or other. [Bodin pp. 194–5]

'Where the rights of the sovereignty are divided betwixt the prince and his subjects, in that confusion of state there is still endless stirs and quarrels for the superiority, until that some one, some few, or all together, have got the sovereignty': *idem*, book 2, chapter 1 [p. 194].

This judgment of Bodin's touching limited and mixed monarchy is not according to the mind of our author, nor yet of the Observator,[j] who useth the strength of his wit to overthrow absolute and arbitrary government in this kingdom, and yet in the main body of his discourse lets fall such truths from his pen as give a deadly wound to the cause he pleads for, if they be indifferently weighed and considered. I will not pick a line or two here and there to wrest against him, but will present a whole page of his book, or more together, that so we may have an entire prospect upon the Observator's mind:

> Without society (saith the Observator) men could not live, without laws men could not be sociable, and without authority somewhere to judge according to law, law was vain. It was soon therefore provided that laws according to the dictate of reason should be ratified by common consent. When it afterward appeared that man was yet subject to unnatural destruction by the tyranny of entrusted magistrates – a mischief almost as fatal as to be without all magistracy – how to provide a wholesome remedy therefore, was not so easy to be invented. It was not difficult to invent laws for the limiting of supreme governors. But to invent how those

---

[j] [i.e. Henry Parker].

laws should be executed, or by whom interpreted, was almost impossible, *'nam quis custodiet ipsos custodes?'* ['for who shall guard the guards themselves?': Juvenal, *Satires* vi, 347]. To place a superior above a supreme was held unnatural. Yet what a lifeless thing would law be without any judge to determine and force it? If it be agreed upon, that limits should be prefixed to princes, and judges to decree according to those limits, yet another inconvenience will presently affront us. For we cannot restrain princes too far, but we shall disable them from some good ... Long it was ere the world could extricate itself out of all these extremities, or find out an orderly means whereby to avoid the danger of unbounded prerogative on this hand, and *[of]*[313] excessive liberty on the other, and scarce has long experience yet fully satisfied the minds of all men in it. In the infancy of the world, when man was not so artificial and obdurate in cruelty and oppression as now, and policy most rude, most nations did choose rather to subject themselves to the mere discretion of their lords than rely upon any limits; and *to*[314] be ruled by arbitrary edicts, than written statutes. But since tyranny being more exquisite, and policy more perfect, especially where learning and religion flourish, few nations will endure the thraldom which usually accompanies unbounded and unconditionate royalty. Yet long it was ere the bounds and conditions of supreme lords *were*[315] so wisely determined, or quietly conserved as now they are. For at first, when as *ephori*,[316] *tribuni, curatores*, etc., were erected to poise against the *scale*[317] of sovereignty, much blood was shed about them, and states were put into new broils by them, and some places the remedy proved worse than the disease. In all great distresses, the body of the people *was*[318] ever constrained to rise, and by force of the major party to put an end to all intestine strifes, and make a redress of all public grievances. But many times calamities grew to a strange height, before so cumbersome a body could be raised; and when it was raised, the motions of it were so distracted and irregular that after much spoil and effusion of blood, sometimes only one tyranny was exchanged for another. Till some *way was*[319] invented to regulate the motions of the people's moliminous[k] body, I think arbitrary rule was most safe for the world. But now since most countries have found ... an art and peaceable order for public assemblies, whereby the people may assume its own power to do itself right, without disturbance to itself or injury to princes, he is very unjust

[k] [massive, cumbrous].

that will oppose this art or order. That princes may not be now beyond all limits and laws, nor yet be ... tied upon those limits by any private parties, the whole community in its underived majesty shall convene to do justice. And that the convention may not be without intelligence, certain times and places and forms shall be appointed for its reglement.*¹* And that the vastness of its own bulk may not breed confusion, by virtue of election and representation a few shall act for many, the wise shall consent for the simple, the virtue of all shall redound to some, and the prudence of some shall redound to all. And surely as this admirably composed court, which is now called a parliament, is more regularly and orderly formed than when it was called mickle*ᵐ* synod *or**³²⁰ witenagemot, or when this real body of the people did throng together at it; so it is not yet perhaps without some defects, which by art and policy might receive further amendment. Some divisions have ... sprung up of late between both Houses, and some between the king and both Houses by reason of uncertainty of jurisdiction, and some lawyers doubt how far the parliament is able to create new forms and precedents, and has a jurisdiction over itself. All these doubts would be solemnly solved. But in the first place, the true privileges of parliament belonging not only to the being and efficacy of it, but to the honour and compliment of it, would be clearly declared. For the very naming of privileges of parliament, as if they were chimeras to the ignorant sort, and utterly unknown unto the learned, hath been entertained with scorn since the beginning of this parliament. [Parker pp. 13–15]

In this large passage taken out of the Observator which concerns the original of all government, two notable propositions may be principally observed.

First, our Observator confesseth arbitrary or absolute government to be the first and the safest government for the world.

Secondly, he acknowledgeth that the jurisdiction is uncertain, and the privileges not clearly declared of limited monarchy.

These two evident truths delivered by him, he labours mainly to disguise. He seems to insinuate that arbitrary government was but in the infancy of the world, for so he terms it. But if we enquire of him how long he will have this infancy of the world to last, he grants it continued above three thousand years, which is an unreason-

---

¹ [for its reglement: in order to regulate it].   *ᵐ* [great].

able time for the world to continue under age. For the first opposers he doth find of arbitrary power were the *ephori, tribuni, curatores,* etc. The *ephori* were above three thousand years after the creation, and the *tribuni* were later. As for his *curatores,* I know not whom he means, except the master of the court of wards. I cannot English the word *curator* better. I do not believe that he can show that any *curatores* or etceteras which he mentions were so ancient as the *ephori.* As for the *tribuni,* he mistakes much if he thinks they were erected to limit and bound monarchy. For the state of Rome was at the least aristocratical (as they call it) if not popular, when tribunes of the people were first hatched. And for the *ephori,* their power did not limit or regulate monarchy but quite take it away. For a 'Lacedaemonian king' in the judgment of Aristotle 'was no king indeed, but in name only, as generalissimo of an army' [1285ᵃ7]; and the best politicians reckon the Spartan commonwealth to have been aristocratical and not monarchical. And if a limited monarchy cannot be found in Lacedaemon, I doubt our Observator will hardly find it anywhere else in the whole world – and in substance he confesseth as much, when he saith '*now* most countries have found out an art and peaceable order for public assemblies' [Parker pp. 14–15], as if it were a thing but new done, and not before, for so the word *now* doth import.

The Observator in confessing the jurisdiction to be uncertain, and the privileges undetermined of that court that should bound and limit monarchy [Parker p. 15] doth in effect acknowledge there is no such court at all. For every court consists of jurisdictions and privileges; it is these two that create a court, and are the essentials of it. If the 'admirably composed court' of parliament have some defects which may receive amendment, as he saith, and if those defects be such as cause divisions both between the Houses, and between the king and both Houses, and these divisions be about so main a matter as jurisdictions and privileges, and power to create new privileges [Parker p. 15], all which are the fundamentals of every court (for until they be agreed upon, the act of every court may not only be uncertain, but invalid, and cause of tumults and sedition); and if 'all these doubts' and divisions have need to be 'solemnly solved', as our Observator confesseth [Parker p. 15], then he hath no reason at all to say that now the conditions of supreme lords are 'wisely determined and quietly conserved' [Parker p. 14], or that now 'most countries have found out an art and peaceable order for public affairs, whereby the people may resume its own power to do itself right without injury unto princes' [Parker 14–15]. For how can the 'underived majesty' of the people by assuming its own power, tell how to do herself right, or how to avoid doing injury to the prince, if her jurisdiction be uncertain, and privileges undetermined?

He tells us '*now* most countries have found an art and peaceable order for public assemblies' [Parker p. 14], and to the intent 'that princes may not be *now* beyond all limits and laws the whole community in *its*[321] underived majesty shall convene to do justice' [Parker p. 15]. But he doth not name so much as one country or kingdom that hath found out this art, where the whole community in its underived majesty did ever convene to do justice. I challenge him, or any other for him, to name but one kingdom that hath either *now* or heretofore found out this art or peaceable order. We do hear a great rumour in this age of moderated and limited kings. Poland, Sweden and Denmark are talked of for such, and in these kingdoms or nowhere is such a moderated government, as our Observator means, to be found. A little enquiry would be made into the manner of the government of these kingdoms. For these northern people, as Bodin observeth, breathe after liberty [Bodin p. 563].

First for Poland, Boterus saith that,

> the government of it is elective altogether, and representeth rather an aristocracy than a kingdom. The nobility, who have great authority in the diets, choosing the king and limiting his authority, making his sovereignty but a slavish royalty. These diminutions of regality began first by default of King Lewis, and Jagello, who to gain the succession in the kingdom contrary to the laws, one for his daughter, and the other for his son, departed with many of his royalties and prerogatives, to buy the voices of the nobility. [Botero pp. 412–13]

The French author of the book called *The Estates of the World* doth inform us that

> the prince's authority was more free, not being subject to any laws, and having absolute power not only of their estates but also of life and death. Since Christian religion was received, it began to be moderated, first by holy admonitions of the bishops and clergy, and then by services of the nobility in war. Religious princes gave many honours and many liberties to the clergy and nobility, and quit much of their rights, the which their successors

have continued ... The superior dignity is reduced to two degrees, that is, the palatinate and chastelleine, for that kings in former times did by little and little call these men to public consultations, notwithstanding that they had absolute power to do all things of themselves – to command, dispose, recompense and punish, of their own motions. Since they have ordained that these dignities should make the body of a senate [D'Avity pp. 641, 643].

the king doth not challenge much right and power over his nobility, nor over their estates, neither hath he any over the clergy.

And though the king's authority depends on the nobility for his election, yet in many things it is absolute after he is chosen. He appoints the diets at what time and place he pleaseth. He chooseth lay-councillors, and nominates the bishops, and whom he will have to be his privy council. He is absolute disposer of the revenues of the crown. He is absolute establisher of the decrees of the diets. It is in his power to advance and reward whom he pleaseth. [Botero pp. 414–15]

He is lord immediate of his subjects, but not of his nobility:

He is sovereign judge of his nobility in criminal causes [p. 642]. The power of the nobility daily increaseth, for that in respect of the king's election, they neither have law, rule, nor form to do it, neither by writing nor tradition [pp. 641–2]. As the king governs his subjects, which are immediately his, with absolute authority; so the nobility dispose immediately of their vassals, over whom every one hath more than a regal power, so as they entreat them like slaves. [D'Avity p. 643]

There be certain men in Poland who are called 'earthly messengers or *nuntios*' [D'Avity p. 644]. They are as it were agents of jurisdictions or circles of the nobility. These have a certain authority, and, as Boterus saith,

in the time of their diets these men assemble in a place near to the senate house, where they choose two marshals, by whom (but with a tribune-like authority) they signify unto the council what their requests are. Not long since, their authority and reputation grew so mightily that they now carry themselves as heads and governors rather than officers and ministers of the public decrees of the state. One of the council refused his senator's place to become one of these officers. [Botero p. 414]

Every palatine, the king requiring it, calls together all the nobility of his palatinate, where having propounded unto them the matters whereon they are to treat, and their will being known, they choose four or six out of the company of the earthly messengers. These deputies meet and make one body, which they call the order of knights [D'Avity pp. 643–4].

This being of late years the manner and order of the government of Poland, it is not possible for the Observator to find among them that the 'whole community in its underived majesty' doth ever 'convene to do justice', nor any election or representation of the community, or that the people assume its own power to do itself right. The earthly messengers, though they may be thought to represent the commons, and of late take much upon them, yet they are elected and chosen by the nobility, as their agents and officers. The community are either vassals to the king, or to the nobility, and enjoy as little freedom or liberty as any nation. But it may be said, perhaps, that though the community do not limit the king, yet the nobility do, and so he is a limited *[monarch]*.[322] The answer is that in truth, though the nobility at the choosing of their king do limit his power and do give him an oath, yet afterwards they have always a desire to please him and to second his will, and this they are forced to do to avoid discord. For by reason of their great power they are subject to great dissensions not only among themselves but between them and the order of knights, which are the earthly messengers. Yea, the provinces are at discord one with another, and as for religion, the diversity of sects in Poland *[breeds]*[323] perpetual jars and hatred among the people, there being as many sects as in Amsterdam itself, or any popular government can desire. The danger of sedition is the cause that though the crown depends on the election of the nobility, yet they have never rejected the king's successor or transferred the realm to any other family but once, when deposing Ladislaus for his idleness (whom yet afterward they restored) they elected Wenceslaus king of Bohemia. But if the nobility do agree to hold their king to his conditions, which is, not to conclude anything but by the advice of his council of nobles, nor to choose any wife without their leaves, then it must be said to be a commonweal, not a royalty; and the king but only the mouth of the kingdom, or, as Queen Christina complained, that 'her husband was but the shadow of a sovereign' [Botero p. 413].

Next, if it be considered how the nobility of Poland came to this great power, it was not by any original contract or popular convention. For it is said they have neither law, rule nor form written or unwritten for the election of their king. They may thank the bishops and clergy, for by their holy admonitions and advice, good and religious princes to show their piety were first brought to give much of their rights and privileges to their subjects, devout kings were merely cheated of some of their royalties. What power soever general assemblies of the estates claim or exercise over and above the bare naked act of counselling, they were first beholding to the popish clergy for it. It is they first brought parliaments into request and power. I cannot find in any kingdom, but only where popery hath been, that parliaments have been of reputation, and in the greatest times of superstition they are first mentioned.

As for the kingdom of Denmark, I read that the senators, who are all chosen out of the nobility, and seldom exceed the number of twenty-eight, with the chief of the realm do choose their king. They have always in a manner set the king's eldest son upon the royal throne. 'The nobility of Denmark withstood the coronation of Frederick, 1559, till he swore not to put any nobleman to death until he were judged of the senate; and that all noblemen should have power of life and death over their subjects without appeal; and the king to give no office without consent of the council' [Bodin p. 100]. There is a chancellor of the realm, before whom they do appeal from all the provinces and islands, and from him to the king himself. I hear of nothing in this kingdom that tends to popularity – no assembly of the commons, no elections or representation of them.

Sweden is governed by a king heretofore elective, but now made hereditary in Gustavus' time. It is divided into provinces. An appeal lieth from the viscount of every territory to a sovereign judge called a lamen; from the lamens to the king's council; and from this council to the king himself.

Now let the Observator bethink himself, whether all or any of these three countries have found out any art at all whereby the people or community may assume its own power. If neither of these kingdoms have, most countries have not, nay none have. The people or community in these three realms are as absolute vassals as any in the world. The regulating power, if any be, is in the nobility, nor is it such in the nobility as it makes show for. The election of kings is rather a formality than any real power. For they dare hardly choose any but the heir, or one of the blood royal. If they should choose one among the nobility it would prove very factious; if a stranger, odious; neither safe. For the government, though the kings be sworn to reign according to the laws, and are not to do anything without the consent of their council in public affairs, yet in regard they have power both to advance and reward whom they please, the nobility and senators do comply with their kings. And Boterus concludes of the kings of Poland, who seem to be most moderated, that 'such as is their valour, dexterity and wisdom, such is their power, authority and government' [Botero p. 415]. Also Bodin saith, that these three kingdoms 'are states changeable and uncertain, as the nobility is stronger than the prince, or the prince than the nobility' [Bodin p. 166]; and the people are so far from liberty, that he saith divers particular lords exact not only customs, but tributes also, which are confirmed and grow stronger both by long prescription of time and use of judgments.

*THE[n]
NECESSITY
OF
The Absolute Power of all KINGS:
And in particular,
OF THE *KING*
OF
ENGLAND*[324]

The Necessity of the Absolute Power of all Kings: and in particular, of the King of England.[325]

[n] [A manuscript of some of this document is in B. L. Harleian 6867, ff.253a–4b; it contains several passages which have been deleted or marked for deletion. All of these passages have indeed been omitted from the printed text – suggesting that the printed version is based either on this manuscript or on a copy of it. One sentence which was *not* deleted in the manuscript was omitted in the printed versions. The manuscript runs from the beginning of the work to p. 174 – 'and reasonable conventions'; resumes at p. 177 – 'as the infinite variety'; and finally ends on p. 179 – 'could be spoke'. In the notes to the text below, BMS is the manuscript; 48B is the bookseller George Thomason's copy of the first printed edition (Wing F917), published in 1648; and 80B is the edition published as *The Power of Kings: and in particular of the King of England*, 1680 (Wing F926). The notes record material differences between these texts. The title-page of some copies of the 1648 edition attributes the work to 'John Bodin, a Protestant according to the church of Geneva', and the manuscript makes a similar attribution. Jean Bodin was not a Protestant, but he was the author of this work, which consists entirely of quotations from Richard Knolles' 1606 translation of Bodin's *Les Six Livres de la Republique*. The manuscript quotes far more accurately from Knolles' text than either of the printed editions, and where it exists it has been used as copy-text. Elsewhere, the text is based on whichever of the two printed editions is closer to Knolles' original – and this is usually the 1648 edition. 80B is the least satisfactory of the three texts, though it was followed in later editions of Filmer's works. It contains an anonymous preface which gives a list of Filmer's works – including *The Free-holders Grand Inquest*. The extracts from Bodin are all taken from the following sections of Knolles' translation: pp. 88–106 (book 1, chapter 8); pp. 185–194 (book 2, chapter 1); pp. 222–5 (book 2, chapter 5); p. 717 (book 6, chapter 4)].

To majesty or sovereignty belongeth an absolute power not subject to any law. [Bodin p. 88][a]

It behoveth him that is a sovereign, not to be in any sort subject to the command of another;[p] whose office *it is*[326] to give laws unto his subjects, to abrogate laws unprofitable, and in their stead to establish other; which he cannot do, that is himself subject *unto*[327] laws, or to others which have command over him: and *that is it for*[328] which the law saith, that the prince is acquitted from the power of the laws. [Bodin p. '73'=91][q]

The laws, ordinances, letters patents, privileges and grants of princes, have no force but during their life; if they be not ratified by the express consent, or at least by sufferance of the prince following, who had knowledge thereof. [Bodin p. '73'=91–2]

If the sovereign prince be exempted from the laws of his predecessors, much less *should*[329] he be bound unto the laws he maketh himself; for a man may well receive a law from another man, but impossible it is in nature for to give a law unto himself, no more than it is to command a man's self in a matter depending of his own will: 'There can be no obligation which taketh state from the mere will of him that promiseth the same'; which is a necessary reason to prove evidently, that a *king or sovereign prince cannot be subject to his own laws; a sovereign prince*[330] cannot bind his own hands, albeit that he would: we see also in the end of all laws these words, 'Because it hath so pleased us': *'quia sic nobis placuit'*[331] to give us to understand, that the laws of a sovereign prince, although they be grounded upon reason, *depend nevertheless*[332] upon nothing but his mere and frank good will. But as for the laws of *God and nature*[333], all princes and people are unto them subject; neither is it in their power to impugn them, if they will not be guilty of high treason *to the divine majesty, making war against God*[334], under the greatness of whom all monarchs of the world ought *to bear the yoke and to*[335] bow their heads in all fear and reverence. [Bodin p. '73'=91–2]

Question[336] may be, whether a prince *be a*[337] subject to the laws

---

[a] [In BMS the following passage has been deleted here; 'The chief power given unto a prince with charge and upon condition is not properly sovereignty nor power absolute, except such condition annexed to the sovereignty be comprehended within the laws of God or nature' [Bodin p. 89]].

[p] [In BMS the following passage has been deleted here: 'which thing Tiberius wisely meaning in these words, reasoned in the senate concerning the right of sovereignty, saying, that "the reason of his doings were no otherwise to be manifested than in that it was to be given to none"' [Bodin p. '73' = 91]].

[q] [In BMS the following passage is deleted here: 'and this word, the "law" in the Latin importeth the commandment of him which hath the sovereignty.
It is certain that' [Bodin p. '73' = 91].

of his country that he hath sworn to keep, or not? If a sovereign prince promise by oath to his subjects to keep the laws, he is bound to keep them; not for that *the*³³⁸ prince is bound to *his laws*,³³⁹ or by his predecessors, but *to*³⁴⁰ the just conventions and promises which he hath *made*,³⁴¹ be it by oath, or without any oath at all, as should a private man be: and for the same causes that a private man may be relieved from his unjust and unreasonable promise, as for that it was *to[o]*³⁴² grievous, or for that he was by deceit or fraud circumvented, or induced *thereinto*³⁴³ by error, or force, or just fear, or by some great hurt. Even for the same causes the prince may be restored in that which toucheth the diminishing of his majesty, and so our maxim resteth, 'that the prince is not subject to his laws, nor to the laws of his predecessors, but well to his own just and reasonable conventions'.ʳ [Bodin p. 92]

The sovereign prince may derogate *unto*³⁴⁴ the laws that he hath promised and sworn to keep, if the equity thereof cease, and that of himself, without consent of his subjects; which his subjects cannot do among themselves, if they be not by the prince relieved. [Bodin p. 93]

The *foreign*³⁴⁵ princes well advised, will never take oath to keep the laws of their predecessors; for otherwise they are not sovereigns. [Bodin p. 93]

Notwithstanding all oaths, the prince may derogate from the laws, or frustrate or disannul the same, the reason and equity of them ceasing. [Bodin p. 94]

There is not any bond for the sovereign prince to keep the laws, more than so far as right and justice requireth. [Bodin p. 94]

Neither is it to be found that the ancient kings of the Hebrews took any oaths, no not they which were anointed by Samuel, Elias and others. [Bodin p. 94]

As for general and particular [laws and customs], which concern the right of men in private, they have not used to be otherwise changed, but after general *assembly*³⁴⁶ of the three estates in France; not for that it is necessary for the *king*³⁴⁷ to rest on their advice, or that he may not do the contrary to that they demand, if natural reason and justice *so*³⁴⁸ require. And in that the greatness and majesty of a true sovereign prince is to be known, when the estates of all the people assembled together

---

ʳ [In BMS the following passage is deleted here: 'Wherein we see many many [*sic*] to be deceived which make a confusion of laws, and of a prince's contracts which they call also laws; as well as he which calleth prince's contracts pactionary laws' [Bodin p. 92]. At this point BMS breaks off].

in all humility present their requests and supplications to their prince, without having any power in anything to command, or determine, or to give voice; but that that which it pleaseth the king to like or dislike, to command or forbid, is holden for law. Wherein they which have written of the duty of magistrates, have deceived themselves, in maintaining that the power of the people is greater than the prince; a thing which oft-times causeth the true subjects to revolt from the obedience which they owe unto their sovereign prince, and ministereth matter of great troubles in commonwealths; of which their opinion, there is neither reason nor ground. [Bodin p. 95]

If the king should be subject unto the assemblies and decrees of the people, he should neither be king nor sovereign, and the commonwealth neither realm nor monarchy; but a mere aristocracy of many lords in power equal, where the greater part commandeth the less; and whereon the laws are not to be published in the name of him that ruleth, but in the name and authority of the estates; as in an aristocratical seignory, where he that is chief hath no power, but oweth obeisance to the seignory; unto whom yet they every one of them feign themselves to owe their faith and obedience: which are all things so absurd, as hard it is *to see*[349] which is furthest from reason. [Bodin p. 95]

When Charles VIII, the French king, then but fourteen years old, held a parliament at Tours, although the power of the parliament was never before nor after so great as in those times; yet Relli, then the Speaker for the people, turning himself to the king, thus beginneth: 'Most high, most mighty and most Christian king, our natural and only lord; we poor, humble and obedient subjects, etc., which are come hither by your command, in all humility, reverence and subjection, present ourselves before you, etc., and have given me in charge from all this noble assembly to declare unto you, the good will and hearty desire they have, with a most fervent resolution to serve, obey and aid you in all your affairs, commandments and pleasures.' All this speech is nothing else but a declaration of their good will towards the king, and of their humble obedience and loyalty. [Bodin pp. 95–6]

The like speech was used in the parliament at Orleans to Charles IX, when he was scarce eleven years old. [Bodin p. 96]

Neither are the parliaments in Spain otherwise holden, but that even a greater obedience of all the people is given to the king; as is to be seen in the acts of the parliament at Toledo by King Philip, 1552, when he yet was scarce twenty-five years old. The answers also of the king of Spain unto the requests and humble supplications of his people, are given in these words: 'We will', or else, 'We decree or ordain'; yea, the subsidies that the subjects pay unto the king of Spain, they call *service*. [Bodin p. 96]

In the parliaments of England, which have commonly been holden every third year, the estates seem to have a great liberty (as the northern people almost all breathe thereafter), yet so it is, that in effect they proceed not but by way of supplications and requests to the king. As in the parliament holden in October 1566, when the *estates**350 by a common consent had resolved (as they gave the queen to understand) not to *entreat**351 of anything, until she had first appointed who should succeed her in the crown; she gave them no other answer, but 'that they were not to make her grave before she were dead'. All whose resolutions were to no purpose without her good liking, neither did she in that anything that they *required*.352 [Bodin p. 96]

Albeit by the sufferance of the king of England, controversies between the king and his people are sometimes determined by the high court of parliament; yet all the estates remain in full subjection to the king, who is no way bound to follow their advice, neither to consent to their requests. [Bodin p. '84'=90]

The estates of England are never otherwise assembled, no more than they are in France or Spain, than by parliament writs and express commandments proceeding from the king; which showeth very well that the estates have no power of themselves to determine, command or decree anything, seeing they cannot so much as assemble themselves, neither being assembled, depart without express commandment from the king. [Bodin p. 96]

Yet this may seem one special thing, that the laws made by the king of England, at the request of the estates, cannot be again repealed, but by calling a parliament *which is much used and done as I have understood by Mr Dale the English ambassador, an honourable gentleman, and a man of good understanding, who yet assured me the king received or rejected the law as seemed best to himself, and stuck not to dispose thereof at his pleasure and contrary to the will of the estates, as*353 we see Henry VIII to have always used his sovereign power, and with his only word to have disannulled the decrees of parliament. [Bodin p. 96]

We conclude the majesty of a prince to be nothing altered or diminished by the calling together or presence of the estates, but to the contrary, his majesty thereby to be much the greater and the more honourable, seeing all his people to acknowledge him for their sovereign. [Bodin p. 98]

We see the principal point of sovereign majesty and absolute power to consist principally in giving laws unto the subjects without their consent. It behoveth that the sovereign prince should have the laws in his power, to change and amend them according as *the case*³⁵⁴ shall require. [Bodin p. 98]

In a monarchy everyone in particular must swear to the observation of the laws, and their allegiance to one sovereign monarch; who, next unto God (of whom he holds his sceptre and power), is bound to no man. For an oath carrieth always with it reverence unto whom, and in whose name it is made, as still given to a superior; and therefore the vassal *giveth*³⁵⁵ such oath unto his lord, but *receiveth*³⁵⁶ none from him again, though they be mutually bound, the one of them to the other. [Bodin p. 99]

Trajan swore to keep the laws, although he *in*³⁵⁷ the name of a sovereign prince *were*³⁵⁸ exempted; but never any of the emperors before him so swore: therefore Pliny the younger, in a *Panegyrical Oration*, speaking of the oath of Trajan, *giveth*³⁵⁹ out: 'a great novelty', saith he, 'and never before heard of, he sweareth by whom we swear'. [Bodin p. 100]

*Of*³⁶⁰ two things the one must *be*,³⁶¹ to wit, the prince that *sweareth*³⁶² to keep the laws of his country, must either not have the sovereignty, or else become a perjured man if he should but abrogate but one law contrary to his oath; whereas it is not only profitable that a prince should sometimes abrogate some such laws, but also necessary for him to alter or correct them,ˢ as the infinite variety of places, times and persons shall require: or if we shall say the prince to be still a sovereign, and yet nevertheless with such *condition as*³⁶³ that he can make no law without the advice of his council or people; he must also be dispensed with by his subjects, for the oath *that*³⁶⁴ he hath made for the observation of the laws; and the subjects again which are obliged to the laws, have also need to be dispensed withal by their prince, for fear they should be perjured: so shall it come to pass, that the majesty of the commonweal inclining now to this side, now to that side; sometimes the prince, sometimes the people bearing sway, shall have no certainty to rest upon; which are notable absurdities, and altogether incompatible with the majesty of absolute sovereignty, and contrary both to law and reason. And yet we see many, *even them*³⁶⁵ that think they see more in the matter than others, *which*³⁶⁶ maintain it to be most necessary that princes *should*³⁶⁷ be bound by oath, to keep the laws and customs of their *country*:³⁶⁸ in which doing, they weaken and overthrow all the rights of sovereign

ˢ [BMS resumes here].

majesty, which ought to be most sacred and holy, and confound the sovereignty of one sovereign monarch, with an aristocracy or democracy. [Bodin pp. 100–101][f]

Publication, or approbation of laws, in the assembly of the estates or parliament, is with us of great importance for the keeping of the laws; not that the prince *is bound to any such approbation, or*[369] cannot of himself make a law without the consent of the *states*[370] or people *(for even all his declarations of war, treaties of peace, valuations of the coin, charters to enable towns to send burgesses to parliament, and his writ of summons to both Houses to assemble, are laws, though made without the consent of the estates or people); but*[371] it is a courteous part to do it by the good liking of the senate. [Bodin p. 103]

What if a prince by law forbid to kill or steal, is he not bound to obey his own laws? I say, that this law is not his, but the law of God, whereunto all princes are more straitly bound than their subjects; God taketh a *straiter*[372] account of princes than others, as Solomon a king hath said; whereto agreeth Marcus Aurelius, saying, 'the magistrates are judges over private men, princes judge the magistrates, and God the princes'. [Bodin p. 104]

It is not only a law of nature, but also oftentimes repeated among the laws of God, that we should be obedient unto the laws of such princes as it hath pleased God to set to rule and reign over us; if their laws be not directly repugnant unto the laws of God, whereunto all princes are as well bound as their subjects.. For as the vassal oweth his oath of fidelity unto his lord, towards and against all men, except his sovereign prince: so the subject oweth his obedience to his sovereign prince, towards and against all, the majesty of God excepted, who is the absolute sovereign of all the princes in the world. [Bodin p. 106]

To confound the state of monarchy, with the popular or aristocratical estate, is a thing impossible, and in effect incompatible, and such as cannot be imagined: for sovereignty being of itself indivisible, how can it at one and the same time be divided betwixt one prince, the nobility and the people in common? The first mark of sovereign majesty is to be of power to give laws, and to command over them unto the subjects: and who should those subjects be that should yield their obedience to

[f] [In BMS the following passage is deleted here: 'whereby it cometh to pass that many princes, seeing that power to be taken from them which properly belongeth to them, and that men would make them subject to the laws of their country, dispense in the end not only with those their country laws, but even with the laws of God and nature, making account of them alike as if they were bound to neither' [Bodin p. 101]].

the law, if they should have also power to make the laws? Who should he be that could give the law, *being*[373] himself constrained to receive it of them, unto whom *he*[374] himself gave it? So that of necessity we must conclude, that as no one in particular hath the power to make the law in such a state, that there the state must needs be popular. [Bodin p. 185]

Never any commonwealth hath been made of *an*[375] aristocracy and popular estate, much less *of*[376] the three estates of a commonwealth. [Bodin p. 193]

Such states, wherein the right[s] of sovereignty *are*[377] divided, are not rightly to be called commonweals, but rather the corruption of commonweals; as Herodotus hath most briefly but truly written. [Bodin p. 194]

Commonweals which change their state, the sovereign right and power of them being divided, find no rest from civil wars. [Bodin pp. 194–5]

Where the rights of the sovereignty are divided between the prince and his subjects, in that confusion of state there is still endless stirs and quarrels for the superiority.[378] [Bodin p. 194]

If the prince be an absolute sovereign, as are the true monarchs of France, of Spain, of England, Scotland, Turkey, Muscovy, Tartary, Persia, Ethiopia, India and almost of all the kingdoms of Africa and Asia; where the kings themselves have the sovereignty, without all doubt or question, not divided with their subjects: in this case it is not lawful for any one of the subjects in particular, or all of them in general, to attempt anything, either by way of fact or of justice, against the honour, life or dignity of the sovereign, albeit *that he*[379] had committed all the wickedness, impiety and cruelty that could be spoke." For as to proceed against him by way of justice, the subject hath not such jurisdiction over his sovereign prince, of whom dependeth all power to command, and who may not only revoke all the power of his magistrates, but even in whose presence the power of all magistrates, corporations, estates and communities cease. [Bodin p. 222]

Now if it be not lawful for the subject by the way of justice to proceed against a king, how should it then be lawful to proceed against him by way of fact or force? For question is not here what men are able to do by strength and force, but what they ought of right to do; as not whether the subject have power and strength, but whether they have lawful power to condemn their sovereign prince. [Bodin p. 222]

The subject is not only guilty of treason in the highest degree who hath slain his sovereign prince, but even he also which hath attempted the

" [BMS ends here].

same, who hath given counsel or consent thereto; yea, if he have concealed the same, or but so much as thought it: which fact the laws have in such detestation, as that when a man guilty of any offence or crime, dieth before he be condemned thereof, he is deemed to have died in whole and perfect estate, except he have conspired against the life and dignity of his sovereign prince. This only thing they have thought to be such, as that for which he may worthily seem to have been now already judged and condemned; yea, even before he was thereof accused. And albeit the laws inflict no punishment upon the evil thoughts of men, but on those only which by word or deed break out into some enormity; yet if any man shall so much as conceit a thought for the violating of the person of his sovereign prince, although he have attempted nothing, they have yet judged this same thought worthy of death, notwithstanding what repentance soever he have had thereof. [Bodin p. 222]

Lest any men should think (kings or princes) themselves to have been the authors of these laws, so the more straitly to provide for their own safety and honour; let us see the laws and examples of holy scripture. [Bodin p. 223]

Nabuchodonosor king of Assyria, with fire and sword destroyed all the country of Palestine, besieged Jerusalem, took it, robbed and razed it down to the ground, *burnt*[380] the temple, and *defiled*[381] the sanctuary of God, slew the king, with the greatest part of the people, carrying away the rest into captivity into Babylon, caused the image of himself made in gold to be set up in public place, commanding all men to adore and worship the same upon pain of being burnt alive, and caused them that refused so to do, to be cast into a burning furnace. And yet for all that, the holy prophets (Baruch i; Jeremy xxix), directing their letters unto their brethren the Jews, then in captivity in Babylon, will them to pray unto God for the good and happy life of Nabuchodonosor and his children, and that they might so long rule and reign over them, as the heavens should endure: yea even God himself doubted not to call Nabuchodonosor his servant, saying, 'that he would make him the most mighty prince of the world'; and yet was there never a more detestable tyrant than he: who not contented to be himself worshipped, but caused his image also to be adored, and that upon pain of being burnt quick. [Bodin p. 223]

We have another rare example of Saul, who possessed with an evil spirit, caused the priests of the Lord to be without just cause slain, for that one of them had received David flying from him; and did what in his power was to kill, or cause to be killed, the same David, a most innocent prince, by whom he had got so many victories; at which time he fell twice himself into David's hands: who blamed of his soldiers for that he would not suffer his so mortal enemy, then in his power, to be slain, being in assured hope to have enjoyed the kingdom after his death; he detested their counsel, saying, 'God forbid that I should suffer the person of a king, the Lord's anointed, to be violated'. Yea, he himself defended the same king persecuting of him, when as he commanded the soldiers of his guard, overcome by wine and sleep, to be wakened. [Bodin p. 223]

And at such time as Saul was slain, and that a soldier, thinking to do David a pleasure, presented him with Saul's head; David caused the same soldier to be slain, which had brought him the head, saying, 'Go thou wicked, how durst thou lay thy impure hands upon the Lord's anointed? Thou shalt surely die therefore'. [Bodin pp. 223–4]

And afterwards, without all dissimulation, mourned himself for the dead king. All which is worth good consideration, for David was by Saul prosecuted to death, and yet wanted not power to have revenged himself, being become stronger than the king. Besides, he was the chosen of God, and anointed by Samuel to be king, and had married the king's daughter, and yet for all that, he abhorred to take upon him the title of a king, and much more to attempt anything against the life or honour of Saul, or to rebel against him; but chose rather to banish himself out of the realm, than in any sort to seek the king's destruction. [Bodin p. 224]

We doubt not but David, a king and a prophet, led by the spirit of God, had always before his eyes the law of God, Exodus xxii, 28: 'Thou shalt not speak evil of thy prince, nor detract the magistrate'; neither is there anything more common in holy scripture, than the forbidding not only to kill or attempt the life or honour of a prince, but even for the very magistrates, although, saith the Scripture, 'they be wicked and naught'. [Bodin p. 224]

The Protestant princes of Germany, before they entered into arms against Charles the Emperor, demanded of Martin Luther, if it were lawful for them so to do or not, who frankly told them that it *was*[382] not lawful, whatsoever tyranny or impiety were pretended. Yet was he not therein by them believed, so thereof ensued a deadly and most lamentable war, the end whereof was most miserable, drawing with it the ruin of many great and noble houses of Germany, with exceeding slaughter of the subjects. [Bodin p. 225]

The prince, whom you may justly call the father of the country, ought to be to every man dearer and more reverend than any father, as one ordained and sent unto us by God. The subject is never to be suffered to attempt anything against the prince, how naughty and cruel soever he be. Lawful it is, not to obey him in things contrary to the laws of God, to fly and hide ourselves from him, but yet to suffer stripes, yea, and death also, rather than to attempt anything against his life and honour. Oh how many tyrants should there be, if it should be lawful for subjects to kill tyrants? How many good and innocent princes should as tyrants perish by the conspiracy of their subjects against them? He that should of his subjects but exact subsidies, should be then, as the vulgar people esteem him, a tyrant. He that should rule and command contrary to the good liking of the people, should be a tyrant. He that should keep strong guards and garrisons for the safety of his person, should be a tyrant. He that should put to death traitors and conspirators against his state, should be also counted a tyrant. How should good princes be assured of their lives, if under colour of tyranny they might be slain by their subjects, by whom they ought to be defended? [Bodin p. 225]

In a well-ordered state, the sovereign power must remain in one only, without communicating any part thereof unto the state (for in that case it should be a popular government and no monarchy). Wise politicians, philosophers, divines and historiographers, have highly commended a monarchy above all other commonweals. It is not to please the prince that they hold this opinion, but for the safety and happiness of the subjects. And contrariwise, when as they shall limit and restrain the sovereign power of a monarch, to subject him to the general estates or to the council, the sovereignty hath no firm foundation, but they frame a popular confusion or a miserable anarchy, which is the plague of all estates and commonweals; the which must be duly considered, not giving credit to their goodly discourses which persuade subjects that it is necessary to subject monarchs, and to *prescribe*[383] their prince a law. For that is not only the ruin of the monarch, but also of the subjects. It is yet more strange, that many hold opinion that the prince is subject to his laws, that is to say, subject to his will, whereon the laws which he hath made depend; a thing *impossible*[384] in nature. And under this colour, and ill-digested opinion, they make a mixture and confusion of civil laws with the laws of nature and of God. [Bodin p. 717]

A pure absolute monarchy is the surest commonweal, and without comparison the best of all. Wherein many are abused, who maintain that an optimacy is the best kind of government, for that many commanders have more judgement, wisdom and counsel than one alone. *But*[385] there is a great difference betwixt counsel and commandment. [Bodin p. 717]

The counsel of many wise men may be better than of one. But to resolve, determine, and to command, one will always perform it better than many.

He which hath advisedly digested all their opinions, will soon resolve without contention; the which many cannot easily perform. It is necessary to have a sovereign prince, which may have power to resolve and determine of the opinions of his council. [Bodin p. 717]

OBSERVATIONS[v]
CONCERNING
THE ORIGINALL
OF
GOVERNMENT,

Upon $\left\{ \begin{array}{l} \text{Mr Hobs } Leviathan \\ \text{Mr Milton against } Salmasius \\ \text{H. Grotius } De\,Jure\,Belli \end{array} \right.$

Aristotle, *Politics* book 4.

'Η πρώτη πολιτεία ἐν τοῖς ῞Ελλησιν ἐγένετο μετὰ τὰς βασιλείας ἐκ τῶν πολεμούντων.

[1297ᵇ16–17: the first form of government amongst the Greeks after monarchy was military rule]

THE PREFACE

With no small content I read Mr Hobbes' book *De Cive*, and his *Leviathan*, about the rights of sovereignty, which no man, that I know, hath so amply and judiciously handled. I consent with him about the rights of exercising government, but I cannot agree to his means of acquiring it. It may seem strange I should praise his building

[B. L. Harleian MS 6867, ff.255a–259a, contains part of the observations on Hobbes, running from immediately after the end of the preface to the close of the first paragraph of section 12, p. 193 below; it has been used as copy-text for the appropriate passages, and is referred to as OMS. The Cambridge manuscript of *Patriarcha*, C.U.L. Add. 7078, pp. 23–43, contains two chapters which were printed with the *Observations* in 1652; it has been used as copy-text for the relevant sections, and is referred to as B. If a reading or omission from OMS or B are recorded in the notes, then the text followed at that point is the first printed edition (Wing F918) referred to as 52H – and this is also the copy-text for those sections where we have no manuscript. Notes record major variants in B, OMS and 52H, and occasionally variants in Wing F913 and 914, the editions of 1679, which are referred to as 79. In passages where the copy-text is 52H and where readings from it are given in the notes, the text is taken from 79].

and yet mislike his foundation, but so it is. His *jus naturae* [right of nature] and his *regnum institutivum* [kingdom by institution] will not down with me, they appear full of contradiction and impossibilities. A few short notes about them I here offer, wishing he would consider whether his building would not stand firmer upon the principles of *regnum patrimoniale* [a paternal kingdom], as he calls it, both according to Scripture and reason – since he confesseth the 'father being before the institution of a commonwealth' was originally an 'absolute sovereign' 'with power of life and death', and that 'a great family, as to the rights of sovereignty is a little monarchy' [Hobbes 2, pp. 121, 178, 105]. If, according to the order of nature, he had handled paternal government before that by institution, there would have been little liberty left in the subjects of the family to consent to institution of government.

In his pleading the cause of the people he arms them with a very large commission of array,*ᵂ* which is a right in nature for every man to war against every man when he please, and also *a*³⁸⁶ right for all the people to govern. This latter point, although he affirm in words, yet by consequence he denies, as to me it seemeth.

He saith a representative may be of*ˣ* all or but of a part of the people [Hobbes 2, p. 94]. If it be of all, he terms it a democracy, which is the government of the people. But how can such a commonwealth be generated? For if every man covenant with every man, who shall be left to be the representative? If all must be representatives, who will remain to covenant? For he that is sovereign makes no covenant by his doctrine. It is not all that will come together that makes the democracy, but all that have power by covenant. Thus his democracy by institution fails.

The same may be said of a democracy by acquisition. For if all be conquerors, who shall covenant for life and liberty? And if all be not conquerors, how can it be a democracy by conquest?

A paternal democracy I am confident he will not affirm, so that in conclusion the poor people are deprived of their government, if there can be no democracy by his principles.

Next, if a representative aristocratical of a part of the people be free from covenanting, then that whole assembly (call it what you

---

ᵂ [a commission of array was a commission issued by the king to mobilise the militia].
ˣ [be of: consist of].

will) though it be never so great, is in the state of nature, and every one of that assembly hath a right not only to kill any of the subjects that they meet with in the streets, but also they all have a natural right to cut one another's throats even while they sit together in council, by his principles. In this miserable condition of war is his representative aristocratical by institution.

A commonwealth by conquest, he teacheth, 'is then acquired when the vanquished, to avoid present death, covenanteth that so long as his life and the liberty of his body is allowed him, the victor shall have the use of it at his pleasure' [Hobbes 2, p. 104]. Here I would know how the liberty of the vanquished can be allowed if the victor have the use of it at pleasure, or how is it possible for the victor to perform his covenant, except he could always stand by every particular man to protect his life and liberty?

In his 'review and conclusion' he resolves that 'an ordinary subject hath liberty to submit when the means of his life is within the guards and garrisons of the enemy' [Hobbes 2, p. 390]. It seems hereby that the rights of sovereignty by institution may be forfeited, for the subject cannot be at liberty to submit to a conqueror, except his former subjection be forfeited for want of protection.

If his conqueror be in the state of nature when he conquers, he hath a right without any covenant made with the conquered. If conquest be defined to be acquiring of right of sovereignty by victory, why is it said the right is acquired in the people's submission, by which they contract with the victor, promising obedience for life and liberty [Hobbes 2, pp. 103–4]? Hath not every one in the state of nature a right to sovereignty, before conquest, which only puts him in possession of his right?

If his conqueror be not in the state of nature, but a subject by covenant, how can he get a right of sovereignty by conquest when neither he himself hath right to conquer, nor subjects a liberty to submit – since a former contract lawfully made cannot lawfully be broken by them?

I wish the title of the book had not been of a commonwealth, but of a weal public, or commonweal, which is the true word carefully observed by our translator of Bodin *De Republica* into English. Many ignorant men are apt by the name of commonwealth to understand a popular government, wherein wealth and all things shall be common, tending to the levelling community in the state of pure nature.

OBSERVATIONS[y] ON MR HOBBES' *LEVIATHAN*: OR HIS ARTIFICIAL MAN A COMMONWEALTH

I

If God created only Adam and of a piece of him made the woman, and if by generation from them two as parts of them all mankind be propagated; if also God gave to Adam not only the dominion over the woman and the children that should issue from them, but also over the whole earth to subdue it, and over all the creatures on it, so that as long as Adam lived no man could claim or enjoy anything but by donation, assignation or permission from him; I wonder how the *right of nature* can be imagined by Mr Hobbes, which, he saith, is a liberty for 'each man to use his own power as he will himself for preservation of his own life'; 'a condition of war of everyone against everyone'; 'a right of every man to everything, even to one another's body' ([Hobbes 2,] p. 64), especially since himself affirms 'that originally the father of every man was also his sovereign lord with power over him of life and death' ([Hobbes 2,] p. 178).

II

Mr Hobbes confesseth *he*[387] believes 'it was never generally so', that there was such a *jus naturae* [right of nature] ([Hobbes 2,] p. 63); and if not generally, then not at all, for one exception bars all if he mark it well. Whereas he imagines such a 'right of nature' may be now practised in America, he confesseth a government there of families, which government how 'small' or 'brutish' soever (as he calls it) is sufficient to destroy his *jus naturale*.

III

I cannot understand how this 'right of nature' can be conceived without imagining a company of men at the very first to have been all created together without any dependency one of another, or as 'mushrooms (*fungorum more*) they all on a sudden were sprung out of the earth without any obligation one to another', as Mr Hobbes' words are in his book *De Cive*, chapter 8, section *1*[388] [Hobbes 1, p. 160]; *when*[389] the Scripture teacheth us otherwise, that all men came

---

[y] [copy-text from here to the end of the first paragraph of section 12 in the observations on Hobbes is OMS].

187

by succession and generation from one man. We must not deny the truth of the history of the creation.

IV

It is not to be thought that God would create man in a condition worse than any beasts, as if he made men to no other end by nature but to destroy one another. A right for the father to destroy *his children or eat them*,[390] and for the children to do the like by their parents, is worse than cannibals. This horrid condition of *mere*[391] nature when Mr Hobbes was charged with, his refuge was to answer 'that no son can be understood to be in *the*[392] state of nature' (*De Cive* chapter I, section 10) [Hobbes I, p. 96] – which is all one with denying his own principle. For if men be not free-born, it is not possible for him to assign and prove any other time for them to claim a right of nature to liberty, if not at their birth.

V

But if it be allowed (which is yet most false) that a company of men were at first without a common power to keep them in awe, I do not see why such a condition must be called a state of war of all men against all men. Indeed if such a multitude of men should be created as the earth could not well nourish, there might be cause for men to destroy one another rather than perish for want of food. But God was no such niggard in the creation, and there being plenty of sustenance and room for all men, there is no cause or use of war till men be hindered in the preservation of life, so that there is no absolute necessity of war in the state of pure nature. It is the right of nature for every man to live in peace, that so he may tend the preservation of his life, which whilst he is in actual war he cannot do. War of itself as it is war preserves no man's life, it only helps *to*[393] preserve and obtain the means to live. If every man tend the right of preserving life, which may be done in peace, there is no cause of war.

VI

But admit the state of nature were the state of war, let us see what help Mr Hobbes hath for it. It is a principle of his that 'the law of nature is a rule found out by reason' (I do think it is given by God), forbidding a man 'to do that which is destructive to his life, and to omit that by which he thinks it may be best preserved' ([Hobbes 2,] p. 64). If the right of nature be a liberty for a man to do anything he thinks fit to preserve his life, then in the first place nature must teach him that life is to be preserved, and so consequently forbids to do that which may destroy or take away the means of life, or to omit that by which it may be preserved – and thus the right of nature and the law of nature will be all one. For I think Mr Hobbes will not say the right of nature is a liberty for a man to destroy his own life. The law of nature might better have been said to consist in a command to preserve or not to omit the means of preserving life, than in a prohibition to destroy, or to omit it.

VII

Another principle I meet with, 'If other men will not lay down their right as well as he, then there is no reason for any one to divest himself of his' ([Hobbes 2,] p. 65). Hence it follows that if all the men in the world do not agree, no commonwealth can be established. It is a thing impossible for all the men in the world every man with every man to covenant to lay down their right. Nay it is not possible *in**394 the smallest kingdom, though all men should spend their whole lives in nothing else but in running up and down to covenant.

VIII

Right may be laid aside but not transferred: for 'he that renounceth or passeth away his right, giveth not to any other man a right which he had not before', and reserves a right in himself against all those with whom he doth not covenant ([Hobbes 2,] p. 65).

IX

The only way to erect a common power, or a commonwealth, is for men to confer all their power and strength upon one man, or one assembly of men, that may reduce all their wills by plurality of voices to one will; which is to appoint one man or an assembly of men to bear their person, to submit their wills to his will. This is a real unity of them all *in**395 one person, made by covenant of every man with every man as if every man should say to every man, I authorise, and give up my right of governing myself to this man, or this assembly of men, on this condition, that thou give up thy right to him, and authorise all his actions. This done, the multitude so united in one person, is called a commonwealth. ([Hobbes 2,] p. 87)

To authorise and give up his right of governing himself, to confer all his power and strength, and to submit his will to another, is to lay down his right of resisting. For if right of nature be a liberty to use power for preservation of life, laying down of that power must be a relinquishing of power to preserve or defend life, otherwise a man relinquisheth nothing.

To reduce all the wills of an assembly by plurality of voices to one will, is not a proper speech, for it is not a plurality but a totality of voices which makes an assembly be of one will – otherwise it is but the one will of a major part of the assembly. The negative voice of any one hinders the being of the one will of the assembly. There is nothing more destructive to the true nature of a lawful assembly than to allow a major part to prevail when the whole only hath right.

For a man to give up his right to one that never covenants to protect is *great*³⁹⁶ folly, since it is neither 'in consideration of some right reciprocally transferred to himself', nor can he hope for any other good by standing out of the way, that the other may enjoy his own original right without hindrance from him, by reason of so much diminution of impediments ([Hobbes 2, pp. 65–]66).

X

'The liberty', saith Mr Hobbes,

whereof there is so frequent and honourable *mention*³⁹⁷ in the histories and philosophy of the ancient Greeks and Romans, and in the writings and discourse of those that from them have received all their learning in the politics, is not the liberty of particular men but the liberty of the commonwealth. Whether a commonwealth be monarchical or popular, the freedom is still the same. ([Hobbes 2,] p. 110)

Here I find Mr Hobbes is much mistaken. For the liberty of the Athenians and Romans *is*³⁹⁸ a liberty only to be found in popular estates, and not in monarchies. This is clear by Aristotle, who calls a city a community of freemen, meaning every particular citizen to be free. Not that every particular man had a liberty to resist his governor or do what he list, but a liberty only for particular men to govern and to be governed by turns, ἄρχειν and ἄρχεσθαι are Aristotle's words [1277ᵇ14–15]. This was a liberty not to be found in hereditary monarchies. So Tacitus mentioning the several governments of Rome, joins the consulship and liberty to be brought in by Brutus, because by the annual election of consuls particular citizens came in their course to govern and to be governed [Tacitus, *Annals* I, 1]. This may be confirmed by the complaint of our author which followeth:

> It is an easy thing for men to be deceived by the specious name of liberty, and for want of judgment to distinguish, mistake that for their private inheritance *and*³⁹⁹ birthright which is the right of the public only; and when the same error is confirmed by the authority of men in reputation for their writings in this subject, it is no wonder if it produce sedition and change of government. In *these*⁴⁰⁰ western parts of the world, we are made to receive our opinions concerning the institution and *rights*⁴⁰¹ of commonwealths from Aristotle and Cicero, and other men, Greeks and Romans, that living under popular estates, derived those rights not from the principles of nature, but transcribed *them*⁴⁰² into their books out of the practice of their own commonwealths, which were popular. And because the Athenians were taught (to keep them from desire of changing their government) that they were freemen, and all that lived under monarchy slaves, therefore Aristotle puts it down in his *Politics*, 'In democracy liberty is to be supposed, for it is commonly held that no man is free in any other government'. So Cicero and other writers *have*⁴⁰³ grounded their civil doctrine on the opinions of the Romans, who were taught to hate monarchy, at first, by them that having deposed their sovereign, shared amongst them the sovereignty of Rome. And by reading of these Greek and Latin authors, men from their childhood have gotten a habit (under a false show of liberty) of favouring tumults, and of licentious controlling the actions of their sovereigns. [Hobbes 2, pp. 110–11].

XI

'Dominion paternal' not attained 'by generation but by contract', which is 'the child's consent, either express or by other sufficient arguments declared' ([Hobbes 2,] p. 102). How a child can express consent, or by other sufficient arguments declare it before it comes to the age of discretion I understand not; yet all men grant it is due before consent can be given, and I take it Mr Hobbes is of the same mind where he teacheth that Abraham's children were bound to obey what Abraham should declare to them for God's law – which *could*[404] not be but in virtue of the obedience they owed to their parents ([Hobbes 2,] p. 249); they *owed*, not that they *covenanted* to give. Also, where he saith the 'father and the master being before the institution of commonweals absolute sovereigns in their own families' ([Hobbes 2,] p. 121), how can it be said that either children or servants were in the state of *jus naturae* [the right of nature] till the institution of commonweals? It is said by Mr Hobbes in his book *De Cive* chapter 9, section 7 [Hobbes 1, p. 166; cf. pp. 164–5, IX, iii], the 'mother originally hath the government of her children, and from her the father derives his right, because she brings forth and first nourisheth them'. But we know that God at the creation gave the sovereignty to the man over the woman, as being the nobler and principal agent in generation. As to the objection that 'it is not known who is the father to the son but by the discovery of the mother', and that 'he is *son to whom*[405] the mother will, and therefore he is the mother's', the answer is that it is not at the will of the mother to make whom she *please*[406] the father, for if the mother be not in the possession of a husband, the child is not reckoned to have any father at all. But if she be in the possession of a man, the child notwithstanding whatsoever the woman discovereth to the contrary is still reputed to be his in whose possession she is. No child naturally and infallibly knows who are his true parents, yet he must obey those that in common reputation are so, otherwise the commandment of 'honour thy father and thy mother' were vain, and no child bound to the obedience of it.

XII

If the government of one man and the government of two men, make two several kinds of government ([Hobbes 2,] p. 94), why may not the government of two and *of*[407] three do the like, and make a third, and so every differing number a *different*[408] kind of commonwealth? If 'an assembly of all' (as Mr Hobbes saith) 'that will come together' be a democracy, and 'an assembly of a part only' an aristocracy, then if all that will come together be but a part only, a democracy and *an**409 aristocracy are all one. And why must an assembly of part be called an aristocracy and not a merocracy?ᶻ

It seems Mr Hobbes is of the mind that there is but one kind of government, and that is monarchy. For he defines a commonwealth to be one person; and an assembly of men, or 'real unity of them all in one and the same person' ([Hobbes 2,] p. 87), the multitude so united he calls a commonwealth. This his moulding of a multitude into one person is the generation of his great *Leviathan*, the king of the children of pride ([Hobbes 2, pp. 166–]167). Thus he concludes the person of a commonwealth to be a monarch.

XIII

I cannot but wonder Mr Hobbes should say 'the consent of a subject to sovereign power is contained in these words, "I authorize and do take upon me all his actions", in which there is no restriction at all of his own former natural liberty' ([Hobbes 2,] p. 112). Surely here Mr Hobbes forgot himself, for before he makes the resignation to go in these words also, I 'give up my right of governing myself to this man' [Hobbes 2, p. 87]. This is a restriction certainly of his own former natural liberty when he gives it away. And if a man allow his sovereign to kill him – which Mr Hobbes seems to confess – how can he reserve a right to defend himself? And if a man have a power and right to kill himself, he doth not authorise and give up his right to his sovereign, if he do not obey him when he commands him to kill himself.

XIV

Mr Hobbes saith 'No man is bound by the words' of his submission

> to kill himself or any other man, and consequently that the obligation a man may sometimes have upon the command of the sovereign to execute any dangerous or dishonourable office, dependeth not on the words of our submission but on the intention which is to be understood by the end thereof. When therefore our refusal to obey frustrates the end for which the sovereignty

ᶻ [OMS ends here].

was ordained, then there is no liberty to refuse; otherwise there is. ([Hobbes 2,] p. 112)

If no man be bound by the words of his subjection to kill any other man, then a sovereign may be denied the benefit of war, and be rendered unable to defend his people – and so the end of government frustrated. If the obligation upon the commands of a sovereign to execute a dangerous or dishonourable office dependeth not on the words of our submission but on the intention, which is to be understood by the end thereof, no man, by Mr Hobbes' rules, is bound but by the words of his *submission*; the intention of the *command* binds not, if the words do not. If the intention should bind, it is necessary the sovereign must discover it, and the people must dispute and judge it – which how well it may consist with the rights of sovereignty, Mr Hobbes may consider. Whereas Mr Hobbes saith the intention is to be understood by the ends, I take it he means the end by effect, for the end and the intention are one and the same thing. And if he mean the effect, the obedience must go before, and not depend on the understanding of the effect, which can never be if the obedience do not precede it. In fine, he resolves refusal to obey may depend upon the judging of what frustrates the end of sovereignty, and what not, of which he cannot mean any other judge but the people.

XV

Mr Hobbes puts a case by way of question:

A great many men together have already resisted the sovereign power unjustly, or committed some capital crime, for which every one of them expecteth death: whether have they not the liberty then to join together and assist and defend one another? Certainly they have, for they but defend their lives, which the guilty man may as well do as the innocent. There was indeed injustice in the first breach of their duty. Their bearing of arms subsequent to it, though it be to maintain what they have done, is no new unjust act, and if it be only to defend their persons it is not unjust at all. ([Hobbes 2,] p. 112[–13])

The only reason here alleged for the bearing of arms is this, that it is no new unjust act – as if the beginning only of a rebellion were an unjust act, and the continuance of it none at all. No better answer can be given to this case than what the author himself hath delivered in the beginning of the same paragraph in these words: 'To resist the sword of the commonwealth in defence of another man, guilty or innocent, no man hath liberty, because such liberty takes away from the sovereign the means of protecting us, and is therefore destructive of the very essence of government'. Thus he first answers the question, and then afterwards makes it, and gives it a contrary answer. Other passages I meet with to the like purpose. He saith 'a man cannot lay down the right of resisting them that assault him by force to take away his life; the same *may*[410] be said of wounds, chains and imprisonment' ([Hobbes 2,] p. 66); 'A covenant *[not]*[411] to defend myself from force by force is void'; right of defending life and means of living can never be abandoned ([Hobbes 2,] p. 69).

These last doctrines are destructive to all government whatsoever, and even to the *Leviathan* itself. Hereby any rogue or villain may murder his sovereign, if the sovereign but offer by force to whip or lay him in the stocks, since whipping may be said to be a wounding, and putting in the stocks an imprisonment. So likewise every man's goods being a means of living, if a man cannot abandon them, no contract among men, be it never so just, can be observed. Thus we are at least in as miserable a condition of war as Mr Hobbes at first by nature found us.

XVI

The kingdom of God signifies, saith Mr Hobbes, a kingdom 'constituted by the votes of the people of Israel in a peculiar manner, wherein they choose God for their king, by covenant made with him, upon God's promising them Canaan' ([Hobbes 2,] p. 216). If we look upon Mr Hobbes' text for this, it will be found that the people did not constitute by votes, and choose God for their king, but by the appointment first of God himself the covenant was to be a God to them. They did not contract with God that if he would give them Canaan they would be his subjects, and he should be their king. It was not in their power to choose whether God should be their God, yea or nay. For it is confessed He reigned naturally over all by his might. If God reigned naturally, He had a kingdom and sovereign power over His subjects, not acquired by their own consent. This kingdom, said to be constituted by the votes of the people of Israel, is but the vote of Abraham only; his single voice carried it, he was the representative of the people. For at this vote, it is confessed that the name of king is not given to God, nor of kingdom to Abraham, yet the thing – if we will believe Mr Hobbes – is all one. If a contract be the mutual transferring of right, I would know what right a people can have to transfer to God by contract. Had the people of Israel at Mount Sinai a right not to obey God's voice? If they had not such a right, what had they to transfer?

The covenant mentioned at Mount Sinai was but a conditional contract, and God but a conditional king, and though the people promised to obey God's word, yet it was more than they were able to perform, for they often disobeyed God's voice – which being a breach of the condition the covenant was void, and God not their king by contract.

It is complained by God, 'They have rejected me that I should not reign over them' [1 Samuel viii, 12]. But it is not said 'according to their contract'. For I do not find that the desiring of a king was a breach of their contract or covenant, or disobedience to the voice of God. There is no such law extant.

The people did not totally reject the Lord, but in part only, out of timorousness. When they saw Nahash king of the children of Ammon come against them, they distrusted that God would not suddenly provide for their deliverance, as if they had had always a king in readiness to go up presently to fight for them. This despair in them who had found so many miraculous deliverances under God's government was that which offended the Lord so highly. They did not desire an alteration of government and to cast off God's laws, but hoped for a certainer and speedier deliverance from danger in time of war. They did not petition that they might choose their king themselves. That had been a greater sin – and yet if they had, it had not been a total rejection of God's reigning over them, as long as they desired not to depart from the worship of God their king, and from the obedience of his laws. I see not that the kingdom of God was cast off by the election of Saul, since Saul was chosen by God himself, and governed according to God's laws. The government from Abraham to Saul is nowhere called the kingdom of God, nor is it said that the kingdom of God was cast off at the election of Saul.

Mr Hobbes allows that 'Moses alone had next under God the sovereignty over the Israelities', [Hobbes 2,] page 252. But he doth not allow it to Joshua, but will have it descend to Eleazar the high priest, Aaron's son. His proof is, God expressly saith concerning Joshua, 'He shall stand before Eleazar, who shall ask counsel *for*[412] him before the Lord' (after the judgment of Urim is omitted by Mr Hobbes), 'at his word *shall they*[413] go out', etc. [Numbers xxvii, 21], 'therefore the supreme power of making peace and war was in the priest' [Hobbes 2, p. 253]. Answer: the work of the high priest was only *ministerial* not *magisterial*. He had no power to command in war, or to judge in peace. Only, when the sovereign or governor did go up to war, he enquired of the Lord by the ministry of the high priest, and, as the Hebrews say, the enquirer with a soft voice as one that prayeth for himself, asked. And forthwith the Holy Ghost came upon the priest, and he beheld the breast-plate, and saw therein by the vision of prophecy, 'go up', or 'go not up', in the letters that showed forth themselves upon the breast-plate before his face. Then the priest answered him, 'go up', or 'go not up'. If this answer gave the priest the sovereignty, then neither King Saul nor King David had the sovereignty, who both asked counsel of the Lord by the priest.

OBSERVATIONS ON MR MILTON AGAINST SALMASIUS

I

Among the many printed books and several discourses touching the right of kings and the liberty of the people, I cannot find that as yet the first and chief point is agreed upon or indeed so much as once disputed. The word 'king' and the word 'people' are familiar, one would think every simple man could tell what they signified. But upon examination it will be found that the learnedest cannot agree of their meaning.

Ask Salmasius what a king is, and he will teach us that 'a king is he who hath the supreme power of the kingdom, and is accountable to none but God, and may do what he please, and is free from the laws' [Milton 7, p. 70]. This definition J[ohn] M[ilton] abominates as being the definition of a tyrant, and I should be of his mind if he would have vouchsafed us a better, or any other definition at all, that would tell us how any king can have a supreme power without being freed from human laws. To find fault with it, without producing any other is to leave us in the dark. But though Mr Milton brings us neither definition nor description of a king, yet we may pick out of several passages of him, something like a definition, if we lay them together. He teacheth us that 'power was therefore given to a king by the people, that he might see by the authority to him committed that nothing be done against law, and that he keeps our laws and not impose upon *us*[414] his own. Therefore there is no regal power but in the courts of the kingdom, and by them', page 155 [Milton 7, p. 430].

And again he affirmeth 'the king cannot imprison, fine or punish any man, except he be first cited into some court – where not the king but the usual judges give sentence', page 168. And before we are told 'not the king but the authority of parliament doth set up and take away all courts', page 167 [Milton 7, p. 462].

Lo, here the description of a king: he is 'one to whom the people give power, to see that nothing be done against law', and yet he saith there is 'no regal power but in the courts of justice, and by them, where not the king but the usual judges give sentence'. This description not only strips the king of all power whatsoever, but puts him in a condition below the meanest of his subjects.

Thus much may show that all men are not agreed what a king is. Next, what the word people means is not agreed upon. Ask Aristotle what the people is, and he will not allow any power to be in any but in free citizens. If we demand who be free citizens, that he cannot resolve us, for he confesseth that he that is a free citizen in one city, is not so in another city. And he is of opinion that 'no artificer should be a free citizen, or have voice in a well ordered commonwealth' [1278[a]8–9]; he accounts a democracy (which word signifies the government of the people) to be a corrupted sort of government [1160[b]16–20]; he thinks many men by nature born to be servants, and not fit to govern as any part of the people. Thus doth Aristotle curtail the people, and can give us no certain rule to know who be the people. Come to our modern politicians,[a] and ask them who the people is – though they talk big of the people, yet they take up and are content with a few representers (as they call them) of the whole people, a point Aristotle was to seek in. Neither are these representers stood upon to be the whole people. But the major part of these representers

---

[a] [people who studied and wrote about politics].

must be reckoned for the whole people. Nay, J[ohn] M[ilton] will not allow the major part of the representers to be the people, but the 'sounder and better part only' of them (p. 126) [Milton 7, p. 356], and in right down terms he tells us, to determine who is a tyrant he leaves 'to magistrates, at least to the uprighter sort of them, and of the people, though in number less by many, to judge as they find cause' (p. 7) [Milton 5, p. 7]. If the 'sounder, the better, and the uprighter' part have the power of the people, how shall we know, or who shall judge who they be?

II

One text is urged by Mr Milton for the people's power: Deuteronomy xvii, 14 – 'When thou art come into the land which thy Lord thy God giveth thee, and shalt say I will set a king over me, like as all the nations about me'. It is said by the *Tenure of Kings* 'these words confirm us that the right of choosing, yea, of changing their own government is by the grant of God himself in the people' [Milton 5, p. 14]. But can the foretelling or forewarning of the Israelites of a wanton and wicked desire of theirs, which God himself condemned, be made an argument that God gave or granted them a right to do such a wicked thing? Or can the narration and reproving of a future fact be a donation and approving of a present right, or the permission of a sin be made a commission for the doing of it? The author in his book against Salmasius, falls from making God the donor or grantor, that he cites him only for a witness: '*Teste ipso Deo penes populos arbitrium semper fuisse, vel ea, quae placeret forma reipublicae utendi, vel hanc in aliam mutandi, de Hebraeis de hoc diserte dicit Deus: de reliquis non abnuit*: That' here in this text 'God himself being witness, there was always a power in the people either to use what form of government they pleased, or of changing it into another. God saith this expressly of the Hebrews, and denies it not of others' [Milton 7, pp. 76–7]. Can any man find that God in this text expressly saith that there was always a right in the people to use what form of government they please? The text not warranting this right of the people, the foundation of the defence of the people is quite taken away – there being no other grant or proof of it pretended.

2. Where it is said that the Israelites desired a king, though then under another form of government, in the next line but one it is

confessed they had a king at the time when they desired a king, which was God himself, and his viceroy Samuel [Milton 5, p. 39], and so saith God: 'They have not rejected thee, but they have rejected me, that I should not reign over them'. Yet in the next verse God saith, as 'they have forsaken me, so do they also unto thee' [1 Samuel viii, 7–8]. Here is no show of any other form of government but monarchy. God by the mediation of Samuel reigned, who 'made his sons judges over Israel' [1 Samuel viii, 1]. When one man constitutes judges we may call him a king, or if the having of judges do alter the government then the government of every kingdom is altered from monarchy. Where judges are appointed by kings, it is now reckoned one of the duties of kings to judge by their judges only.

3. Where it is said, 'he shall not multiply to himself horses [Deuteronomy xvii, 16], nor wives, nor riches, that he might understand that he had no power over others, who could decree nothing of himself *extra legem* [outside the law]' [Milton 7, p. 76], if it had said *contra legem Dei* [against the law of God], it had been true, but if it meant *extra legem humanam* [outside human law], it is false.

4. If there had been any right given to the people, it seems it was to the elders only. For it is said it was 'the elders of Israel gathered together' [1 Samuel viii, 4] petitioned for a king. It is not said it was all the people, nor that the people did choose the elders, who were the fathers and heads of families authorised by the judges.

5. Where it is said, 'I will set a king over me like as all the nations about me' [Deuteronomy xvii, 14], 'to set a king' is not to choose a king but by some solemn public act of coronation or otherwise to acknowledge their allegiance to the king chosen. It is said, thou shalt 'set him king whom the Lord thy God shall choose' [Deuteronomy xvii, 15]. The elders did not desire to choose a king like other nations, but they say 'now make us a king to judge us like all the nations' [1 Samuel viii, 5].[b]

III

As for David's covenant with the elders when he was anointed, it was not to observe any laws or conditions made by the people, for

---

[b] [Milton 5, p. 14 argued that Deuteronomy xvii, 14 gave the people a right to choose their king. Filmer replies that it was God who chose the king; the people merely acknowledged their allegiance to the man chosen].

ought appears, but to keep God's laws and serve Him, and to seek the good of the people as they were to protect him.

6. The Reubenites and Gadites promise their obedience, not according to their laws or conditions agreed upon, but in these words: 'All that thou commandest us we will do, and whithersoever thou sendest us *we**⁴¹⁵ will go; as we hearkened [un]to Moses in all things, so will we hearken unto thee. Only the Lord thy God be with thee as He was with Moses' [Joshua i, 16–17]. Where is there any condition of any human law expressed? Though the rebellious tribes offered conditions to Rehoboam, where can we find that 'for like conditions not performed, all Israel deposed Samuel'? I wonder Mr M[ilton] should say this, when within a few lines after he professeth that 'Samuel had governed them uprightly' [Milton 5, p. 15].

IV

Jus regni is much stumbled at, and the definition of a king which saith 'his power is supreme in the kingdom, and he is accountable to none but to God, and that he may do what he please, and is not bound by laws'. It is said, if this definition be good, no man is or ever was, who may be said to be a tyrant (p. 14). For 'when he hath violated all divine and human laws, nevertheless he is a king, and guiltless *jure regio* [by royal right]' [Milton 7, p. 72]. To this may be answered that the definition confesseth he is accountable to God, and therefore not guiltless if he violate divine laws. Human laws must not be shuffled in with divine, they are not of the same authority. If human laws bind a king, it is impossible for him to have supreme power amongst men. If any man can find us out such a kind of government wherein the supreme power can be without being freed from human laws, they should first teach us that. But if all sorts of popular government that can be invented cannot be one minute without an arbitrary power freed from all human laws, what reason can be given why a royal government should not have the like freedom? If it be tyranny for one man to govern arbitrarily, why should it not be far greater tyranny for a multitude of men to govern without being accountable or bound by laws? It would be further enquired how it is possible for any government at all to be in the world without an arbitrary power. It is not power except it be arbitrary. A legislative power cannot be without being absolved from human laws. It cannot be showed how a king can have any power at all but an arbitrary power. We are taught that 'power was therefore given to a king by the people, that he might see by the authority to him committed that nothing be done against law, and that he keep our laws, and not impose upon us his own. Therefore there is no royal power but in the courts of the kingdom, and by them', page 155 [Milton 7, p. 430]. And again it is said 'the king cannot imprison, fine or punish any man except he be first cited into some court, where not the king but the usual judges give sentence', page 168 [Milton 7, p. 462]. And before we are told 'not the king, but the authority of parliament doth set up and take away all courts', page 167 [Milton 7, p. 462].

Lo, here we have Mr Milton's perfect definition of a king: he is one to whom the people gave 'power to see that nothing be done against law, and that he keep our laws, and not impose his own'. Whereas all other men have the faculty of seeing by nature, the king only hath it by the gift of the people. Other power he hath none. He may see the judges keep the laws if they will; he cannot compel them, for he may not imprison, fine, nor punish any man. The courts of justice may, and they are set up and put down by the parliament. Yet in this very definition of a king we may spy an arbitrary power in the king, for he may wink if he will – and no other power doth this description of a king give, but only a power to see. Whereas it is said Aristotle 'doth mention an absolute kingdom for no other cause but to show how absurd, unjust and most tyrannical it is' [Milton 7, p. 88], there is no such thing said by Aristotle, but the contrary, where he saith that 'a king according to law makes no sort of government' [1287ᵃ3–4]; and after he had reckoned up five sorts of kings he concludes that there were in a manner but two sorts, the Lacedaemonian king and the absolute king, whereof the first was but as a general in an army, and therefore no king at all, and then fixes and rests upon the 'absolute king, who ruleth according to his own will' [1287ᵃ9–10].

V

If it be demanded what is meant by this word people? 1. Sometimes it is *populus universus* [the whole people], and then every child must have his consent asked, which is impossible. 2. Sometimes it is *pars major* [the greater part], and sometimes it is *pars potior et sanior* [the better and sounder part]. How the major part, where all are alike free, can bind the minor part, is not yet proved.

But it seems the major part will not carry it, nor be allowed except they be the 'better part and the sounder part' [Milton 7, p. 356]. We are told 'the sounder part implored the help of the army when it saw itself and the commonwealth betrayed', and that the 'soldiers judged better than the great council, and by arms saved the commonwealth, which the great council had almost damned by their votes', page 7 [Milton 7, p. 54].

Here we see what the people is – to wit, 'the sounder part of which the army is the judge'. Thus upon the matter the soldiers are the people – which being so, we may discern where the liberty of the people lieth, which we are taught to consist 'all for the most part in the power of the people's choosing what form of government they please' (p. 61) [Milton 7, p. 192]. A miserable liberty, which is only to choose to whom we will give our liberty, which we may not keep. See more concerning the people in the book entitled *The Anarchy*, pages 8, 9, 10, 11, 12, 13, 14 [pp. 139–46 above].

VI

We are taught that 'a father and a king are things most diverse. The father begets us, but not the king; but we create the king. Nature gives a father to the people, the people give themselves a king. If the father kill his son he loseth his life, why should not the king also?' page 34 [Milton 7, pp. 44–6].

Answer: father and king are not so diverse. It is confessed that at first they were all one, for there is confessed *paternum imperium et haereditarium* [a paternal and hereditary empire], page 141 [Milton 7, p. 394], and this fatherly empire, as it was of itself *hereditary*, so it was *alienable* by the parent, and *seizable* by a usurper as other goods are. And thus every king that now is hath a paternal empire, either by inheritance, or by translation or usurpation. So a father and a king may be all one.

A father may die for the murder of his son where there is a superior father to them both, or the right of such a supreme father. But where there are only father and sons, no sons can question the father for the death of their brother. The reason why a king cannot be punished is not because he is excepted from punishment, or doth not deserve it, but because there is no superior to judge him but God only to whom he is reserved.

VII

It is said thus, 'He that takes away from the people the power of choosing for themselves what form of government they please, he doth take away that wherein all civil liberty almost consists', page 65 [Milton 7, p. 192]. If almost all liberty be in choosing of the kind of government, the people have but a poor bargain of it – who cannot exercise their liberty but in chopping and changing their government, and have liberty only to give away their liberty, than which there is not a greater mischief, as being the cause of endless sedition.

VIII

'If there be any statute in our law by which thou canst find that tyrannical power is given to a king, that statute – being contrary to God's will, to nature and reason – understand that by that general and primary law of ours, that statute to be repealed, and not of force with us', page 153 [Milton 7, p. 426]. Here if any man may be judge what law is contrary to God's will, or to nature, or to reason, it will soon bring in confusion. Most men that offend, if they be to be punished or fined, will think that statute that gives all fines and forfeitures to a king to be a tyrannical law. Thus most statutes would be judged void, and all our forefathers taken for fools or madmen to make all our laws to give all penalties to the king.

IX

The sin of the children of Israel did lie not in desiring a king, but in desiring such a king like as the nations round about had. They distrusted God almighty that governed them by the monarchical power of Samuel, in time of oppression, when God provided a judge for them. But they desired a perpetual and an hereditary king that they might never want. In desiring a king they could not sin, for it was but desiring what they enjoyed by God's special providence.

X

Men are persuaded that in the making of a covenant, something is to be performed on both parts by mutual stipulation, which is not always true. For we find God made a covenant with Noah and his seed, with all the fowl and the cattle, not to destroy the earth any more by a flood [Genesis ix, 8–11]. This covenant was to be kept on God's part. Neither Noah, nor the fowl, nor the cattle, were to perform anything by this covenant. On the other side, Genesis xvii, 9, 10, God covenants with Abraham, saying 'Thou shalt keep my covenant ... every male child among you shall be circumcised'. Here it is called God's covenant, though it be to be performed only by Abraham. So a covenant may be called the king's covenant, because it is made to him, and yet to be performed only by the people. So also, 2 Kings xi, 17, 'Jehoiada made a covenant between the Lord and the king and the people, that they should be the Lord's people; between the king also and the people' – which might well be that the people should be the king's servants, and not for the king's covenanting to keep any human laws. For it is not likely the king should either covenant or take any oath to the people when he was but seven years of age, and that never any king of Israel took a coronation oath that can be showed. When Jehoiada showed the king to the rulers in the house of the Lord, he took an oath of the people. He did not article with them, but – saith the next verse – commanded them to keep a 'watch of the king's house', and that they should 'compass the king round about, every man with his weapons in his hand: and he that cometh within the ranges, let him be slain' [2 Kings xi, 5–8].

XI

To the text, 'Where the word of a king is, there is power, and who may say *to*⁴¹⁶ him, what doest thou?' [Ecclesiastes viii, 4], J[ohn] M[ilton] gives this answer: 'It is apparent enough that the preacher in this place gives precepts to every private man, not to the great sanhedrin, nor to the senate ... shall not the nobles, shall not all the other magistrates, shall not the whole people dare to mutter, so oft as the king pleaseth to dote?' [Milton 7, pp. 80, 82]. We must here note that the great council and all other magistrates or nobles, or the whole people, compared to the king are all but private men if they derive their power from him. They are magistrates under him, and out of his presence. For when he is in place they are but so many private men. J[ohn] M[ilton] asks, 'Who swears to a king, unless the king on the other side be sworn to keep God's laws and the laws of the country?' [Milton 7, p. 80]. We find that the rulers of Israel took an oath at the coronation of Jehoash. But we find no oath taken by that king – no, not so much as to God's laws, much less to the laws of the country.

XII

'A tyrant is he, who regarding neither law nor the common good, reigns only for himself and his faction', page 19 [Milton 5, p. 19]. In his *Defence* he expresseth himself thus, 'he is a tyrant who looks after only his own and not his people's profit. [Aristotle's] *Ethics*, book 10' (p. 189) [Milton 5, p. 18].

1. If it be tyranny not to regard the law, then all courts of equity, and pardons for any offences must be taken away. There are far more suits for relief against the laws than there be for the observation of the laws. There can be no such tyranny in the world as the law, if there were no equity to abate the rigour of it. *Summum jus* [law pushed to extremes] is *summa injuria* [extreme injustice]. If the penalties and forfeitures of all laws should still be exacted by all kings, it would be found that greatest tyranny would be for a king to govern according to law. The fines, penalties and forfeitures of all laws are due to the supreme power only, and were they duly paid they would far exceed the taxes in all places. It is the chief happiness of a kingdom, and their chief liberty, not to be governed by the laws only.

2. 'Not to regard the common good but to reign only for himself', is the supposition of an impossibility in the judgment of Aristotle, who teacheth us that 'the despotical power cannot be preserved, except the servant, or he in subjection, be also preserved' [1278^{b}36–8]. The truth of this strongly proves that it is in nature impossible to have a form of government that can be for the destruction of a people, as tyranny is supposed. If we will allow people to be governed, we must grant they must in the first place be preserved, or else they cannot be governed.

Kings have been and may be vicious men, and the government of one not so good as the government of another. Yet it doth not follow that the form of government is or can be in its own nature ill, because the governor is so. It is anarchy, or want of government, that can totally destroy a nation. We cannot find any such government as tyranny mentioned or named in Scripture, or any word in the

Hebrew tongue to express it. After such time as the cities of Greece practised to shake off monarchy, then and not till then, (which was after Homer's time) the name of tyrant was taken up for a word of disgrace for such men as by craft or force wrested the power of a city from a multitude to one man only – and not for the *exercising* but for the *ill obtaining* of the government. But now every man that is but thought to govern ill, or to be an ill man, is presently termed a tyrant, and so judged by his subjects. Few remember the prohibition, Exodus xxii, 28, 'Thou shalt not revile the Gods, nor curse the ruler of thy people', and fewer understand the reason of it. Though we may not judge one another, yet we may speak evil or revile one another, in that which hath been lawfully judged, and upon a trial wherein they have been heard condemned. This is not to judge, but only to relate the judgment of the ruler. To speak evil, or to revile a supreme judge, cannot be without judging him who hath no superior on earth to judge him – and in that regard must always be presumed innocent, though never so ill, if he cannot lawfully be heard.

J[ohn] M[ilton] that will have it tyranny in a king not to regard the laws, doth himself give as little regard to them as any man, where he reckons that 'contesting for privileges, customs, forms and that old entanglement of iniquity, their gibberish laws' are 'the badges of ancient slavery': *Tenure*, page 3 [Milton 5, p. 3]; [cf.] 'a disputing precedents, forms and circumstances' page 5 [Milton 5, p. 4].

J[ohn] M[ilton] is also of opinion that 'if at any time our forefathers, out of baseness, have lost anything of their right, that ought not hurt us. They might if they would promise slavery for themselves. For us certainly they could not, who have always the same right to free ourselves that they had to give themselves to any man in slavery' [Milton 7, p. 412]. This doctrine well practised, layeth all open to constant anarchy.

Lastly, if any desire to know what the liberty of the people is, which J[ohn] M[ilton] pleads for, he resolves us, saying that 'he that takes away from the people the right of choosing what form of government they please, takes away truly that in which all liberty doth almost consist' [Milton 7, p. 192]. It is well said by J[ohn] M[ilton] that all liberty doth *almost* consist in choosing their form of government. For there is another liberty exercised by the people, which he mentions not – which is the liberty of the people's choosing their religion. Every man may be of any religion, or of no religion. Greece and

Rome have been as famous for polytheism, or multitudes of gods, as of governors; and imagining aristocracy and democracy in heaven, as on earth.

OBSERVATIONS UPON H. GROTIUS
DE JURE BELLI & PACIS

In most questions of weight and difficulty concerning the right of war, or peace, or supreme power, Grotius hath recourse to the law of nature, or of nations, or to the primitive will of those men who first joined in society. It is necessary therefore a little to lay open the variety or contrariety in the civil and canon law, and in Grotius himself, about the law of nature and nations, not with a purpose to raise any contention about words or phrases but with a desire to reconcile or expound the sense of different terms.

Civilians,^{c} canonists, politicians and divines are not a little perplexed in distinguishing between the law of nature and the law of nations. About *jus naturae* and *jus gentium* there is much dispute by such as handle the original of government, and of property and community.

The civil law in one text allows a threefold division of law into *jus naturae*, *jus gentium* and *jus civile*. But in another text of the same law we find only a twofold division, into *jus civile* and *jus gentium*. This latter division the law takes from Gaius, the former from Ulpian, who will have *jus naturale* to be 'that which nature hath taught all creatures': '*quod natura omnia animalia docuit*' [*Digest* I, i, 1, 3; p. 29]. but for this he is confuted by Grotius, Salmasius and others who restrain the law of nature only to men using reason, which makes it all one with the law of nations – to which the canon law consents, and saith that '*jus naturale est commune omnium nationum* [natural law is common to all nations]' [*Decreti* dist. I, c.vii]. 'That which natural reason appoints all men to use, is the law of nations' [*Institutes* I, ii, 1; p. 1], saith Theophilus in the text of the civil law, and in the second book of the *Institutes*, chapter 1, *jus naturae* is confounded with *jus gentium*.

As the civilians sometimes confound, and sometimes separate the law of nature and the law of nations, so other-whiles they make them

---

^{c} [Civil lawyers; writers on civil – i.e. Roman – law].

also contrary one to the other. 'By the law of nature all men are born free': *'jure naturali omnes liberi nascuntur'*; but servitude is by the law of nations: *'jure gentium servitus invasit'* [by the law of nations servitude came in], saith Ulpian [*Digest* I, i, 4; p. 29].

And the civil law not only makes the law of nature and of nations contrary, but also will have the law of nations contrary to itself. 'War', saith the law, 'was brought in by the law of nations': *'ex jure gentium introducta bella'* [*Digest* I, i, 5; p. 29]. And yet the law of nations saith, 'since nature hath made us all of one kindred, it follows it is not lawful for one man to lie in wait for another': *'cum inter nos cognitionem quandam natura constituit, consequens est hominem homini insidiare nefas esse'*, saith Florentinus [*Digest* I, i, 3; p. 29].

Again, the civil law teacheth that 'from the law of nature proceeds the conjunction of man and woman, the procreation and education of children' [*Digest* I, i, 1, 3; p. 29]. But as for 'religion to God, and obedience to parents' [*Digest* I, i, 2; p. 29] it makes it to be by the law of nations.

To touch now the canon law, we may find in one place that 'men are governed either by the law of nature, or by customs': *'homines reguntur naturali jure, aut moribus'* [*Decreti* dist. I]. The law of nature, they call 'a divine law, the customs a human law': *'leges aut divinae sunt aut humanae; divinae naturae, humanae moribus constant'* [*Decreti* dist. I, c.i]. But in the next place the canon law makes *jus* to be either *'naturale, aut civile, aut gentium'* [*Decreti* dist. I, c.vi]. Though this division agree in terms with that of Ulpian in the civil law, yet in the explication of the terms there is diversity. For, what one law makes to belong to the law of nature, the other refers to the law of nations – as may easily appear to him that will take the pains to compare the civil and canon law in these points.

A principal ground of these diversities and contrarieties of divisions was an error which the heathens taught, that 'all things at first were common', and that 'all men were equal'. This mistake was not so heinous in those ethnic[d] authors of the civil laws, who wanting the guide of the history of Moses were fain to follow poets and fables for their leaders. But for Christians, who have read the Scriptures, to dream either of a community of all things, or an equality of all persons, is a fault scarce pardonable.

---

[d] [pagan; neither Christian nor Jewish, and so lacking knowledge of the Scriptures].

To salve these apparent contrarieties of community and property, *of**417 equality and subjection, the law of *jus gentium* was first invented. When that could not satisfy, to mend the matter this *jus gentium* was divided into a natural law of nations, and an human law of nations; and the law of nature into a primary and a secondary law of nature – distinctions which make a great sound, but edify not at all if they come under examination.

If there hath been a time when all things were common and all men equal, and that it be otherwise now, we must needs conclude that the law by which things were common, and men equal, was contrary to the law by which now things are proper*ᵉ* and men subject.

If we will allow Adam to have been lord of the world and of his children, there will need no such distinctions of the law of nature and of nations. For the truth will be that whatsoever the heathens comprehended under these two laws, is comprised in the moral law.

That the law of nature is one and the same with the moral may appear by a definition given by Grotius. The 'law of nature', saith he, 'is the dictate of reason, showing that in every action by the agreeing or disagreeing of it with natural reason there is a moral honesty or dishonesty, and consequently that such an action is commanded or forbidden by God the author of nature' (Grotius I, i, x, I). I cannot tell how Grotius would otherwise have defined the moral law. And the canon law grants as much, teaching that 'the law of nature is contained in the law and the gospel' [*Decreti* dist. I] 'whatsoever ye will that men do', etc., Matthew vii[, 12].*ᶠ*

The term of *jus naturae* is not originally to be found in Scripture. For though Thomas Aquinas takes upon him to prove out of the second [epistle] to the Romans that there is a *jus naturae*, yet Saint Paul doth not use those express terms. His words are, 'the gentiles which have not the law, do by nature the things contained in the law, these, having not the law are a law unto themselves' [Romans ii, 14]. He doth not say nature is a law unto them, but they are a law unto themselves. As for that which they call the law of nations, it is not a law distinct, much less opposite to the law of nature. But it is a small branch or parcel of that great law, for it is nothing but the law of nature or the moral law between nations. The same com-

---

ᵉ [privately owned].
ᶠ [Matthew vii, 12: 'Therefore all things whatsoever ye would that men should do to you, do ye even so to them: for this is the law and the prophets'].

mandment that forbids one private man to rob another, or one corporation to hurt another corporation, obliges also one king not to rob another king, and one commonwealth not to spoil another. The same law that enjoins charity to all men, even to enemies, binds princes and states to show charity to one another, as well as private persons.

And as the common or civil laws of each kingdom, which are made against treason, theft, murder, adultery, or the like, are all and every one of them grounded upon some particular commandment of the moral law; so all the laws of nations must be subordinate and reducible to the moral law.

The law of nature or the moral law is like the main ocean, which though it be one entire body, yet several parts of it have distinct names according to the diversity of the coasts on which they border. So it comes to pass that the law of nations, which is but a part of the law of nature, may be sub-divided almost *in infinitum* according to the variety of the persons or matters about which it is conversant.

The law of nature or the divine law is general, and doth only comprehend some principles of morality notoriously known of themselves, or at the most is extended to those things which by necessary and evident inference are consequent to those principles. Besides these, many other things are necessary to the well governing of a commonwealth, and therefore it was necessary that by human reason something more in particular should be determined concerning those things which could not be defined by natural reason alone. Hence it is that human laws be necessary as comments upon the text of the moral law – and of this judgment is Aquinas, who teacheth that*

> [the necessity of human law flows from this, that natural or divine law comprehends certain self-evident principles of morality and extends at the most to what follows from those principles by necessary and evident consequence. But besides these there are many other things necessary to good government in a commonwealth. And so it was necessary that by human reason some things should be determined more particularly concerning what could

---

* 'necessitas legis humanae manat ex eo, quod lex naturalis, vel divina, generalis est, et solum complectitur quaedam principia morum per se nota, et ad summum extenditur ad ea quae necessaria et evidenti elatione ex illis principiis consequuntur: praeter illa vero multa alia sunt necessaria in republica ad ejus rectam gubernationem: et ideo necessarium fuit ut per humanam rationem aliqua magis in particulari determinarentur circa ea quae per solam rationem naturalem definiri non possunt.'

not be decided by natural reason alone] (Ludovicus Molina *De Justitia*)

Thus much may suffice to show the distractions in and between the civil and common laws about the law of nature and nations. In the next place we are to consider how Grotius distinguisheth these laws.

To maintain the community of things to be natural, Grotius hath framed new divisions of the law of nature. First, in his preface to his books *De Jure Belli & Pacis* he produceth a definition of the law of nature in such doubtful, obscure and reserved terms, as if he were diffident of his undertaking. Next, in his first book and first chapter he gives us another distribution, which differs from his doctrine in his preface.

In his preface his first principle is that the 'appetite of society, that is to say, of community, is an action proper to man'. Here he presently corrects himself with an exception, that 'some other creatures are found to desire society', and withal he answers the objection thus – that 'this desire of society in brute beasts comes from some external principle' [Grotius, Prolegomena 6–7]. What he means by *'principium intelligens extrinsecum* [intelligent external principle]' I understand not, nor doth he explain, nor is it material, nor is the argument he useth to any purpose. For admitting all he saith to be true, yet his principle fails, for the question is not from what principle this desire of society proceeds in beasts, but whether there be such a desire or no. Besides, here he takes the appetite of society and community to be all one, whereas many live in society which live not in community.

Next, he teacheth that 'the keeping of society (*custodia societatis*) which in a rude manner', saith he, 'we have now expressed, is the fountain of that law which is properly so called'. I conceive by the law properly so called he intends the law of nature, though he express not so much; and to this appetite of sociable community he refers *alieni abstinentia* [abstaining from what belongs to others] [Grotius, Prolegomena 8]. But herein it may be he forgets himself, for where there is community there is neither *meum* nor *tuum* [mine nor thine], nor yet *alienum* [another's] – and if there be no *alienum* there can be no *alieni abstinentia*. To the same purpose, he saith that 'by the law of nature men must stand to bargains': '*juris naturae sit stare pactis*'

[Grotius, Prolegomena 15]. But if all things were common by nature, how could there be any bargain?

Again, Grotius tells us that 'from this signification of the law there hath flowed another larger', which consists, saith he, 'in discerning what delights us or hurts us, and in judging how things should be wisely distributed to each one'. This latter he calls the 'looser law of nature'; the former, '*jus sociale*, the law of nature, strictly, or properly taken'. 'And these two laws of nature should have place', saith he, 'though men should deny there were a God. But to them that believe there is a God, there is another original of law beside the natural, coming from the free will of God, to the which our own understanding tells us we must be subject' [Grotius, Prolegomena 9–12].

Thus have I gathered the substance of what is most material concerning the law of nature in his preface.

If we turn to the book itself, we have a division of law into

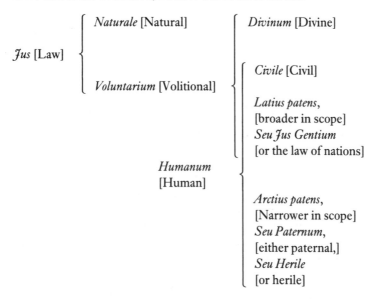

Jus [Law]

— *Naturale* [Natural]

— *Voluntarium* [Volitional]

— *Divinum* [Divine]

— *Humanum* [Human]

— *Civile* [Civil]

Latius patens, [broader in scope] *Seu Jus Gentium* [or the law of nations]

Arctius patens, [Narrower in scope] *Seu Paternum,* [either paternal,] *Seu Herile* [or herile]

In the definition of *jus naturale* he omits those subtleties of *jus naturae proprie dictum* [the law of nature properly so called], and *quod laxius ita dicitur* [what is more loosely so called], which we find in his preface, and gives such a plain definition, as may fitly agree to the moral law. By this it seems the law of nature and the moral law are one and the same. Whereas he affirmeth that

> the actions about which the law of nature is conversant are lawful or unlawful of themselves, and therefore are necessarily commanded or forbidden by God – by which mark, this law of nature doth not only differ from human law but from the divine voluntary law, which doth not command or forbid those things which of themselves and by their own nature are lawful or unlawful, but makes them unlawful by forbidding them and due by commanding them. [Grotius I, i, x, 2]

in this he seems to make the law of nature to differ from God's voluntary law, whereas in God necessary and voluntary are all one. Salmasius *De Usuris* in the twentieth chapter condemns this opinion of Grotius. Though he name him not, yet he means him, if I mistake not.

In the next place, I observe his saying that some things are by the law of nature not *proprie* [properly] but *reductive* [by reduction], and that the law of

> nature deals not only with those things which are beside the will of man but also with many things which follow the act of man's will. So dominion, such as is now in use, man's will brought in. But now that it is brought in, it is against the law of nature to take that from thee against thy will which is in thy dominion. [Grotius I, i, x, 3–4]

Yet for all this, Grotius maintains that 'the law of nature is so immutable that it cannot be changed by God himself' [I, i, x, 5]. He means to make it good with a distinction: 'some things', saith he, 'are by the law of nature, but not simply, but according to the certain state of things. So the common use of things was natural as long as dominion was not brought in, and right for every man to take his own by force before laws were made' [Grotius I, i, x, 7]. Here, if Grotius would have spoken plain, instead of 'but not simply, but according to the certain state of things', he would have said 'but not immutably, but for a certain time'. And then this distinction would have run thus: 'some things are by the law of nature, but not immutably, but for a certain time'. This must needs be the naked sense of his distinction, as appears by his explication in the words following, where he saith that 'the common use of things was natural so long as dominion was not brought in'. Dominion, he saith, was brought in by the will of man, whom by this doctrine Grotius makes to be able to change that law which God himself cannot change, as he saith. He gives a double ability to man: first, to make that no law of nature which God made to be the law of nature; and next, to make that a law of nature which God made not. For now that dominion is brought in, he maintains, it is against the law of nature to take that which is in another man's dominion.

Besides, I find no coherence in these words: 'by the law of nature it was right for every man to take his own by force, before laws made', since by the law of nature no man had anything of his own, and until laws were made there was no property according to his doctrine.

'*Jus humanum voluntarium latius patens* [volitional human law which is broader in scope]', he makes to be the law of nations, which, saith he, 'by the will of all or many nations hath received a power to bind'. He adds 'of many' because there is, as he grants, 'scarce any law to be found common to all nations besides the law of nature – which also is wont to be called the law of nations, being common to all nations'. Nay, as he confesseth 'often that is the law in one part of the world which in another part of the world is not the law of nations' [Grotius I, i, xiv, 1].

By these sentences it seems Grotius can scarce tell what to make to be the law of nations or where to find it.

Whereas he makes the law of nations to have a binding power from the will of men, it must be remembered that it is not sufficient for men to have a will to bind, but it is necessary also to have a power to bind.

Though several nations have one and the same law – for instance, let it be granted that theft is punished by death in many countries – yet this doth not make it to be a law of nations, because each nation hath it but as a national or civil law of their own country, and though it have a binding power from the will of many nations, yet because each nation hath but a will and power to bind themselves, and may without prejudice, consent, or consulting of any neighbour-nation alter this law if they find cause, it cannot properly be called the law of nations. That which is the foundation of the law of nations is to have it concern 'such things as belong to the mutual society of nations among themselves', as Grotius confesseth (book 2, chapter 8) [Grotius II, viii, i, 2] – and not of such things as have no further relation than to the particular benefit of each kingdom. For, as private men must neglect their own profit for the good of their country, so particular nations must sometimes remit part of their benefit for the good of many nations.

True it is that in particular kingdoms and commonwealths there be civil and national laws, and also customs that obtain the force of laws. But yet such laws are ordained by some supreme power, and the customs are examined, judged and allowed by the same supreme power. Where there is no supreme power that extends over all or many nations but only God himself, there can be no laws made to bind nations, but such as are made by God himself. We cannot find that God made any laws to bind nations, but only the moral law. As for the judicial law, though it were ordained by God, yet it was not the law of nations but of one nation only, and fitted to that commonwealth.

If any think that the customs wherein many nations do consent may be called the law of nations, as well as the customs of any one nation may be esteemed for national laws, they are to consider that it is not the being of a custom that makes it lawful – for then all customs, even evil customs, would be lawful. But it is the approbation of the supreme power that gives a legality to the custom. Where there is no supreme power over many nations, their customs cannot be made legal.

The*g* doctrine of Grotius is that

> God immediately after the creation did bestow upon mankind in general a right over things of inferior nature … From whence it came to pass that presently every man might snatch what he would for his own use, and spend what he could – and such an universal right was then instead of property. For what every one so catched another could not take from him but by injury. (*De Jure Belli* book 2, chapter 2, [ii, 1])

How repugnant this assertion of Grotius is to the truth of holy

---

g [The section also included in B begins here. Copy-text is B, which at p. ix gives as the title of the first part of this section, ending at p. 219 below: The Opinions of Hugo Grotius and Mr Selden about natural community and voluntary property examined].

Scripture, Mr Selden teacheth us in his *Mare Clausum* (book 1, chapter 4), saying that Adam 'by donation from God', Genesis i, 28,

> was made the general lord of all things, not without such a private dominion to himself as (without his grant) did exclude his children. And by donation and assignation, or some kind of cession (before he was dead or left any heir to succeed him) his children had their distinct territories by right of private dominion. Abel had his flocks, and pastures for them. Cain had his fields for corn, and the land of Nod where he built himself a city. [Selden 2, pp.19–20]

This determination of Mr Selden's being consonant to the history of the Bible, and to natural reason, doth contradict the doctrine of Grotius. I cannot conceive why Mr Selden should afterwards affirm that 'neither the law of nature nor the divine law do command or forbid either communion of all things or private dominion, but permitteth both' [Selden 2, p. 20].

As for the general community between Noah and his sons which Mr Selden will have to be granted to them [Selden 2, p. 18], Genesis ix, 2, the text doth not warrant it. For although the sons are there mentioned with Noah in the blessing, yet it may best be understood with a subordination or a benediction in succession. The blessing might truly be fulfilled if the sons, either under or after their father, enjoyed a private dominion. It is not probable that the private dominion which God gave to Adam – and by his donation, assignation or cession, to his children – was abrogated, and a community of all things instituted between Noah and his sons. At the time of the Flood, Noah was left the sole heir of the world. Why should it be thought that God would disinherit him of his birthright, and make him of all the men in the world the only tenant in common with his children? If the blessing given to Adam, Genesis i, 28, be compared to that given to Noah and his sons, Genesis ix, 2, there will be found a considerable difference between those two texts. In the benediction of Adam we find expressed a 'subduing of the earth, and a dominion over the creatures', neither of which are expressed in the blessing of Noah, nor the earth there once named. It is only said, the 'fear of you shall be upon the creatures, and into your hands are they delivered'. Then immediately it follows, 'Every moving thing shall be meat for you, as the green herb'. The first blessing gave Adam dominion over the earth and all creatures, the later allows Noah liberty to use the living creatures for food. Here is no alteration or diminishing of his title to a property of all things, but an enlargement only of his commons.

But whether with Grotius, community came in at the creation, or with Mr Selden at the Flood, they both agree it did not long continue. '*Sed veri non est simile hujusmodi communionem diu obtinuisse*' [but it is not true that this kind of common ownership lasted for long] is the confession of Mr Selden [Selden 2, p. 18]. It seems strange that Grotius should maintain that community of all things should be by the law of nature, of which God is the author, and yet such community should not be able to continue. Doth it not derogate from the providence of God Almighty to ordain a community which could not continue? Or doth it not make the act of our forefathers, in abrogating the natural law of community by introducing that of property, to be a sin of a high presumption?

The prime duties of the second table[h] are conversant about the right of property. But if property be brought in by a human law, as Grotius teacheth, then the moral law depends upon the will of man. There could be no law against adultery or theft if women and all things were common.

Mr Selden saith that the law of nature or of God '*nec vetuit nec jubebat, sed permisit utrumque, tam nempe rerum communionem quam privatum dominium*' [neither forbade nor commanded, but equally permitted both, that is to say common ownership as well as the private dominion of things] [Selden 2, p. 20]. And yet for property (which he terms '*primaeva rerum dominia*' [the form of ownership in the earliest times]) he teacheth that 'Adam received it from God' (*a numine acceperat*) [Selden 2, p. 19]. And for community he saith: 'We meet with evident footsteps of the community of things in that donation of God by which Noah and his three sons are made *domini pro indiviso rerum omnium* [lords in common of all things]' [Selden 2, pp. 17–18]. Thus he makes the private dominion of Adam as well as the common dominion of Noah and his sons to be both by the will of God. Nor doth he show how Noah or his sons, or their posterity, had any authority to alter the law of community which was given them by God.

---

[h] [The last six of the Ten Commandments (Exodus xx, 3–17), dealing with duties between people. The first table – the first four Commandments – dealt with duties towards God].

'In distributing territories', Mr Selden saith, 'the consent as it were of mankind (passing their promise which should also bind their posterity) did intervene. So that men departed from their common right of communion of those things, which were so distributed to particular lords or masters' [Selden 2, p. 21]. This distribution by consent of mankind we must take upon credit, for there is not the least proof offered for it out of antiquity.

How the consent of mankind could bind posterity when all things were common is a point not so evident. Where children take nothing by gift or by descent from their parents, but have an equal and common interest with them, there is no reason in such cases that the acts of the fathers should bind the sons.

I find no cause why Mr Selden should call community a pristine right, since he makes it but to begin in Noah and to end in Noah's children or grandchildren at the most. For he confesseth the earth '*a Noachidis seculis aliquot post diluvium esse divisam*' [was divided by Noah's descendants some centuries after the Flood] [Selden 2, p. 18].

That ancient tradition which by Mr Selden's acknowledgment hath *received**[418] reputation everywhere, seems most reasonable, in that it tells us that

> Noah himself, as lord of all, was author of the distribution of the world, and of private dominion, and that by the appointment of an oracle from God he did confirm this distribution by his last will and testament, which at his death he left in the hands of his eldest son Shem. And also warned all his sons that none of them should invade any of their brothers' dominions, or injure one another, because from thence discord and civil war would necessarily follow. [Selden 2, p. 19]

Many[i] conclusions in Grotius his book *De Jure Belli ac Pacis* are built upon the foundation of these two principles:

1   The first is that '*communis rerum usus naturalis fuit*' [the use of things in common was natural] [Grotius I, i, x, 7].

2   The second is that '*dominium quale nunc in usu est, voluntas humana introduxit*' [property as it now exists was introduced by human will] [Grotius I, i, x, 4].

---

[i] [At p. 9 in B the title of the section which begins here and ends at p. 227 is given as: Dangerous Conclusions of Grotius against Monarchy Censured].

Upon these two propositions of natural community and voluntary property depend divers dangerous and seditious conclusions, which are dispersed in several places. In the fourth chapter of the first book, the title of which chapter is of the war of subjects against their superiors, Grotius handleth the question 'Whether the law of not resisting superiors do bind us in most grievous and most certain danger' [Grotius I, iv, vii, I], and his determination is that

> This law of not resisting superiors seems to depend upon the will of those men who at first joined themselves in a civil society, from whom the right of government doth come to them that govern. If those had been at first asked if their will were to impose this burden upon all, that they should choose rather to die than in any case *by arms*[419] to repel the force of superiors, I know not whether they would answer that it was their will unless perhaps with this addition: if resistance cannot be made but with the great disturbance of the commonwealth, and destruction of many innocents. [I, iv, vii, 2]

Here we have his resolution that in great and certain danger men may resist their governors, if it may be without disturbance of the commonwealth. If you would know who should be judge of the greatness and certainty of the danger, or how we may know it, Grotius hath not one word of it. So that for ought appears to the contrary, his mind may be that every private man may be judge of the danger – for other judge he appoints none. It had been a foul fault in so desperate a piece of service as the resisting of superiors, to have concealed the lawful means by which we may judge of the greatness of certainty of public danger before we lift up our hands against authority, considering how prone most of us are to censure and mistake those things for great and certain dangers which in truth many times are no dangers at all, or at the most but very small ones; and *to*[420] flatter ourselves that by resisting our superiors we may do our country laudable service without disturbance of the commonwealth, since the effects of sedition cannot be certainly judged of but by the events only.

Grotius proceeds to answer an objection against this doctrine of resisting superiors. 'If', saith he,

> any man shall say that this rigid doctrine of dying rather than resisting any injuries of superiors is no human but a divine law,

it is to be noted that men at first, not by any precept of God, but of their own accord, led by experience of the infirmities of separated families against violence, did meet together in civil society, from whence civil power took beginning. Which therefore St Peter calls an human ordinance, although elsewhere it be called a divine ordinance, because God approveth the wholesome institutions of men. God in approving a human law is to be thought to approve it as human, and in a human manner. [Grotius I, iv, vii, 3]

And again in another place he goeth further, and teacheth us that 'if the question happen to be concerning the primitive will of the people, it will not be amiss for the people that now are, and which are accounted the same with them that were long ago, to express their meaning in this matter which is to be followed, unless it certainly appear that the people long ago willed otherwise' (book 2, chapter 2) [Grotius II, vii, xxvii, 2].

For fuller explication of his judgment about resisting superiors, he concludes thus:

The greater the thing is which is to be preserved, the greater is the equity which reacheth forth an exception against the words of the law. Yet I dare not (saith Grotius) without difference condemn either *single*[421] men or a lesser part of the people, who in the last refuge of necessity do so use this equity as *in*[422] the meantime they do not forsake the respect of the common good. [Grotius I, iv, vii, 4]

Another doctrine of Grotius is that 'the empire which is exercised by kings doth not cease to be the empire of the people' [Grotius II, xvi, xvi, 1]. 'That kings who in a lawful *manner*[423] succeed those who were elected have the supreme power by an usufructuary right only and no property' [Grotius I, iii, xi, 1].

Furthermore, he teacheth that 'the people may choose what form of government they please, and their will is the rule of right: *Populus eligere potest qualem vult gubernationis formam, neque ex praestantia formae, sed ex voluntate jus metiendum est*' [Grotius] (book 1, chapter 3, [viii, 2]).

Also that:

The people choosing a king may reserve some acts to themselves and may bestow others upon the king with full authority if either an express partition be appointed, or if the people being yet free do command their future king by way of a standing command, or if anything be added by which it may be understood that the king may be compelled or else punished. [Grotius I, iii, xvii, I]

In these passages of Grotius which I have cited, we find evidently these doctrines:

1   That civil power depends on the will of the people.

2   That private men or petty multitudes may take up arms against their princes.

3   That the *lawful*[424] kings have no property in their kingdoms, but an usufructuary right only as if the people were the lords and kings but their tenants.

4   That the law of not resisting superiors is a human law, depending on the will of the people at first.

5   That the will of the first people, if it be not known, may be expounded by the people that now are.

No doubt but Grotius foresaw what uses the people might make of these doctrines by concluding if the chief power be in the people that then it is lawful for them to compel and punish kings as oft as they misuse their power. Therefore he tells us he 'rejects the opinion of them who everywhere and without exception will have the chief power to be so the people's that it is lawful for them to compel and punish kings as oft as they misuse their power'. And 'this opinion', he confesseth, 'if it be altogether received, hath been and may be the cause of many evils' [Grotius] (book 1, chapter 3, [viii, I]). This cautelous[j] rejection, qualified with these terms of *everywhere, without exception* and *altogether*, makes but a mixed negation – partly negative and partly affirmative (which our lawyers call a negative pregnant).[k] Which brings forth this modal proposition, *that in some places with some exception, and in some sort the people may compel and punish their kings.*

But let us see how Grotius doth refute the general opinion that people may correct kings. He frames his argument in these words:

[j] [wily, circumspect].

[k] [negative pregnant: a legal term for a negative which implies an affirmative – for example, a denial that you have committed a certain crime on a particular day, implying that you have committed the crime, though not then].

It is lawful for every man to yield himself to be a private servant to whom he please. What should hinder but that also it may be lawful for a free people so to yield themselves to one or *to*[*425] more, that the right of governing them be fully set over without retaining any part of the right? And you must not say 'that this may not be presumed', for we do not now seek what in a doubtful case may be presumed, but what by right may be done. [Grotius I, iii, viii, I]

Thus far is the argument, in which the most that is proved (if we gratify him and yield his whole argument for good) is this, *that the people may grant away their power without retaining any part.* But what is this to what the people *have* done? For though the people may give away their power without reservation of any part to themselves, yet if they have not so done, but have reserved a part, Grotius must confess that the people may compel and punish their kings if they transgress. So that, by his favour, the point will be, not what by right *may* be done, but what in this doubtful case *hath* been done – since by his own rule it is the will and meaning of the first people that joined in society that must regulate the power of their successors.

But on Grotius' side it may be urged that in all presumption the people have given away their whole power to kings, unless they can prove they have reserved a part. For if they will have any benefit of a reservation or exception, it lies on their part to prove their exception, and not on the kings' parts who are in possession.

This answer, though in itself it be most just and good, yet of all men Grotius may not use it. For he saves the people the labour of proving the primitive reservation of their forefathers, by making the people that now are, competent expositors of the meaning of those first ancestors; who may justly be presumed not to have been either so improvident for themselves or so negligent of all their posterity, when, by the law of nature, they were free and had all things common, *as*[*426] at *an*[*427] instant without any condition or limitation to give away that liberty and right of community and to make themselves and their children eternally subject to the will of such governors as might misuse them without control.

On the behalf of the people it may be further answered to Grotius that although our ancestors had made an absolute grant of their liberty, without any condition expressed, yet it must *necessarily be*[*428] implied that it was upon condition to be well governed, and that the non-performance of that implied condition makes the grant void. Or, if we will not allow an implicit condition, then it may be said that the grant in itself was a void grant for being unreasonable and a violation of the law of nature, without any valuable consideration. What sound reply Grotius can return to such answers I cannot conceive, if he keep himself to his first principle of natural community.

As Grotius' argument against the people is not sound, so his answer to the argument that is made for the people is not satisfactory. It is objected that 'he that ordains is above him that is ordained'. Grotius answers:†

> [this is true only in the case of a grant of authority where the effect continues to depend on the will of the person who made the grant, and not in a case where the arrangement at first arose by the will of the grantor but later continued by necessity – as when a woman chooses a husband, whom she must then by necessity obey]. [Grotius I, iii, viii, 13]

The reply may be that by Grotius' former doctrine the very effect of the constitution of kings by the people depends perpetually upon the will of them that constitute, and upon no other necessity. He will not say that it is by any necessity of the law of nature, or by any positive law of God. He teacheth that: '*Non Dei precepto sed sponte*' [not by God's decree but of their own accord], men entered into civil society; that it is **an**[429] human ordinance; that God doth only approve it '*ut humanum*' [as human], and '*humano modo*' [in a human way] [Grotius I, iv, vii, 3]. He tells us further that '*Populus potest eligere qualem vult gubernationis formam, et ex voluntate jus metiendum est*': [the people can choose what form of government they please, and the government's right is to be measured by the people's will] [Grotius I, iii, viii, 2]; that the people may give the king as little power as they will and for as little time as they please; that they **may**[430] make temporary kings, as dictators and protectors – '*jus quovis tempore revocabile, id est precarium*' [a right which can be recalled at any time, that is to say, an impermanent right], as the Vandals in Africa and the Goths in Spain would depose their kings as oft as they displeased **them**,[131] '*horum enim actus irriti possunt reddi ab his, qui potestatem revocabiliter*

---

† '*verum duntaxat est in ea constitutione cujus effectus perpetuo pendet a voluntate constituentis, non etiam in ea quae ab initio est voluntatis, postea vero effectum habet necessitatis: quomodo mulier virum sibi constituit, cui parere semper habet necesse.*'

dederunt, ac proinde non idem est effectus, nec jus idem' [for their acts can be rendered invalid by those who gave them revocable power, and so the effect is not the same, nor the right] [Grotius I, iii, xi, 3]. Here he doth teach in plain words, the effect doth depend upon the will of the people. By this we may judge how improperly he useth the instance of a woman that appoints herself a husband, whom she must always necessarily obey [Grotius I, iii, viii, 13] – since the necessity of the continuance of the wife's obedience depends upon the law of God, which hath made the bond of matrimony indissolvable. Grotius will not say the like for the continuance of the subject's obedience to the prince, neither will he say that women may choose husbands as he tells us the people may choose kings, by giving their husbands as little power and for as little a time as they please.

Next, it is objected that tutors who are set over pupils may be removed if they abuse their power. Grotius answers: *'In tutore hoc procedit qui superiorem habet, at in imperiis quia progressus non datur in infinitum'* [this occurs since the tutor has a superior, but in matters of government because there is no infinite progression] *'omnino in aliqua persona, aut coetu consistendum est'*: 'we must stay in some one person, or in a multitude, whose faults (because they have no superior judge above them) God hath witnessed that He will have a particular care of, either to revenge them if He judge it needful, or to tolerate them either for the punishment or trial of the people' [Grotius I, iii, viii, 14]. It is true in kingdoms we cannot proceed *in infinitum*. Yet we may and must go to the highest, which by Grotius' rule is the people, because they first made kings. So that there is no need to stay *in aliqua persona* [in some one person], but *in coetu*, in the people – so that by his doctrine kings may be punished by the people, but the faults of the people must be left to the judgment of God.

I have briefly presented here the desperate inconveniences which attend upon the doctrine of the natural freedom and community of all things. These and many more absurdities are easily removed if on the contrary we maintain the natural and private dominion of Adam to be the fountain of all government and property. And if we mark it well we shall find that Grotius doth in part grant as much. The ground why those that now live do obey their governors is the will of their forefathers, who at the first ordained princes – and in obedience to that will the children continue in subjection. This is according to the mind of Grotius, so that the question is not *whether* kings have a fatherly power over their subjects, but *how* kings first came by it. Grotius will have it that our forefathers, being all free, made an assignment of their power to kings. The other opinion denies any such general freedom of our forefathers, but derives the power of kings from the original dominion of Adam.

This natural dominion of Adam maybe proved out of Grotius himself, who teacheth that *'generatione jus acquiritur parentibus in liberos'* [by generation parents acquire rights over their children; Grotius II, v, i], and that 'naturally no other can be found but the parents to whom the government should belong' [Grotius II, v, ii, I], and the right of ruling and compelling them doth belong to parents. And in another place he hath these words, speaking of the fifth commandment: *'Parentum nomine qui naturales sunt *magistratus*,*[432] *etiam alios rectores par est intelligi quorum authoritas societatem humanam continet'* [by the word parents – who are natural magistrates – should also be understood other rulers whose authority binds together human society; Grotius II, xx, xxx, 2]. And if parents be natural magistrates, children must needs be born natural subjects.

But *though*[433] Grotius acknowledges parents to be natural magistrates, yet he will have it that children when they come to full age and are separated from their parents are free from natural subjection. For this he offers proof out of Aristotle and out of Scripture [Grotius II, v, ii, I; II, v, vii].

First, for Aristotle. We must note he doth not teach that every separation of children of full age is an obtaining of liberty, as if that men when they come to years might voluntarily separate themselves and cast off their natural obedience. But Aristotle speaks only of a passive separation. For he doth not say that children are subject to parents until they *do separate*, but he saith until they *be separated* – *χωρισθῇ*[434] in the verb of the passive voice. That is, until *by law* they be separated. For the law (which is nothing else but the will of him that hath the power of the supreme father) doth in many cases for the public benefit of society free children from subjection to the subordinate parent. So that the natural subjection, by such emancipation of children, is not extinguished but only assumed and regulated by the parent paramount.

Secondly, Grotius cites Numbers xxx to prove that the 'power of the fathers over the sons and daughters, to dissolve their vows, was not perpetual, but during the time only whilst the children were part of the father's family' [Grotius II, v, vii]. But if we turn to the chapter we may find that Grotius either deceives himself or us. For there is not one word in that chapter concerning *vows*[435] of sons, but of daughters only, being in their father's family. And the being of the *daughter*[436] in the father's house meaneth only the daughter's being a virgin and not married, which may be gathered by the argument of the whole chapter – which taketh particular order for the vows of women of all estates. First for virgins, in the third verse. Secondly, for wives in general, in the sixth verse. Thirdly, for widows and women divorced, in the ninth verse. There is no law for virgins out of their fathers' houses; we may not think they would have been omitted if they had been free from their fathers. We find no freedom in the text for women till after marriage – and if they were married, though they were in their fathers' houses, *yet*[437] fathers had no power of their vows, but their husbands.

If by the law of nature departure from the father's house had emancipated children, why doth the civil law, contrary to the law of nature, give power and remedy to fathers *to*[438] recover by action of law their children that depart, or are taken from them without their consent? Without the consent of parents the civil law allows no emancipation.[^l]

Concerning subjection of children to parents, Grotius distinguisheth three several times:

The first is the time of 'imperfect judgment'.

The second is the time of 'perfect judgment', but 'whilst the son remains a part of the father's family'.

The third is 'the time after he hath departed out of his father's family'.

In the first time, he saith, 'all the actions of children are under the dominion of the parents' [Grotius II, v, ii, 1].

During the second time,

> when they are of the age of mature judgment they are under their fathers' command in those actions only which are of moment for their parents' family. In other actions the children have a power or moral faculty of doing, but they are bound in those also to study always to please their parents. But since this duty is not by force of any moral faculty, as those former are, but only of piety, observance and duty of repaying thanks, it doth

[^l]: [The section included in B ends here. Copy-text from here is 52H].

227

not make anything void which is done against it, as neither a gift of anything is void being made by any owner whatsoever against the rules of parsimony. [Grotius II, v, iii]

In both these times, the right of ruling and compelling is (as Grotius acknowledgeth) comprehended so far forth as children are to be compelled to their duty, or amended. Although the power of a parent doth so follow the person of a father that it cannot be pulled away and transferred upon another, yet the father may naturally pawn or also sell his son if there be need. [Grotius II, v, iv–v]

In the third time, he saith, 'the son is in all things free and of his own authority, always that duty remaining of piety and observance, the cause of which is perpetual' [Grotius II, v, vi]. In this triple distinction, though Grotius allow children in some cases during the second, and in all cases during the third time to be free and of their own power by a moral faculty, yet, in that he confesseth in all cases children are bound to study always to please their parents out of piety and duty, – 'the cause of which', as he saith, 'is perpetual' – I cannot conceive how in any case children can naturally have any power or moral faculty of doing what they please without their parents' leave, since they are always bound to study to please their parents. And though by the laws of some nations children when they attain to years of discretion have power and liberty in many actions, yet this liberty is granted them by positive and human laws only – which are made by the supreme fatherly power of princes, who regulate, limit or assume the authority of inferior fathers for the public benefit of the commonwealth. So that naturally the power of parents over their children never ceaseth by any separation, but only by the permission of the transcendent fatherly power of the supreme prince children may be dispensed with or privileged in some cases from obedience to subordinate parents.

Touching the point of dissolving the vows of children, Grotius in his last edition of his book hath corrected his first. For in the first he teacheth 'that the power of the father was greater over the daughter dwelling with him than over the son, for her vow he might make void, but not his'. But instead of these words, in his last edition he saith 'that the power over the son or daughter to dissolve vows, was not perpetual but did endure as long as the children were a part of their father's family' [Grotius II, v, vii]. About the meaning of the text out of which he draws this conclusion, I have already spoken.*ᵐ*

Three ways Grotius propoundeth, whereby supreme power may be had:

> First, by full right of property.
> Secondly, by an usufructuary right.
> Thirdly, by a temporary right.

The Roman dictators, saith he,

> had supreme power by a temporary right. As well those kings who are first elected as those that in a lawful right succeed to kings elected have supreme power by a usufructuary right. Some kings that have got supreme power by a just war, or into whose power some people for avoiding a greater evil have so yielded themselves as that they have excepted nothing, have a full right of property. [Grotius I, iii, xi, 1]

Thus we find but two means acknowledged by Grotius whereby a king may obtain a full right of property in a kingdom. That is, either by a just war or by donation of the people.

How a war can be just without a precedent title in the conqueror, Grotius doth now show. And if the title only make the war just, then no other right can be obtained by war than what the title bringeth. For a just war doth only put the conqueror in possession of his old right, but not create a new. The like which Grotius saith of succession may be said of war. 'Succession', saith he, 'is no title of a kingdom, which gives a form to the kingdom, but a continuation of the old, for the right which began by the election of the family is continued by succession, wherefore so much as the first election gave, so much the succession brings' [Grotius I, iii, x, 5]. So to a conqueror that hath a title, war doth not give but put him in possession of a right, and except the conqueror had a full right of property at first, his conquest cannot give it him. For if originally he and his ancestors had but an usufructuary right, and were outed of the possession of the kingdom by an usurper, here, though the re-conquest be a most just war, yet shall not the conqueror in this case gain any full right of property, but must be remitted to his usufructuary right only. For

---

ᵐ [See above pp. 226–7. The passage referred to is from one of the chapters that was included in B].

what justice can it be that the injustice of a third person – an usurper – should prejudice the people to the divesting of them of that right of property which was reserved in their first donation to their elected king, to whom they gave but an usufructuary right, as Grotius conceiveth? Wherefore it seems impossible that there can be a just war whereby a full right of property may be gained, according to Grotius' principles. For if a king come in by conquest, he must either conquer them that have a governor, or those people that have none. If they have no governor, then they are a free people, and so the war will be unjust to conquer those that are free, especially if the freedom of the people be by the primary law of nature as Grotius teacheth. But if the people conquered have a governor, that governor hath either a title or not. If he have a title, it is an unjust war that takes the kingdom from him. If he have no title, but only the possession of a kingdom, yet it is unjust for any other man that wants a title also, to conquer him that is but in possession. For it is a just rule that 'where the cases are alike, he that is in possession is in the better condition': '*in pari causa possidentis melior conditio*' (book 2, chapter 23) [Grotius II, xxiii, II]. And this by the law of nature, even in the judgment of Grotius. But if it be admitted that he that attempts to conquer have a title and he that is in possession hath none, here the conquest is but in nature of a possessory action, to put the conqueror in possession of a primer right and not to raise a new title. For war begins where the law fails: '*ubi judicia deficiunt incipit bellum*' (book 2, chapter 1) [Grotius II, ii, I]. And thus upon the matter I cannot find in Grotius' book *De Jure Belli* how that any case can be put wherein by a just war a man may become a king *pleno jure proprietatis* [by full right of property].

All government and supreme power is founded upon public subjection, which is thus defined by Grotius: '*Publica subjectio est, qua se populus homini alicui, aut pluribus hominibus, aut etiam populo alteri in ditionem dat*' [public subjection occurs when a people gives itself into the power of one or more men, or into that of another people] (book 2, chapter 5) [Grotius II, v, xxxi]. If subjection be the gift of the people, how can supreme power *pleno jure*, in full right, be got by a just war?

As to the other means whereby kings may get supreme power in full right of property, Grotius will have it to be 'when some people for avoiding a greater evil do so yield themselves into another's power as that they do except nothing' [Grotius I, iii, xi, I]. It would be considered how, without war, any people can be brought into such danger of life as that because they can find no other ways to defend themselves, or because they are so pressed with poverty as they cannot otherwise have means to sustain themselves, they are forced to renounce all right of governing themselves and deliver it to a king.

But if such a case cannot happen but by *war*[439] only, which reduceth a people to such terms of extremity as compels them to an absolute abrenunciation of all sovereignty, then war – which causeth that necessity – is the prime means of extorting such sovereignty, and not the free gift of the people, who cannot otherwise choose but give away that power which they cannot keep.

Thus upon the reckoning, the two ways propounded by Grotius are but one way – and that one way, in conclusion, is no way whereby supreme power may be had in full right of property. His two ways are, a just war or a donation of the people. A just war cannot be without a title, no title without *the*[440] donation of the people, no donation without such a necessity as nothing can bring upon the donors but a war. So that howsoever Grotius in words acknowledge that kings may have *full*[441] right of property, yet by consequence he denies it by such circular suppositions as by coincidence destroy each other. And in effect he leaves all people a right to plead in bar against the right of property of any prince, either *per minas* [by threats] or *per dures*.

Many times, saith Grotius, it happens that war is grounded upon 'expletive justice, *justitiam expletricem*', which is 'when a man cannot obtain that he ought, he takes that which is as much in value, which in moral estimation is the same' [Grotius II, vii, ii, I]. For in war, when the same province cannot be recovered to the which a man hath a title, he recovers another of the like value. This recovery cannot give a full right of property, because the justice of such a war reacheth no farther than to a compensation for a former right to another thing, and therefore can give no new right.

I am bound to take notice of a case put by Grotius amongst those causes which he thinks should move the people to renounce all their right of governing and give it to another. 'It may also happen', saith he, 'that a father of a family possessing large territories will not receive any man to dwell within his land upon *any*[442] other condition' [Grotius I, iii, viii, 3]. And in another place he saith that 'all kings are not made by the people' [Grotius I, viii, iii, 13], which may be sufficiently understood by the examples of a father of a family receiving strangers under the law of obedience. In both these passages we have a close and curt acknowledgment that a father of a family may be an absolute king over strangers, without the choice of the people. Now I would know whether such fathers of families have not the same absolute power over their own children without the people's choice, which he allows them over strangers. If they have, I cannot but call them absolute proprietary kings, though Grotius be not willing to give them that title in plain terms. For indeed, to allow such kings were to condemn his own principle that 'dominion came in by the will of the people' [I, i, x, 4], and so consequently to overthrow his usufructuary kings – of whom I am next to speak.

Grotius saith that 'the law of obeying or resisting princes depends upon the will of them who first met in civil society, from whom power doth flow to kings' [Grotius I, iv, vii, 2]; and that 'men of their own accord came together into civil society, from whence springs civil power' [Grotius I, iv, vii, 3]; and 'the people may choose what form of government they please' [Grotius I, iii, viii, 2]. Upon these suppositions he concludes that kings elected by the people have but an usufructuary right, that is, a right to take the profit or fruit of the kingdom, but not a right of property or power to alienate it. But why doth he call it an usufructuary right? It seems to me a term too mean or base to express the right of any king, and is derogatory to the dignity of supreme majesty. The word usufructuary is used by the lawyers to signify him that hath the use, profit or fruit of some corporal thing that may be used without the property, for of fungible things (*res fungibiles*, the civilians" call them) that are spent or consumed in the use, as corn, wine, oil, money, there cannot be an usufructuary right.

It is to make a kingdom all one with a farm, as if it had no other use but to be let out to him that can make most of it. Whereas in truth it is the part and duty of a king to govern, and he hath a right so to do, and to that end supreme power is given unto him. The taking of the profit or making use of the patrimony of the crown is but as a means only to enable him to perform that great work of government.

" [Civil lawyers; writers on civil – i.e. Roman – law].

Besides, Grotius will not only have an elected king but also his lawful successors to have but an usufructuary right, so that though a king hath a crown to him and to his heirs, yet he will allow him no property, because he hath no power to alienate it. For he supposeth the primary will of the people to have been to bestow supreme power to go in succession, and not to be alienable. But for this he hath no better proof than a naked presumption, *'in regnis quae populi voluntate delata sunt concedo non esse praesumendum eam fuisse populi voluntatem ut alienatio imperii sui regi permitteretur'* [in kingdoms which have been granted by the will of the people, I admit that it is not to be presumed that it was the wish of the people that the king be permitted to alienate his power; Grotius I, iii, xiii, I].

But though he will not allow kings a right of property in their kingdoms, yet a right of property there must be in somebody, and in whom but in the people? For he saith, 'the empire which is exercised by kings doth not cease to be the empire of the people' [II, xvi, xvi, I]. His meaning is, the use is the king's, but the property is the people's.

But if the power to alienate the kingdom be in him that hath the property, this may prove a comfortable doctrine to the people. But yet to allow a right of succession in kings and still to reserve a right of property in the people may make some contradiction. For the succession must either hinder the right of alienation which is in the people, or the alienation must destroy that right of succession which, by Grotius' confession, may attend upon elected kings.

Though Grotius confess that supreme power be *'unum quiddam* [a unity], and in itself indivisible', yet he saith, 'sometimes it may be divided either by parts potential, or *subjective'*[443] [Grotius I, iii, xvii, I]. I take his meaning to be that the government, or the governed may be divided. An example he gives of the Roman Empire which was divided into the east and west. But whereas he saith *'fieri potest,* etc. It may be, the people choosing a king may reserve some actions to themselves, and in others they may give full power to the king' [Grotius I, iii, xvii, I], the example he brings out of Plato of the Heraclides doth not prove it, and it is to dream of such a form of government as never yet had name nor was ever found in any settled kingdom, nor *[can]*[444] *possibly*[445] be without strange confusion.

If it were a thing so voluntary and at the pleasure of men when they were free to put themselves under subjection, why may they not as voluntarily leave subjection when they please, and be free again?

If they had a liberty to change their natural freedom into a voluntary subjection, there is stronger reason that they may change their voluntary subjection into natural freedom – since it is as lawful for men to alter their wills as their judgments.

Certainly it was a rare felicity that all the men in the world at one instant of time should agree together in one mind to change the natural community of all things into private dominion. For without such an unanimous consent it was not possible for community to be altered. For if but one man in the world had dissented, the alteration had been unjust, because that man by the law of nature had a right to the common use of all things in the world, so that to have given a property of any one thing to any other had been to have robbed him of his right to the common use of all things. And of this judgment the Jesuit Ludovicus Molina seems to be in his book *De Justitia*, where he saith, '*si aliquis de cohabitantibus*, etc. If one of the neighbours will not give his consent to it, the commonwealth should have no authority over him, because *then**[446] every other man hath no right or authority over him, and therefore can they not give authority to the commonwealth over him'.

If our first parents, or some other of our forefathers did voluntarily bring in property of goods and subjection to governors, and it were in their power either to bring them in or not, or having brought them in to alter their minds and restore them to their first condition of community and liberty, what reason can there be alleged that men that now live should not have the same power? So that if any one man in the world, be he never so mean or base, will but alter his will and say he will resume his natural right to community, and be restored unto his natural liberty, and consequently take what he please and do what he list, who can say that such a man doth more than by right he may? And then it will be lawful for every man, when he please, to dissolve all government, and destroy all property.

Whereas Grotius saith that by the law of nature all things were at first common [Grotius I, i, x, 7] and yet teacheth that after property was brought in it was against the law of nature to use community [Grotius I, i, x, 4], he doth thereby not only make the law of nature changeable, which he saith God cannot do, but he also makes the law of nature contrary to itself.

OBSERVATIONS[a]
UPON
Aristotles Politiques,
TOUCHING
Forms of Government,
Together with
DIRECTIONS
FOR
OBEDIENCE TO GOVERNOURS
in dangerous and doubtfull Times.

SOPHOCLES.
Ἀναρχίας γὰρ μεῖζον οὐκ ἔστιν κακόν;
[Antigone 672: what evils are not caused by anarchy?]

PLATO.
Ὁ βασιλεὺς ὡς θεὸς ἐξ ἀνθρώπων.
[the king is as a god amongst men]

THE PREFACE

In every alteration of government there is something new, which none can either divine or judge of till time hath tried it. We read of many several ways of government. But they have all, or most of them, been of particular cities, with none or very small territories at first belonging to them. At this present the government of the Low Countries and of Switzerland are not appropriated either of them to any one city. For they are compounded of several petty principalities which have special and different laws and privileges each of them. Insomuch

[a] [Copy-text for the *Observations* is the first edition of 1652 (Wing F921), referred to in the notes as 52A. Where the notes record readings or omissions in this edition, the text is taken from the editions of 1679 (Wing F913 and 914), referred to as 79. A manuscript exists of some of the *Directions* – see below p. 281, n. *v*].

235

that the United Provinces and united cantons are but confederacies and leaguers, and not two entire commonweals; associates only for mutual defence. Nay, the cantons of Switzerland are not only several republics, but reputed to have different forms of commonweals – some being said to be aristocratically governed, and others democratically, as the mountaineers. And some of the cantons are papists, and some Protestants, and some mixed of both. We do not find that any large or great dominion or kingdom united in *one*[447] government and under the same laws, was ever reduced at *once*[448] to any kind of popular government, and not confined to the subjection of one city. This being a thing not yet done, requires the abler men to settle such a peaceable government as is to be desired, there being no precedent in the case. All that can be done in it is at first to enquire into such other governments as have been existent in the world. As a preface to such an enquiry the sacred Scripture (if it be but for the antiquity of it) would be consulted, and then Aristotle – the grand master of politics. And after him the Greek and Latin historians that lived in popular times would be diligently examined. To excite others of greater abilities to an exacter disquisition, I presume to offer a taste of some doctrines of Aristotle, which are ushered in with a briefer touch of the holy Scriptures.

It is not probable that any sure direction of the beginning of government can be found either in Plato, Aristotle, Cicero, Polybius, or in any other of the heathen authors, who were ignorant of the manner of the creation of the world. We must not neglect the Scriptures and search in philosophers for the grounds of dominion and property, which are the main principles of government and justice. The first government in the world was monarchical, in the father of all flesh. Adam, being commanded to multiply, and people the earth, and to subdue it, and having dominion given him over all creatures, was thereby the monarch of the whole world. None of his posterity had any right to possess anything but by his grant or permission, or by succession from him. The 'earth', saith the Psalmist, 'hath he given to the children of men' [Psalms xcv, 16] – which shows the title comes from the fatherhood. There never was any such thing as an independent multitude, who at first had a natural right to a community. This is but a fiction or fancy of too many in these days, who please themselves in running after the opinions of philosophers and poets to find out such an original of government as might promise them some title to liberty, to the great scandal of Christianity and bringing in of atheism – since a natural freedom of mankind cannot be supposed without the denial of the creation of Adam. And yet this conceit of original freedom is the only ground upon which not only the heathen philosophers but also the authors of the principles of the civil law, and Grotius, Selden, Hobbes, Ascham and others, raise and build their doctrines of government and of the several sorts or kinds, as they call them, of commonwealths.

Adam was the father, king and lord over his family. A son, a subject and a servant or a slave, were one and the same thing at first. The father had power to dispose or sell his children or servants. Whence we find that at the first reckoning up of goods in Scripture, the man-servant and the maidservant are numbered among the possessions and substance of the owner, as other goods were. As for the names of subject, slave and tyrant, they are not found in Scripture, but what we now call a subject or a slave is there named no other than a servant. I cannot learn that either the Hebrew, Greek or Latin have any proper and original word for a tyrant or a slave. It seems these are names of later invention, and taken up in disgrace of monarchical government.

I cannot find any one place or text in the Bible, where any power or commission is given to a people either to govern themselves, or to choose themselves governors, or to alter the manner of government at their pleasure. The power of government is settled and fixed by the commandment of 'honour thy father'. If there were a higher power than the fatherly, then this commandment could not stand and be observed. Whereas we read in Scripture of some actions of the people in setting up of kings, further than to a naked declaration by a part of the people of their obedience such actions could not amount – since we find no commission they have to bestow any right. A true representation of the people to be made is as impossible as for *a*[449] whole people to govern. The names of an aristocracy, a democracy, a commonweal, a state, or any other of like signification, are not to be met either in the law or gospel.

That there is a ground in nature for monarchy, Aristotle himself affirmeth, saying the first kings were fathers of families [1252^{b}18–21]. As for any ground of any other form of government, there hath been none yet alleged but a supposed natural freedom of mankind, the proof whereof I find none do undertake, but only beg it to be granted.

We find the government of God's own people varied under the several titles of patriarchs, captains, Judges and kings. But in all these the supreme power rested still in one person only. We nowhere find any supreme power given to the people or to a multitude in Scripture, or ever exercised by them. The people were never the Lord's anointed, nor called gods, nor crowned, nor had the title of nursing fathers [Isaiah xlix, 23; on kings see also] Genesis xxxv, 11. The supreme power being an indivisible beam of majesty cannot be divided among, or settled upon a multitude. God would have it fixed in one person, not sometimes in one part of the people and sometimes in another, and sometimes – and that for the most part – nowhere, as when the assembly is dissolved it must rest in the air or in the walls of the chamber where they were assembled.

If there were anything like a popular government among God's people it was about the time of the Judges, when there was 'no king in Israel'. For they had then some small show of government, such as it was, but it was so poor and beggarly that the Scripture brands it with this note, that 'every man did what was right in his own eyes because there was no king in Israel' [Judges xvii, 6]. It is not said 'because there was no government' but because there was no king. It seems no government but the government of a king, in the judgment of the Scriptures, could restrain men from doing what they listed. Where every man doth what he pleaseth it may be truly said there is no government. For the end of *the*[450] government is that every man should not do what he pleaseth or be his own judge in his own case. For the Scripture to say there was no king is to say there was no form of government in Israel.

And what the Old Testament teacheth us, we have confirmed in the New. If Saint Paul had only said 'let every soul be subject to the higher powers' [Romans xiii, 1] and said no more, then men might have disputed whether Saint Paul by 'higher powers' had not meant as well other governors as kings, or other forms of government as monarchy. But the good luck is, Saint Paul hath been his own interpreter or comment. For after the general doctrine of obedience to be given by all men to the higher powers, he proceeds next to charge it home and lay it to the conscience under pain of damnation, and applies it to each particular man's conscience, saying, 'wilt thou not be afraid of the power?' – which power he expounds in the singular number, restraining it to one person, saying, 'he is the minister of

God to thee': it is not, 'they are the ministers to thee'. And then again, 'he beareth not the sword in vain'; and then a third time in the same verse, lest thou shouldest forget it, he saith, for 'he is the minister of God, a revenger to wrath, etc., upon thee'. If Saint Paul had said, 'they are the ministers of God', or 'they bear not the sword in vain', it might be doubted whether 'they' were meant of kings only, or of other governors also. But this scruple is taken away by the apostle himself. And as Saint Paul hath expounded what he means by higher powers, so Saint Peter also doth the like. For the self-same word that Saint Paul useth for 'higher' in Saint Peter is translated 'supreme', so that though in our English Bibles the words differ, yet in the original they are both the same. So that Saint Paul might have been Englished, 'let every soul be subject to the supreme power', or Saint Peter might have been translated, 'whether to the king as to the higher'. Yet there is this difference, that whereas Saint Paul useth the word in the plural number, Saint Peter hath it in the singular and with application to the king [Romans xiii, 1–4; 1 Peter ii, 13].

It will be said, though Saint Peter make the king supreme, yet he tells us the king is a 'human ordinance', or a creature of the people's. But it is answered, kings may be called an human ordinance for being made of one of the people, and not by the people – and so are human in regard of their material cause, not of their efficient. If Saint Peter had meant that kings had been made by the people, he must also have meant that governors had been made by the people, for he calls the governors as well an ordinance of man, as the king. For his words are, 'submit yourselves to every ordinance of man for the Lord's sake, whether it be to the king as supreme, or whether it be to governors'. But Saint Peter showeth that governors are not made by the people, for he saith 'they that are sent by him' (not by them) 'for the punishment of evil doers'. So that governors are sent by the king and not by the people. Some would have 'sent by him' to be 'sent by God', but the relative must be referred to the next antecedent, which is the king and not God [1 Peter ii, 13]. Besides, if governors be sent by God, and kings by the people, then governors would be supreme, which is contrary to Saint Peter's doctrine; and it will follow that the people have not the power of choosing repre-senters to govern, if governors must be sent of God.

The safest sense of Saint Peter's words is: submit yourselves to all human laws whether made by the king or by his subordinate governors. So the king may be called a human ordinance, as being all one with a speaking law. The word in the original is, be subject to every human creation. It is more proper to call a law made by a king a creation of an ordinance, than the people's choosing or declaring of a king, a creation of him.

But take the words in what sense soever you will, it is most evident that Saint Peter in this place takes no notice of any government or governors but of a king and governors sent by him, but not by the people. And it is to be noted that Saint Peter and Saint Paul, the two chief of the apostles, *writ*[451] their epistles at such *time*[452] when the name of a popular government, or of the power of the people of Rome, was at least so much in show and in name that many do believe that notwithstanding the emperors by strong hand usurped a military power, yet the government was for a long time in most things then in the senate and people of Rome. But for all this, neither of the two apostles take any notice of any such popular government – no, nor our Saviour himself, who divides all between God and Caesar, and allows nothing that we can find for the people.

OBSERVATIONS UPON ARISTOTLE'S POLITICS TOUCHING FORMS OF GOVERNMENT

What cannot be found in Scripture many do look for in Aristotle. For if there be any other form of government besides monarchy, he is the man best able to tell what it is, and to let us know by what name to call it, since the Greek tongue is most happy in compounding names most significant to express the nature of most things. The usual terms in this age – of aristocracy and democracy – are taken up from him to express forms of government most different from monarchy. We must therefore make enquiry into Aristotle touching these two terms.

True it is, Aristotle seems to make three sorts of government which he distinguisheth by 'the sovereignty of one man, or of a few, or of many, for the common good'* (book 3, chapter 7) [1279ᵃ27–9]. 'These', he saith, 'are right or perfect governments, but those that are for the private good of one, or of a few, or of a multitude, are

---

* ''Ανάγκη δ'εἶναι κύριον ἢ ἕνα, ἢ ὀλίγους, ἢ τοὺς πολλοὺς πρὸς τὸ κοινὸν συμφέρον.'

transgressions'* [1279ᵃ29–31]. The government of a monarch for the common good he calls a kingdom. The government

> of a few more than one, an aristocracy, either because the best men govern or because it is for the best of the governed. When a multitude governs for the common good, it is called by the common name of all governments, a polity. It is possible that one or a few may excel in virtue, but it is difficult for many to excel in all virtue except in war-like affairs, for this is natural in a multitude. Therefore, in this sort of government their principal use is to war one for another, and to possess the arms or ammunition. The transgressions of government before spoken of are these: tyranny is the transgression of the kingdom, *and*⁴⁵³ democracy is the transgression of the polity. For tyranny is a monarchy for the benefit of the monarch; the oligarchy for the profit of the rich; the democracy for the benefit of the poor. None of these are for the common good. (book 3, chapter 7) [1279ᵃ34–1279ᵇ10]

Here Aristotle if he had stood to his own principles should have said 'an oligarchy should be for the benefit of a few, and those the best, and not for the benefit of the rich; and a democracy for the benefit of many, and not of the poor only'; for so the opposition lieth. But then Aristotle saw his democracy would prove to be no transgression, but a perfect polity, and his oligarchy would not be for the benefit of a few, and those the best men. For they cannot be the best men that seek only their private profit. In this chapter the mind of Aristotle about the several kinds of government is clearliest delivered, as being the foundation of all his books of *Politics*. It is the more necessary to make a curious observation of these his doctrines. In the first place, he acknowledgeth the government of one man, or of a monarchy, and that it is a perfect form of government.

Concerning monarchy, Aristotle teacheth us the beginning of it. For, saith he, the 'first society made of many houses is a colony, which seems most naturally to be a colony of families or foster-brethren of children and children's children. And therefore at the beginning cities were under the government of kings. The eldest in every

---

* 'Ταύτας μὲν ὀρθὰς εἶναι πολιτείας τὰς πρὸς τὸ ἴδιον ἢ τοῦ ἑνὸς, ἢ τῶν ὀλίγων, ἢ τοῦ πλήθος παρεκβάσεις. Τῶν μὲν ἀρχῶν τὴν πρὸς τὸ κοινὸν ἀποβλέπουσαν συμφέρον βασιλείαν. &c.'

house is king, and so for kindred sake it is in colonies'* (book I, chapter 2) [1252ᵇ16–21].

Thus he deduced the original of government from the power of the fatherhood, not from the election of the people. This it seems he learnt of his master Plato, who in his third book of *Laws* affirms that the true and first reason of authority is that the father and mother, and simply those that beget and engender, do command and rule over all their children [*Laws* 3.680e–681b]. Aristotle also tells us from Homer 'that every man gives laws to his wife and children'† [1252ᵇ22–3].

In the fourth book of his *Politics*, chapter 2, he gives to monarchy the title of the 'first and divinest sort of government', defining tyranny to be 'a transgression from the first and divinest'‡ [1289ᵃ39–41].

Again, Aristotle in the eighth book of his *Ethics*, in the twelfth chapter saith that of 'the right kinds of government, a monarchy was the best, and a popular estate the worst'§ [1160ᵃ35–6].

Lastly, in the third book of his *Politics* and the sixteenth chapter, concerning monarchy, he saith that 'a perfect kingdom is that wherein the king rules all things according to his own will' 'for he that is called a king according to the law makes no kind of government'|| [1287ᵃ8–10, 3–4].

Secondly, he saith there is a government of a *few* men, but doth not tell us how many those few men may or must be. Only he saith they must be more than one man, but how many, that he leaves uncertain.

This perfect government of a few, any man would think Aristotle should have called an oligarchy, for that this word properly signifies so much. But instead of the government of a few, Aristotle gives it a quite other name and terms it an aristocracy, which signifies the power of the best. The reason why it is called an aristocracy,

---

* 'Μάλιστα δὲ κατὰ φύσιν ἔοικεν ἡ κώμη ἀποικία οἰκείας εἶναι, οὕς καλοῦσί τινες ὁμογάλακτας παῖδάς τε καὶ παίδων παῖδας. Διὸ καὶ τὸ πρῶτον ἐβασιλεύοντο ἂι πόλεις καὶ νυν ἔτι τὰ ἔθνη. πᾶσα γὰρ οἰκεία βασιλεύεται ὑπὸ τοῦ πρεσβυτάτου, ὥστε καὶ δι' ἀποικίαι διὰ τὴν συγγένειαν.'

† 'θεμιστεύει δὲ ἕκαστος παίδων ἠδ' ἀλόχων.'

‡ ''Ανάγκη γὰρ τὴν μὲν τῆς πρώτης καὶ θειοτάτης παρέκβασιν εἶναι χειρίστην.'

§ 'Τούτων δὲ βελτίστη ἡ βασιλεία, χειρίστη δὲ τιμοκρατία.'

|| 'Περὶ δὲ τῆς παμβασιλείας καλουμένης, αὕτη δ'ἐστι καθ' ἣν ἄρχει πάντων κατὰ τὴν ἑαυτοῦ βούλησιν ὁ βασιλεύς. ὁ μὲν γὰρ κατὰ νόμον λεγόμενος βασιλεὺς οὐκ ἔστιν εἶδος καθάπερ εἴπομεν πολιτείας.'

saith Aristotle, is for that there the best men govern, or (because that is not always true) 'for that it is for the best of the governed' [1279ª36–7]. By this latter reason any government, and most especially a monarchy, may be called an aristocracy – because the end of monarchy is for the best of the governed, as well as the end of an aristocracy. So that of these two reasons for calling the government of a few an aristocracy the first is seldom true, and the latter is never sufficient to frame a distinction. This Aristotle himself confesseth in his next chapter, saying 'that the causes aforesaid do not make a difference, and that it is poverty and riches, and not few and many, that makes the difference between an oligarchy and democracy. There must be an oligarchy where rich men rule, whether they be few or many; and wheresoever the poor have the sovereignty, there must be a democracy'* (book 3, chapter 8) [1279ᵇ38–1280ª1].

Now if Aristotle will allow riches and poverty to make a difference between an oligarchy and a democracy, these two must likewise make the difference between an aristocracy and a polity, for the only difference Aristotle makes between them is in their ends, and not in their matter. For the same few men may make an aristocracy if their end be the common good, and they may be an oligarchy if they aim only at their private benefit.

Thus is Aristotle distracted and perplexed how to distinguish his aristocracy, whether by the smallness of their number or by the greatness of their estates. Nay, if we look into Aristotle's *Rhetorics* (book 1, chapter 8) we shall find a new conceit, not only about aristocracy but also about the sorts of government. For whereas he has taught us in his *Politics* that there be three sorts of right or perfect government and as many sorts of wrong, which he calls transgressions or corruptions, he comes in his *Rhetorics* (book 1, chapter 8) and teacheth us that there be four sorts of government:

'1   A democracy, where magistracies are distributed by lots.

2   In an oligarchy by their wealth.

3   In an aristocracy by their instructions in the law. It is necessary for these to appear the best, from whence they have their name.†

---

* 'Διὸ καὶ οὐ συμβαίνει τὰς ῥηθείσας αἰτίας γίνεσθαι διαφορᾶς ᾧ δὲ διαφέρουσιν ἥ τε δημοκρατία καὶ ἡ ὀλιγαρχία ἀλλήλων πενία καὶ πλοῦτός ἐστιν, &c.'
† 'ἔστι δὲ δημοκρατία πολιτεία ἐν ᾗ κλήρῳ διανέμονται τὰς ἀρχάς, ὀλιγαρχία δὲ ἐν ᾗ οἱ ἀπὸ τιμημάτων, ἀριστοκρατία δὲ ἐν ᾗ οἱ κατὰ παιδειαν.'

4   A monarchy according to the name, wherein one is lord over all'* [1365ᵇ31–1366ᵃ1].

Here we see aristocracy is not distinguished by smallness of number nor by riches, but by skill in the laws. For he saith those that are instructed in the laws govern in an aristocracy,† a point not dreamt of in his *Politics*. By which it seems Aristotle himself did not know well what he would have to be an aristocracy. And as he cannot teach us truly what an aristocracy is, so he is to seek to tell us where any aristocracy ever was. Even himself seems to doubt whether there be any such form of government, where he saith in his third book of *Politics*, chapter 5, it is impossible for any mechanical man to be a citizen in an aristocracy, 'if there be any such government as they call aristocratical'‡ [1278ᵃ18–19].

His 'if' makes him seem to doubt of it. Yet I find him affirm that the commonwealth of Carthage was aristocratical. He doth not say it was an aristocracy, for he confesseth it had many of the transgressions which other commonwealths had and did incline either to a democracy or an oligarchy:

'The government of Carthage did transgress from an aristocracy to an oligarchy'§ (book 2, chapter 11) [1273ᵃ21–2].

And he concludes that if by misfortune there should happen any discord among the Carthaginians themselves there would be no medicine by law found out to give it rest. Wherein methinks Aristotle was a kind of prophet, for the discords between the citizens of Carthage were the main cause that Hannibal lost not only Italy, but Carthage itself.

By these few collections we may find how uncertain Aristotle is in determining what an aristocracy is, or where, or when any such government was. It may justly be doubted whether there ever was or can be any such government.

Let us pass from his aristocracy to his third sort of perfect or right government, for which he finds no particular name but only the common name of all government, *politia*. It seems the Greeks

---

* 'Μοναρχία δὲ ἐστὶ κατὰ τοὔνομα ἐν ᾗ εἷς ἁπάντων κύριός ἐστιν.'

† 'οἱ γὰρ ἐμμεμενηκότες ἐν τοῖς νομίμοις ἐν τῇ Ἀριστοκρατίᾳ ἄρχουσιν.'

‡ 'Εἰ τις ἐστιν ἣν καλοῦσιν ἀριστοκρατικήν.'

§ 'Παρεκβαίνει δὲ τῆς ἀριστοκρατίας ἡ τάξις τῶν Καρχηδονίων μάλιστα πρὸς τὴν ὀλιγαρχίαν.'

were wonderfully to seek, that they of all men should not be able to compound a name for such a perfect form of government. Unless we should believe that they esteemed this kind of commonwealth so superlatively excellent, as to be called, κατ᾽ ἐξοχὴν, the government of governments, or polity of polities.

But howsoever Aristotle in his books of *Politics* vouchsafe us not a name, yet in his books of *Ethics* he affirmeth it may very properly be called 'a timocratical government, where magistrates are chosen by their wealth'* (book 8, chapter 12) [1160ᵃ33–4]. But why Aristotle should give it such a name I can find no reason. For a polity by his doctrine is the government of many, or of a multitude, and the multitude he will have to be the poorer sort, insomuch that except they be poor he will not allow it to be the government of a multitude, though they be never so many. For he makes poverty the truest note of a popular estate, and as if to be poor and to be free were all one, he makes liberty likewise to be a mark of a popular estate, for in his fourth book, and fourth chapter, he resolves that 'a popular state is where free men govern, and an oligarchy where rich men rule'† [1290ᵇ1–2] – as if rich men could not be free men. Now how magistrates should be chosen for their wealth, ἀπὸ τιμημάτων among all poor men, is to me a riddle.

Here I cannot but wonder why all our modern politicians, who pretend themselves Aristotelians, should forsake their great master and account a democracy a right or perfect form of government, when Aristotle brands it for a transgression, or a depraved or corrupted manner of government. They had done better to have followed Aristotle, who (though other Grecians could not, yet he) could find out the name of a timocracy for a right popular government. But it may be our politicians forbear to use the word timocracy because he affords an ill character of it, saying that of all the right kinds of government a 'monarchy was the best, and a timocracy the worst'‡ [1160ᵃ35–6]. Yet afterwards Aristotle in the same chapter makes amends for it in saying a 'democracy is the least vicious, because it doth but a little transgress from a timocracy' [1160ᵇ19–21].

But not to insist longer on the name of this nameless form of government, let enquiry be made into the thing itself, that we may

---

* 'Τρίτη δ᾽ἡ ἀπὸ τιμημάτων ἥν τιμοκρατικὴν λέγειν δικεῖον φαίνεται.'
† '"Οτι δῆμος ἐστιν ὅταν ἐλεύθεροι κύριοι ὦσιν, ὀλιγαρχία δ᾽ὅταν ὁι πλούσιοι.'
‡ 'βελτίστη ἡ βασιλεία, χειριστη ἡ τιμοκρατία.'

know what Aristotle saith is the 'government of many or of a multitude, for the common good'.

This many or multitude is not the whole people, nor the major part of the people, or any chosen by the people to be their representers. No, Aristotle never saith or meaneth any such thing. For he tells us 'the best city doth not make any artificer or handicraftsman a citizen'* (book 3, chapter 5) [1278ª8–9].

And if these be excluded out of the number of citizens, there will be but a few left in every city to make his timocratical government, since artificers or mercenary men make far the greatest part of a city; or to say 'a city is a community of free men'† (book 3, chapter 7) [1279ª21] and yet to exclude the greatest part of the inhabitants from being citizens, is but a mockery of freedom. For any man would think that a city being a society of men assembled to the end to live well, that such men without whom a city cannot subsist, and who perform necessary works and minister to all in public, should *not be*¹⁵¹ barred from being citizens. Yet says Aristotle, 'all those are not to be deemed citizens without whom a city cannot subsist'‡ (book 3, chapter 5) [1278ª3–4], except they abstain from necessary works; for he resolves it 'impossible for him to exercise the work of virtue, that useth a mechanical or mercenary trade'§ [1278ª20–1].

And he makes it one of his conclusions that 'in ancient times among some men no public workman did partake of the government until the worst of democracies were brought in'‖ (book 3, chapter 4) [1277ᵇ1–3].

Again, Aristotle will have his best popular government consist of free men, and accounts the poorer sort of people to be free men. How then will he exclude poor artificers, who work for the public, from participating of the government?

Further, it is observable in Aristotle that quite contrary to the signification of the Greek names, the government of a multitude may be termed an oligarchy if they be rich, and the rule of a few a democracy if they be poor and free.

---

* '*Ἡ δὲ βελτίστη πόλις οὐ ποιήσει βάναυσον πολίτην.*'
† '*Ἡ δὲ πόλις κοίνωνια τῶν ἐλευθέρων ἐστιν.*'
‡ '*Οὐ πάντας θετέον πολίτας ὧν ἄνευ οὐκ ἄν εἴη πόλις.*'
§ *Οὐ γὰρ δῖον τ' ἐπιτηδεῦυαι τὰ τῆς ἀρετῆς ζῶντα βίον βάναυσον ἢ θητικόν.*'
‖ '*Διὸ παρ' ἐνίοις οὐ μετεῖχον δι δημιουργοὶ τὸ παλαιὸν ἀρχῶν πρὶν δῆμον γενέσθαι τὸν ἔσκατον.*'

After much uncertainty of the nature of this politic government which wants a name, Aristotle at last resolves that this general commonweal or *politia* is compounded of a 'democracy and oligarchy', for 'to speak plainly, a polity is a mixture of a democracy and an oligarchy'* (book 4, chapter 8) [1293^{b}33–4]. That is, one perfect form is made of two imperfect ones. This is rather a confounding than compounding of government, to patch it up of two corrupt ones by appointing an oligarchical penalty for the rich magistrates that are chosen by election, and a democratical fee for the poor magistrates that are chosen by lot.

Lastly, it is to be noted that Aristotle doth not offer to name any one city or commonweal in the world where ever there was any such government as he calls a polity. For him to reckon it for a perfect form of government, and of such excellency as to carry the name from all other, and yet never to have been extant in the world, may seem a wonder. And a man may be excused for doubting or for denying any such form to be possible in nature, if it cannot be made manifest what it is, nor when, nor where it ever was.

In conclusion, since Aristotle reckons but three kinds of perfect government, which are, first, a monarchy of one; secondly, an aristocracy of a few; thirdly, a polity of a multitude. And if these two latter cannot be made good by him, there will remain but one right form of government only which is monarchy. And it seems to me that Aristotle in a manner doth confess as much where he informs us 'that the first commonweals among the Grecians, after kingdoms, was made of those that waged war'† (book 4, chapter 13) [1297^{b}16–17] – meaning that the Grecians, when they left to be governed by kings, fell to be governed by an army. Their monarchy was changed into a stratocracy,^{p} and not into an aristocracy or democracy. For if unity in government, which is only found in monarchy, be once broken, there is no stay or *bounds*,^{455} until it come to a constant standing army. For 'the people or multitude', as Aristotle teacheth us, 'can excel in no virtue but military', and that 'that is natural to them', and therefore in a popular estate 'the sovereign power is in

---

* Ἔστι γὰρ ἡ πολιτεία ὡς ἁπλῶς εἰπεῖν, μίξις ὀλιγαρχίας καὶ δημοκρατίας.'
† 'καὶ ἡ πρώτη δὲ πολιτεία ἐν τοῖς Ἕλλησιν ἐγένετο μετὰ τὰς βασίλειας ἐκ τῶν πολεμούντων.'
^{p} [rule by an army; Filmer has in mind the army's power in England after the abolition
  of monarchy in 1649].

the sword and those that are possessed of the arms'* (book 3, chapter 7) [1279ᵃ40–1279ᵇ4]. So that any nation or kingdom that is not charged with the keeping of a king must perpetually be at the charge of paying and keeping of an army.

These brief observations upon Aristotle's perfect forms of government may direct what to judge of those corrupted or imperfect forms which he mentions, for *rectum est index sui et obliqui* [what is right is a guide to itself and to deviations], and he reckons them to be all one in matter and form, and to differ only in their end – the end of the perfect forms being for the good of the governed, and of the imperfect for the benefit only of the governors. Now since Aristotle could not tell how to define or describe his right *and**⁴⁵⁶ perfect forms of government, it cannot be expected he can satisfy us concerning those he calls imperfect. Yet he labours and bestirs himself mainly in the business, though to little purpose. For howsoever the title of his book be πολιτικῶν, of *Politics*, and that he mentions πολιτεία for a special form of government, which hath the common name of a polity, yet when he comes to dispute in particular of government he argues only about democracies and oligarchies, and therein he is copious because only those which he calls corrupt forms of governments were common in Greece in his days. As for an aristocracy or a polity which he mentions, they are only speculative notions or airy names, invented to delude the world and to persuade the people that under those quaint terms there might be found some subtle government which might at least equal, if not excel, monarchy. And the inventors of those fine names were all but rebels to monarchy, by Aristotle's confession, where he saith 'the first commonweals of Greece, after kings were left, were made of those that waged war' (book 4, chapter 13) [1297ᵇ16–17].

As Aristotle is irresolute to determine what are truly perfect aristocracies and polities, so he is to seek in describing his imperfect forms of government, as well oligarchies as democracies. And therefore he is driven to invent several sorts of them, and to confound himself with subdivisions. We will allege some of his words.

The cause why there be many kinds of commonweals is for that

---

* 'Πλείους δ'ἤδη χαλεπὸν ἠκριβῶσθαι πρὸς πᾶσαν ἀρετήν, ἀλλὰ μάλιστα τὴν πολεμικήν· αὕτη γὰρ ἐν πλήθει γίγνεται · διόπερ κατὰ ταύτην τὴν πολιτείαν κυριώτατον τὸ προπολεμοῦν κἀι μετέχουσιν αὐτῆς οἱ κεκτημένοι τὰ ὅπλα.'

there are many parts of every city. Sometimes all these parts are in a commonweal, sometimes more of them, sometimes fewer. Whence it is manifest that there are many commonweals differing from each other in kind, because the parts of them differ after the same manner. For a commonweal is the order of magistrates distributed either according to the power of them that are partakers of it, or according to some other common equality belonging to poor and rich, or some other thing common to both. It is therefore necessary that there be so many commonweals as there are orders, according to the excellencies and differences of parts. But it seemeth principally there are but two chief kinds of commonweals, the democracy and the oligarchy. For they make the aristocracy a branch of oligarchy, as if it were a kind of oligarchy; and that other which is properly a polity, to be a branch of democracy. So they are wont to esteem of commonweals. But it is both truer and better that there being two right forms, or one, that all the other be transgressions. [1289^{b}27–1290^{a}26]

Here we find Aristotle of several minds. Sometimes he is for many commonweals, sometimes for two, or sometimes for one. As for his many commonweals, if he allow them according to the several parts of a city, he may as well make three thousand kinds of commonweals, as three. If two artificers and three soldiers should govern, that should be one kind of commonweal. If four husbandmen and five merchants, that would be a second sort; or six tailors and ten carpenters, a third sort; or a dozen sailors and a dozen porters, a fourth, and so *in infinitum*. For Aristotle is not resolved how many parts to make of a city or how many combinations of those parts, and therefore in his reckoning of them he differs from himself, sometimes makes more, sometimes fewer parts, and oft concluding at the end of his account with *etceteras*, and confessing that one and the same man may act several parts – as he that is a soldier may be a husbandman and an artificer. And in his fourth book and fourth chapter he seems to reckon up eight parts of a city, but in the tale of them he misses or forgets the sixth: 1. He names the ploughman. 2. The artificer. 3. The tradesman or merchant. 4. The mercenary hireling. 5. The soldier (here Aristotle falls foul upon Plato for making but four parts of a city: 1. The weaver. 2. The ploughman. 3. The tailor. 4. The carpenter. Afterwards, as if these were not sufficient, he addeth the smith and the feeder of necessary cattle, the merchant and the ingrosser or retailer). Whilst Aristotle was busy in this reprehension of Plato, he forgets himself and skips over his sixth part of a city and names the 7. rich men, 8. the magistrates [1290ᵇ39–1291ᵃ36]. In the same chapter he offers at another division of the parts of a city or commonweal, first dividing it into a populacy and nobility. The people he divides first into 'husbandmen. 2. Into artificers. 3. Into merchants or those that use buying or selling. 4. Into those that frequent the seas', of whom 'some follow the war, others seek for gain'; some are 'carriers or transporters', others 'fishermen. 5. Handicraftsmen that possess so little goods that they cannot be idle. 6. Those that are not free on both sides, and any other suchlike multitude of people'. The kinds of noblemen are distinguished 'by riches, by lineage, by virtue, by learning and other suchlike things' [1291ᵇ17–29].

That there may be more parts of a commonweal than are here numbered, Aristotle confesseth or supposeth; and of a multitude of parts, and of a multitude of mixtures of such parts may be made a world of forms of oligarchies and democracies.

This confusion of the parts and kinds of commonweals drove Aristotle rather to rest upon the division of rich and poor for the main parts of a commonweal, than any other. The distinction of a few and of a multitude or the whole people, might seem more proper to distinguish between an oligarchy and a democracy. But the truth is, Aristotle looking upon the cities of Greece and finding that in every of them, even in Athens itself, there were many of the people that were not allowed to be citizens and to participate in the government, and that many times he was a citizen in one sort of government who was not a citizen in another, and that citizens differed according to every commonweal; he considered that if he should place a right in the whole people either to govern or to choose their form of government or the parties that should govern, he should hereby condemn the government of all the cities in Greece, and especially of aristocracy which, as he saith, allows no artificer to be a citizen. And besides, he should thereby confute a main principle of his own *Politics*, which is that some men are born slaves by nature – which quite contradicts the position that all men are born equal and free. And therefore Aristotle thought it fitter to allow all imaginable forms of government, that so he might not disparage any one city, than to propound such a form as might condemn and destroy all the rest.

Though Aristotle allow so many several forms of corrupted governments, yet he insists upon no one form of all those that he can define or describe, in such sort that he is able to say that any one city in all Greece was governed just according to such a form. His diligence is only to make as many forms as the giddy or inconstant humour of a city could happen upon. He freely gives the people liberty to invent as many kinds of government as they please, provided he may have liberty to find fault with every one of them. It proved an easier work for him to find fault with every form, than to tell how to *amend*[457] any one of them. He found so many imperfections in all sorts of commonweals that he could not hold from reproving them before ever he tells us what a commonweal is or how many sorts there are. And to this purpose he spends his whole second book in setting out and correcting the chief commonweals of Greece, and among others the Lacedaemonian, the Cretan and Carthaginian commonweals, which three he esteems to be much alike, and better than any other. Yet he spares not to lay open their imperfections, and doth the like to the Athenian. Wherein he breaks the rule of method, by delivering the faults of commonweals before he teach us what a commonweal is. For in his first book he speaks only of the parts of which a city or a commonweal is made, but tells us not what a city or commonweal is until he come to his third book, and there in handling the sorts of government he observes no method at all, but in a disorderly way flies backward and forward from one sort to another. And howsoever there may be observed in him many rules of policy touching government in general, yet without doubt where he comes to discourse of particular forms he is full of contradiction, or confusion, or both. It is true he is brief and difficult. The best right a man can do him is to confess he understands him not. Yet a diligent reader may readily discern so many irregularities and breaches in Aristotle's books of *Politics* as tend to such distraction or confusion that none of our new politicians can make advantage of his principles for the confirmation of an original power by nature in the people, which is the only theme now in fashion. For Aristotle's discourse is of such commonweals as were founded by particular persons – as the Chalcedonian by Phaleas, the Milesian by Hippodamas, the Lacedaemonian by Lycurgus, the Cretan by Minos, the Athenian by Solon, and the like. But the natural right of the people to found or elect their kind of government is not once disputed by him. It seems the 'underived majesty' [Parker p. 15] of the people was such a metaphysical piece of speculation as our grand philosopher was not acquainted with. He speaks very contemptuously of the multitude in several places. He affirms that the 'people are base or wicked judges in their own cases'* (book 3, chapter 9) [1280ᵃ15–16] and that 'many of them differ nothing from beast[s]'† (book 3, chapter 11) [1281ᵇ19–20]. And again he saith 'the common people or freemen are such as are neither rich nor in reputation for virtue, and it is not safe to commit to them great governments, for by reason of their injustice and unskilfulness they would do much injustice and commit many errors, and it is pleasanter to the multitude to live disorderly than soberly'‡ (book 6, chapter 4) [1319ᵇ31–2]. If Aristotle had believed a public interest to have been in the people to the enabling them to be their own carvers in point of government, he would never have entangled himself with such intricate and ambiguous forms of commonweals as himself cannot tell how to explain, nor any of his commentators how to understand or make use of.

This one benefit I have found by reading Aristotle, that his books of *Politics* serve for an admirable commentary upon that text of Scripture which saith 'In those days there was no king in Israel; every man did that which was right in his own eyes' [Judges xvii, 6]. For he grants a liberty in every city for any man or multitude of men either by cunning or force to set up what government they please, and he will allow some name or other of a commonweal, which in effect is to allow every man to do what he lists, if he be able. Hence it is that by the confession of Aristotle 'the first commonweals in Greece, after kings were given over, were made of those that waged war' [1297ᵇ16–17]. Those several kinds of commonweals were all summed up into the government of an army. For 'it is', saith Aristotle, 'in their power who manage arms to continue or not continue the form of government whereby the estate is governed'§ (book 7, chapter 9) [1329ᵃ11–12], which is nothing else but a *stratocratic*[458] or military government. We cannot much blame Aristotle for the incertainty and contrariety in him about the sorts of government if we consider him as a heathen. For it is not possible for the wit of man to search out the first grounds or principles of government (which necessarily depend upon the original of property) except he know that at the

---

* 'ὅι πλεῖστοι φαῦλοι κριταὶ περὶ τῶν ὁικειων.'
† 'τί διαφέρουσιν ἔνιοι τῶν θηριων.' [52A, 79: beast].
‡ 'ἥδιον γὰρ τοῖς πολλοῖς τὸ ζῆν ἀτάκτως ἢ τὸ σωφρόνως.'
§ 'Ὁι γὰρ τῶν ὅπλων κύριοι κὰι μὴ μένειν κύριοι τὴν πολιτείαν.'

creation one man alone was made, to whom the dominion of all things was given and from whom all men derive their title. This point can be learnt only from the Scriptures. As for the imaginary contract of people, it is a fancy not improbable only, but impossible, except a multitude of men at first had sprung out and were engendered of the earth, which Aristotle knows not whether he may believe or no (book 2, chapter 8) [1269ª4–8]. If justice (which is to give every man his due) be the end of government, there must necessarily be a rule to know how any man at first came to have a right to anything to have it truly called his. This is a point Aristotle disputes not, nor so much as ever dreamt of an original contract among people. He looked no further in every city than to a scambling*q* among the citizens, whereby every one snatched what he could get, so that a violent possession was the first and best title that he knew.

The main distinction of Aristotle touching perfect or right forms of government from those that are imperfect or corrupt consists solely in this point, that where the profit of the governed is respected there is a right government, but where the profit of the governors is regarded there is a corruption or transgression of government. By this it is supposed by Aristotle that there may be a government only for the benefit of the governors. This supposition to be false may *be*[459] proved from Aristotle himself; I will instance about the point of tyranny.

'Tyranny', saith Aristotle, 'is a despotical or masterly monarchy' (book 3, chapter 7) [1279ᵇ16–17]. Now he confesseth that 'in truth the masterly government is profitable both to the servant by nature and the master by nature' (book 4, chapter 10) [1278ᵇ33–5], and he yields a solid reason for it, saying, 'It is not possible *if*[460] the servant be destroyed that the mastership can be saved' (book 3, chapter 6) [1278ᵇ37–8]. Whence it may be inferred that if the masterly government of tyrants cannot be safe without the preservation of them whom they govern, it will follow that a tyrant cannot govern for his own profit only. And thus his main definition of tyranny fails, as being grounded upon an impossible supposition by his own confession. No example can be showed of any such government that ever was in the world as Aristotle describes a tyranny to be. For under the worst of kings, though many particular men have unjustly suffered, yet the multitude

---

q [disorderly struggle].

253

or the people in general have found benefit and profit by the government.

It being apparent that the different kinds of government in Aristotle arise only from the difference of the number of governors – whether one, a few or many – there may be as many several forms of governments as there be several numbers, which are infinite. So that not only the several parts of a city or commonweal but also the several numbers of such parts may cause multiplicity of forms of government by Aristotle's principles.

It is further observable in assemblies that it is not the whole assembly but the major part only of the assembly that hath the government. For 'that which pleaseth the most is always ratified', saith Aristotle (book 4, chapter 4) [1291^{b}37–8]. By this means one and the same assembly may make at one *sitting*$*^{461}$ several forms of commonweals. For in several debates and votes the same number of men, or all the self-same men do not ordinarily agree in their votes; and the least disagreement, either in the persons of the men or in their number, alters the form of government. Thus in a commonweal one part of the public affairs shall be ordered by one form of government, and another part by another form, and a third part by a third form, and so *in infinitum*. How can that have the denomination of a form of government which lasts but for a moment only about one fraction of business? For in the very instant, as it were in the twinkling of an eye, while their vote lasteth the government must begin and end.

To be governed is nothing else but to be obedient and subject to the will or command of another: it is the will in *man*$*^{462}$ that governs. Ordinarily men's wills are divided according to their several ends or interests, which most times are different and many times contrary the one to the other. And in such cases, where the wills of the major part of the assembly do unite and agree in one will there is a monarchy of many wills in one, though it be called an aristocracy or democracy in regard of the several persons. It is not the many bodies but the one will or soul of the multitude that governs. 'Where one is set up out of many the people becometh a monarch, because many are lords not separately but altogether as one. Therefore such a people, as if it were a monarch, seeks to bear rule alone'* (book 4, chapter 4) [1292^{a}11–13, 15–16].

* 'Μόναρχος γὰρ ὁ δῆμος γινεται, σύνθετος εἷς ἐκ πολλῶν· δὶ γὰρ πολλοὶ κύριοι εἰσὶν οὐχ ὡς ἕκαστος ἀλλὰ πάντες. ὁ δὲ οὖν τοιουτος δῆμος ἅτε μόναρχος ὢν ζητεῖ μοναρχεῖν.'

It is a false and improper speech to say that a whole multitude, senate, council or any multitude whatsoever doth govern where the major part only rules; because many of the multitude that are so assembled are so far from having any part in the government that they themselves are governed against and contrary to their wills. There being in all government various and different debates and consultations, it comes to pass ofttimes that the major part in every assembly differs according to the several humours or fancies of men. Those who agree in one mind, in one point, are of different opinions in another. Every change of business or new matter begets a new major part, and is a change both of the government and governors. The difference in the number or in the qualities of the persons that govern is the only thing that causes different governments, according to Aristotle, who divides his kinds of government to the number of one, a few or many. As amongst the Romans their tribunitial laws had several titles according to the names of those tribunes of the people that preferred and made them, so in other governments the body of their acts and ordinances is composed of a multitude of momentary monarchs, who by the strength and power of their parties or factions are still under a kind of a civil war, fighting and scratching for the legislative miscellany or medley of several governments. If we consider each government according to the nobler part of which it is composed, it is nothing else but a monarchy of monothelites[r] or of many men of one will, most commonly in one point only. But if we regard only the baser part or bodies of such persons as govern there is an interrupted succession of a multitude of short-lived governments, with as many intervals of anarchy. So that no man can say at any time that he is under any form of government, for in a shorter time than the word can be spoken, every government is begun and ended. Furthermore in all assemblies, of what quality soever they be, whether aristocratical or democratical, as they call them, they all agree in this one point, to give that honourable regard to monarchy that they do interpret the major or prevailing part in every assembly to be but as one man, and so do feign to themselves a kind of monarchy.

Though there be neither precept nor practice in Scripture, nor yet any reason alleged by Aristotle for any form of government but only monarchy, yet it is said that it is evident to common sense that

---

[r] [heretics of the seventh century who held that Christ had only one will].

of old time Rome, and in this present age Venice and the Low Countries, enjoy a form of government different from monarchy.

Hereunto it may be answered that a people may live together in society and help one another, and yet not be under any form of government; as we see herds of cattle do, and yet we may not say they live under government. For government is not a society only to live, but to live well and virtuously. This is acknowledged by Aristotle who teacheth that 'the end of a city is to live blessedly and honestly. Political communities are ordained for honest actions, but not for living together only'* [1280ᵇ39–1281ᵃ4].

Now there be two things principally required to a blessed and honest life – religion towards God and peace towards men; that is, 'a quiet and peaceable life in all godliness and honesty', 1 Timothy ii, 2. Here then will be the question: whether godliness and peace can be found under any government but monarchy, or whether Rome, Venice or the Low Countries did enjoy these under any popular government? In these two points let us first briefly examine the Roman government, which is thought to have been the most glorious.

For religion, we find presently after the building of the city by Romulus, the next king, Numa, most devoutly established a religion and began his kingdom with the service of the gods. He forbade the Romans to make any images of God, which law lasted and was observed 170 years; there being in all that time no image or picture of God in any temple or chapel of Rome. Also, he erected the pontifical college and was himself the first bishop or *pontifex*. These bishops were to render no account either to the senate or commonalty. They determined all questions concerning religion, as well between priests as between private men. They punished inferior priests if they either added or detracted from the established rites or ceremonies, *or**⁴⁶³ brought in any new thing into religion. The chief bishop, *pontifex maximus*, taught every man how to honour and serve the gods. This care had monarchy of religion.

But after the expulsion of kings, we do not find during the power of the people any one law made for the benefit or exercise of religion. There be two tribunitian laws concerning religion, but they are merely for the benefit of the power of the people and not of religion. L.

---

* Τέλος πόλεως τὸ ἔυ ζῆν εὐδαιμόνως καὶ καλῶς. τῶν καλῶν πράξεων χάριν θετέον εἶναι τὴν πολιτικὴν κοινωνίαν, ἀλλὰ οὐ τοῦ συζῆν.'

Papirius, a tribune, made a law called *Lex Papiria*, that it should not be lawful for any to consecrate either houses, grounds, altars or any other things without the determination of the people [Cicero, *De Domo sua* 50 (128–9)]. Domitius Ænobarbus, another tribune, enacted a law called *Domitia Lex*, that the pontifical college should not, as they were wont, admit whom they would into the order of priesthood, but it should be in the power of the people. And because it was contrary to their religion that church dignities should be bestowed by the common people, hence for very shame he ordained that the lesser part of the people, namely seventeen tribes, should elect whom they thought fit, and afterwards the party elected should have his confirmation or admission from the college [Cicero, *De lege agraria* II, 7, 18]. Thus by a committee of seventeen tribes taken out of thirty-five the ancient form of religion was altered and reduced to the power of the lesser part of the people. This was the great care of the people to bring ordination and consecration to the laity.

The religion in Venice and the Low Countries is sufficiently known; much need not be said of them. They admirably agree under a seeming contrariety. It is commonly said that one of them hath all religions and the other no religion; the atheist of Venice may shake hands with the sectary of Amsterdam. This is the liberty that a popular estate can brag of, every man may be of any religion, or no religion, if he please. Their main devotion is exercised only in opposing and suppressing monarchy. They both agree to exclude the clergy from meddling in government, whereas in all monarchies both before the law of Moses and under it, and ever since, all barbarians, Grecians, Romans, infidels, Turks and Indians, have with one consent given such respect and reverence to their priests as to trust them with their laws. And in this our nation, the first priests we read of before Christianity were the Druids who, as Caesar saith, 'decided and determined controversies in murder, in case of inheritance, of bounds of lands, as they in their discretion judged meet; they grant rewards and punishments' [Caesar, *De Bello Gallico* book 6, 13, 5]. It is a wonder to see what high respect even the great Turk giveth to his mufti or chief bishop, so necessary is religion to strengthen and direct laws.

To consider of the point of peace, it is well known that no people ever enjoyed it without monarchy. Aristotle saith the Lacedaemonians 'preserved themselves by warring, and after they had gotten to themselves the empire then were they presently undone, for that they could not live at rest nor do any better exercise than the exercise of war' (book 2, chapter 7) [1271ᵇ3–6]. After Rome had expelled kings it was in perpetual war till the time of the emperors. Once only was the temple of Janus shut, after the end of the first Punic War, but not so long as for one year, but for some months. It is true, as Orosius saith, that 'for almost 700 years, that is, from Tullus Hostilius to Augustus Caesar, only for one summer the bowels of Rome did not sweat blood' [Orosius *Historiarum adversus paganos* IV, 12, 9]. On the behalf of the Romans it may be said that though the bowels of Rome did always sweat blood, yet they did obtain most glorious victories abroad. But it may be truly answered, if all the Roman conquests had no other foundation but injustice, this alone soils all the glory of her warlike actions. The most glorious war that ever Rome had was with Carthage, the beginning of which war Sir Walter Raleigh proves to have been most unjustly undertaken by the Romans, in confederating with the Mamertines and aiding of rebels, under the title of protecting their confederates [Raleigh I, V, I, iii]. Whereas kings many times may have just cause of war for recovering and preserving their rights to such dominions as fall to them by inheritance or marriage, a popular estate, that can neither marry nor be heir to another, can have no such title to a war in a foreign kingdom. And to speak the truth, if it be rightly considered the whole time of the popularity of Rome the Romans were no other than the only prosperous and glorious thieves and robbers of the world.

If we look more narrowly into the Roman government, it will appear that in that very age wherein Rome was most victorious and seemed to be most popular, she owed most of her glory to an apparent kind of monarchy. For it was the kingly power of the consuls who, as Livy saith, had the same royal jurisdiction or absolute power that the kings had, not any whit diminished or abated, and held all the same regal ensigns of supreme dignity [Livy II, i, 7–8], which helped Rome to all her conquests. Whiles the tribunes of the people were struggling at home with the senate about election of magistrates, enacting of laws and calling to account, or such other popular affairs, the kingly consuls gained all the victories abroad. Thus Rome at one and the same time was broken and distracted into two shows of government – the popular, which served only to raise seditions and discords within the walls, whilst the regal achieved the conquests of foreign nations and kingdoms. Rome was so sensible of the benefit and necessity of monarchy that in her most desperate condition and danger, when all other hopes failed her, she had still resort to the creation of a dictator who for the time was an absolute king, and from whom no appeal to the people was granted – which is the royallest evidence for monarchy in the world. For they who were drawn to swear they would suffer no king of Rome, found no security but in perjury and breaking their oath by admitting the kingly power in spite of their teeth, under a new name of a dictator or consul – a just reward for their wanton expelling their king for no other crime they could pretend but pride, which is most tolerable in a king of all men. And yet we find no particular point of pride charged upon him but that he enjoined the Romans to labour in cleansing and casting of ditches, and paving their sinks – an act both for the benefit and ornament of the city, and therefore commendable in the king. But the citizens of Rome, who had been conquerors of all nations round about them, could not endure of warriors to become quarriers and day-labourers. Whereas it is said that Tarquin was expelled for the rape committed by his son on Lucrece, it is unjust to condemn the father for the crime of his son. It had been fit to have petitioned the father for the punishment of the offender. The fact of young Tarquin cannot be excused, yet without wrong to the reputation of so chaste a lady as Lucrece is reputed to be, it may be said she had a greater desire to be thought chaste than to be chaste. She might have died untouched and unspotted in her body if she had not been afraid to be slandered for inchastity. Both Dionysius Halicarnasseus and Livy, who both are her friends, so tell the tale of her as if she had chosen rather to be a whore than to be thought a whore. To say truth, we find no other cause of the expulsion of Tarquin than the wantonness and licentiousness of the people of Rome.

This is further to be considered in the Roman government, that all the time between their kings and their emperors there lasted a continued strife between the nobility and commons, wherein by degrees the commons prevailed at last so to weaken the authority of the consuls and senate that even the last sparks of monarchy were in a manner extinguished, and then instantly began the civil war which lasted till the regal power was quickly brought home and settled in monarchy. So long as the power of the senate stood good for the election of consuls, the regal power was preserved in them, for the senate had their first institution from monarchy. It is worth the noting that in all those places that have seemed to be most popular, that weak degree of government that hath been exercised among them, hath been founded upon and been *beholding*[464] unto monarchical principles both for the power of assembling and manner of consulting. For the entire and gross body of any people is such an unwieldy and diffused thing as is not capable of uniting, or congregating, or deliberating in an entire lump, but in broken parts, which at first were regulated by monarchy.

Furthermore, it is observable that Rome in her chief popularity was oft *beholding*[465] for her preservation to the monarchical power of the father over the children. By means of this fatherly power, saith Bodin, the Romans flourished in all honour and virtue, and oftentimes was their commonweal thereby delivered from most imminent destruction, when the fathers drew out of the *consistories*[466] their sons, being tribunes publishing laws tending to sedition. Amongst others Cassius 'threw his son headlong out of the consistory, publishing the law *agraria* (for the division of lands) in the behoof of the people, and after by his own private judgment put him to death' [Bodin p. 23] – the magistrates, serjeants and people standing thereat astonished, and not daring to withstand his fatherly authority, although they would with all their power have had that law for division of lands; which is sufficient proof this power of the father not only to have been sacred and inviolable, but also to have been lawful for him either by right or wrong to dispose of the life and death of his children, even contrary to the will of the magistrates and people.

It is generally believed that the government of Rome, after the expulsion of kings, was popular. Bodin endeavours to prove it, but I am not satisfied with his arguments, and though it will be thought a paradox, yet I must maintain it was never truly popular.

First, it is difficult to agree what a popular government is. Aristotle saith it is where many or a multitude do rule; he doth not say where the people, or the major part of the people, or the representers of the people govern.

Bodin affirms, 'if all the people be interested in the government it is a popular estate' (Bodin book 2, chapter 1, [p. 183]), but after in the same chapter he resolves that 'it is a popular estate when all the people, or the greater part thereof hath the sovereignty' [p. 184], and he puts the case that if there be three-score thousand citizens, and forty thousand of them have the sovereignty, and twenty thousand be excluded, it shall be called a popular estate [p. 196]. But I must tell him, though fifty-nine thousand, nine hundred and ninety-nine of them govern, yet it is no popular estate. For if but one man be excluded, the same reason that excludes that one man may exclude many hundreds, and many thousands, yea, and the major part itself. If it be admitted that the people are or ever were free by nature, and not to be governed but by their own consent, it is most unjust to exclude any one man from his right in government; and to suppose the people so unnatural as at the first to have all consented to give away their right to a major part (as if they had liberty given them only to give away, and not to use it themselves) is not only improbable but impossible. For the whole people is a thing so uncertain and changeable that it alters every moment. So that it is necessary to ask of every infant *as*[467] soon as it is born its consent to government, if you will ever have the consent of the whole people.

Moreover, if the arbitrary trial by a jury of twelve men be a thing of that admirable perfection and justice as is commonly believed, wherein the negative voice of every single person is preserved, so that the dissent of any of the twelve frustrates the whole judgment; how much more ought the natural freedom of each man be preserved by allowing him his negative voice, which is but a continuing him in that estate wherein, it is confessed, nature at first placed him? Justice requires that no one law should bind all, except all consent to it. There is nothing more violent and contrary to nature than to allow a major part, or any other greater part less than the whole, to bind all the people.

The next difficulty to discovering what a popular estate is, is to find out where the supreme power in the Roman government rested. It is Bodin's opinion that 'in the Roman state the government was in the magistrates, the authority and council in the senate, but the sovereign power and majesty in the people' (Bodin book 2, chapter 1 [p. 190]). So in his first book his doctrine is that 'the ancient Romans said "*imperium in magistratibus, authoritatem in senatu, potestatem in plebe, majestatem in populo jure esse dicebant* [they said that by right command is in the magistrates, authority in the senate, power in the plebeians, and majesty in the people]"' [Bodin p. 157]. These four words, *command, authority, power* and *majesty* signify ordinarily one and the same thing, to wit, the sovereignty or supreme power. I cannot find that Bodin knows how to distinguish them. For they were not distinct faculties placed in several subjects, but one and the same thing diversely qualified. For *imperium, authoritas, potestas* and *majestas* were all originally in the consuls, although for the greater show the consuls would have the opinion and consent of the senate – who were never called together nor had their advice asked, but when and in what points only it pleased the consuls to propound. So that properly *senatusconsultum* [a decree of the senate] was only a decree of the consuls with the advice of the senators. And so likewise the consuls, when they had a mind to have the countenance of an ampler council, they assembled the centuries, who were reckoned as the whole people, and were never to be assembled but when the consuls thought fit to propound some business of great weight unto them. So that *jussus populi* – the command of the people – which Bodin so much magnifies, was properly *jussus consulum* – the command of the consuls, by the advice or consent of the assembly of the centuries, who were a body composed of the senators and the rest of the patricians, knights and gentlemen, or whole nobility together with the commons. For the same men who had voices in senate had also their votes allowed in the assembly of the centuries, according to their several capacities.

It may further appear that the Roman government was never truly popular, for that in her greatest show of popularity there were to be found above ten servants for every citizen or freeman, and of those servants not one of them was allowed any place or voice in government. If it be said that the Roman servants were slaves taken in war, and therefore not fit to be freemen; to this it may be answered that if the opinion of our modern politicians be good, which holds that all men are born free by nature, or if but the opinion of Aristotle be sound, who saith that 'by nature some men are servants and some are masters' [1255^{a}1–2], then it may be unnatural or unjust to make all prisoners in war servants, or (as they are now called) slaves – a term not used in the popular governments, either of Rome or Greece. For in both languages the usual word that doth answer to our late term of slave is but *servus* in Latin, and δοῦλος in Greek. Besides, if the wars of the Romans by which they gained so many servants were unjust, as I take all offensive war to be without a special commission from God, and as I believe all the Roman wars were that were made for the enlargement of their empire, then we may conclude that the Romans were the notablest plagiaries[s] or men-stealers in the world.

But to allow the lesser part of the people of Rome, who called themselves citizens, to have had a just right to exclude all servants from being a part of the people of Rome, let us enquire whether the major part of those whom they allowed to be citizens had the government of Rome – whereby we may discover easily how notoriously the poorer and greater part of the citizens were gulled of their share in government. There were two famous manners of their assembling the people of Rome. The first was by classes, as they called them, which were divided into centuries. The second was by tribes, or wards. The former of these was a ranking of the people according to their abilities or wealth. The latter according to the place or ward wherein every citizen dwelt. In the assemblies of neither of these had the major part of the people the power of government, as *may*[468] thus be made appear.

First, for the assembly of the centuries, there were six degrees or classes of men according to their wealth. The first classis was of the richest men in Rome, none whereof were under two hundred pounds in value. The valuation of the second classis was not under fourscore pounds; and so the third, the fourth and the fifth classis were each a degree one under another. The sixth classis contained the poorer sort and all the rabble. These six classes were subdivided into hundreds or centuries.

The first classis had	98	
The second had	22	
The third classis had	20	centuries
The fourth classis had	22	
The fifth classis had	30	
The sixth classis had	1	
	193	

The classes and centuries being thus ordered, when the assembly came to give their votes they did not give their voices by the poll, which is the true popular way. But each century voted by itself. Each century having one voice, the major part of the centuries carried

[s] [kidnappers].

the business. Now there being fourscore and eighteen centuries in the first classis – in which all the patricians, senators, noblemen, knights and gentlemen of Rome were enrolled – being more in number, and above half the centuries, must needs have the government if they agreed all together in their votes, because they voted first. For when ninety-seven centuries had agreed in their votes, the other centuries of the inferior classis were never called to vote. Thus the nobles and richer men who were but few in comparison of the common people did bear the chief sway, because all the poorer sort, or proletarian rabble, were clapped into the sixth classis – which in reckoning were allowed but the single voice of one century, which never came to voting, whereas in number they did far exceed all the five other classes or centuries. And if they had been allowed the liberty of other citizens they might have been justly numbered for a thousand centuries or voices in the assembly. This device of packing so many thousands into one century did exclude far the greatest part of the people from having a part in the government.

Next, for the assembly of the people of Rome by tribes, it must be considered that the tribes did not give their voices by the poll all together, which is the true way of popular voting, but each tribe or ward did vote by itself, and the votes of the major part (not of the people but) of the tribes did sway the government. For the tribes being unequal, as all divisions by wards usually are, because the number of the people of one tribe is not just the same with the number of the people of each other tribe; whence it followed that the major number of the tribes might possibly be the minor number of the people, which is a destroying of the power of the major part of the people.

Add hereunto that the nobility of Rome were excluded from being present at the assembly of the tribes, and so the most considerable part of the people was wanting. Therefore it could not be the voices of the major part of the people, where a great part of the people were allowed no voices at all. For it must be the major part of the *whole* and not of a *part* of the people that must denominate a popular government.

Moreover, it must be noted that the assembly of the tribes was not originally the power of the people of Rome, for it was almost forty years after the rejection of kings before an assembly of tribes were thought on or spoken of. For it was the assembly of the people by centuries that agreed to the expulsion of kings and creating of consuls in their room. Also the famous laws of the twelve tables were ratified by the assembly of the centuries. This assembly by centuries, as it was more ancient than that by tribes so it was more truly popular, because all the nobility as well as the commons had voices in it. The assembly by tribes was pretended at first only to elect tribunes of the people and other inferior magistrates to determine of lesser crimes that were not capital but only fineable, and to decree that peace should be made. But they did not meddle with denouncing war to be made, for that high point did belong only to the assembly of the centuries, and so also did the judging of treason and other capital crimes. The difference between the assembly of the tribes and of the centuries is very material, for though it be commonly thought that either of these two assemblies were esteemed to be the people, yet in reality it was not so. For the assembly of the centuries only could be said to be the people, because all the nobility were included in it as well as the commons, whereas they were excluded out of the assembly of the tribes. And yet in effect the assembly of the centuries was but as the assembly of the lords or nobles only, because the lesser and richer part of the people had the sovereignty, as the assembly of the tribes was but the commons only.

In maintenance of the popular government of Rome, Bodin objects that there could be no regal power in the two consuls, 'who could neither make law, nor peace, nor war' [Bodin p. 188]. The answer is, though there were two consuls yet but one of them had the regality, for they governed by turns, one consul one month, the other consul another month; or the first one day, and the second another day. That the consuls could make no laws is false. It is plain by Livy that they had the power to make laws, or war, and did execute that power, though they were often hindered by the tribunes of the people. Not for that the power of making laws or war, was ever taken away from the consuls or communicated to the tribunes, but only the exercise of the consular power was suspended by a seeming humble way of intercession of the tribunes. The consuls by their first institution had a lawful right to do those things, which yet they would not do by reason of the shortness of their reigns, but chose rather to countenance their actions with the title of a decree of the senate (who were their private council), yea, and sometimes with the decree of the assembly of the centuries (who were their public council). For both the assembling of the senate and of the centuries was at the pleasure of the consuls, and nothing was to be propounded in either of them but at the will of the consuls – which argues a sovereignty in them over the senate and centuries. The senate of Rome was like the House of Lords, the assembly of the tribes resembled the House of Commons, but the assembling of the centuries was a body composed of Lords and Commons united to vote together.

The tribunes of the people bore all the sway among the tribes. They called them together when they pleased, without any order, whereas the centuries were never assembled without ceremony and religious observation of the birds by the augurs, and by the approbation of the senate, and therefore were said to be *auspicata* [auspicious], and *ex authoritate patrum* [by the authority of the senate].

These things considered, it appears that the assembly of the centuries was the only legitimate and great meeting of the people of Rome. As for any assembling or electing of any trustees or representers of the people of Rome, in nature of the modern parliaments, it was not in use or ever known in Rome.

Above two hundred and twenty years after the expulsion of kings a sullen humour took the commons of Rome, that they would needs depart the city to Janiculum, on the other side of Tiber. They would not be brought back into the city until a law was made that a *plebiscitum*, or a decree of the commons, might be observed for a law. This law was made by the dictator Hortensius to quiet the sedition by giving a part of the legislative power to the commons in such inferior matters only as by toleration and usurpation had been practised by the commons. I find not that they desired an enlargement of the points which were the object of their power, but of the persons or nobility that should be subject to their decrees. The great power of making war, of creating the greater magistrates, of judging in capital crimes, remained in the consuls with the senate and assembly of the centuries.

For further manifestation of the broken and distracted government of Rome, it is fit to consider the original power of the consuls, and of the tribunes of the commons, who are ordinarily called the tribunes of the people.

First, it is undeniable that upon the expulsion of kings, kingly power was not taken away but only made annual and changeable between two consuls, who in their turns and by course had the sovereignty and all regal power. This appears plainly in Livy, who tells us that Valerius Publicola being consul, he himself alone ordained a law and then assembled a general session.

Terentilius Harsa[469] inveighed and complained against 'the consuls' government, as being so absolute, and in name only less odious than that of kings, but in fact more cruel. For instead of one lord the city had received twain, having authority beyond all measure, unlimited and infinite' [Livy III, ix, 2–4]. Sextius and Licinius complain that there would never be any indifferent course so long as the nobles kept the sovereign place of command, and the sword to strike, whiles the poor commons have only the buckler [Livy VI, xxxvii, 4]. Their conclusion was that 'it remains that the commons bear the office of consuls too, for that were a fortress of their liberty. From that day forward shall the commons be partakers of those things wherein the nobles now surpass them, namely sovereign rule and authority' [Livy VI, xxxvii, 10–11].

The law of the twelve tables affirms, '*Regio imperio duo sunto, iique consules appellantor*': 'let two have regal power, and let them be called consuls' [Cicero, *De Republica* III, iii, 8]. Also, the judgment of Livy is that 'the sovereign power was translated from consuls to decemvirs, as before from kings to consuls' [Livy III, xxxiii, 1]. These are proofs sufficient to show the royal power of the consuls.

About sixteen years after the first creation of consuls, the commons finding themselves much run into debt by wasting their estates in following the wars, and so becoming, as they thought, oppressed by usury, and cast into prison by the judgment and sentence of the consuls, they grievously complained of usury and of the power of the consuls, and by sedition prevailed, and obtained leave to choose among themselves magistrates called tribunes of the people, who by their intercession might preserve the commons from being oppressed and suffering wrong from the consuls. And it was further agreed that the persons of those tribunes should be sacred, and not to be touched by any. By means of this immunity of the bodies of the tribunes from all arrests or other violence, they grew in time by degrees to such boldness that by stopping the legal proceedings of the consuls (when they pleased to intercede) they raised such an anarchy ofttimes in government that they themselves might act and take upon them what power soever they pleased (though it belonged not to them). This gallantry of the tribunes was the cause that the commons of Rome, who were diligent pretenders to liberty, and the great masters of this part of politics, were thought the only famous preservers and keepers of the liberty of Rome. And to do them right, it must be confessed they were the only men that truly understood the rights of a negative voice. If we will allow every man to be naturally free till they give their consent to be bound, we must allow every particular person a negative voice. So that when as all have equal power, and are as it were fellow magistrates or officers, each man may impeach or stop his fellow officers in their proceedings. This is grounded upon the general reason of all them which have anything in common, where he which forbiddeth, or denieth, hath most right – because his condition in that case is better than his which commandeth, or moveth to proceed. For every law or command is in itself an innovation, and a diminution of some part of popular liberty – for it is no law except it restrain liberty. He that by his negative voice doth forbid or hinder the proceeding of a new law doth but preserve himself in that condition of liberty wherein nature hath placed him, and whereof he is in present possession. The condition of him thus in possession being the better the stronger is his prohibition, any single man hath a juster title to his negative voice than any multitude can have to their affirmative. To say the people are free, and not to be governed but by their own consent, and yet to allow a major part to rule the whole, is a plain contradiction, or a destruction of natural freedom. This the commons of Rome rightly understood – and therefore the transcendent power of the negative voice of any one tribune, being able of itself to stay all the proceedings not of the consuls and senate only, and other magistrates, but also of the rest of his fellow tribunes, made them seem the powerfullest men in all Rome. And yet in truth they had no power or jurisdiction at all, nor were they any magistrates, nor could they lawfully call any man before them. For they were not appointed for administration of justice, but only to oppose the violence and abuse of magistrates by interceding for such as appealed, being unjustly oppressed. For which purpose at first they sat only without the door of the senate, and were not permitted to come within the doors. This negative power of theirs was of force only to hinder but not to help the proceedings in courts of justice; to ungovern, and not to govern the people. And though they had no power to make laws, yet they took upon them to propound laws, and flattered and humoured the commons by the agrarian and frumentarian laws. By the first they divided the common fields and conquered lands among the common people; and by the latter they afforded them corn at a cheaper or lower price. By these means these demagogues or tribunes of the commons led the vulgar by the noses, to allow whatsoever usurpations they pleased to make in government.

The royal power of the consuls was never taken away from them by any law that I hear of, but continued in them all the time of their pretended popular government, to the very last – though repined at, and opposed in some particulars by the commons.

The no-power or negative power of the tribunes did not long give content to the commons, and therefore they desired that one of the consuls might be chosen out of the commonalty. The eager propounding of this point for the commons, and the diligent opposing of it by the nobility or senate, argues how much both parties regarded the sovereign power of a consul. The dispute lasted fourscore years within two. The tribunes, pressing it upon all advantages of opportunity, never gave over till they carried it by strong hand, or stubbornness, hindering all elections of the *curule* or greater magistrates for five years together; whereby the nobles were forced to yield the commons a consul's place, or else an anarchy was ready to destroy them all. And yet the nobility had for a good while allowed the commons military tribunes with consular power, which in effect or substance was all one with having one of the consuls a commoner, so that it was the bare *name**[470] of a consul which the commons so long strived for with the nobility. In this contention, some years consuls were chosen, some years military tribunes, in such confusion that the Roman historians cannot agree among themselves what consuls to assign or name for each year, although they have Capitoline tables, Sicilian and Greek registers, and calendars, fragments of Capitoline marbles, linen books or records to help them. A good while the commons were content with the liberty of having one of the consuls a commoner. But about four score years after they enjoyed this privilege, a desire took them to have it enacted that a decree of the commons, called a *plebiscitum*, might be observed for a law. Hortensius the dictator yielded to enact it thereby to bring back the seditious commons, who departed to Janiculum on the other side of Tiber, because they were deeply engaged in debt in regard of long seditions and dissensions. The eleventh book of Livy, where this sedition is set down, is lost; we have only a touch of it in Florus his epitome [Livy XI,

Periocha], and Saint Augustine mentions the plundering of many houses by the commons at their departing [Augustine, *Civitas Dei* III, 17]. This sedition was above 220 years after the expulsion of kings, in all which time the people of Rome got the spoil of almost all Italy and the wealth of very many rich cities. And yet the commons were in so great penury, and overwhelmed with debts, that they fell to plunder the rich houses of the citizens, which sounds not much for the honour of a popular government. This communicating of a legislative power to the commons, touching power of enfranchising allies, judgments penal, and fines, and those ordinances that concerned the good of the commons – called *plebiscita* – was a dividing of the supreme power and the giving a share of it to others as well as to the consuls, and was in effect to destroy the legislative power. For to have two supremes is to have none, because the one may destroy the other, and is quite contrary to the indivisible nature of sovereignty. The truth is, the consuls having but annual sovereignty were glad, for their own safety and ease in matters of great importance and weight, to call together sometimes the senate, who were their ordinary council, and many times the centuries of the people, who were their council extraordinary, that by their advice they might countenance and strengthen such actions as were full of danger and envy. And thus the consuls by weakening their original power brought the government to confusion, civil dissension and utter ruin. So dangerous a thing it is to show favour to common people, who interpret all graces and favours for their rights and just liberties. The consuls following the advice of the senate or people, did not take away their right of governing no more than kings lose their supremacy by taking advice in parliaments.

Not only the consuls but also the praetors and censors (two great offices, ordained only for the case of the consuls, from whom an appeal lay to the consuls) did in many things exercise an arbitrary or legislative power in the absence of the consuls. They had no laws to limit them. For, many years after the creation of consuls, ten men were sent into Greece to choose laws. And after the twelve tables were confirmed, whatsoever the praetors – who were but the consuls' substitutes – did command was called *jus honorarium* [an honorary law]; and they were wont at the entrance into their office to collect and hang up for public view a form of administration of justice which they would observe. And though the *edictum praetoris* [praetor's edict] expired with the praetor's office, yet it was called *edictum perpetuum* [a perpetual edict].

What peace the Low Countries have found since their revolt is visible. It is near about an hundred years since they set up for themselves, of all which time only twelve years they had a truce with the Spaniard. Yet in the next year after the truce was agreed upon, the war of Juliers broke forth, which engaged both parties. So that upon the matter, they have lived in a continued war for almost one hundred years. Had it not been for the aid of their neighbours, they had been long ago swallowed up, when they were glad humbly to offer their new hatched commonweal and themselves vassals to the Queen of England, after that the French king, Henry III, had refused to accept them as his subjects. That little truce they had was almost as costly as a war, they being forced to keep about thirty thousand soldiers continually in garrison. Two things they say they first fought about, religion and taxes – and they have prevailed, it seems, in both, for they have gotten all the religions in Christendom, and pay the greatest taxes in the world. They pay tribute half in half for food, and most necessary things, paying as much for tribute as the price of the thing sold. Excise is paid by all retailers of wine and other commodities. For each tun of beer six shillings; for each cow for the pail two stivers every week; for oxen, horses, sheep and other beasts sold in the market the twelfth part at least; be they never so oft sold by the year to and fro, the new master still pays as much. They pay five stivers for every bushel of their own wheat, which they use to grind in public mills. These are the fruits of the Low Country war.

It will be said that Venice is a commonwealth that enjoys peace. She indeed of all other states hath enjoyed of late the greatest peace. But she owes it not to her kind of government but to the natural situation of the city, having such a bank in the sea of near three score miles, and such marshes towards the land, as make her unapproachable by land or sea. To these she is indebted for her peace at home – and what peace she hath abroad she buys at a dear rate. And yet her peace is little better than a continued war. The city always is in such perpetual fears that many besieged cities are in more security. A senator or gentleman dares not converse with any stranger in Venice, shuns acquaintance, or dares not own it. They are no better than banditos to all human society. Nay, no people in the world live in such jealousy one of another. Hence are their intricate solemnities or rather lotteries in election of their magistrates, which in any other place would be ridiculous and useless. The senators or gentlemen arc not only jealous of the common people, whom they keep disarmed, but of one another. They dare not trust any of their own citizens to be a leader of their army, but are forced to hire and entertain foreign princes for their generals, excepting their citizens from their wars and hiring others in their places. It cannot be said that people live in peace which are in such miserable fears continually.

The Venetians at first were subject to the Roman Emperor, and for fear of the invasion of the Huns forsook Padua and other places in Italy, and retired with all their substance to those islands where now Venice stands. I do not read they had any leave to desert the defence of their prince and country where they had got their wealth, much less to set up a government of their own. It was no better than a rebellion or revolting from the Roman Empire. At first they lived under a kind of oligarchy, for several islands had each a tribune, who all met and governed in common. But the dangerous seditions of their tribunes put a necessity upon them to choose a duke for life, who for many hundreds of years had an absolute power – under whose government Venice flourished most, and got great victories and rich possessions. But by insensible degrees the great council of the gentlemen have for many years been lessening the power of their dukes and have at last quite taken it away. It is a strange error for any man to believe that the government of Venice hath been always the same *that*⁴⁷¹ it is now. He that reads but the history of Venice may find for a long time a sovereign power in their dukes, and that for these last two hundred years, since the diminishing of that power, there hath been no great victories and conquests obtained by that estate.

That which exceeds admiration is that Contarini hath the confidence to affirm the present government of Venice to be a mixed form of monarchy, democracy and aristocracy. For whereas he makes the duke to have the person and show of a king, he after confesseth that the duke can do nothing at all alone, and being joined with other magistrates he hath no more authority than any of them. Also, the power of the magistrates is so small that no one of them, how great soever he be, can determine of anything of moment without the allowance of the council. So that this duke is but a man dressed up in purple, a king only in pomp and ornament, in power but a senator, within the city a captive, without a traitor, if he go without leave. As little reason is there to think a popular estate is to be found in the great council of Venice, or S.P.Q.V. [the senate and people of Venice] for it doth not consist of the fortieth part of the people, but only of those they call patricians or gentlemen. For the commons neither by themselves nor by any chosen by them for their representers, are admitted to be any part of the great council. And if the gentlemen of Venice have any right to keep the government in their own hands and to exclude the commons, they never had it given them by the people, but at first were beholding to monarchy for their nobility. This may further be noted, that though Venice of late enjoyed peace abroad, yet it had been with that charge – either for fortification and defence, or in bribery so excessive (whereby of late upon any terms they purchased their peace) – that it is said their taxes are such that Christians generally live better under the Turk than under the Venetians. For there is not a grain of corn, a spoonful of wine, salt, eggs, birds, beasts, fowl or fish sold, that payeth not a certain custom. Upon occasions the labourers and craftsmen pay a rate by the poll monthly. They receive incredible gains by usury of the Jews, for in every city they keep open shops of interest, taking pawns after fifteen in the hundred, and if at the year's end it be not redeemed it is forfeited, or at the least sold at great loss. The revenues which the very courtesans pay for toleration maintains no less than a dozen of galleys.

By what hath been said, it may be judged how unagreeable the popular government of Rome heretofore, and of Venice and the United Provinces at the present, are either for religion or peace (which two are the principal ingredients of government), and so consequently not fit to be reckoned for forms – since whatsoever is either good or tolerable in either of their governments is borrowed or patched up of a broken and distracted monarchy. Lastly, though Venice and the Low Countries are the only remarkable places in this age that reject monarchy, yet neither of them pretend their government to be founded upon any original right of the people, or have the common people any power amongst them, or any chosen by them. Never was any popular estate in the world famous for keeping themselves in peace; all their glory hath been for quarrelling and fighting.

Those that are willing to be persuaded that the power of government is originally in the people, finding how impossible it is for any people to exercise such power, do surmise that though the people cannot govern, yet they may choose representers or trustees, that may manage this power for the people — and such representers must be surmised to be the people. And since such representers cannot truly be chosen by the people, they are fain to divide the people into several parts, as of provinces, cities and borough towns, and to allow to every one of those parts to choose one representer or more of their own. And such representers, though not any of them be chosen by the whole or major part of the people, yet still must be surmised to be the people. Nay, though not one of them be chosen either by the people or the major part of the people of any province, city or borough for which they serve, but only *by*[472] a smaller part, still it must be said to be the people. Now when such representers of the people do assemble or meet, it is never seen that all of them can at one time meet together, and so there never appears a true or full representation of the whole people of the nation, the representers of one part or other being absent. But still they must be imagined to be the people. And when such imperfect assemblies be met – though not half be present – they proceed, and though their number be never so small, yet it is so big that in the debate of any business of moment they know not how to handle it without referring it to a fewer number than themselves, though themselves are not so many as they should be. Thus those that are chosen to represent the people are necessitated to choose others to represent the representers themselves. A trustee of the north doth delegate his power to a trustee of the south; and one of the east may substitute one of the west for his proxy. Hereby it comes to pass that public debates which are imagined to be referred to a general assembly of a kingdom, are contracted into a particular or private assembly – than which nothing can be more destructive or contrary to the nature of public assemblies. Each company of such trustees hath a prolocutor or speaker, who by the help of three or four of his fellows that are most active may easily comply in gratifying one the other. So that each of them in their turns may sway the trustees, whilst one man, for himself or his friend, may rule in one business, and another man for himself or his friend prevail in another cause, till such a number of trustees be reduced to so many petty monarchs as there be men of it. So in all popularities where a general council or great assembly of the people meet, they find it impossible to dispatch any great action either with expedition or secrecy if a public free debate be admitted; and therefore are constrained to epitomise and sub-epitomise themselves so long till at last they crumble away into the atoms of monarchy, which is the next degree to anarchy – for anarchy is nothing else but a broken monarchy, where every man is his own monarch or governor.

Whereas the power of the people in choosing both their government and governors is of late highly magnified, as if they were able to choose the best and excellentest men for that purpose, we shall find it true what Aristotle hath affirmed, that 'to choose well is the office of him that hath knowledge; none can choose a geometrician but he that hath skill in geometry' (book 3, chapter 11) [1282^{a}8–10]. For, saith he, 'all men esteem not excellency to be one and the same' (book 3, chapter 17) [1288^{a}23–4].

A great deal of talk there is in the world of the freedom and liberty that they say is to be found in popular commonweals. It is worth the enquiry how far and in what sense this speech of liberty is true: 'true liberty is for every man to do what he list, or to live as he please, and not to be tied to any laws'. But such liberty is not to be found in any commonweal, for there are more laws in popular estates than anywhere else, and so consequently less liberty; and government, many say, was invented to take away liberty, and not to give it to every man. Such liberty cannot be; if it should, there would be no government at all. Therefore Aristotle, book 6, chapter 4: 'It is profitable not to be lawful to do everything that we will, for power to do what one will cannot restrain that evil that is in every man' [1318^{b}38–1319^{a}1]. So that true liberty cannot nor should not be in any estate. But the only liberty that the talkers of liberty can mean is a liberty for some men 'to rule and to be ruled' [1277^{b}14–15], for so Aristotle expounds it; one while to govern, another while to be governed; to be a king in the forenoon, and a subject in the afternoon. This is the only liberty that a popular estate can brag of, that where a monarchy hath but one king, their government hath the liberty to have many kings by turns. If the common people look for any other liberty, either of their persons or their purses, they are pitifully deceived. For a perpetual army and taxes are the principal materials of all popular regiments: never yet any stood without them, and very seldom continued with them. Many popular estates have started up, but few have lasted – 'it is no hard matter for any kind of government to last one, or two, or three days' (book 6, chapter 5) [1319^{b}35–6].

For all such as out of hope of liberty attempt to erect new forms of government, he gives this prudent lesson: 'We must look well into the continuance of time, and remembrance of many years, wherein the means tending to establish community had not lain hid if they had been good and useful. For almost all things have been found out, albeit some have not been received, and other some have been rejected after men have had experience of them' (book 2, chapter 5) [1264^{a}1–5].

It is believed by many that at the very first assembling of the people it was unanimously agreed in the first place that the consent of the major part should bind the whole; and that though this first agreement cannot possibly be proved, either how or by whom it could be made, yet it must necessarily be believed or supposed because otherwise there could be no lawful government at all. That there could be no lawful government, except a general consent of the whole people be first surmised, is no sound proposition. Yet true it is that there could be no popular government without it. But if there were at first a government without being *beholding*[473] to the people for their consent, as all men confess there was, I find no reason but that there may be so still, without asking leave of the multitude.

If it be true that men are by nature free-born, and not to be governed without their own consents, and that self-preservation is to be regarded in the first place, it is not lawful for any government but self-government to be in the world. It were sin in the people to desire, or attempt to consent to any other government. If the fathers will promise for themselves to be slaves, yet for their children they cannot, who have always the same right to set themselves at liberty which their fathers had to enslave themselves.

To pretend that a major part, or the silent consent of any part, may be interpreted to bind the whole people, is both unreasonable and unnatural. It is against all reason for men to bind others where it is against nature for men to bind themselves. Men that boast so much of natural freedom are not willing to consider how contradictory and destructive the power of a major part is to the natural liberty of the whole people. The two grand favourites of the subjects, liberty and property (for which most men pretend to strive), are as contrary as fire to water, and cannot stand together. Though by human laws, in voluntary actions a major part may be tolerated to bind the whole multitude, yet in necessary actions – such as those of nature are

– it cannot be so. Besides, if it were possible for a whole people to choose their representers, then either every each one of those representers ought to be particularly chosen by the whole people, and not one representer by one part, and another representer by another part of the people, or else it is necessary that continually the entire number of the representers be present – because otherwise the whole people is never represented.

Again, it is impossible for the people, though they might and would choose a government or governors, ever to be able to do it. For the people, to speak truly and properly, is a thing or body in continual alteration and change. It never continues one minute the same, being composed of a multitude of parts whereof divers continually decay and perish, and others renew and succeed in their places. They which are the people this minute, are not the people the next minute. If it be answered, that it is impossible to stand so strictly as to have the consent of the whole people, and therefore that which cannot be must be supposed to be the act of the whole people; this is a strange answer, first to affirm a necessity of having the people's consent, then to confess an impossibility of having it. If but once that liberty – which is esteemed so sacred – be broken or taken away but from one of the meanest or basest of all the people, a wide gap is thereby opened for any multitude whatsoever that is able to call themselves (or whomsoever they please) the people.

Howsoever men are naturally willing to be persuaded that all sovereignty flows from the consent of the people, and that without it no true title can be made to any supremacy; and that it is so current an axiom of late, that it will certainly pass without contradiction, as a late exercitator' tells us; yet there are many and great difficulties in the point never yet determined *[nor]*[474] so much as disputed, all which the exercitator waives and declines, professing he will 'not insist upon the distinctions touching the manner of the people's passing their consent, nor determine which of them is sufficient, and which not to make the right or title; whether it must be antecedent to possession or may be consequent: express or tacit: collective or representative: absolute or conditionated: free or enforced: revocable or irrevocable' [Gee chapter 1]. All these are material doubts

---

' [The exercitator was Edward Gee, who in 1650 published *An Exercitation concerning Usurped Powers*].

concerning the people's title, and though the exercitator will not himself determine what consent is sufficient and what not to make a right or title, yet he might have been so courteous as to have directed us to whom we might go for resolution in these cases. But the truth is, that amongst all them that plead the necessity of the consent of the people, not one of them hath ever touched upon these so necessary doctrines. It is a task, it seems, too difficult, otherwise surely it would not have been neglected, considering how necessary it is to resolve the conscience touching the manner of the people's passing their consent, and what is sufficient and what not to make or derive a right or title from the people.

No multitude or great assembly of any nation, though they be all of them never so good and virtuous, can possibly govern. This may be evidently discovered by considering the actions of great and numerous assemblies, how they are necessitated to relinquish that supreme power which they think they exercise, and to delegate it to a few. There are two parts of the supreme power, the *legislative* and the *executive*. Neither of these can a great assembly truly act. If a new law be to be made it may in the general receive the proposal of it from one or more of the general assembly, but the forming, penning or framing it into a law is committed to a few, because a great number of persons cannot without tedious and dilatory debates examine the benefits and mischiefs of a law. Thus in the very first beginning, the intention of a general assembly is frustrated. Then after a law is penned or framed, when it comes to be questioned whether it shall pass or nay, though it be voted in a full assembly yet by the rules of the assembly they are all so tied up and barred from a free and full debate that when any man hath given the reasons of his opinion, if those reasons be argued against, he is not permitted to reply in justification or explanation of them, but when he hath once spoken he must be heard no more – which is a main denial of that freedom of debate for which the great assembly is alleged to be ordained in the high point of *legislative* power.[a]

The same may be said, touching the *executive* power. If a cause be brought before a great assembly, the first thing done is to refer or commit it to some few of the assembly, who are trusted with the examining the proofs and witnesses, and to make report to the general

---

[a] [Filmer has in mind the procedure of the English parliament].

assembly – who upon the report proceed to give their judgments without any public hearing or interrogating the witnesses, upon whose testimonies diligently examined every man that will pass a conscientious judgment is to rely. Thus the *legislative* and *executive* power are never truly practised in a great assembly. The true reason whereof is, if freedom be given to debate, never anything could be agreed upon without endless disputes. Mere necessity compels to refer main transactions of business to particular congregations and committees.

Those governments that seem to be popular are kinds of petty monarchies, which may thus appear: government is a relation between the governors and the governed, the one cannot be without the other, *mutuo se ponunt et auferunt* [they rise and fall together]. Where a command or law proceeds from a major part, there those individual persons that concurred in the vote are the governors, because the law is only their will in particular. The power of a major part, being a contingent or casual thing, expires in the very act itself of voting, which power of a major part is grounded upon a supposition that they are the stronger part. When the vote is passed, these voters – which are the major part – return again, and are incorporated into the whole assembly, and are buried as it were in that lump, and no otherwise considered. The act or law ordained by such a vote loseth the makers of it before it comes to be obeyed. For when it comes to be put in execution it becomes the will of those who enjoin it and force obedience to it, not by virtue of any power derived from the makers of the law. No man can say that during the reign of the late Queen Elizabeth, that King Henry VIII or Edward VI did govern, although that many of the laws that were made in those two former princes' times were observed and executed under her government. But those laws, though made by her predecessors, yet became the laws of her present government, who willed and commanded the execution of them, and had the same power to correct, interpret or mitigate them, which the first makers of them had. Every law must always have some present known person in being, whose will it must be to make it a law for the present. This cannot be said of the major part of any assembly, because that major part instantly ceaseth as soon as ever it hath voted – an infallible argument whereof is this, that the same major part, after the vote given, hath no power to correct, alter or mitigate it, or to cause it to be put in execution. So that he that shall act or cause that law to be executed makes himself the commander or willer of it, which was originally the will of others. It is said by Mr Hobbes in his *Leviathan*, page 141: 'Nothing is law where the legislator cannot be known', for there must 'be manifest signs that it proceedeth from the will of the sovereign; there is requisite not only a declaration of the law, but also sufficient signs of the author and the authority' [Hobbes 2, p. 141].

That senate or great council, wherein it is conceived the supreme or legislative power doth rest, consists of those persons who are actually subjects at the very same time wherein they exercise their legislative power, and at the same instant may be guilty of breaking one law, whilst they are making another law. For it is not the whole and entire will of every particular person in the assembly, but that part only of his will which accidentally falls out to concur with the will of the greater part. So that the sharers of the legislative power have each of them perhaps not a hundredth part of the legislative power (which in itself is indivisible), and that not in *act* but in *possibility*, only in one particular point, for that moment whilst they give their vote. To close this point, which may seem strange and new to some, I will produce the judgment of Bodin. In his sixth book of a common-weal, and the fourth chapter, his words are,

> The chief point of a commonweal, which is the right of sover-eignty, cannot be nor subsist, to speak properly, but in monarchy. For none can be sovereign in a commonweal but one alone. If they be two, or three, or more, no one is sovereign, for that no one of them can give or take a law from his companion; and although we imagine a body of many lords or of a whole people to hold the sovereignty, yet hath it no true ground nor support if there be not a head with absolute power to unite them together, which a simple magistrate without sovereign authority cannot do. And if it chance that the lords or tribes of the people be divided (as it often falls out) then must they fall to arms one against another, and although the greatest part be of one opinion, yet may it so happen as the lesser part, having many legions and making a head, may oppose itself against the greater number and get the victory. We see the difficulties which are and always have been in popular estates, whereas they hold contrary parts and for divers magistrates. Some demand peace, others war; some will have this law, others that; some will have one commander, others another; some will treat a league with the king of France, others with the king of Spain; corrupted or drawn some one

way, some another, making open war – as hath been seen in our age amongst the Grisons, etc. [Bodin p. 715]

Upon these texts of Aristotle fore-cited, and from the mutability of the Roman popularity, which Aristotle lived not to see, I leave the learned to consider whether it be not probable that these or the like paradoxes may be inferred to be the plain mind of Aristotle, viz. 1. That there is no form of government but monarchy only. 2. That there is no monarchy, but paternal. 3. That there is no paternal monarchy, but absolute or arbitrary. 4. That there is no such thing as an aristocracy or democracy. 5. That there is no such form of government as a tyranny. 6. That the people are not born free by nature.

DIRECTIONS FOR OBEDIENCE TO GOVERNMENT IN DANGEROUS OR DOUBTFUL TIMES[v]

All those who *in these times*[475] so eagerly strive for an original power to be in the people *do*[476] with one consent acknowledge that originally the supreme power was in the fatherhood; and that the first kings were fathers of families. This is not only evident, and affirmed by Aristotle, but yielded unto by Grotius, *Mr Selden, Mr Hobbes, Mr Ascham*[477] and all others of that party, not one excepted, that I know of.

Now for those that confess an original subjection in children to be governed by their parents, to dream of an original freedom in mankind is to contradict themselves. And to make subjects to be free, and kings to be limited; to imagine such pactions and contracts between kings and people as cannot be proved ever to have been made, or can ever be described or fancied how it is possible for such contracts ever to have been, is a boldness to be wondered at.

Mr Selden confesseth that Adam

---

[v] [A manuscript of a section of this work is in British Library, Harleian MS 4685, f.75a–b. In the notes, DMS is the manuscript version, 52A and 79 the first edition of 1652 (Wing F921) and the editions of 1679 (Wing F913 and 914). DMS contains the text from the title and opening words to p. 283 – 'destruction of the'. The notes record variants in DMS and 52A. In the case of passages not in DMS, if a reading from 52A is given in the notes, then the text is taken from 79].

by donation from God was made the general lord of all things, not without such a private dominion to himself as (without his grant) did exclude his children. And by donation or assignation, or some kind of *cession*[478] (before he was dead or left any heir to succeed him) his children had their distinct territories *by right of private dominion. Abel had his flocks, and pastures*[479] for them. Cain had his fields for corn, and the land of Nod where he built himself a city. [Selden 2, p. 19–20]

It is confessed that in the infancy of the world the paternal government was monarchical. But when the world was replenished with multitude of people, then the paternal government ceased and was lost, and *an*[480] elective kind of government by the people was brought into the world. To this it may be answered that the paternal power cannot be lost. It may either be transferred or usurped, but never lost, or ceaseth. God, who is the giver of power, may transfer it from the father to some other. He gave to Saul a fatherly power over his father Kish. God also hath given to the father a right or liberty to alien his power over his children to any other, whence we find the sale and gift of children to have been much in use in the beginning of the world, when men had their servants for a possession and an inheritance as well as other goods. Whereupon we find the power of castrating and making eunuchs much in use in old times. As the power of the father may be lawfully transferred or aliened so it may be unjustly usurped, and in usurpation the title of an usurper is before and better than the title of any other than of him that had a former right. For he hath a possession by the permissive will of God, which permission how long it may endure no man ordinarily knows. Every man is to preserve his own life for the service of God and of his king or father, and is so far to obey an usurper as may tend not only to the preservation of his king and father, but sometimes even to the preservation of the usurper himself when probably he may thereby be reserved to the correction or mercy of his true superior. Though by human laws a long prescription may take away right, yet divine right never dies nor can be lost or taken away.

Every man that is born is so far from being free-born that by his very birth he becomes a subject to him that begets him. Under which subjection he is always to live unless by immediate appointment from God or by the grant or death of his father he become possessed of that power to which he was subject.

The right of fatherly government was ordained by God for the preservation of mankind. If it be usurped, the usurper may be so far obeyed *as may tend to the preservation of the subjects, who may thereby be enabled*[481] to perform their duty to their true and right sovereign when time shall serve. In such cases to obey an usurper is properly to obey the first and right governor, who must be presumed to desire the safety of his subjects. The command of an usurper[w] is not to be obeyed in anything tending to the destruction of the[w] person of the governor, whose being in the first place is to be looked after.

It hath been said that there have been so many usurpations by conquest in all kingdoms that all kings are usurpers, or the heirs or successors of usurpers; and therefore any usurper if he can but get the possession of a kingdom hath as good a title as any other.[x] Answer: The first usurper hath the best title, being, as was said, in possession by the permission of God; and where an usurper hath continued so long that the knowledge of the right heir be lost by all the subjects, in such a case an usurper in possession is to be taken and reputed by such subjects for the true heir, and is to be obeyed by them as their father. As no man hath an infallible certitude but only a moral knowledge, which is no other than a probable persuasion grounded upon a peaceable possession, which is a warrant for subjection to parents and governors. For we may not say, because children have no infallible or necessary certainty who are their true parents, that therefore they need not obey, because they are uncertain. It is sufficient, and as much as human nature is capable of, for children to rely upon a credible persuasion. For otherwise the commandment of 'honour thy father' would be a vain commandment, and not possible to be observed.

By human positive laws a possession time out of mind takes away or bars a former right – to avoid a general mischief of bringing all right into a disputation not decidable by proof and consequently to the overthrow of all civil government – in grants, gifts and contracts between man and man. But in grants and gifts that have their original from God or nature, as the power of the father hath, no inferior power of man can limit nor make any law of prescription against

---

[w] [DMS ends here].
[x] [A new paragraph begins here in 79].

them. Upon this ground is built that common maxim, that *nullum tempus occurrit regi*, no time bars a king.

All power on earth is either derived or usurped from the fatherly power, there being no other original to be found of any power whatsoever. For if there should be granted two sorts of power without any subordination of one to the other, they would be in perpetual strife which should be supreme – for two supremes cannot agree. If the fatherly power be supreme, then the power of the people must be subordinate, and depend on it. If the power of the people be supreme, then the fatherly power must submit to it, and cannot be exercised without the licence of the people – which must quite destroy the frame and course of nature. Even the power which God himself exerciseth over mankind is by right of fatherhood: he is both the king and father of us all. As God hath exalted the dignity of earthly kings, by communicating to them his own title by saying they 'are gods' [Psalms lxxxii, 6]; so on the other side he hath been pleased as it were to humble himself by assuming the title of a king to express his power, and not the title of any popular government. We find it is a punishment to have 'no king', Hosea iii, 4, and promised as a blessing to Abraham, Genesis xvii, 6, 'that kings shall come out of thee'.

Every man hath a part or share in the preservation of mankind in general. He that usurps the power of a superior thereby puts upon himself a necessity of acting the duty of a superior in the preservation of them over whom he hath usurped, unless he will aggravate one heinous crime by committing another more horrid. He that takes upon him the power of a superior sins sufficiently, and to the purpose; but he that proceeds to destroy both his superior and those under the superior's protection goeth a strain higher, by adding murder to robbery. If government be hindered, mankind perisheth. An usurper by hindering the government of another brings a necessity upon himself to govern. His duty before usurpation was only to be ministerial or instrumental in the preservation of others by his obedience. But when he denies his own and hinders the obedience of others, he doth not only not help but is the cause of the distraction in hindering his superior to perform his duty. He makes the duty his own. If a superior cannot protect it is his part to desire to be able to do it, which he cannot do in the future if in the present they be destroyed for want of government. Therefore it is to be presumed that the superior desires the preservation of them that should be subject to him, and so likewise it may be presumed that an usurper in *general*[482] doth the will of his superior by preserving the people by government. And it is not improper to say that in obeying an usurper we may obey primarily the true superior, so long as our obedience aims at the preservation of those in subjection and not at the destruction of the true governor. Not only the usurper but those also over whom power is usurped may join in the preservation of themselves, yea, and in the preservation sometimes of the usurper himself.

Thus there may be a conditional duty or right in an usurper to govern. That is to say, supposing him to be so wicked as to usurp, and not willing to surrender or forgo his usurpation, he is then bound to protect by government, or else he increaseth and multiplieth his sin.

Though an usurper can never gain a right from the true superior, yet from those that are subjects he may. For if they know no other hath a better title than the usurper, then as to them the usurper in possession hath a true right.

Such a qualified right is found at first in all usurpers, as is in thieves who have stolen goods and during the time they are possessed of them have a title in law against all others but the true owners. And such usurpers to divers intents and purposes may be obeyed.

Neither is he only an usurper who obtains the government, but all they are partakers in the usurpation who have either failed to give assistance to their lawful sovereign, or have given aid either by their persons, estates or counsels for the destroying of that governor under whose protection they have been born and preserved. For although it should be granted that *protection* and *subjection* are reciprocal, so that where the first fails the latter ceaseth, yet it must be remembered that where a man hath been born under the protection of a long and peaceable government, he owes an assistance for the preservation of that government that hath protected him, and is the author of his own disobedience.

It is said by some that an usurped power may be obeyed in things that are lawful. But it may *be*[483] obeyed not only in lawful things but also in things indifferent.[y] Obedience in things indifferent is

[y] [things indifferent: things neither commanded nor forbidden by God].

necessary, not indifferent. For in things necessarily good God is immediately obeyed, superiors only by consequence. If men command things evil, obedience is due only by *tolerating* what thcy inflict, not by *performing* what they require. In the first, they declare what God commands to be *done*, in the latter what to be *suffered*. So it remains that things indifferent only are the proper object of human laws. Actions are to be considered simply and alone, and so are good as being motions depending on the first mover; or jointly with circumstances, and that in a double manner: 1. In regard of the *ability* or *possibility*, whilst they may be done. 2. In the *act* when they be performed. Before they be done they be indifferent, but once breaking out into act they become distinctly good or evil according to the circumstances which determine the same. Now an action commanded is supposed as not yet done (whereupon the Hebrews call the imperative mood the first future) and so remaineth many times indifferent.

Some may be of opinion that if obedience may be given to an usurper in things indifferent, as well as to a lawful power, that then there is as much obedience due to an usurped power as to a lawful. But it is a mistake, for though it be granted that in things indifferent an usurper may be obeyed as well as a lawful governor, yet herein lieth a main difference – that some things are indifferent for a lawful superior, which are not indifferent but unlawful to an usurper to enjoin. Usurpation is the resisting and taking away the power from him who hath such a former right to govern the usurper as cannot be lawfully taken away. So that it cannot be just for an usurper to take advantage of his own unlawful act or create himself a title by continuation of his own injustice, which aggravates and never extenuates his crime. And if it never can be an act indifferent for the usurper himself to disobey his lawful sovereign, much less can it be indifferent for him to command another to do that to which he hath no right himself. It is only then a matter indifferent for an usurper to command, when the actions enjoined are such as the lawful superior is commanded by the law of God to provide for the benefit of his subjects by the same or other like restriction of such indifferent things, and it is to be presumed, if he had not been hindered, would have commanded the same, or the like laws.

Select biographical notes

ARISTOTLE (384–322 B.C.)

The most influential of the ancient Greek philosophers, Aristotle wrote prolifically on a very wide range of subjects. He was commonly regarded as *the* philosopher in the later Middle Ages and early modern period, and his works long lay at the centre of the university curriculum. Filmer drew on three of these works the *Rhetoric*, the *Nichomachean Ethics* and especially the *Politics*. Filmer is typical of his age in regarding Aristotle as the greatest of non-Christian thinkers, but he went well beyond most contemporary political theorists in the detailed attention which he gave to Aristotle's political ideas. In Filmer's opinion, Aristotle's ignorance of the Bible, and the social and political circumstances of his times, led him into confusions; but if his teaching was reconstructed in such a way as to take account of these defects, the message which remained was that absolute monarchy was the best form of government.

BARCLAY, JOHN (1582–1621)

John Barclay was the son of William Barclay, a Scotsman who taught civil law in France and Lorraine, and who published *De Regno* (1600) in which he defended the rights of kings against George Buchanan and other 'monarchomachs' (king-killers) as he called them. William died in 1608, and in the following year John published his father's posthumous *De Potestate Papae* as a contribution to the controversy over the oath of allegiance of 1606. This book attacked the idea that the pope has the authority to depose kings, and it soon attracted a reply from Cardinal Bellarmine. John then defended William in *Pietas* (1612), which rebutted the theories of Bellarmine and re-affirmed those of his father. Later, John went to Rome and made his peace with the Cardinal. In 1621 he published his best-known work, the extremely popular Latin satire *Argenis*. It is possible that Filmer confused the two Barclays.

BELLARMINE, ROBERT (1542–1621)

An Italian Jesuit theologian whose prolific writings against Protestants were extremely influential in the later sixteenth and early seventeenth centuries. Bellarmine was the nephew of a pope, and himself rose to high office in the church. After holding academic appointments at Louvain and Rome he became a Cardinal and Archbishop. His chief work, the *Disputationes de Controversiis* (3 volumes, Ingolstadt 1586–9, and many other editions), attacked the ideas of the Protestant Reformers on a wide variety of points relating to theology and church government. Bellarmine held that the pope was empowered to depose heretical kings, and claimed that whereas the pope derived his powers directly from God, kings drew theirs from the people. He maintained the papal position in the controversy over the Venetian Interdict of 1606, and again shortly afterwards in books published against James I and William Barclay. Bellarmine was in turn attacked by many supporters of James – including Marc' Antonio De Dominis – and the arguments of these writers were often very similar to those later employed by Filmer.

BLACKWOOD, ADAM (1539–1613)

A Scotsman who went to France where he studied civil law. For a while he taught philosophy at Paris, and later he gained legal office at Poitiers through the patronage of Mary Queen of Scots. In 1581 he published *Apologia pro Regibus*, an attack on the theory of legitimate resistance put forward by George Buchanan. Six years later he brought out a defence of Mary Queen of Scots, of whom he had long been a loyal follower. Blackwood was one of the best-known opponents of ideas of limited and resistible monarchy in the later sixteenth century.

BODIN, JEAN (c. 1530–96)

A French lawyer and scholar, and one of the most influential political theorists of the early modern period. Bodin studied at Paris and then at Toulouse – where for a while he taught law. Later, he returned to Paris to practise law, and in 1571 joined the household of the king's brother, the Duke of Alençon – in whose service he visited England. In the course of the French religious wars Bodin came to believe that only strong monarchical authority could restore order. In 1576 he published his most famous work, the *Six Livres de la République*. This massive book was packed with information and reflections on ancient and recent laws, politics and constitutions. It argued that an unlimited and indivisible sovereign was necessary in every state. In 1606 Bodin's book was translated into English by Richard Knolles. Filmer drew very extensively on this translation.

BOTERO, GIOVANNI (1544–1617)

An Italian cleric and writer. For a while Botero taught philosophy and rhetoric in Jesuit schools, but he fell out with the Jesuits, and in 1580 became secretary to Archbishop Charles Borromeo of Milan. In 1599 he entered the service of the Duke of Savoy. Amongst Botero's many publications were works on the greatness of cities, on reason of state, and on oceanography. He took a pragmatic and empirical approach to politics, but unlike Machiavelli he tried to ensure that his conclusions were compatible with the teachings of the Catholic church. His *Relazioni Universali* (Rome 1591–3 and many later editions) surveyed the geography and institutions of states throughout the world. In the *Anarchy* Filmer drew on the 1630 translation of this work – *Relations of the Most Famous Kingdoms and Common-wealthes thorowout the World.*

BRACTON, HENRY DE (HENRY OF BRATTON) (*c.* 1210–68)
In the seventeenth century it was commonly supposed that the important medieval legal treatise *De Legibus et Consuetudinibus Angliae* (on the laws and customs of England) had been written by Henry de Bracton, who served Henry III as a judge. In fact the book was probably drawn up while Martin of Patishall was Henry's chief judge, between 1218 and 1229. It had great influence on English law in subsequent centuries and was first printed in 1568 and again in 1640. Filmer drew on it to prove that Bracton – a major authority on English common law – believed that the king's power was unlimited and that he had no superior except God.

BUCHANAN, GEORGE (1506–82)
A Scotsman who studied at St Andrews and Paris, where he taught for a while. Later, he held various appointments on the Continent and then returned to Scotland. A Protestant, Buchanan took part in the events of the Reformation and wrote against Mary Queen of Scots. For a while he was tutor to the young King James VI – who later reacted strongly against his mentor's political opinions. In 1579 Buchanan published *De Jure Regni apud Scotos*, in which he argued that the king derived his power from the people, to whom he was accountable. These ideas were documented from the Scottish past in Buchanan's Latin history of Scotland, published in 1582. Buchanan's ideas circulated widely and were vigorously attacked by British and Continental apologists for extensive monarchical power.

CALVIN, JOHN (1509–64)
A French Protestant who led the Reformation in Geneva. Calvin's many works included the well-known *Institutes of the Christian Religion*, first printed in 1536 and later extended. The final edition of this work was published in 1559. Filmer cited the *Institutes* to show that Calvin inclined towards theories of original popular sovereignty and legitimate resistance.

CAMDEN, WILLIAM (1551–1623)
One of the major historians in early modern England. Camden was headmaster of Westminster school, and also held the heraldic office of Clarenceux king-of-arms. According to the biographer John Aubrey, Filmer was 'very intimately acquainted' with Camden. In 1610 Camden was appointed along with John Hayward as historian to Chelsea College – which was instituted to organise English controversial efforts against Roman Catholics. In 1615 Camden published the first part of his *Annales* of Elizabeth's reign, and a second part followed posthumously in 1628. His most famous work – on

which Filmer drew – was *Britannia*, first published in Latin in 1586. This book was later extended, and in 1610 was translated into English.

COKE, SIR EDWARD (1552–1634)

Coke was the most influential legal writer of the early seventeenth century. Under James I he held the offices of chief justice of the common pleas and later of the king's bench, until he was dismissed in 1616 as a result of disagreements with the king over royal power, and with Thomas Egerton (lord chancellor Ellesmere) and others over the extent of the jurisdiction of the common law courts. In the parliaments of the 1620s Coke was a leading critic of royal policies. His *Reports* (thirteen parts, 1600–15; two further parts 1656–9) and *Institutes* (four parts, 1628–44) commented on many aspects of the common law, and portrayed the king's power as limited by English custom. *The Freeholders Grand Inquest* takes issue with Coke's views, and also where possible cites his authority to confirm its interpretation of English constitutional history.

COTTON, SIR ROBERT (1571–1631)

A leading antiquarian scholar of the Elizabethan and Jacobean periods. Cotton was knighted in 1603 by James I who consulted him on historical and legal precedents, as did James' adviser the Earl of Northampton. He sat in the House of Commons in the parliaments of 1624, 1625 and 1628–9. Cotton was an avid collector of manuscripts and his library became a great centre for historical research, much used by scholars including Camden, Selden and Raleigh. His own works consist largely of short essays on legal and historical topics. Most of these circulated only in manuscript during his lifetime. *The Free-holders Grand Inquest* drew on two of these writings. Filmer possessed at least one of Cotton's works in manuscript.

EGERTON, THOMAS, BARON ELLESMERE AND VISCOUNT BRACKLEY (1540–1617)

Egerton was a lawyer who rose to become solicitor general, attorney general and finally lord chancellor of England. On questions of royal power he inclined towards the views of James I rather than those of Sir Edward Coke. In 1609 he published a speech maintaining that those Scots who had been born since the succession of James I to the English crown were naturalised as subjects in England. This book contained a great many legal precedents supporting a high view of the king's power. Both *Patriarcha* and *The Freeholders Grand Inquest* borrowed freely from Egerton's speech.

FERNE, HENRY (1602–62)

A royalist clergyman who became one of the leading pamphleteers on the king's side in the early 1640s. In 1642 he published *The Resolving of Conscience* which argued that no one who reflected on the nature of royal authority could conscientiously side with parliament in the Civil War. This book led to a controversy between Ferne and the parliamentarian cleric Charles Herle, and during this Herle produced the *Fuller Answer to a Treatise written by Dr Ferne* to which Filmer refers. Ferne and Filmer shared many opinions, but Ferne's aim was to win waverers over to the king's cause and he stressed the moderation of royalism, while Filmer had few qualms about spelling out the implications of absolutist theory. In 1656 Ferne attacked James Harrington's *Oceana*. At the Restoration he became master of Trinity College and vice-chancellor of Cambridge University, and shortly before his death he was appointed Bishop of Chester.

GROTIUS, HUGO (HUIG VAN GROOT) (1583–1645)
A Dutch lawyer and scholar, most famous for his work on international law. In 1613 he became pensionary of Rotterdam, but five years later he was arrested because of his association with the Remonstrants – who held views antagonistic to the Calvinist theory of predestination. He was sentenced to imprisonment for life, but escaped to France where in 1625 he published his great treatise on international law, the *De Jure Belli ac Pacis*. This book derived royal power from a grant by the people, and argued that the earth was at first held by mankind in common. Filmer replied to Grotius' arguments on these points in two chapters of the Cambridge manuscript of *Patriarcha* and again in his *Observations* on Hobbes, Milton and Grotius.

HAYWARD, SIR JOHN (1564? -1627)
A civil lawyer and historian. In 1599 he published the *First Part of the Life and Raigne of Henrie the IIII*. Though this work did not explicitly defend the deposition of Richard II, its treatment of that event angered Queen Elizabeth and led to Hayward's imprisonment. Under James I, Hayward was careful to make clear his detestation of ideas of legitimate resistance and limited monarchy. In 1603 he published *An Answer to the First Part of a Certaine Conference*, which attacked the political ideas of Robert Parsons, and denied that kings are accountable to their subjects. In 1610 Hayward and William Camden were appointed as the two historian members of Chelsea College – an institution founded to organise English controversial efforts against Roman Catholics. In 1617 he became a master in chancery, and in 1626 he was appointed a member of the most powerful ecclesiastical court, the High Commission. His ideas on English constitutional history differed sharply from those of Sir Edward Coke, for Hayward denied that the common law was immemorial, and held that the king was above the law. Filmer refers to Hayward's *Answer* to Parsons, and also to his *The Lives of the III. Normans, Kings of England*, published in 1613.

HOOKER, RICHARD (1554? -1600)
One of the most famous of Elizabethan apologists for the church of England. Hooker's *Of the Laws of Ecclesiastical Polity* (5 books, 1594–7; books six and eight, 1648; book seven 1662) set out the case in favour of Elizabeth's church settlement in classic form, taking issue especially with puritan critics of the church. Hooker was an Oxford academic who later became master of the

Temple, and then rector of Bishopsbourne in Kent. Filmer's praise for Hooker is typical of those who supported the established church against puritan criticisms, and reveals much about Filmer's stance on religious questions. But Hooker held that royal authority was derived from a grant by the people, and Filmer differed sharply from him on this question. Filmer quotes from a manuscript of Hooker's eighth book.

HUNTON, PHILIP (1604?-82)
A clergyman, and one of the most important parliamentarian pamphleteers in the Civil War. Hunton was vicar of Westbury, and in 1657 was appointed head of Cromwell's newly founded college at Durham. After the Restoration, Hunton lost his offices. His principal work was *A Treatise of Monarchie*, published in 1643. This book is the main target of Filmer's *Anarchy*. It argued that the English constitution was a mixed monarchy, in which power was shared between king, Lords and Commons. Hunton hoped to attract moderates to the parliamentarian cause by advocating a system which would grant the king a large share of power, while at the same time preventing tyranny by ensuring that royal power was limited. Filmer argued that Hunton's system was a recipe for anarchy, since it included no satisfactory mechanism for resolving disputes between the three sharers in sovereign power.

JAMES I (1566-1625)
James VI of Scotland became king of England in 1603. While in Scotland, James published *The True Law of Free Monarchies* (1598) – a work on which Filmer drew. In England, James re-published the *True Law,* and also wrote a number of other political works, including a famous speech to parliament delivered on 21 March 1610, and a declaration of his reasons for dissolving the parliament of 1621. Filmer cited both of these works. James I's views were close to Filmer's on a great many questions. Both men believed that the king's power was derived from God alone, and both claimed that the monarch alone makes law, though he might choose to consult his subjects in doing so. But James placed very much less emphasis than Filmer on the patriarchal origins of royal power.

LAMBARDE, WILLIAM (1536-1601)
A leading Elizabethan antiquarian scholar. Lambarde wrote a famous history of his (and Filmer's) county, Kent, which was published in 1574 and in a new edition in 1596. A lawyer, Lambarde edited an influential collection of Anglo-Saxon laws in 1568, and in 1581 he published what soon became the standard work on the office of justice of the peace. In 1591 Lambarde completed his *Archeion or, a Discourse upon the High Courts of Justice in England.* This work contained very many citations from legal sources, and both *Patriarcha* and *The Free-holders Grand Inquest* drew freely on this material. The *Archeion* was first published in 1635 – in two separate editions – but Filmer used a manuscript of the book.

Select biographical notes

MILTON, JOHN (1608–72)
Milton was one of the greatest of English poets and a competent pamphleteer. In 1649 he became Latin secretary to the council of state, and in the same year he published *The Tenure of Kings and Magistrates*, on which Filmer drew. In this work and in his *Eikonoklastes* (1649) Milton asserted that all political power is derived from the people, who could resist their rulers if they judged them to be acting tyrannically. Milton argued that if the mass of the people became corrupted it could be justifiable for a righteous few to act in the name of the whole, and on these grounds he defended the army's intervention in politics, the purging of parliament, and the trial and execution of the king. In 1650 Milton was commissioned to write a reply to Salmasius' attack on those who were responsible for the king's death. The bulk of Filmer's *Observations on Mr Milton against Salmasius* is devoted to replying to this book, the *Pro Populo Anglicano Defensio* (1651).

PARKER, HENRY (1604–52)
Parker was a lawyer who became one of the most famous parliamentarian pamphleteers in the Civil War period. Amongst his many publications, the best-known is the anonymous *Observations upon some of his Majesties late Answers and Expresses* (1642), which sparked off a prolonged controversy between royalist and parliamentarian propagandists on the nature and origins of royal authority, and on the English constitution. Parker asserted that all political power stemmed from the people, and he granted the two Houses of parliament ultimate authority in England. Filmer took issue with the *Observations* in the *Anarchy*, calling its anonymous author 'the Observator'.

PARSONS (OR PERSONS), ROBERT (1546–1610)
Parsons was the leading English Elizabethan Jesuit. He spent much of his life on the Continent, where he encouraged the king of Spain to invade England and oust the heretical queen. He wrote a number of pamphlets denouncing the Elizabethan regime, and in 1594 produced *A Conference about the Next Succession to the Crown of Ingland*, which argued that the authority of monarchs is derived from the people. The people were consequently empowered to call their rulers to account, and could alter the succession. The purpose of Parsons' book was to oppose the succession of the Protestant James VI of Scots to the English throne, and his work was soon attacked by those who hoped for favour from James, including Sir John Hayward.

PRYNNE, WILLIAM (1600–69)
Prynne was a lawyer who became one of the best-known and most prolific pamphleteers of the Civil War period. He lobbied for religious reform in the 1620s and 30s, suffering imprisonment and the loss of his ears as a result. During the Civil War he sided with parliament, and in 1643 published *The Sovereign Power of Parliaments and Kingdoms* in four parts, of which the first (*The Treachery of Papists to their Soveraignes*) was attacked in *The Free-holders Grand Inquest*. Prynne maintained the sovereignty of the people represented

in parliament, and their right to resist a tyrannical king. But he opposed the execution of Charles I, and the abolition of monarchy and the House of Lords. In defending the Lords, he drew extensively on *The Free-holders Grand Inquest.*

RALEIGH, SIR WALTER (1552?-1618)

An Elizabethan politician, adventurer and writer, Raleigh benefited greatly from the Queen's favour, but lost most of his influence on the accession of James I. In 1603 he was found guilty of treason on dubious grounds. For the next thirteen years he was imprisoned in the Tower of London. Then, in 1616 the king allowed him to lead an expedition to the Orinoco in search of gold. The expedition was a failure, and Raleigh disobeyed royal orders by attacking Spaniards. At the request of the Spanish ambassador he was executed on his return to England in 1618. Filmer drew on Raleigh's *History of the World* – a survey of biblical and ancient history, first published in 1614 – and on his *The Prerogative of Parliaments in England,* published posthumously in 1628. This work, written in dialogue form, argued that the king's power was unlimited, but also that it would be extremely foolish for James to ignore the wishes of Parliament.

SALMASIUS, CLAUDIUS (CLAUDE DE SAUMAISE) (1588–1653)

A French classical scholar. Salmasius studied at Paris and Heidelberg. He became a Protestant, and in 1631 took up a professorship at Leiden. In addition to his work on classical authors, Salmasius wrote a defence of usury – *De Usuris* (1638) – which Filmer cited. In 1649 Salmasius was commissioned by Charles II to write the *Defensio Regia pro Carolo I.* This book defended absolute monarchy and attacked the ideas and actions of the English Independents, and particularly their execution of Charles I. Milton replied to Salmasius in his *Pro Populo Anglicano Defensio* (1651). Filmer and others in turn answered Milton.

SELDEN, JOHN (1584–1654)

One of the greatest legal scholars in early modern England, Selden was a lawyer and historian who antagonised many of the clergy in 1618 by publishing *The Historie of Tithes,* which cast doubt on the idea that tithes were due to clerics by divine right. An opponent of royal policy in the parliament of 1628–9, Selden was gaoled for seditious conduct in 1629. During the 1630s he made his peace with the court, befriending Archbishop Laud, one of the king's most prominent advisers. In 1635 he published *Mare Clausum* which took issue with Hugo Grotius' arguments for the freedom of the seas. Filmer drew on this book's account of the origins of property. Amongst Selden's many other works was a history of noble and other titles, called *Titles of Honor.* This was first published in 1614. A revised and greatly extended edition was printed in 1631, and this edition was one of the major sources of historical information used in *The Free-holders Grand Inquest,* and in a section of the Cambridge manuscript of *Patriarcha.*

SPELMAN, SIR HENRY (1564?–1641)
Spelman was one of the most important antiquarian scholars in early modern England. His *Archaeologus* (from which *The Free-holders Grand Inquest* quotes) is a dictionary of medieval legal terms, published in 1626 (covering the letters A–L), and in complete form as *Glossarium Archaiologium* in 1664. Spelman's work is of great importance in the history of English historiography, and he made significant advances in the understanding of medieval society and institutions. His other writings include several works decrying sacrilege and arguing that divine providence struck down those who held ex-monastic land.

SUAREZ, FRANCISCO (1548–1617)
One of the greatest Jesuit philosophers and theologians. Suarez taught at a number of universities including Rome (1580–5) and Coimbra (1597–1616). Amongst his very voluminous writings were *Tractatus De Legibus ac Deo Legislatore* (Coimbra 1612), and *Defensio Fidei Catholicae* (Coimbra 1613). The *Defensio* was a reply to James I's defence of the English oath of allegiance, which required Catholics to renounce the pope's claims to be able to depose heretical rulers. Suarez vigorously defended the papal deposing power. The *Defensio* was publicly burned in London. In both the *Defensio* and the *De Legibus* Suarez asserted that royal power springs from a grant by the people, and that the people can in certain circumstances take up arms against their rulers. *Patriarcha* drew on the *De Legibus*.

Textual notes

1. [B: A defence of the natural power of kings against the unnatural liberty of the people].
2. [B omits
    A defective contents list of all three chapters occurs at the beginning of A; this is largely identical with the lists given at the beginning of each chapter, and is omitted here].
3. [B: Within this last hundred of years many of the schoolmen and other divines have published and maintained an opinion that:]
4. [B omits].
5. [B: for good divinity, hath been fostered by succeeding papists].
6. [B omits].
7. [B omits].
8. [B omits].
9. [B: zealous
    C, D: other zealous].
10. [A omits].
11. [A omits].
12. [B omits].
13. [B: they do].
14. [B: principle].
15. [B: main foundation of popular sedition would be taken away].
16. [A omits].
17. [B omits].
18. [B: detract not].
19. [B: was ever].
20. [B: Mr Hooker].
21. [A: are].
22. [A omits].
23. [B omits].
24. [B: an observation or two upon the].
25. [B: the].
26. [B: make].
27. [B omits].
28. [A omits].
29. [B omits].
30. [A: my].
31. [A omits].
32. [B omits].
33. [B omits].
34. [B omits].
35. [B: subordination].
36. [B: from whence it].
37. [B: assigning].

38. [B: or].
39. [A omits].
40. [B: with].
41. [A omits].
42. [B: of].
43. [A: them].
44. [B omits].
45. [B omits].
46. [B: the names of their].
47. [B: we].
48. [B: made of].
49. [A omits].
50. [A omits].
51. [B: to aid].
52. [A: our].
53. [B omits].
54. [B omits].
55. [B omits].
56. [B omits].
57. [B: of].
58. [D]. [B here adds: So we find that at the offering of princes at the dedication of the tabernacle the princes of Israel are said to be heads of the houses of their fathers, as Eliab the son of Helon was prince of the children of his father Zebulun. Numbers vii, 2 and 24.]
59. [B omits].
60. [B: Secondly, this].
61. [A: is devolved].
62. [A: princes].
63. [B: principals].
64. [A: return again].
65. [B: and].
66. [A omits].
67. [B: a].
68. [B omits].
69. [B omits].
70. [B: translation].
71. [B: his].
72. [B omits].
73. [A omits].
74. [A omits].
75. [B omits].
76. [B: in].
77. [D. A and B: no].
78. [B: to].
79. [B omits].
80. [B: his].
81. [B: one].

82. [B omits].
83. [C, D. A, B: arguments].
84. [A: preservation].
85. [A: the].
86. [B: and to].
87. [A: doth].
88. [B: Judaical].
89. [B omits].
90. [B: he meaneth by this 'complete economical power'].
91. [B omits].
92. [B: and Grotius and].
93. [B: men].
94. [B: and it].
95. [B: any].
96. [A: Is].
97. [A: than than].
98. [C, D. A and B omit].
99. [B: third parts].
100. [B: any history].
101. [B: are to be found of it].
102. [A omits].
103. [A: maintained].
104. [B: you in mind of what Bellarmine affirms].
105. [A: he had].
106. [B: that].
107. [B: of a].
108. [B omits].
109. [B omits].
110. [A omits].
111. [A: most].
112. [B omits].
113. [A: until the].
114. [B omits].
115. [A omits].
116. [A omits].
117. [B: the].
118. [B: monarchs].
119. [B omits].
120. [B: state].
121. [A: assembly].
122. [B: every].
123. [A: manlike].
124. [A: they].
125. [B: of years].
126. [B omits].
127. [B: fourteen].
128. [A omits].

129. [A omits].
130. [A omits].
131. [B: or].
132. [A: tendered].
133. [B omits].
134. [A: in the].
135. [B omits].
136. [B omits].
137. [B omits].
138. [A: hath likewise].
139. [A omits].
140. [B: of].
141. [C, D. A, B: a contract cannot].
142. [A omits].
143. [B omits].
144. [A, B: Vitellus].
145. [B omits].
146. [A: But].
147. [A omits].
148. [A: nature and virtuous].
149. [B: and more].
150. [B: spilt].
151. [A omits].
152. [A: but]
153. [A omits]
154. [B omits].
155. [A omits].
156. [B: that].
157. [A omits].
158. [B, C, D: literally
      A: liberally].
159. [A omits].
160. [B omits].
161. [B: complaints and cries].
162. [A: be].
163. [B: *opposuit*].
164. [B: who lived].
165. [A omits].
166. [A omits].
167. [B: unto].
168. [B: of higher power to]
169. [B: or].
170. [A omits].
171. [A: an].
172. [A: the king].
173. [A: the].
174. [A: estates].

175. [A: by the].
176. [B: the king's].
177. [B: and].
178. [A: he is].
179. [A: and].
180. [A: by].
181. [A: and].
182. [A, C, D: mischevable
     B: mischeivable
     The *Oxford English Dictionary* cites this passage as its sole authority
     for the word 'mischievable'].
183. [B: the Lord's].
184. [A: it].
185. [B: at].
186. [A omits].
187. [A omits].
188. [A omits].
189. [B omits].
190. [B: ~~that~~].
191. [B: regulate].
192. [A: absolute].
193. [B: some things fall].
194. [B: besides].
195. [A: he].
196. [A omits].
197. [A omits].
198. [B: For].
199. [B omits].
200. [A: his].
201. [A: *impetrari*
     The Latin does not occur in the printed versions of Lambarde's
     Archeion, though the English translation is there. However, the Latin
     is in Lambarde's *ARXAIONOMIA, sive de priscis anglorum legibus*, 1568,
     f. 79a, where the reading is: *impetrare*].
202. [A: some parliaments].
203. [C, D: need
     A, B: need of].
204. [A: absolute ~~and irregular~~
     C: absolute].
205. [A: hath been].
206. [A: serving only in a few].
207. [A: occasions].
208. [A: be].
209. [B omits].
210. [A: 13].
211. [A omits].
212. [A: The].

213. [B omits].
214. [A: upon cause].
215. [A: was].
216. [B: that].
217. [B: omits].
218. [B: in].
219. [A: an or].
220. [B: all their].
221. [B omits].
222. [B: find].
223. [B: nobility, clergy and the king's council].
224. [A omits].
225. [A omits].
226. [A: wisemen the].
227. [A: do].
228. [A omits].
229. [B: By the word *witena* it is very likely the thanes were meant, who were the same in the Saxon times that the barons were in the times of the Normans, as the Saxon ealdormen were those that were afterwards Norman earls. As for those ancient boroughs that might be decayed at the time of the Conquest, it is possible that for their antiquity or some other reason they might receive the privileges of sending burgesses after the Conquest. The like may be said for the contrary privilege for lands in ancient demesne.]
230. [B omits].
231. [B omits].
232. [B omits].
233. [B omits this passage and instead has the passage printed above in the Appendix, section (3), pp. 66–8].
234. [B: better than that of King Henry I].
235. [B: first calling the people to parliament].
236. [B: got].
237. [B omits].
238. [A omits].
239. [B omits, but has this material in the passage printed at p. 67].
240. [A: gave].
241. [A: call it the natural liberty of the people with a mischief].
242. [A: in].
243. [A omits].
244. [B: not or to alter it].
245. [B: chose or set down].
246. [B: Which seems to prove that in ancient times the assent of the Commons was not always requisite, for though their assent may seem to ratify, yet it doth not follow that therefore their dissent must nullify an act of parliament. Those may have deliberative voices which have not always a negative].
   [B here has the passage printed as the last paragraph of section

16, p. 60].
247. [B: have].
248. [B omits].
249. [B: out of].
250. [C, D. A and B omit].
251. [A omits].
252. [A omits].
253. [A: he should].
254. [B: regal].
255. [A omits].
256. [A omits].
257. [B: We].
258. [A omits].
259. [B omits].
260. [A: institutions].
261. [B omits].
262. [B omits].
263. [B: the].
264. [B: this].
265. [B: this].
266. [A: found].
267. [B: mend].
268. [A: disherison].
269. [B omits].
270. [B omits].
271. [A: Blacknett].
272. [A omits].
273. [A: opinions].
274. [A omits; C: according to law, and].
275. [Egerton p. 23: Newport-Panell
       i.e. Newport Pagnell].
276. [B omits].
277. [B: people].
278. [B: thing].
279. [B: writes it].
280. [B: were].
281. [48F, 79: or].
282. [79: they think fit
       Statutes of Ireland: them seemeth].
283. [48F omits].
284. [48F, 79: *cunctique*].
285. [79: *emendat*].
286. [79: undue].
287. [79: lose].
288. [79: the].
289. [48F: *d'esslier*].
290. [79 omits].

291. [48F, 79: Ethelbert].
292. [48F: do all].
293. [79: by the].
294. [48F: sometimes passed].
295. [79: part
     Glanville: and part].
296. [79: and part
     Glanville: part].
297. [48F: precedent].
298. [48F: sunder].
299. [79: doth].
300. [48F: primative].
301. [79: a great].
302. [79: a].
303. [79: by].
304. [48A: never].
305. [48A, 79: or].
306. [48A, 79: neither].
307. [48A: transcends].
308. [48A: person].
309. [79: a].
310. [Here and throughout this paragraph 48A prints: authorative].
311. [48A: accur].
312. [48A, 79: monarchy].
313. [48A, 79: to
     Parker: to].
314. [48A, 79: so
     Parker: to].
315. [48A, 79: was
     Parker: were].
316. [48A: *euphori*].
317. [48A: seale].
318. [48A, 79: were
     Parker: was].
319. [48A, 79: was
     Parker: way was].
320. [48A, 79: of
     Parker: or].
321. [48A: tis].
322. [48A, 79: monarchy].
323. [48A: bred
     79: breed].
324. [The title is taken from Thomason's copy of the 1648 edition. A variant title-page adds at the end: By John Bodin A Protestant according to the Church of Geneva].
     [BMS begins:
     John Bodin a protestant according to the with the

Ge Church of Geneva, a famous Politician and
learned Lawyer.
His Judgment of the Absolut Power
Majesty or Soveraignty of Kings or
Princes and particularly of the King
of England.]

325. [80B: The Power of Kings: and in particular, of the King of England].
326. [48B, 80B: is].
327. [48B, 80B: to].
328. [80B: this is that].
329. [48B, 80B: shall].
330. [48B, 80B, king].
331. [48B, 80B omit].
332. [48B, 80B: yet depend].
333. [48B, 80B, God].
334. [48B, 80B: against God].
335. [48B, 80B, to].
336. [80B: A question].
337. [48B, 80B: be].
338. [48B, 80B: a].
339. [BMS: ~~keep the~~ his laws].
     [48B: keep his laws].
     [80B: keep his laws by himself].
340. [BMS, 80B: by].
341. [80B: made himself].
342. [48B, 80B: so].
343. [48B, 80B: thereunto].
344. [80B: from].
345. [Bodin p. 93: sovereign].
346. [80B: assemblies].
347. [80B: kings].
348. [80B: do so].
349. [48B omits
     Bodin p. 95: to say].
350. [48B: states].
351. [80B: treat].
352. [80B: requested].
353. [80B: though].
354. [80B: occasion].
355. [80B: gives].
356. [80B: receives].
357. [80B: under].
358. [80B: was].
359. [80B: gives
     Bodin p. 100: crieth].
360. [80B: Of these].

361. [80B: come to pass].
362. [80B: swears].
363. [80B: conditions].
364. [48B, 80B: which].
365. [48B, 80B: men].
366. [48B, 80B: will].
367. [BMS: should should].
368. [48B, 80B: countries].
369. [80B omits].
370. [48B, 80B: estates].
371. [BMS, 48B: yet].
372. [48B, 80B: stricter].
373. [80B: being he].
374. [BMS omits].
375. [BMS: a].
376. [80B: of all].
377. [80B: is].
378. [48B, 80B omit].
379. [48B, 80B: he].
380. [48B: burns].
381. [48B: defiles].
382. [48B: were].
383. [80B: give].
384. [48B: unpossible].
385. [80B: For].
386. [52H omits].
387. [52H: and].
388. [52H: 3].
389. [52H omits].
390. [52H: or eat his children].
391. [52H: pure].
392. [52H: this].
393. [52H: us to].
394. [52H: to be done in].
395. [OMS: into].
396. [52H: a great].
397. [OMS omits].
398. [52H: was].
399. [52H: or
      Hobbes 2: and].
400. [52H: the
      Hobbes 2: these].
401. [52H: right
      Hobbes 2: rights].
402. [OMS omits].
403. [52H omits
      Hobbes 2 includes].

404. [52H: they could].
405. [52H: his son whom].
406. [52H: will].
407. [52H: the government of].
408. [52H: differing].
409. [52H omits].
410. [52H omits].
411. [52H, 79 omit].
412. [52H: from
        Hobbes 2: for].
413. [79: they shall
        Hobbes 2: shall they].
414. [52H omits].
415. [52H omits].
416. [79: unto].
417. [79: or].
418. [52H: obtained].
419. [B: by force of arms].
420. [52H: so].
421. [52H: simple].
422. [52H: that in].
423. [52H: order].
424. [52H: lawfullest].
425. [52H omits].
426. [52H omits].
427. [B omits].
428. [52H: be necessarily].
429. [B: a].
430. [52H omits].
431. [B omits].
432. [52H: *magistratuus*].
433. [52H: although].
434. [B omits].
435. [52H: the vows].
436. [B: daughters].
437. [52H: yet the].
438. [52H: for to].
439. [79: a war].
440. [52H omits].
441. [79: a full].
442. [52H omits]
443. [79: subjunctive].
444. [52H, 79: cannot].
445. [52H: possible].
446. [52H: when].
447. [52A: once].
448. [52A: one].

449. [79: the].
450. [79 omits].
451. [79: wrote].
452. [79: a time].
453. [52A: and the].
454. [52A: be].
455. [79: bound].
456. [79: or].
457. [52A: mend].
458. [79: stratocratie].
459. [52A: he].
460. [52A: that if].
461. [52A: setting].
462. [79: a man].
463. [52A omits].
464. [79: beholden].
465. [79: beholden].
466. [79: consistory].
467. [79: so].
468. [52A: may be].
469. [52A, 79: Turentillus Arsa].
470. [52A: names].
471. [52A omits].
472. [79 omits].
473. [79: beholden].
474. [52A, 79: not].
475. [52A omits].
476. [DMS: will].
477. [DMS: Selden, Hobbes, Ascham].
478. [52A: concession].
479. [DMS omits].
480. [DMS: a].
481. [DMS omits].
482. [52A: the general].
483. [79: not be].

Index

Index

CAMBRIDGE TEXTS IN THE
HISTORY OF POLITICAL THOUGHT

Titles published in the series thus far